ALSO BY JOHN FEINSTEIN

Moment of Glory

Are You Kidding Me?

Living on the Black

Tales from Q School

Last Dance

Let Me Tell You a Story

Caddy for Life

Open

The Punch

The Last Amateurs

The Majors

A March to Madness

A Civil War

A Good Walk Spoiled

Play Ball

Hard Courts

Forever's Team

A Season Inside

Last Shot: A Final Four Mystery

Vanishing Act: Mystery at the U.S. Open

Cover-up: Mystery at the Super Bowl

Change-up: Mystery at the World Series

Running Mates: A Mystery

Winter Games: A Mystery

The Rivalry: Mystery at the Army-Navy Game

A Season on the Brink

A Year with Bob Knight and the Indiana Hoosiers

JOHN FEINSTEIN

With a new introduction

SIMON & SCHUSTER PAPERBACKS
New York London Toronto Sydney New Delhi

Simon & Schuster Paperbacks
A Division of Simon & Schuster, Inc.
1230 Avenue of the Americas
New York, NY 10020

This Simon & Schuster trade paperback edition November 2011

SIMON & SCHUSTER PAPERBACKS and colophon are registered
trademarks of Simon & Schuster, Inc.

For information about special discounts for bulk purchases,
please contact Simon & Schuster Special Sales at
1-866-506-1949 or business@simonandschuster.com.

The Simon & Schuster Speakers Bureau can bring authors
to your live event. For more information or to book an event,
contact the Simon & Schuster Speakers Bureau at
1-866-248-3049 or visit our website at www.simonspeakers.com.

Manufactured in the United States of America

10   9   8   7   6

Library of Congress Control Number: 86-18033

ISBN 978-0-0253-7230-6
ISBN 978-1-4516-5025-9 (pbk)

For Mom and Dad. . . .
and that's non-negotiable.

Contents

Introduction

Almost from the minute _A Season on the Brink_ hit book-stores twenty-five years ago, I have been asked the same question repeatedly: Why did it strike such a chord? Why do people still come up to me years later and tell me they just reread the book for a second, fifth, or tenth time? Why did it start out with a first printing of 17,500 books and end up selling into the millions?

There is no doubt that the access Bob Knight gave me in the winter of 1985–86 had a good deal to do with the book's success. Back then it was unheard of for a reporter to be granted that sort of access to a basketball coach, much less a wildly controversial one who had won two national championships and an Olympic gold medal.

Nowadays, you can turn on almost any basketball game on TV and hear what a coach is saying to his team in the locker room. Everything is about "inside access," whether it is watching Olympic athletes sitting nervously with their headphones on just before they are called on to compete or getting information from an athlete's website.

Back then, when I told people I had complete access to Knight, including standing in the locker room with my tape recorder running before, during, and after games and listening in to what was said in the huddle during timeouts, few people actually believed me.

I still remember the look on CBS analyst Billy Packer's face when I walked onto the court at Michigan with Knight and took my seat on the end of the bench for the Big Ten–deciding game that season.

"What are you doing there?" he asked me at halftime.

"Researching my book," I answered.

"Oh boy," he said. "Bob's going to be sorry about this."

Of course we all know now that Knight was more angry than sorry when the book came out. He wrote in his autobiography that giving me access was the worst mistake he ever made because I turned out to be a bad guy and I violated our agreement by leaving (some of) his profanity in the book. Trust me, if I'd left it all in there I'd still be writing.

There isn't any doubt in my mind that Knight honestly believed we had some sort of agreement on profanity. When I told him the book *had* to include profanity in order to have credibility, he said he understood. But he didn't. People who use a lot of profanity—I speak, unfortunately, from personal experience—rarely understand just how often they use it.

Knight was stunned one night during my winter with him when he told a friend of his that he really thought he had done a good job cutting down on his profanity that season and the friend (in a rare moment for someone in Knight's inner circle) told him he was wrong. For the record, the friend was Bob Murrey, who put on his clinics. Bob Hammel would have swallowed his tongue before he would have contradicted Knight.

When Knight read chapter one, in which I described the locker room scene in which he completely went off on Daryl

Thomas, he couldn't believe how much profanity there was in his rant. What he didn't know was that I had removed about 80 percent of the f—— in the speech and had completely removed his repeated use of a word that rhymes with *bunt*.

So he called me a lot of names—many of them profane—after the book came out. There are still people who believe Knight's name-calling made the book a bestseller, forgetting it was already #2 on *The New York Times* list before he said anything publicly. Others say I was lucky because Indiana won the national championship in 1987. A nice theory but the book takes place a year earlier when Indiana lost in the first round of the NCAA Tournament to Cleveland State. And there are many who believe the access I had was critical. I buy that theory—up to a point.

What made *A Season on the Brink* so successful was the access I had to *Knight*. The book would not have sold as well if I had the same access to Dean Smith or John Thompson—the two highest profile coaches along with Knight back then—or even Jim Valvano, who had become a major figure in the college game after North Carolina State's stunning national title run in 1983. If I had waited six years and had that same access to Mike Krzyzewski after his back-to-back national titles at Duke, the book still would not have become a publishing phenomenon.

There just isn't anyone like Knight—for better and worse. That's why people are so fascinated by him even today when he's little more than another retired coach still looking for a sliver of the spotlight by working on TV. The irony of Knight being a member of the media—in any form—is almost too funny for words. Of course, Knight would insist he's different than anyone else working on TV, and he's right. Most color commentators show up for pregame shootarounds, try to talk to coaches before a game about their team, and try to get a sense of who the players are before the game starts.

Knight does none of that. He just shows up—in a sweater of course, which has created the reality TV–like comedy of ESPN putting play-by-play men in sweaters rather than telling Knight he has to wear a coat and tie like everyone else—and watches the game. Fortunately for him, his understanding of basketball is so keen that he can figure out what both teams are trying to do very quickly and explain it eloquently. If *anyone* else in TV tried to pull off Knight's act, they'd be fired before they ever did a second game.

At the end of *A Season on the Brink*, I wondered if Knight would ultimately self destruct. Sadly, even though he would vehemently deny it, he did. Can you imagine any coach with Knight's on-court and off-court record at Indiana managing to get himself fired after twenty-eight years on the job? He won three national titles, an Olympics, an NIT, and dominated the Big Ten. Almost all his players graduated. There was never the smallest hint of any sort of NCAA rules violation—Steve Alford's charity calendar appearance aside—from the first day he was in Bloomington until the day he walked out the door.

Knight should have coached his last game at Indiana and on the night of his final game at Assembly Hall the school should have announced that the court would be forevermore known as Bob Knight Court. He should have broken Dean Smith's all-time record for victories at Indiana, one of *the* basketball schools, not at Texas Tech, a basketball desert where the athletic department literally had to take out ads begging people to show up for Knight's record-breaking games.

Even now, because he can't ever admit he might have made

a mistake, he has refused to come back to be inducted into the Indiana Hall of Fame. He remains bitter and angry even though the president who fired him, Myles Brand, is dead and almost everyone involved in his banishment from IU is no longer at the school.

Of course, that's why people can never get enough of Knight. His good qualities are *so* good, his bad ones *so* bad. If I had a dollar for every time someone told me a story about encountering Knight and finding him gracious and charming and funny, I would never have to work another day in my life. If I also had a dollar for every time I've been told a story about Knight being a bully or being rude and obnoxious, I'd be Bill Gates.

People rarely encounter a Knight who is innocuous. They encounter a Knight who leaves them with their mouths agape—in awe or in agony. There's no in-between.

I'm often asked what my relationship with Knight is like today. It has—not surprisingly—ebbed and flowed through the years. Eight years after the book was published, Knight apparently decided to forgive me. We began exchanging hellos when we encountered each other, even occasionally engaging in small talk. In 2003, when I was writing my book on Red Auerbach, we talked about Red on the phone for almost two hours and—as is always the case with the good Knight—he was funny, insightful, and full of anecdotes that aided the book immeasurably.

At the end of the conversation I said, "Bob, I know you did this for Red, but I want you to know I really appreciate it."

"No John, I really should thank you," he answered. "It's almost impossible to do anything for Red, and I'm really glad you gave me the chance to do this. I hope the book is great."

Can you ask for anything more than that?

Six years later, I had to introduce Knight at the annual Army Sports Hall of Fame Banquet. Mike Krzyzewski was being inducted and Knight was giving his induction speech. I was the emcee.

The end of my introduction went like this: "So please welcome college basketball's all-time winningest coach, a member of the Army Sports Hall of Fame and the Basketball Hall of Fame—but most important, the man who built my house . . . Bob Knight."

Everyone in the room laughed—except for the one man there *not* dressed in a tuxedo.

You can guess who that was. The sweater was blue.

Maybe on the fiftieth anniversary of the book we can get together and toast each other. But I'm not counting on it.

—John Feinstein
June 2011

A
Season
on the
Brink

Foreword

By Al McGuire

My first memory of Bob Knight is a vivid one. This was back in 1970, when my Marquette team was getting ready to play in the NIT semifinals against Louisiana State, which starred Pistol Pete Maravich. We were playing the second game of the semifinal doubleheader.

The first game was between Army and St. John's. It was one of those games that make coaches old, a one- or two-point game the whole way. Bob was coaching Army, and his teams were known for this type of game. They never had very much talent, but they were always very hard to play against because they were so aggressive and tenacious on defense. They were like a little dog that grabs hold of your leg and won't let go.

I was standing in the tunnel leading from the locker rooms to the floor when the game ended, waiting to go out for the second game. I don't remember exactly what happened (I'm sure Bob does in detail) but Army lost the game at the buzzer and I think there may have been a touch call that went against them at the end to lose the game. Either way, a killer to lose. I've been through a few of those myself.

As the teams came off the floor, I saw Bob. In a situation like that, maybe you shake a hand, offer a word of condolence. I didn't say anything. The reason was because I had never seen anyone look so drained, so *beaten*, in my life. It was a look I'll never forget because I can't remember seeing another coach with that look. He had given the game everything he could and losing it just destroyed him. You could see it all over his face. Bob couldn't have been more than thirty back then but when he came off the floor, he looked like an old man I've never forgotten that look.

If Bob Knight retired today, he would be a lock for a place in the basketball Hall of Fame. On any list of the great coaches that the game has ever known, the name Bob Knight is going to be somewhere near the top. With luck, someday it might be at the very top. He's that good a coach.

Bob Knight knows so much basketball that I never talk about the game with him. I don't know enough about it to do so. I feel the game more than I know it, that's the way I've always been. I can talk one thing—winning. But don't ask me how. My assistant, Hank Raymonds, was in charge of that. I never studied the game. Bob has studied it, dissected it, and in many ways changed it over the years. If he wants to talk basketball, I listen. But I never argue with him about the game. About people, maybe. About basketball, never.

When I was at Marquette, we played some of his best Indiana teams. In 1976, in fact, we played his undefeated team in the Mideast regional final. That was one of my best teams, probably a more talented team than the one that won the national championship a year later. I was so uptight during the game that I got two technical fouls that certainly didn't do my team any good. I doubt we would have won, though. Bob had a great *team*, and I put that word in italics because that's what they were. None of the individuals on that team was a superstar—Quinn Buckner, Scott May, Bobby Wilkerson, Tom Abernethy, and Kent Benson—but as a group they were unbeatable. They had been coached to play a certain way and they never deviated. They also never lost.

What Bob did then was to take you out of your game. If he had a week to prepare for you, he would find a way to take away the things you did best. If you had to play one of his teams in the NCAAs, you always wanted to play him on the second game of the weekend because that way he had less time to prepare. Give Bob time to prepare and most often he would figure out a way to beat you.

I think that's changed over the years. Bob is as good as he ever was, but other coaches have gotten better. They know how to prepare better and that makes it harder for Bob to dominate as a coach the way he once did. He still gets 100 percent out of his team at all times. The difference is that other coaches are coming closer and closer to doing that all the time. He hasn't come down, but they have gone up.

I'm not sure he understands that. His feeling has always been that if he knows his business, then if the kids listen to him, you get the job done. One of his great frustrations at West Point was not understanding that at West Point you couldn't get the job done a lot of the time just because it was West Point. Bob always believed you could and that's why losing tore him up so much. That's why he looked the way he did that year at the NIT.

Losing still tears him up. This is his greatest asset and his greatest albatross all at once. Bob thinks he can beat the game. Nobody can beat the game. If you could, there would be no game. But Bob keeps trying to beat it anyway and when he doesn't he thinks of it as failure, *his* failure, and it tears him apart.

I remember a few years ago I arrived in Bloomington early on a Friday morning to tape a spot we were doing for NBC with Bob. I picked up the morning paper and read that Indiana had lost the night before to Iowa by one in overtime. I thought, "Oh boy, is he going to be in a lousy mood." When we got to Indiana, I went downstairs to his locker room and I knocked on the door.

Bob asked who it was and I said, "It's Al." He said, "Hey, Al, can we do this another day, we're real busy." I couldn't do that. We had the crew, we were all set, our schedule was too tight. I explained that. Finally, the door opened. There was the entire coaching staff. They looked like death. They had been sitting in that room all night looking at tape over and over and over again. I thought the assistant coaches were going to kiss me just for showing up and rescuing them. God knows how long they might have stayed in there wrestling with that tape if we hadn't shown up. Bob just can't let go of a loss. He has to have answers. The trouble is sometimes the answer is obvious: the other team was better.

But that's also what makes Bob great. I saw his team practice last November and I thought he was going to have serious problems. They had no size, little experience, and very little quickness. I was worried. I thought it was going to be another very tough season for him. So, they go out and win twenty-one games. That was a great coaching job, maybe as good a job as Bob has ever done. He's still a brilliant coach. Different from other coaches today, but brilliant.

When I think of Bob Knight, I think of Vince Lombardi and I think of Red Auerbach. Personally, I don't think either one of them could have coached the way he did in this day and age.

Maybe they would have adjusted because the great ones can do that. Bob is a throwback, he's from that school. He's a complete disciplinarian. He demands complete loyalty and dedication and he gives it in return.

I guess I'm like all of Bob's friends in that I look at his dedication and his work ethic and I admire them but I also worry because of them. I wish he didn't put so much of himself into the game. I wish he had more outside interests. I know he hunts and fishes and enjoys doing both. But if he's going to fish on Tuesday, he has to be completely successful with basketball on the other six days to really enjoy Tuesday.

I've told him that I honestly don't see what's left for him in college coaching. He has won every championship there is to win, including the Olympics; he's proved his greatness over and over, including this last season. What's left? Bob reminds me of Alexander the Great, who conquered the world and then sat down and cried because there was nothing left to conquer. I don't think he has any true goals left in the college game.

I would love to see him get into television. I know he's flirted with it in the past and I think he would be terrific. He's so bright, so articulate, and so good at stringing thoughts together when he wants to. I've been with him when he's done TV on All-Star games during the off-season and he's been terrific. I'd be happy to see him make the switch because I'm like everyone else, I don't want to see someone with a $2 Saturday night special knock him off the coaching pedestal he deserves.

What I mean by that is this: Suppose some referee decides that the way to make a name for himself is to draw Bob Knight into some kind of fight or battle. Or suppose some fan decides to pick a fight with him. Or suppose some administrator comes to Indiana and decides he's the guy to prove once and for all that he's Bob Knight's boss. If anything like that happens, Bob is going to be judged wrong no matter what he does because of the past. He deserves better than that.

What people don't see, what they don't understand about Bob is that he's a warm, sensitive, and funny guy. Yes funny. The problem with Bob's sense of humor most of the time is that he never smiles when he tells a joke. Half the time people don't know he's joking because they look at his face and all they see is this deadpan. By the time they realize he's kidding it's too late.

I think some people know about the warm and sensitive side. I think this book will show that side quite a bit and and I'm glad. Bob always tried to act so tough—all the screaming and yelling. He's really not tough, not at all. Get by that and ask for help—or don't ask for help—and he'll be the first one to offer it. All the critical things he says about his players—try and criticize one of them and see what kind of response you get. Be ready to duck, too.

What Bob is, more than anything, is intense. He is intense about everything he does. If he takes you to a restaurant he wants you to love that restaurant just the way he does. If you watch his basketball team he wants you to think he's a great basketball team —unless he doesn't think it's great. He loves to compete. He loves to win. But it's never that simple with him because nothing is simple with Bob. He wants to know *how* you won and *why* you won. And he has to know *how* you lost and *why* you lost. That's to make sure it doesn't happen again. I always used to say just, "let's win and get the hell out of here." Bob can't do that. He has to ask all the questions *and* get all the answers. Until he does that, he isn't satisfied.

I've never really tried to give Bob advice because among his older friends, I'm fairly young at fifty-eight. Bob likes to surround himself with older coaches. He's happy with them around, comfortable. He respects them, he feels he learns from them. Once though, I was at a clinic with him in Cherry Hill, New Jersey, and I told him I thought a day would come when he needed to calm down at least a little, that if he rode the razor's edge all the time the way he did, sooner or later, he would slip over.

I think he listens when people tell him things like that, but he's gotten so good at riding the edge over the years that it's hard for him to pull off it. When he threw the chair, he slipped over the edge, no doubt about it. That's what I mean when I say that anyone who rides the edge that long, even someone as intelligent as Bob, will slip at some point.

I hope that was a one-time thing. I tend to think it was because I have so much faith in Bob. He's always come out a winner in the end. At times, people have questioned his methods, but no one has ever questioned his results either in terms of wins and losses or in the kind of kid he produces and has produced over the years. I think as long as Bob learns to understand, at least to some degree, that even he can never beat the game, he can coach and coach successfully as long as he wants to. And if he wants to get out he's got a place in the Hall of Fame and in the broadcast booth waiting for him. He's not only one of basketball's great coaches, but one of its most compelling and fascinating figures.

When I had dinner last November with Bob and John Feinstein, I made two predictions. The first one was that with all the time they were going to spend together, they wouldn't be speaking to each other by March. Apparently, I was wrong on that one—but not by much. My second prediction was that if John survived the season, he would have a terrific book on his hands. To get to watch a master at work up close is a rare opportunity.

Undoubtedly, John saw Bob at his best and at his worst. To understand someone you have to see everything, not just the good. Even great coaches have bad days. Even good people are human and make mistakes. The point of this book is to give people an idea of what makes a great coach, one as complex as Bob Knight, tick. And to give people an idea of how the people around him survive, or thrive and why they are willing to put up with all his foibles.

Living through a season, especially a season of change, as the one just past was for Bob Knight, strikes me as a wonderful way to do that. I told John if he survived the season, I would eagerly look forward to reading his book because when you are a fan of Bob Knight's—and I am one—you want to know all you can about the man. And, even if you aren't a fan, this is a story about a complex, brilliant, and difficult man.

Bob Knight is unique. In another time, he would have been a superb general. He never made it past private in the Army, but he has proved himself to be a fantastic leader throughout his career. He may well be the last of the great coaching dictators. The last of a breed.

But also the first of a breed. After all, there is only one Bob Knight.

On the Brink

NOVEMBER 24, 1985. . . . The day was no different from any other that fall. A cold rain had been falling steadily all morning and all afternoon, and the wind cut holes in their faces as they raced from their cars to the warmth of the lobby, and then into the locker room a moment later. This was Sunday. In six days, Indiana would begin its basketball season, and no one connected with the team had any idea what the season would hold. The only thing everyone knew for certain was that no one could live through another season like the last one.

Bob Knight knew this better than any of them. The 1984–85 season had been the most painful he had lived through in twenty years as a coach. Nine months after what might have been his most glorious night in coaching, he had suffered through his most ignominious. He had gone from Olympic hero to national buffoon, from being canonized in editorials to being lampooned in cartoons.

In the summer of 1984, Knight had coached perhaps the best amateur team in the history of basketball. His U.S. Olympic team had destroyed every opponent it faced on the way to the Olympic gold medal. And yet, because of the Soviet boycott, Knight could not feel, even in his greatest moment, complete satisfaction.

He had returned to coach at Indiana and had experienced his worst season. He benched starters, threw his leading rebounder off the team, and generally acted like a man who was burned out—scorched out might be a better term. Some friends urged him to quit, or at least take a year off. But Knight couldn't quit; he had to prove himself—again.

At age forty-five, Knight was starting over. Not from scratch, but not that far from it. He knew by the end of the previous season that he had to change. He knew he could not lash out at his team every time it failed. He surely knew that he could never again throw a chair during a game as he had done in February during a loss to Purdue. He had to work harder than he had worked in recent years. He had to be certain that he still wanted to coach and act that way. He had to get his team playing the way it had played during his six years at West Point and during his first thirteen years at Indiana. Above all, he had to be more patient.

For Knight, the last was the most difficult. Bob Knight was many things: brilliant, driven, compassionate—but not patient. His explosions at players and officials on the bench during games were legendary. To those who knew him, his eruptions in practice and the locker room were frightening. Friends worried after he threw the chair that he was destined to end up like Woody Hayes, the Ohio State football coach whose career had ended when he slugged an opposing player in frustration at the end of a bowl game.

Knight had come to practice on October 15, eager to begin again. Players and assistant coaches noticed right away that he was teaching more, that he spent less time talking to buddies on the sidelines and more time caught up in the work. He *was* more patient. He seemed to understand that this was a young team, an inexperienced team, a fragile team. It was a team that had to be nurtured, not bullied.

Now, though, the season was just six days away. When Knight looked onto the floor he saw a team that in no way resembled the great teams he had coached in the mid 1970s or, for that matter, the team he had coached in 1981, when he won his second national championship. They couldn't attack defensively the way Knight liked to attack. They couldn't intimidate. Worse than that, he thought, they could be intimidated. Every day he came to practice wanting to see them get better, looking for hope. Some days he found it: Steve Alford was a brilliant shooter, a gritty player who could score against almost any defense. Daryl Thomas, the 6-foot-7-inch center, and Andre Harris, the 6-6 forward recruited out of a junior college, were superb athletes, blessed with great quickness around the basket. Rick Calloway, the rail-thin freshman, was going to be a wonderful player some day.

But all of them had up days and down days. And the rest of the team was too young or too slow or too small. The vulnerability preyed on Knight's mind. The last thing in the world Bob Knight ever wanted to be was vulnerable. He had felt vulnerable, beatable, mortal the previous season when his team had finished under .500 in Big Ten play (7–11) for the first time in fourteen years. The NCAA had invited sixty-four teams to its postseason tournament, more than at any time in history. Indiana wasn't one of them.

Knight was incapable of accepting failure. Every defeat was personal; *his* team lost, a team *he* had selected and coached. None of the victories or milestones of the past mattered. The fact that he could quit right then and know that his place in history was secure didn't matter. Failure on any level all but destroyed him, especially failure in coaching because it was coaching that gave him his identity, made him special, set him apart.

And so on this rainy, ugly Sunday, beginning the final week of preparation for another season, Knight was angry. He was angry because as his team scrimmaged he could see its flaws. Even playing perfectly, following every instruction he gave, this team would be beatable. How could that be? Knight believed—and his record seemed to back him up—that the system he had devised over the years was the best way there was to play basketball. He always told his players that. "Follow our rules, do exactly what we tell you and you will not lose," he would say. "But boys, you have to listen to me."

The boys listened. Always, they listened. But they didn't always assimilate, and sometimes, even when they did, they could not execute what they had been told. That was what frightened Knight—yes, frightened him—about this team. It might do everything it was told and still not be very good. He liked these players; there wasn't, in his view, a bad kid on the team. But he wondered about their potential as basketball players.

Today the player bothering him most was Daryl Thomas. In Thomas, Knight saw a player of huge potential. Thomas has what coaches call a "million dollar body." He was strong and wide, yet quick. He could shoot the basketball with both hands, and when he went past bigger men to the basket, they had little choice but to foul him.

But Thomas was not one of those basketball players who like to get up on game day and eat nails for breakfast to get ready. He was a middle-class kid from Chicago, extremely bright and sensitive. Knight's angry words often hurt him. Other Indiana players, Alford for one, knew that Knight would say almost anything when he was angry and that the only way to deal with that was to ignore the words of anger and listen to the words of wisdom. Dan Dakich, who had graduated the previous spring to become a graduate assistant coach, had told the freshman Calloway, "When he's calling you an asshole, don't listen. But when he starts telling you *why* you're an asshole, listen. That way you'll get better."

Thomas couldn't shut off some words and hear others. He heard them all, and they hurt.

Knight didn't want to hurt Thomas. He wanted to make him a better player, but he honestly believed that some days Thomas had to be hurt if he was going to get better. He had used this tactic on Landon Turner, another sensitive black youngster with immense ability. Turner, 6-10 and 250 pounds, had emerged from a shell of mediocrity as a junior to play a key role in Indiana's 1981 run to the national championship. That summer he was crippled in an automobile accident. Knight, who had once put Tampax in Turner's locker, who had cursed him and called him names for three years, spent the next six months raising money to pay Landon Turner's medical bills.

Now, he was hoping that Thomas would bloom as a junior the way Turner had. Some days he cajoled. Other days he joked. Today, though, he raged. Practice had not gone well; after three straight good practices, the team had been sluggish. Intellectually, Knight knew this was inevitable. Emotionally, it drove him to the brink of complete hysteria.

First, he screamed at Thomas for playing carelessly. Then, he banished him from the scrimmage, sending him to a lone basket at the end of the court to practice with Magnus Pelkowski, a 6-10 sophomore who was not scrimmaging because of an injury.

"Daryl," he screamed as Thomas walked toward where Pelkowski was working, "get the f— out of my sight. If that's the best you can give us after two days' rest, get away from me. There is absolutely no way you'll start on Saturday. No way. You cost yourself that chance today by f—— around. You are so terrible, it's just awful. I don't know what the f— you are thinking about. You think I was mad last year? You saw me, I was the maddest sonofabitch you ever saw. You want another year like that? Just get the f— out of my sight."

When Knight is angry, he spews profanities so fast they're hard to keep track of. In the right mood, he can talk for hours without ever using an obscenity. In this mood, every other word was one. Turning to his assistant coaches, Knight added, "F— Daryl Thomas. Don't even mess with him anymore. We've worked three years with the sonofabitch. Use him to make Magnus a better player. At least *he* wants to play."

They played on without Thomas. Finally, after about twenty minutes, he was allowed to return. But he was tight. Some players react to Knight's anger with anger of their own and play better. Not Thomas; he tightens up. When Courtney Witte, a backup forward with far less natural ability than Thomas, scored over him from inside, Knight blew up again. "Daryl, get in the game or get out! Do you know you haven't scored a basket inside since Jesus Christ was lecturing in Omaha? Just get out, Daryl. Get him the f— in the locker room. He hasn't done a f—— thing since we got out here."

Thomas departed. His teammates felt for him, because every one of them had been in his shoes at some point. Especially the better players; Knight rarely picks on the second teamers. The rest of the team lasted two plays before Knight blew up again and told them all to join Thomas in the locker room. Knight was genuinely angry, but he was also playing a game with his team. It was a dangerous game, but one he had played successfully for twenty years: put pressure on them now so they will react well to pressure from opponents later. But this was a delicate team and a delicate situation. Last year's team had folded under Knight's pressure. Knight knew that. Some days this fall he restrained himself because of that. But not today.

In the locker room, Knight ordered the assistant coaches to play back the tape of the day's practice. As often happens when Knight is angry, he began invoking the past. "I'd like to know when somebody in here is going to go up and grab somebody and punch them when they watch this bullshit. [Quinn] Buckner would have hit somebody by now. Do you know that? He just would have gone up and hit one of you f——. People I played with in college would have killed you people if you pulled that shit on them."

Quinn Buckner had been the captain of the 1976 national championship team. He was, without question, Knight's all-time favorite player. He had been a leader, a coach on the floor, but no one could remember him hitting a teammate. Part of that was because any time two players squared off in practice, Knight would say to them, "Anybody who wants to fight, you can fight me." No one wanted to fight Knight.

Knight stormed out, leaving the assistants to go through the tape with the players. The room was dark, almost quiet. The four assistant coaches, Kohn Smith, Joby Wright, Royce Waltman, and Ron Felling, gingerly began pointing out mistakes. With the exception of Felling, they had all lived through the nightmare of the previous year, and they didn't want a repeat, either. But no one was really listening as the coaches droned on about missed screens and lack of concentration. Everyone in the room knew Knight was going to be back. Most people get angry, scream and yell, and then calm down. Knight, more often than not, gets even angrier.

Sure enough, five minutes later, he returned. Thomas was on his mind. "Daryl, you know you are a f—— joke," he said. "I have no more confidence in your ability to go out and play hard than I did when you were a freshman. I don't know how you've f—— up your head in the last two weeks but you're as f—— up now as you've ever been. I wouldn't turn you loose in a game if you were the last guy I had because of your f—— head. This is just bullshit.

"*Honest to Christ I want to just go home and cry when I watch this shit. Don't you boys understand? Don't you know how bad I want to see Indiana play basketball? I want to see Indiana play so bad I can f—— taste it. I want a good team so bad it hurts. I want to go out there and kick somebody's ass.*"

He looked at Winston Morgan, a fifth-year senior playing without a scholarship. "Do you?" Morgan nodded assent. "*Bullshit. Lying sonofabitch. Show me out there and I'll believe it. I come out here to practice and see this and I just want to quit. Just go home and never come back.*"

Knight was hoarse from yelling. His voice was almost choking with emotion. He stopped. The tape started. It ran for one play. "Stop, stop it," Knight said. "Daryl, look at that. You don't even run back down the floor hard. That's all I need to know about you, Daryl. All you want to be out there is comfortable. You don't work, you don't sprint back. Look at that! You never push yourself. You know what you are Daryl? You are the worst f—— pussy I've ever seen play basketball at this school. The absolute worst pussy ever. You have more goddamn ability than 95 percent of the players we've had here but you are a pussy from the top of your head to the bottom of your feet. An absolute f—— pussy. That's my assessment of you after three years."

Finally, with Thomas fighting back tears, Knight turned on the rest of his team. For ten more minutes he railed at them, called them names, told them they couldn't beat anybody. He told them not to bother coming to practice the next day, or the day after. He didn't care what they did. "Get them out of here," he finally told the assistants. "Get them the f— out."

Knight walked out onto the floor. He was drained. He turned to Kohn Smith. "Go talk to Daryl," he said. Knight knew he had gone too far with Thomas, and undoubtedly he had regretted many of the words as soon as they were out of his mouth. But he couldn't take them back. Instead, he would send Smith, who was as quiet and gentle as Knight was loud and brutal, to talk to Thomas.

Thomas cried. Smith comforted him. Thomas was facing the same question everyone who comes in contact with Knight faces sooner or later: Is it worth it? Does the end justify the means? He knew Knight just wanted him to be a better player. He knew Knight liked him and cared about him. He knew that if anyone ever attacked him, Knight would come to his defense. But was all that worth it for this? This was Knight at his meanest. Every player who comes to Indiana faces the screaming, raving Knight at some point in his life. Some leave because it isn't worth it to them, but most stay. And most leave convinced Knight's way is the right way. But now Daryl Thomas wondered. He had to wonder; he wouldn't have been human if he hadn't wondered, if he hadn't cried.

They practiced early the next morning, but without Knight: he stayed home, not wanting to put himself or his team through another emotional trauma.

One morning later, Knight called Thomas into his locker room. He put his arm around Thomas and told him to sit down. He spoke softly, gently. There were no other coaches, no teammates in the room. "Daryl, I hate it when I get on you the way I did Sunday, I really do," he said. "But do you know why I do it?"

Thomas shook his head. "Because, Daryl, sometimes I think I want you to be a great player more than you want you to be a great player. And that just tears me up inside. Because there is no way you will ever be a great player unless *you* want it. You have the ability. But I can coach, teach, scream, and yell from now until Doomsday and you won't be any good unless you want it as bad as I do. Right now, I *know* you don't want it as bad as I do. Somehow, I have to convince you to feel that way. I don't know if this is the right way, but it's my way. You know it's worked for other people in the past. Try, Daryl, please try. That's all I ask. If you try just as hard as you can, I promise you it will be worth it. I know it will. Don't try for me, Daryl. Try for you."

Thomas listened to all this. Unlike some players who might not understand what Knight was saying, he understood. This was the way his coach coached; that would never change. Thomas was going through the same emotional swings that other gifted Knight players had gone through. One in particular, Isiah Thomas (no relation to Daryl) had come out of the Chicago ghetto and had lit up Indiana basketball for two years with his talent and his personality. He and Knight had fought for two years while Thomas starred for Indiana, and had continued to fight after Thomas left Indiana early to turn pro.

At a clinic once, someone asked Isiah Thomas what he really thought about Knight. "You know there were times," Isiah Thomas answered, "when if I had had a gun, I think I would have shot him. And there were other times when I wanted to put my arms around him, hug him, and tell him that I loved him."

Those words, perhaps better than any others, sum up the love-hate relationship between Knight and his players, even between Knight and his friends. To know Bob Knight is to love him. To know Bob Knight is to hate him. Because he views the world and everyone in it in strict black-and-white terms, he is inevitably viewed that way by others.

In less than forty-eight hours, Daryl Thomas had seen the black and the white. He had felt the full range of emotions. That Saturday, when Indiana played its first game of the season, Daryl Thomas was Indiana's best player. Not for Knight. For himself. But it was only one game. A long season lay ahead.

2.

Rise and Fall

Bob Knight spent the fall of 1985 driven and haunted by the year just past. The high was so high, and the low so low, that the memories were vivid and sharp. Partly because of his prodigious memory, but more because it provided much-needed comfort, he could recall the Olympics in almost minute-by-minute detail, especially the climax.

It was warm in Los Angeles on August 10, warm yet comfortable, just as it had been throughout the 1984 Summer Olympics. Miraculously, there had been no smog, no giant traffic snafus, and no serious security problems throughout the two weeks.

Knight awoke that morning feeling the way he always feels on the morning of a basketball game: keyed up, excited, nervous, perhaps even a little more than usual, because this was not merely another game. This was a game, a night, a moment he had waited for his entire life.

That night he would coach the United States of America in a

basketball game to decide the winner of an Olympic gold medal. In speeches long after that game had been won, Knight would say often, "If you cannot fight for your country in war, then I can think of no greater honor than to represent it in the Olympic Games."

For Knight, a true, red-white-and-blue patriot, this was far more than a basketball game. This was the culmination of a crusade, one that he had once believed he would never get the chance to carry out. Even though Knight had been recognized for years as a superb coach, the best there was in the opinion of many, his controversial temperament had brought him as much derision as his coaching ability had acclaim.

Nothing in Knight's career had drawn more fire than his first experience representing his country as coach of an international team. It was in Puerto Rico in 1979. While leading the U.S. team to the gold medal in the Pan American Games, Knight was arrested for assaulting a Puerto Rican police officer. Witnesses to the incident, which took place during a U.S. practice session, are unanimous in saying that the policeman was far more at fault than Knight, that the policeman was rude and officious and practically begged Knight to get into an altercation with him.

Even though Knight was put through the humiliation of being dragged from the practice floor in handcuffs, he probably would have been judged a victim in that incident had he simply allowed the witnesses to tell the story. But that isn't Knight's way. He is completely incapable of letting an incident—any incident—simply die a natural death. Indiana University vice-president Edgar Williams, one of Knight's best friends, describes that side of him best: "Bob always—always—has to have the last word. And more often than not, it's that last word that gets him in trouble."

Puerto Rico was a perfect demonstration of Williams's words. In speeches long after he had left San Juan behind, Knight was still taking shots. He talked about mooning Puerto Rico as he left it, made crude jokes about Puerto Rico, and, ultimately, turned public sentiment around: instead of being the victim of an officious cop, he made himself the Ugly American. Knight thought he was being funny; he couldn't understand that many found his brand of humor offensive. And because he chose not to understand, the person he hurt most was Robert Montgomery Knight. It was almost as if he wanted to testify against himself after a dozen witnesses had proved his innocence.

Because of Puerto Rico, Knight thought he would never be named Olympic coach. In 1978, when the coach for 1980 was selected, he thought he would get the job. He had coached Indiana to the national championship in 1976 and had built a program that won sixty-three of sixty-four games over two seasons. But, in a close vote that went to a second ballot, Providence coach Dave Gavitt was named. Knight was crushed by the choice because he wanted more than anything to take a U.S. team to Moscow—site of the 1980 Games—and beat the hell out of the Russians. As it turned out, Gavitt never got that chance either.

As runner-up for the Olympic job in 1978, Knight became the Pan-Am coach. That led to Puerto Rico and, in Knight's mind, finished his chances to be Olympic coach. When the selection committee met in May 1982 there were two major candidates: Knight and John Thompson, the Georgetown coach. It took three ballots, but the committee named Knight. It was testimony to his extraordinary ability as a coach that, in spite of Puerto Rico and the aftermath, he was given another chance.

When Knight learned he had been selected he called three people: Pete Newell and Fred Taylor, his coaching mentors, and Bob Hammel, sports editor of *The Bloomington Herald-Telephone*— his best friend. All three men remember the emotion in his voice that evening, rare emotion from a man who doesn't like to admit to being emotional.

"He was like a little kid," Hammel said. "I had been at a track meet in Minneapolis, and when I called my office, they said he had called, which wasn't unusual. What was unusual was that he had left his home phone number with the desk. Usually, he's very sensitive about giving strangers his number but he had just changed it and wanted to be sure I reached him. When I called, the first thing he said was, 'You'll never guess what just happened. They've named me Olympic coach.'

"I knew how disappointed he had been in '78, and I knew he felt that the scars of San Juan would be too much to overcome. In fact, I didn't even know that was the weekend they were picking the coach because he never mentioned it to me. He was as private about that as he's ever been."

Once he had the job, Knight was a man with a mission: to destroy the hated Russians, to make sure the world knew that the U.S. played basketball on one level and the rest of the world on another. He would study all the opponents, study every player available to him, select twelve players who would play the game *his* way, and then he wouldn't just beat the rest of the world, he would obliterate it.

He selected three friends as his assistant coaches: C. M. Newton of Vanderbilt, Don Donoher of Dayton, and George Raveling of Iowa. He scouted, organized, and prepared on every level.

Knight was very much a general preparing to do battle. In the summer of 1983, when Donoher and Knight were in France to scout the European championships, they took a side trip that spoke volumes for Knight's secret dreams. "I picked Bob up at the airport," recalled Donoher, "and the first thing he told me was that we were going to Bastogne (site of the Battle of the Bulge). We had to drive all the way across France to get there, but that's what we did. He knew roads that weren't on the map we had. He would say, 'There's a road coming up here on the left that Patton took en route . . .' and sure enough the road would be there. After we finished there, we drove back across France because he was determined to go to Normandy. We spent an entire day at Normandy. We must have examined every gun, every foxhole, every cave, every piece of barbed wire. It was like having a history book talk to you. He knew everything. Finally, near the end of the day, we were standing looking out at Omaha Beach. Bob had this faraway look in his eyes. He looked all around and then he looked at me and said, 'Can you imagine how great it would have been to have been here in a command position on D-Day?' "

But at the last minute, fate and politics tossed a giant wrench into his plans: the Russians, getting even for Jimmy Carter's 1980 boycott in Moscow, decided to boycott Los Angeles. Even after the April announcement, Knight kept preparing for the Russians right up until the day in July when it was no longer possible for them to come. Ed Williams, watching his friend during this period, saw him as a general who had prepared the perfect battle plan, trained his troops, raised his sword to lead the charge, and then saw the enemy waving a white flag. Playing Canada and Spain in the medal round of the Olympics was a little like sailing into Tokyo Bay after the atomic bombs had been dropped.

But Knight never let himself approach the Olympics that way. For one thing, he couldn't afford to; if, by some chance, he slipped and his team lost to Spain or Canada or West Germany, he would never live it down. He knew how much Henry Iba, the coach of the 1972 Olympic team, had suffered after the stupefying loss to the Russians in Munich. Knight thought Iba a great coach, and looked up to him. It hurt Knight to hear people say that Iba, who had coached the U.S. to easy gold medals in 1964 and 1968, was too old to coach that team and had, because of his conservative style, cost the U.S. the gold medal. Knight was angered by the loss in Munich because he thought the U.S. had been cheated. *Cheated by the Russians.* To the boy from Orrville, Ohio, that was one small step short of letting the Russians invade. Knight cannot bear defeat on any level; to suffer one on the Olympic level would have destroyed him.

And so, he drove everyone connected with the Olympic team as if they would be facing a combination of the Russians, the Bill Russell–era Boston Celtics, and Lew Alcindor's UCLA team. The Olympic Trials, held during an ugly, rainy week in Bloomington in April, were brutal. Seventy-six players practiced and played three times a day in Indiana's dark, dingy field house, as Knight and his assistants watched from a football-coaching tower.

The players were pushed into a state of complete exhaustion; by week's end, Knight had what he wanted. Some wondered why players like Charles Barkley and Antoine Carr weren't selected while players like Jeff Turner and John Koncak were. The answer was simple: Knight wanted players who would take his orders without question. Barkley and Carr, though more talented than Turner and Koncak, might follow orders, but might not. There would be no maybes on Knight's Olympic team.

It was still a team of breathtaking talent: Michael Jordan, the 6-foot-6 skywalker from North Carolina; Patrick Ewing, the intimidating 7-1 center from Georgetown; Wayman Tisdale, 6-9 and unstoppable, from Oklahoma; Sam Perkins, Jordan's brilliant

Carolina teammate; Alvin Robertson, the 6-4 defensive whiz from Arkansas; and Steve Alford, Knight's own freshman point guard. Alford was easily the team's best shooter and earned his spot with tough play that belied his baby-faced good looks.

Knight took his team and demanded more of it than any team he had ever coached—which is saying a lot. He pushed the players, insulted them, yelled at them. Some of them had never been spoken to this way before. None, with the exception of Alford, had ever been pushed this way before. Some of them hated him for it, and cursed the day they had ever shown up at the Olympic Trials. But that was how Knight wanted it. He wanted each of them to understand that this would happen to all of them only once in their lives, and that they had to give him absolutely everything they had. He wanted no close calls, nothing left to chance.

As it turned out, the team did everything Knight could possibly have asked. It raced through a nine-game exhibition series against players from the National Basketball Association, never beaten and rarely challenged. The preliminary round of the Olympics— five games—was a mere formality. In the quarterfinals against West Germany, they were sloppy but still won by eleven, their closest game. They annihilated Canada in the semifinals, leaving only Spain, a team they had beaten by twenty-five points in preliminary play, between them and the gold medal.

The team looked unbeatable, but there were still nerves that last Friday. The U.S. hockey team had proved in 1980 that miracles can happen; Knight wanted no miracles in this game. The tip-off was scheduled for 7 P.M. The team arrived at the Forum shortly after 5 P.M. There was a problem, though: Jordan had brought a wrong-colored uniform and several players had brought the wrong warmups.

"Jesus Christ," Knight said to his coaches, "these guys aren't ready to play. All they're thinking about is going home tomorrow."

Donoher, with police escort, was dispatched to go back to downtown Los Angeles to the Olympic Village at the University of Southern California to find Jordan's uniform. Ater turning Jordan's room upside down and finding nothing, he returned to the

Forum, distraught. Only then did trainer Tim Garl tell him that the people at the front desk had been holding the uniform. They hadn't recognized Donoher, and therefore hadn't stopped him to give him the uniform.

Nerve endings were frayed. Donoher was doing a decent Knight imitation, spraying obscenities off the locker-room walls. But, uniforms and warmups aside, this team was ready to play. When Knight walked into the locker room for his final pep talk, he was ready to breathe fire. Already that day, Willie Davis, the former Green Bay Packer, had been the last of a long list of people who had spoken to the team. Davis told them that they might never do anything as important the rest of their lives as what they would do on this night.

Now Knight was ready to deliver some final words of inspiration. But when he flipped over the blackboard on which he would normally write the names of the other teams' starters, he found a note scotch-taped to the board. It had been written by Jordan: "Coach," it said, "after all the shit we've been through, there is no way we lose tonight."

Knight looked at the twelve players and ditched his speech. "Let's go play," he said. Walking onto the floor, Knight folded Jordan's note into a pocket (he still has it in his office today) and told his coaches, "This game will be over in about ten minutes."

He was wrong. It took five. The final score was 101–68. Spain never had a chance. The general sent his troops out to annihilate and they did just that. When it was over, when he had finally reached that golden moment, Knight's first thought wasn't, *I've done it, I've won the Olympic gold medal.* It was, *Where is Henry Iba?* Knight had made certain the old coach was with the team every step of the way from the Olympic Trials right through each Olympic game. Now, when the players came to him to carry him off the floor on their shoulders, Knight had one more order left for them: "Coach Iba first." And so, following their orders to the end, the players carried Henry Iba around the floor first. Then they gave Knight a ride. Then, and only then, did he smile.

It was, Bob Hammel thought as he watched, more a half smile, a look of relief more than a look of joy. They hadn't so much won as they had not lost. But still, there was a satisfaction. He had now coached an Olympic gold medal winner, a Pan American Games gold medal winner, two NCAA champions, and an NIT champion. He had won every championship there was to win in amateur basketball. He had reached the pinnacle. He was, without question, the best college basketball coach in the world. Maybe he was the best college basketball coach *ever*.

The next morning, as he had said he would all along, he flew to Montana, put on his waders, and sat in the middle of a river by himself and fished. This was his reward. His release. He sat in the river, having done everything he had set out to do in life.

He was forty-three years old.

———

Practice began at Indiana that fall with a mixture of anticipation and trepidation in the air. A great team was anticipated. The previous season, a too-young Indiana team had gone 22–9 and had reached the Final Eight of the NCAA tournament with a victory over top-ranked North Carolina that had to rank among the great upsets in tournament history. North Carolina, led by Jordan and Perkins, had a 28–2 record, and some had already declared it one of the great teams of all time.

But Alford, just a freshman, scored twenty-seven points and Dan Dakich, the prototype slow white kid who couldn't run or jump, kept Jordan under control. Knight completely outcoached Dean Smith, the one man considered in his class as a coach, and the Hoosiers won the game. That they lost in the next round to a Virginia team that wasn't in the same class with North Carolina was disappointing. But it didn't change the promise the team had shown in the North Carolina game.

And so, as the 1984–85 team gathered on October 15, there was that sense of anticipation. But trepidation was there, too, because neither the players nor the coaches knew quite how the Olympic experience would affect Knight. He had put so much energy into the summer that they were afraid it might affect his winter. Knight seemed conscious of this, too; during the early practices he was less involved than usual, often content to sit on the sidelines with Hammel, Williams, professor friends who came to practice, or whoever that day's visitor might be. Jim Crews, the first assistant coach, knew his boss expected the coaches to take some of the burden off him.

"He made that clear to us from the first day," Crews said. "We were an experienced staff and an experienced team. There was no reason why he had to supervise every little thing that went on. He wanted us to do more of the coaching and, really, there was no reason why we shouldn't."

It wasn't quite that simple, though. To start with, Knight's staff had worked just about as hard as he had in preparing for the Olympics. They had scouted, organized, looked at tapes, done all the drudge work. They too began the season a little fatigued. The same was true of Alford. A true gym rat, Alford had been playing pickup basketball at home two days after the gold medal game. If he had known just how hard other guards were going to play against an Olympic hero, he might have preferred to rest a little.

The first hint of trouble came early, in the opening game against Louisville. Knight had agreed to a four-year series against Louisville partly because CBS-TV wanted to do the game, and partly because Crews had convinced him Louisville would be a good pre–Big Ten warmup game. Louisville took control of the game before halftime, and Knight angrily benched three starters in the second half in favor of freshmen. They made a run, but fell back, and the game was lost.

Still, the early part of the season went well. Indiana went into Big Ten play with an 8–2 record (the other loss was at Notre Dame) and immediately annihilated Michigan—at Michigan—in the Big Ten opener, winning by an astonishing twenty-five points. Soon, their league record was 3–1, the only loss at Michigan State. Typical Knight team, everyone thought. Knight thought so, too.

But within the team there were some problems. Mike Giomi, a 6-10 junior and the team's best rebounder, had been having academic problems. He was also getting into trouble around town, failing to pay parking tickets, failing to return library books. He was in and out of the Knight doghouse, a condition not uncommon for Indiana players, but more extreme in Giomi's case.

The same was true of Winston Morgan. Morgan was then a fourth-year junior, having sat out the 1983–84 season because of a foot injury. Knight moaned all year about how good the team could be if it just had Morgan. But once Morgan was healthy, he became far less wonderful. In fact, he got worse and worse. This was also not uncommon at Indiana; players often joke that the best way to get better is to get hurt. The more Knight sees his players play, the more convinced he becomes that they aren't any good. But Morgan was also having problems away from the court. He was involved in a messy relationship with a female student, messy enough that she eventually went to talk to Knight about what she saw as Morgan's dishonesty. There are only three crimes an Indiana player can commit that will get him in serious trouble with Knight: drug use, skipping class, and lying. The incident put Morgan so deep in Knight's doghouse that his Indiana career seemed over.

Marty Simmons, a promising freshman in 1984, had been a step slower all season, mystifying the coaches. He looked heavier to them, but his weight chart said he still weighed 218, about the same weight he had played at the year before. Finally, exasperated after a loss, Knight had Tim Garl personally weigh Simmons. He weighed 238. Scared to admit that he had eaten himself onto the bench, Simmons had been lying about his weight. His days, not to mention his meals, were numbered.

There was more: Knight wasn't happy with Alford. He kept harping on the fact that Alford couldn't play defense, couldn't pass very well, and wasn't getting better. Alford was in fact struggling. He was still leading the team in scoring, but some nights he simply couldn't get shots because defenses were geared to stop him. Dakich, the hero of the North Carolina game, was in and out of the lineup. Uwe Blab, the 7-3 senior center, had worked and worked to improve, but was still awkward, still had trouble catching the ball in traffic, and still left Knight exasperated.

And yet, they were winning. Even though Knight claims that winning doesn't necessarily make him happy, it goes a long way toward getting him there. His famous quote, "You play basketball against yourself; your opponent is your potential," sounds pretty, but really isn't so. Knight coaches basketball to win. If he gets upset during a victory, it is usually when he sees something that he thinks may lead to defeat on another night.

But after the 11–3 start, the winning stopped. They went to Ohio State, Knight's alma mater, a place where Knight cannot stand to lose, and lost; the final score was 86–84. Furious, Knight refused to let Giomi and Morgan ride home with the team, putting them on the second of the two small charter planes Indiana uses to fly to games. Morgan's memory of that night is of a horrible game, a screaming coach, and a nightmarish ride home on the eight-seat plane, the weather bouncing them all over the sky.

It got worse at Purdue. They blew a big lead because no one rebounded. This was unforgivable; rebounding, to Knight, is directly related to effort. If you lose because you make no effort, you are in big trouble. Indiana came out of Purdue in big trouble.

Then came Illinois. A Sunday afternoon on national TV. An opponent Knight despised because he didn't think Coach Lou Henson ran a clean program. When the coaches met to pick a lineup, Knight asked—as he always does—for suggestions. But his mind was made up: bench everyone but Blab and start four freshmen. Bench Alford, too, because, "He doesn't guard anybody."

The four freshmen played as hard as they could. They played good defense, but they had little chance to win, losing 52–41. The day after the game, Knight announced that he had thrown Giomi off the team for cutting class. Giomi had met NCAA academic requirements and he had met Indiana's requirements, but he had not met Knight's requirements. The team's leading rebounder, a player the team needed to be successful, was gone.

Suddenly, Knight was being excoriated nationwide. Some people claimed he had started the freshmen to show up Henson. Others implied he had thrown the game to make a point to his team. For perhaps the first time since Knight had become Indiana coach in 1971, his *coaching* was called into question. Indiana was 3–4 in the Big Ten. Alford, the Olympic hero, had been benched. Had Knight lost control? Was it really just six months ago that he sat atop the coaching world?

Another loss to Iowa—with the starters back starting—was followed by three victories over the bottom of the Big Ten: Minnesota, Northwestern, and Wisconsin. That brought Indiana to a three-game home stretch that would decide the fate of the season. Indiana was 6–5 in the Big Ten and 14–7 overall, with Ohio State, Illinois, and Purdue coming to Assembly Hall. There was still plenty of time to bounce back from the problems of January.

They didn't. They lost to Ohio State. They lost to Illinois—

badly—and Knight put his foot through a chair in frustration. And then Purdue came to town.

Purdue is Indiana's archrival, the in-state school the Hoosiers love to look down their noses at. Purdue almost always beats Indiana in football, so basketball is Indiana's only chance to get even. But Purdue is always competitive, always a problem. Even Knight, with all his great teams, has never dominated Purdue; his record going into that day's game against Purdue was 16–12. With the season fading fast, a victory at home over Purdue was imperative.

Saturday, February 23, was an unseasonably warm day in Bloomington after a typical winter week full of cold rain and snow flurries. Knight, who had made plaid sport coats famous, decided to wear just a short-sleeved shirt for the game that afternoon. It reminded him of outfits he had worn during the glory days of the previous summer when he had been Olympic coach.

The game started horribly for Indiana. Purdue was up, 12–2, when there was a scramble for a loose ball. When the whistle finally blew, referee London Bradley called a foul on Indiana. Knight, who often uses bad officiating to rationalize defeat—and, in all fairness, the officiating in the Big Ten is awful—went crazy. He screamed and yelled and drew a technical foul.

Purdue guard Steve Reid walked to the foul line in front of the Indiana bench to shoot the technical. Knight stood frozen for a few seconds. Later, he would remember thinking that if he had been wearing a sport coat, he could have thrown it. But he wasn't. So, he turned around and, before anyone on the Indiana bench could stop him, he picked up the plastic orange chair he had been sitting on and threw it.

The chair throw was hardly Olympian. In fact, Knight side-armed it, grabbing it with both hands but never raising it above waist level. The chair skittered in front of Reid and ran out of steam just as it reached the far side of the court. It hit no one. One Indiana manager went to recover it while another put a second chair down in the original's place. On the Indiana bench, there was no visible reaction. Everyone just watched, waiting to see what would happen next.

Knight insists he threw the chair the way he did intentionally, carefully tossing it and aiming it so it would land where it did. But he had thrown a chair. *Thrown a chair.* More than 17,000 people in Assembly Hall saw it, as did millions of others watching on cable TV nationwide. Standing in front of her television set in Orrville, eighty-one-year-old Hazel Knight saw her son throw the chair and cried out, "Oh, Bobby, oh no."

Others who care about Knight had the same thought. Hammel, shocked, thought later that the worst thing about it was the symbolic nature of the whole thing: wild man coach throws chair. Always, forever more, Knight and that chair would be linked. "The worst thing about it," Hammel said a year later, "was that he didn't do just what he constantly begs his players to do: anticipate. He never anticipated the consequences. Bob Knight is too smart not to anticipate the consequences of something like that."

The initial consequence was immediate ejection from the game. Knight walked off to the privacy of the coaches' locker room. He came to see his players at halftime and calmly told them what they needed to do to win the game, not even mentioning the incident. To his players, the chair throw was not that big a deal, because they had seen him throw so many chairs in practice. The unofficial record was thirteen: Knight had lit into a stack of twenty chairs one day, and his players were disappointed when he ran out of steam with seven unthrown.

But everywhere else, shock waves were forming. As soon as Knight left the game—Purdue went on to win easily—Indiana athletic director Ralph Floyd, a close friend of Knight's, went to the locker room. "He was in tears," Floyd would say later. "He knew he had made a mistake. He understood what he had done."

Close behind Floyd came Ed Williams and Indiana president John Ryan. When Ryan walked into the locker room, Knight looked at him, tears in his eyes, and said, "Dr. Ryan, I'm sorry."

"If his response had been anything else, I'm not certain what I would have done ultimately," Ryan said. "But he understood right away that he had made a terrible mistake."

That night, Knight, looking to escape, went to Kansas on a recruiting trip. But the nightmare of the chair was only beginning. Donoher called. He wanted to drive the 175 miles to Bloomington to talk to Knight. He felt his friend needed help. "When you are in trouble, Bob Knight is the ultimate friend," Donoher said. "He'll do anything he can to help you. But a lot of the time when he's in trouble, he'll have you believe he doesn't need help from his friends. Only he does. He's like anyone else that way."

Notre Dame coach Digger Phelps called that night. He wanted Knight to meet him the next day in Indianapolis to talk. When Phelps had heard what Knight had done his stomach had twisted in fear. "I worry that he's going to go out like MacArthur did," Phelps said later. "One day the President is going to say, 'General, enough. Come home. You are relieved of your command.' "

Ryan, the president, is a small, soft-spoken man whom the players have trouble figuring out because whenever he comes into the locker room after a game, win or lose, he simply walks around shaking hands and saying, "Thank you." Ryan has been president of I.U. for the same fifteen years that Knight has been basketball coach. It is a long-standing joke around the state that Ryan considers himself very fortunate that Knight has allowed him to retain his job for so long.

Now, Ryan had to act. Ed Williams went to see Knight after he returned from Kansas. Williams loves Bob Knight, respects him, and worries about him. "I couldn't feel closer to him if he were my first-born son," he says. Williams thought it important that Indiana—and Knight—act decisively. He suggested to Knight that Ryan should suspend him for one game, saying that Indiana fully supported Knight and everything he stood for as a basketball coach but that everyone, including Ryan and Knight, recognized that a mistake had been made. The chair should not have been thrown.

"I told Bob I thought we should keep this in the family," Williams said. "Why let [Big Ten Commissioner] Wayne Duke get involved? If John Ryan didn't suspend him, Wayne Duke would. So why not let Indiana do it? At the time, I thought Bob would go along. He said that sounded right to him."

But a day later, Knight changed his mind. He told Williams that he could not deal with a public rebuke, no matter how mild, from Ryan. If Ryan suspended him he would feel compelled to resign on the spot. Williams took this information back to Ryan, advising him to go ahead with the suspension. "For Bob's sake and for Indiana's," Williams said a year later. "I thought then, I think now, that the University had to take some action. It could not publicly condone what Bob did. And Bob needed to be told that. He needed to be told, 'Bob, we love you, we want you here forever, but there is a line, there is a point where we say no more. And you just came close to it.' "

John Ryan took no action. Instead, he let Duke play the heavy, suspending Knight for one game. Williams, although saying he disagrees with what the president did, disagrees with those who saw it as a sign of weakness. "The easy thing was to suspend him. John Ryan did not take the easy way out. He did what he believed was best for Bob and for the school."

"I don't think we condoned what Bob did in any way," Ryan said. "It was wrong. He knew it, I knew it, we all knew it. I believed though that given that it was one incident, the Big Ten should mete out the penalty. I didn't tell Bob at the time, but I would not have appealed any penalty Wayne Duke handed down. I would have accepted it. A reprimand, a penalty was in order. My one concern was that if Bob was suspended it be for a road game. I was afraid that we might have a crowd control problem if he was not present for our next home game."

Knight sat out a 70–50 loss to Iowa, as Crews ran the team. The other assistants, looking for any kind of light touch, kidded him afterward that, judging from that performance, he would never get a job as a head coach. But there were few laughs around Assembly Hall that February. "It was," Alford says now, "as if a black cloud settled on top of the building and just stayed and stayed and stayed."

Everyone dreaded coming to practice. Each day seemed worse than the last. The season, it seemed, would never end. Two weeks after the chair throw, Dave Knight, the man who had introduced Knight to basketball when he was eleven years old, was visiting. The two are not related, but Dave Knight is one of many older-brother figures in the coach's life. As he sat in the coaches' locker room before practice one day, Dave Knight pitched forward, stricken by a heart attack. The players were on the floor warming up when assistant coach Kohn Smith came running out screaming for Garl. "Quick, it's an emergency, run," he yelled.

Every player on the floor had the exact same thought: *It's Coach.*

He's had a heart attack. Knight was white-faced with fear when Garl and student trainer Steve Dayton charged in to attend to Dave Knight. They brought him back, saving his life. But they, too, when the call first came, had been convinced that the traumas of the season had finally done the coach in.

The debacle dragged on. Indiana finished the regular season with a 15–13 record, 7–11 in the Big Ten, putting the Hoosiers seventh in their own league after being rated fourth in the nation in preseason. It was the first time in Knight's fourteen seasons that Indiana had finished below .500 in Big Ten play or out of the first division. Indiana was passed over for the NCAA tournament, and settled for the National Invitation Tournament.

The Hoosiers reached the semifinals in New York, where they beat a struggling Tennessee team. After that game, Knight did a TV interview with Bill Raftery, a former coach at Seton Hall. Raftery asked Knight what he liked best about the way his team had played to reach the NIT final. "What I like best about this team right now," Knight answered sincerely, "is the fact that I only have to watch it play one more time."

The feeling was mutual. If the coach couldn't wait for the season to be over, neither could the players. The final was a microcosm of the season: mistakes, bad defense, a loss. UCLA, the kind of undisciplined team Knight thinks his team should never lose to, won the game and the championship, 65–63. The last chance to salvage something from a lost season had produced another loss.

The plane trip home lasted forever. The twenty-seat Indiana University foundation plane bounced all over the sky. Alford was so stir-crazy he wanted to jump out a window. Dakich still swears the flight took twelve hours. Finally they landed, and the team bus took them to Assembly Hall. It was 4 A.M. when they gathered in their meeting room for final words from Knight. This was part of the tradition. The team gathered here after every trip for a summation—in this case, for a summation of the season. Knight had little to say. He excused Dakich and Blab, the seniors, and told the remaining players he could not—and would not—go through another season like the one just ended. The players felt the same way.

When the team had been dismissed, Knight asked Morgan to

stay behind. Morgan had played a total of fifty-eight seconds in the last eleven games. He had one more year of eligibility, but Knight didn't want him back. Knight was convinced that his attitude toward basketball and college was messed up. Shortly after 4 A.M., Knight told Morgan he didn't want him back the next season, and that he would try to help him get into school somewhere else. Morgan nodded; this was hardly a shock.

When Knight finished, Morgan turned to go. Jim Crews was slumped in a chair by the door. He had just coached his last game at Indiana because—in spite of the Iowa game—he was about to be named head coach at Evansville. Morgan stopped in front of Crews. "Coach," he said softly, "I want to thank you for working with me and wish you luck at Evansville. I know you'll do great."

Watching that scene, Knight changed his mind about Morgan on the spot. "This kid," he thought, "is worth trying to save. I tell him at 4 in the morning that he's through and he stops to wish Jimmy luck. He really isn't a bad kid."

It would be two months before Morgan would learn of his reprieve. At that moment, he walked out the door, not knowing his future. A few moments later, the coach who had owned the basketball world nine months earlier also walked out the door. His future was just as uncertain as Winston Morgan's.

3.
Square One

Although Knight would never admit it, the horrific 1984–85 season changed him. It changed his attitude toward coaching, toward recruiting, even toward some of his cherished mind games. It reminded him how much coaching—real coaching—meant to him.

After he won his second national championship in 1981, Knight almost quit coaching. He was forty at the time, and since he didn't think he had any chance to be Olympic coach, he saw no tangible reason to keep coaching.

That spring, CBS Sports acquired the rights to the NCAA basketball tournament. College basketball had been owned and dominated by NBC Sports for years, but CBS paid $48 million to steal the tournament from NBC. It desperately needed someone who would give its telecasts impact and credibility. Kevin O'Malley, executive producer of CBS Sports, decided to go for the biggest name in the game: Bob Knight.

Knight was willing to listen. He was restless in Bloomington. His oldest son, Tim, would begin his senior year of high school in the fall. His younger son, Patrick, was 10; moving at that age would hardly be a problem. It would be a new challenge, and CBS was willing to give him big money—about $500,000 annually—and control of the telecasts: scheduling, halftime shows, all of it. At one point, O'Malley was convinced he had his man. "It was late one night and I really thought he was going to do it," O'Malley said. "I asked him why he wanted to do it, because I had become fascinated by him. He's just so extraordinarily bright. He asked me if I had ever seen Ted Williams play baseball. I said I had. 'Greatest hitter ever,' Knight said. 'And now, he's the best fisherman there is. The best. No doubt about it.'

"And then he looked at me and said, 'How many people have ever been the absolute best there is at *two* things?'"

But Knight never signed with CBS. On the morning of July 25, Landon Turner was driving his car down Route 46, a winding road in central Indiana. It was early in the morning, and he was sleepy. For a brief second, he lost control of the car and went off the road. He jerked the wheel to try to regain control, but the car fishtailed across the two-lane road and hit a restraining wall. Turner's 6-foot-10-inch, 250-pound body was folded like an accordian inside the tiny car. He was taken to the hospital, paralyzed from the waist down. Knight was out west on a fishing and hunting trip, trying to sort out his future, when the phone call about Turner came. He flew immediately to Indianapolis, arriving late at night. Hammel picked him up at the airport and the two men drove straight to the hospital. Turner wasn't conscious, but Knight went in to see him briefly. When he came out, his eyes were red with tears. Hammel knew then that Knight would not—could not—leave Indiana.

Knight devoted most of his waking hours during the next few months to what became the Landon Turner Fund. Before he was through, more than $400,000 had been raised. Turner, paralyzed for life, had a motorized wheelchair and a van. His parents' home was redone with ramps throughout so he could get around, and a condominium was purchased for him to live in. When he was ready to return to school, his scholarship was waiting; Knight named him captain of the 1982 team he would never play for.

Knight stayed in coaching because of Landon Turner. Turner's injury, and Knight's instinctive, protective, caring reaction to it, eliminated any thoughts of leaving Bloomington. But this meant that his staying in coaching did not come from a drive to succeed. He had already succeeded. So while on the surface he was the same obsessed person he had always been, still spending long hours looking at tape, meeting with coaches, preparing for opponents, and still finding defeat unacceptable, Knight was not the same coach after the 1981 championship. This showed up most clearly in his avoiding the most important function of any college coach: recruiting. No one—not Bob Knight, not John Wooden, not Adolph Rupp—can win without recruiting well. But he never liked recruiting very much, and now he turned it over almost completely to his assistant coaches. Players the head coach had never seen play were offered scholarships to Indiana. Now Knight only wanted to know two things: Is he a good kid? Is he interested in Indiana first and foremost? If the answer to both questions was yes, offer him a scholarship. To some degree, Knight had come to believe his own press clippings, the ones that said, "Give him five guys who can walk and talk and he'll outcoach everyone else."

While Knight was backing off a little bit, the rest of the Big Ten was catching up. Illinois seemed to be getting every blue-chip player in the Midwest. Michigan, under Bill Frieder, was also getting a bunch. Gene Keady, a solid, aggressive coach, had taken over at Purdue. The results of Knight's recruiting in the late 1970s could carry Indiana through 1983, but no further. Knight had worked as he had never worked in his life to get Isiah Thomas out of Chicago in 1979. Thomas, the magical, baby-faced guard, had been the key player in the 1981 championship but had turned pro after his sophomore season. Knight hadn't worked like that in recruiting in the early 1980s. His recruiting of Alford, who joined the program in the fall of 1983, had consisted of one phone call to Alford's father. When Sam Alford told his son, then a junior on the New Castle High School team coached by his father, that Bob Knight wanted him to play at Indiana, Steve Alford was ready to walk to Bloomington. He had gone to Knight's summer camp since the age of nine, and the chance to play at Indiana was all he ever dreamed about.

But recruiting required more than an occasional phone call, and a major part of the problem in 1985 had been the talent gap created by Knight's laissez-faire approach. Knight realized this during 1985 and made a momentous decision: he would recruit junior college players. He reached the decision on a cold morning in Madison, Wisconsin, during the first three-game losing streak of the season. He told assistant coaches Jim Crews and Joby Wright to put together a list of junior college players who could be recruited by Indiana.

This was a major step for Knight. In his entire coaching career, he had recruited only one junior college player. That was Courtney Witte, a senior on the 1985–86 team, and his had been an exceptional situation: Witte's father had played at Indiana in the 1950s and his uncle, Jerry Memering, had played for Knight's first team there. Witte was considered a little too small and a little too slow when he came out of high school in Vincennes, Indiana. But when 6-10 John Flowers decided to transfer during the 1983 season, Indiana needed a big man for the next season quickly. Witte had grown to 6-8 by the time he was a sophomore at Vincennes Junior College, and Knight offered him a scholarship without ever having seen him play.

But now Knight was saying, "We need better athletes." The best athletes in junior college were players who had been unable to meet minimum NCAA academic requirements as high school seniors. At best, they were academic risks. But Knight believed that if you looked carefully, you could find one or two JUCOs who had either learned their lesson or had changed their attitude. "If you find the right junior college kid, he's going to be so thrilled to have a chance to play at a place like Indiana that he may come in here with a better attitude than the freshmen," Knight insisted.

"A junior college kid is older, he's been kicked around a little. He may be a little tougher."

It was a wonderful rationalization. But it was also a gamble Knight felt he had to take. Shortly after the 1985 season ended, Knight signed three junior college players.

Knight's change of life, or midlife crisis, call it what you will, went even further. During the Final Four in Lexington, he talked seriously with his coaching mentor, Pete Newell, about playing zone defense. *Bob Knight playing zone defense.* It was easier to imagine Spiro Agnew becoming a Democrat or Elizabeth Taylor swearing off marriage. But Knight was serious. He had taken man-to-man defense to a new level of sophistication, but much of that sophistication lay in the zone principles inherent in his man-to-man. With a forty-five-second clock voted into the college rules for 1986, he thought playing some zone would make it a little easier on his players, who at times had looked overmatched playing man-to-man.

There was more: Knight also wanted to change the tempo of his offense. Rather than walk the ball up and then run his "motion" offense against a waiting defense, he wanted to push the ball up the floor at every opportunity to try to get shots off before the defense could set up. This would at the very least help Alford, who at 6-1 and 160 pounds had found himself hounded all over the court by bigger, stronger players throughout his sophomore season. If they couldn't catch up to him, they couldn't guard him. With Uwe Blab gone, Indiana would have a smaller, quicker team anyway; it made sense to use speed to their advantage.

It was all reasonable and rational. But it also demonstrated that after twenty years as a coach, after knowing almost nothing but success, Bob Knight was stepping back and taking a close look at himself. He knew he still wanted to coach, if only because he could not bear walking away after a season he considered a complete failure. But even though he told friends repeatedly that the 1985 team just wasn't very good, he acted like a man who also thought that the coach of that team hadn't been very good.

And so he went back to square one: He had never recruited junior college players; he started recruiting them. He had never considered playing a zone defense; he considered playing zone.

He had almost always played the game at a controlled pace; he considered quickening that pace. And, without saying so at the time, he also was beginning to rethink his twenty-four-hour-a-day mind games with his players. The ravings and rantings of 1985 had not brought the team back as they had in the past. Making an issue of losing had simply produced more losing. Knight always believed that the tougher he made things for his players during practice, the better they would deal with adversity during games. The formula had worked and worked and worked, but not in 1985. Maybe, just maybe, it needed some adjusting, some tinkering.

Knight had always known that his brinksmanship would be tolerated in most quarters only as long as he won. One more major incident, a chair toss or anything even slightly similar, and he was gone. One more awful season and, quite possibly, he would have to walk away because the losing tore him up so much. "Suppose the chair had bounced funny and hit someone," mused Bob Hammel, as loyal a friend as Knight has. "If it does, that's it, it's over. Here's a man who has spent his whole life making certain he had control of things, and he allowed things to get that far out of his control. That could have been the end."

Hammel spoke for all of Knight's friends—coaches, professors, ex-players, journalists. The loyalty of Knight's friends is unsurpassed because his loyalty to them is unsurpassed. Without exception, they can talk about acts of warmth and compassion that he has performed on their behalf. He is incapable of saying no to a friend.

And, just as much as they revere him, Knight's friends worry about him. Many of them expect a Woody Hayes-type ending for him. Hayes, who had been one of Knight's teachers at Ohio State, had punched an opposing player on national television at the end of the 1978 Gator Bowl. That act had finished his lengthy coaching career. Some see that ending as inevitable. As quickly as they say that, they add, "Don't ever let him find out I said that." But they say it. They all agree that he has had a lifelong knack for walking right to the brink of disaster and then pulling back. But in 1985 he had stepped across the line and almost gone tumbling over it. If he was going to survive 1986, he had to change. He had to take a step back. He had to bring his life under control. There were no more chances left.

If ever a basketball team needed an off-season to regroup, it was Indiana. If ever a coach needed a summer off, it was Knight. But prior to the 1985 disaster, Knight had made plans for a summer trip for the team around the world. It would be a thirty-eight-day trip that would start in Canada and proceed to Japan, China, Yugoslavia, and Finland before returning home. There would be eighteen games, including two in Japan against the Russians.

Several friends tried to talk Knight out of the trip, telling him he needed a rest. But Indiana had made a commitment and, what's more, Knight thought the experience would help the younger players who hadn't played that much the previous season. He also thought the chance to go around the world would be a good experience for everyone.

It didn't start off well. On the June day when the team gathered to begin practice in preparation for the trip, Knight was almost out of control. Every time someone made a mistake he would begin harping on the season that had ended in March. It was as if no time at all had passed; everyone was still guilty of the sins of the winter. There would be no forgiveness.

Winston Morgan was one exception. Knight had all but decided to give him another chance after that final team meeting, but he didn't tell him about the decision until May. That is Knight's way: He doesn't believe in making anything easy for anyone. His mind games, he feels, will make them tougher. When Knight did tell Morgan he could come back, Morgan was thrilled. There would be no scholarship, though. Morgan would have to work part-time and pay his own way, and, except for game days, he couldn't eat at the training table with the team. But he would get another chance if he wanted it. Morgan was thankful for the chance.

He may have had second thoughts during the first part of the trip. Indiana didn't play well in Japan. During games, Knight let the assistants coach and sat either at the end of the court or up in the stands. Adjustments were being made: Daryl Thomas, about to become a junior, was trying to learn to play the center position at 6-7. Stew Robinson was hurt part of the time. Morgan was relearning the game. The four players who would join the team in the fall—two junior college players (only two of Knight's three JUCO recruits had gotten into Indiana) and two freshmen—were not allowed to make the trip under NCAA rules. Witte, who had sat out 1985 with a broken foot, was on the trip, but also not eligible to play because of NCAA rules. In all, there were only eleven players available, and six of them had just completed their freshman season. Indiana was a small, inexperienced team, feeling its way.

Indiana lost six of its first eight games, including two to the Russians. After the first Russian game, someone asked Knight to compare the Russians to the 1984 U.S. Olympic team. "There *is* no comparison," Knight snapped. "Next question."

Even though the games were only practice, the losses were eating at Knight. His temper was worse than it had been during the season, and when Ed Williams joined the entourage in the second week he had serious doubts about whether anyone would survive the trip.

The bottom seemed to drop out in Hiroshima. After the team played a bad half without the injured Robinson and with Alford resting, Knight stormed from the stands and banished the assistants from the bench. They spent the rest of the game in the stands wondering about their futures. The three of them—Kohn Smith, Joby Wright, and Royce Waltman—walked the streets that night, wondering if Knight was going to fire them as he had sworn he would. They talked about what they would do if they were fired—"I'll go back down South and pick cotton," Wright declared at one point—and decided they had better find Garl to get some money in case they were sent home.

"It was one of those nights where you hope someone tries to mug you," Smith said. "Because they always say the most dangerous man in a fight is the one who doesn't care if he lives or dies. That was us."

Later, the three of them would laugh about that phase of the trip, but it hardly seemed funny at the time. Wright's description of Knight during that period was simple: "You ever been in a five-by-five cage with a wounded tiger, who has just had salt poured on the wound and is very hungry, too? Think about that and then think about someone rollin' a live grenade in there and that's what it was like."

Hearing this description, Waltman would shake his head, laugh, and say, "If you were smart, you jumped right on top of that grenade, because it was an easier way to die."

At night, the players often sat around telling each other where they would have gone if they hadn't been foolish enough to choose Indiana. Everyone was miserable. When Tim Garl, as trainer the one person on the trip who could get a true reading every day of the feelings of both the players and the coaches, suggested to Knight that he might be riding the players too hard, Knight suggested he find another job.

The coaches assumed this was just another late-night Knight firing. Over the years he had fired everyone, including himself, several times. The next day on a train trip Knight called Garl over for a talk. The coaches figured peace was being made.

"Everything all right now?" Waltman asked Garl when he returned a few minutes later.

"Yeah," Garl answered. "Now I'm fired for sure."

But he didn't stay fired and neither did the coaches. The team got out of Japan alive and won the last ten games on the trip to finish 12–6. There was noticeable improvement, especially in Thomas, who was adjusting to playing with his back to the basket, and Morgan, who had also been on the verge of being fired in Japan. They even had some fun during the last three weeks. Knight is a superb tour guide because he has read so many history books, and he made certain the players saw all the sights.

Nonetheless, when the team returned home to the U.S., Stew Robinson jumped off the plane when it landed and kissed the ground.

———

During the trip, Knight made some decisions about the upcoming season. He didn't think he could ask the players to learn an entirely new offense and defense all at once. He had toyed with some zone defense in practice on the trip, but decided to put off teaching it for at least another year. But he did want a push-it-up offense, and he would emphasize that when practice began on October 15.

Knight also thought that two of the new players would have

to be starters. Knight thought one of the junior college players was the best athlete he had ever recruited. That was Andre Harris, a slender 6-6 jumping jack. Harris was from Grand Rapids, Michigan, but had spent two years at Barton County Junior College in Kansas because he had failed to meet the NCAA's required 2.0 grade-point average. He graduated from Barton County and could now enroll at Indiana as a junior.

The other potential starter was Rick Calloway. Calloway wasn't slender, he was skinny, a rail-thin 6-5, 180 pounds. He was from Cincinnati, a gifted, instinctive player who had almost gone to Georgetown but changed his mind after Knight's visit to his home the previous fall. Knight didn't know it at the time, but Calloway was a better jumper than Harris and a precocious, rarely intimidated freshman.

There would be two other new players. One was Todd Jadlow, a teammate of Harris's at Barton County. Jadlow was 6-9 and 215 pounds with a mean streak in him that Knight liked. He could also shoot. He was a good student who had opted for junior college for a year because he was only 6-6 and 185 pounds when he left high school and his only major scholarship offer, from Kansas State, had been withdrawn.

The fourth recruit was perhaps the most intriguing. Jeff Oliphant was 6-6 and 180 pounds, from a small town in southern Indiana. He had played for his father at tiny L&M High School, about an hour from Bloomington, and was one of those players that others saw simply as a slow white kid. But Knight saw him as a potential star. Oliphant could shoot, his vision of the game was perhaps the best on the team, and he was a natural guard who was already 6-6 and perhaps still growing. He would be redshirted as a freshman—a redshirt is a player who participates in no games for a season and thereby gains a fifth year of eligibility—so that he could mature physically. At times during the season when Oliphant made passes that no one else on the team had the vision to see, Knight would compare him to Larry Bird.

Oliphant was in fact a potential star, but Bird is a once-in-a-lifetime player. The three-time NBA Most Valuable Player had also come out of a small Indiana high school and had signed with Indiana, but the "big-city" atmosphere in Bloomington had been too much for the kid from French Lick, and Bird left within four weeks of enrolling. He later enrolled at Indiana State, became a superstar, and left people wondering what might have happened if he had ever played for Knight. The best coach and the best player. The smartest coach and the smartest player. The combination might have been mind-boggling.

It was very unlikely that Oliphant would become Bird, though they did have a lot in common: Both were 6-6 kids from small Indiana towns who could shoot and had a natural flair for passing. Like Bird, Oliphant was almost painfully quiet. But Oliphant did not have Bird's drive, his passion for the game. He worked hard and was intelligent, but he wasn't Bird.

Comparing an Oliphant to a Bird was another common Knight syndrome. Knight's players often joke about how good they were in high school, how terrible they were in college, and how wonderful they became again as soon as they were out of college. When Knight recruits a player he is almost always convinced he will become a great player. Often, when an Indiana player is struggling, Knight will reminisce about previous players who have played that position, or he will begin to project how good the next player at that spot will be.

When Knight's former players gather, they all tell war stories. One night during the fall, Steve Green, who had been part of Knight's first recruiting class at Indiana and a captain on the 31–1 1975 team, told about a game in which he made a huge mistake. "I came out of the game for a rest and I sat down next to Coach," he said. "Very bad move. The next thing I know, the guys playing screw up a couple times and he starts yelling at me, 'Green, how can you let those sonsofbitches play like that? What the hell kind of example are you setting? What kind of leader are you anyway?' "

Hearing Green tell this story, Dakich began to laugh. "Last year when I was the captain, whenever we started playing badly he would turn to me and say, 'Goddammit Dakich, what kind of leader are you? Do you think Steve Green would ever allow *his* team to play that way? He'd have kicked somebody's ass by now!' "

Players learn to accept the fact that for four years, they will be terrible basketball players most of the time. Ted Kitchel, who graduated in 1983, sums that up best. "I played on [imitating Knight's voice] 'the four worst f—— teams in the *history* of Indiana basketball. *The worst.*' We won three Big Ten championships and the national championship in 1981. But believe me, we were, *'the worst.'* "

Knight picks out targets on each team. Usually, it is a player he knows can handle the abuse, and it is almost always a very good player. Kitchel had been a major target, with Randy Wittman not far behind. During 1985–86, Alford would be Public Enemy Number 1. More than one tape session became "The Steve Alford Show." And, when Knight wanted to tell Alford what a terrible leader he was, he used Kitchel and Wittman as examples of the kind of leader he wanted.

The coaches would giggle whenever Knight brought up Wittman, as he often did. At the end of 1982, Knight had told Wittman, who had a fifth year of eligibility because of an injury, that he should skip that year, turn pro, and leave Indiana. He had not, of course, meant it. And with each passing year, Kitchel and Wittman became, retroactively, better and tougher.

But even they couldn't reach the plateau of the players on the 1975 and 1976 teams. The 1975 senior class—Green, John Laskowski, and Steve Ahlfeld—were all still close to Knight. All three lived in Indianapolis. Laskowski did the color commentary on Indiana's telecasts, and when he wasn't available Green did it. Ahlfeld was one of the team's doctors. The 1976 class consisted of Crews, who became an assistant for eight years after graduating, Quinn Buckner, Scott May, Bobby Wilkerson, and Tom Abernethy. Only Wilkerson was no longer a close member of the extended Knight/I.U. family. Of all his players, Knight talked about Buckner more than any other. Buckner was smart, savvy, tough: a coach on the court.

When Buckner was a senior, Knight benched him for two games. Buckner was so distraught that when he went into one of those games he had trouble breathing; he was so upset about the benching that he was hyperventilating. But Buckner ended his career jumping into Knight's arms in Philadelphia after capping a 32–0 season with the national championship. Knight is his second father; Buckner is Knight's oldest son.

The players who came later heard about those two teams so much they had the speeches memorized. Laskowski remembers walking into the locker room once and having Kitchel and Wittman come over and begin examining his head. "They were checking for my halo."

Alford is bright enough to understand his coach. Yet their relationship is tempestuous to say the least. One reason for that is Alford's unique standing among Indiana basketball fans. He is the perfect boy next door. He is small by basketball standards, and he is baby-faced. He is neatly dressed, always polite, and a resolute churchgoer. He is also white; in most parts of the state, that alone makes him special.

He is a coach's son. "I learned to count on a basketball scoreboard," he says. He is as pure a shooter as you can imagine, having worked for hours and hours and hours on his shot. He almost never misses a free throw—he was once twenty-five for twenty-five in a high school playoff game—and any opening for his jump shot is almost always a basket. As a senior in high school he averaged thirty-eight points a game and won the coveted Mr. Basketball Award as the best player in the state. Then he went to Indiana and became a starter and the leading scorer as a freshman. Then he made the Olympic team and starred again. In short, before he began his sophomore year in college, Alford had lived the American dream and, even more than that, the Indiana dream: Mr. Basketball; starter at I.U.; Olympic hero.

Knight knew all that and knew how hard it would be for any kid, even one as levelheaded as Alford, to deal with all the adulation. And adulation it is: People stop at Alford's house in New Castle to take pictures of their son standing under the hoop where Alford shot baskets as a boy. Girls squeal when he is introduced as if he were a rock star. Dan Dakich calls him the Shaun Cassidy of college basketball.

Alford didn't have a great sophomore year. He was better than the team, but not as good as he could be. Knight harped constantly on his poor defense, and told him again and again that he wasn't working hard enough. Alford thought he was working hard. Knight told him he wasn't. Knight understood what Alford was going through. "Hell, the kid's eighteen years old and he's got an Olympic gold medal. Julius Erving doesn't have an Olympic gold medal. He's everyone's hero in an entire state. That's not easy." But he also felt the need to push Alford as much as he could get away with if only for his own good. "He just doesn't understand how hard it is for someone like him to play well," Knight told the coaches repeatedly that season.

For Alford to get better as a player, Knight believed, he had to do everything Knight told him to do without hesitation. Alford hadn't done that as a sophomore. He had questioned the coach; not openly, but by his actions. Knight is not a coach who accepts questioning from his players on any level. Knight didn't want Alford to take anything for granted as a junior. He knew that for Indiana to be good, Alford had to be his best player and the team's leader. But that's not what he told Alford. As the plane flew home from Europe in late July, Knight took Alford aside and told him in no uncertain terms that this year the five best defensive players would start, period. "And you, Steve, are not one of those five players right now."

Did Alford think Knight was serious, or just playing a mind game? "I was convinced," Alford said, "that he had never been more serious in his life."

4.

October 15

In college basketball, no date means more than October 15. On that day, basketball teams all around the country begin formal preparations for the upcoming season. The players have probably played against each other every afternoon from the day school opened, but October 15 is the real thing. The coaches no longer sit high in the stands to observe—though even doing that is a violation of a universally ignored NCAA rule—but are down on the floor, teaching, coaching, and yelling.

October 15 fell on a Tuesday, and it also fell right in the middle of a week when Indiana was staging a major fundraising event in Assembly Hall. That meant that the first four days of practice would take place away from Assembly Hall, in the Indiana Middle School Building. The players dressed in the Assembly Hall locker room, then drove to practice.

When they arrived, they were greeted by a total of eight coaches: Knight, Kohn Smith, Royce Waltman, and Joby Wright were the holdovers from the previous season. Crews was gone to Evansville, replaced by Ron Felling. There were also three graduate assistants: Dan Dakich; Murry Bartow, son of Knight's close friend Gene Bartow, the coach at Alabama-Birmingham; and Julio Salazar, a Colombian who had worked Knight's summer camp for several years after meeting him in San Juan during the Pan-American Games.

The status of the graduate assistants was quite different from that of the four full-time coaches. They didn't dress in the comfortable coaches' locker room, but in a tiny office a few feet down the hall from the players' locker room. They didn't look at tape with the other coaches; their job was to gather the tape and help prepare it to be used. They only occasionally went on the road with the team. They were coaches training to be coaches, paying their dues by doing scut work for the older coaches. One of Dakich's assignments each morning during the fall semester was to pick up Andre Harris, who lived off campus, to make sure he got to his first class or to a study hall.

Felling turned out to be a delight for the players. He was forty-five, a curly-haired ex–high school coach who loved to talk about two things: basketball and women. Felling had won four state championships in Illinois at tiny Lawrenceville High School, but had retired in 1983. He had coached, among others, Marty Simmons, who had come to Indiana as a future star only to move on to Evansville with Crews after his weight problems the previous season. Over the years, Felling and Knight had become friends through clinics and camps, and when Crews got the Evansville job, Knight called Felling at 2 A.M.

Sound asleep, Felling picked up the phone and heard a voice say, "Well, are you gonna come work for me or not?" It was Knight, and that was the job offer. Felling took it.

Knight had been serious about Alford; he began the first practice in a white uniform. At Indiana, the starting team wears red uniforms in practice, and the subs wear white. During the course of the season, every player will spend some time in red and some time in white; there are days when the entire starting five finds itself in white.

But putting Alford in white was a clear signal from coach to player. The talk on the airplane coming home from Europe wasn't just talk. Knight was going to make the preseason difficult for Alford. Everyone on the team understood what was going on; they also understood that if anyone on the team was tough enough to handle the situation, it was Alford.

Alford, with his baby face and short-cropped, always neat brown hair, doesn't look very tough, but he is. He takes a physical pounding in every game he plays because he is small and his great shooting ability makes him the target of a lot of tough defense. Beyond that, though, Alford had earned the respect of his teammates because he didn't let Knight get to him. Every time Knight told Alford how bad he was, Alford just shrugged and played a little better. Which was exactly what Knight wanted.

"When I first came here, with his reputation and everything he had won, I figured Steve would be spoiled and not too tough at all," said Daryl Thomas. "But he proved himself to me. In fact, I think he proved himself to everybody."

Ironically, Thomas was the one whose toughness Knight questioned. Like Alford, Thomas was exceptionally bright, but he wasn't nearly as driven as Alford. He liked basketball, but wasn't obsessed with it. He wanted to be good, but he didn't *live* to be good. Where Alford would just set his jaw and think, "You're crazy," when Knight told him how bad he was, Thomas tended to believe it.

Even before the late November blowup when Knight brought Thomas to tears, he had called Thomas every name there was. Knight knew this wasn't always good strategy with Thomas. "The problem with calling Daryl Thomas a pussy," he said one night, "is that he believes you."

Much had been made over the years of Knight's use of profanity with the players. It is no exaggeration. Knight uses profanity when he is angry, when he is happy, and whenever he feels like it. He once taped an outtake for a TV show explaining why he used the word *fuck* so much. "I just think," he said, "that *fuck* is the most expressive word in the English language. It can be used to express surprise as in, 'Well I'll be *fucked!*' Or, it can be used to express anger, as in '*Fuck* you!' Or, it can express dismay as in, 'Oh, *fuck!*' "

Knight used it to express all these things and more. Some of his friends had talked to him over the years about trying to curb that language, and he had gone through periods of trying to do so. But when things went bad in practice, Knight would backslide, occasionally reeling off seven or eight of them in one sentence. Once, in a fit of temper, Knight decided he wanted the floor cleared of everyone except his players and coaches. This was a typical Indiana practice: several professors, Knight hunting cronies, and other assorted friends were present. So was Ed Williams.

"I want all these cocksuckers out of here right now," Knight yelled.

When a manager politely asked Williams if he would please leave, the I.U. vice president shook his head. "You heard what he said," Williams told the manager indignantly. "For his sake, I hope he wasn't referring to me." When the manager told Knight what Williams had said, Knight broke up.

———

But even Thomas would admit that Knight's number one target during the first days of practice was Alford. The little kid, as Bob Hammel affectionately called him, could do little right. He was shooting superbly and consistently, but Knight wanted more. He wanted defense. He wanted better vision on offense. He wanted better passes. He wanted him to take a charge. And take charge.

Twice, during the first ten days, Knight threw Alford out of practice. Throwing a player out of practice, especially in preseason, is not uncommon. Sometimes Knight will throw the whole team out of practice. But there was a lot of tension between Knight and Alford. The second kickout came early in practice when Knight didn't think Alford had fought through a screen properly. Alford thought he had, but before he could say a word he was banished.

When an Indiana player is thrown out of practice he is supposed to go to the locker room and wait. He may be called back, or Knight may come in to add some comments to what he has already said, or he may just sit there until the rest of the team arrives. This time, though, Alford didn't wait. He was frustrated. He got dressed and went home. Shortly after he left, Knight sent a manager in to get him. The manager reported back that there was no sign of Alford, only his practice clothes piled in a heap in front of his locker.

"Call him and get him back here," Knight ordered. Alford was called and came back. More angry words. Alford listened and didn't answer, but he was furious. Finally, Knight told him, "You can just get out and don't bother coming back until I call you. I don't want to see you."

This is another Knight test. The proper response is to show up at practice the next day as if nothing has happened. In this case, though, Knight was taking a risk. Alford had spent ten days in white. He had been thrown out twice and then called back to receive more abuse. Maybe, just maybe, he would call Knight's bluff and not come back.

"It may run through your mind," Alford said later. "But, hey, my dad still leads Coach 7–5 in kicking me out. I understand what they're both doing when they do it. I don't always like it, I don't always think it's fair. But I understand. I have to be an example."

And so the next day Alford came back. He was sitting on a training table having his ankles taped before practice when Knight walked in. "Did I have a dream that I called you and told you to come back?" Knight said. Alford didn't answer. Knight walked out. Practice started. About fifteen minutes into the workout, Knight said quietly, "Steve, put on a red shirt."

Alford was a starter again. He had passed his first test of the season.

———

There was, during those early days of practice, an unspoken tension that was felt by everyone. Every player, every coach knew that another season like '85 would be unbearable. Yet this was a team full of question marks. On some days, even at only 6–7, Thomas looked unstoppable playing the low post; on others, he looked helpless. Some days, Harris was a wonder to watch; on others, he was a disaster. Both would have to play well against bigger players for Indiana to be successful. Calloway was also up and down. The two seniors who would be doing a lot of playing, Morgan and Robinson, were working as hard as could be asked, but both had their bad days, too.

The only real thread of consistency was Alford, who just showed up every day regardless of shirt color and knocked in jump shots from all over the floor. With each passing day, Knight had less and less to say to Alford. He even began complimenting him in his speeches to the public.

Preseason often seemed to Knight like one long speech. He spoke to alumni groups, charity groups, and whenever friends asked him to. He spoke all over the state, more often than not for nothing. Every night it seemed there was another speech. Vincennes one night, Petersburg the next. Indianapolis at lunch, the rotary club in Bloomington at dinner. Chicago to talk to five hundred alumni on Wednesday, a local restaurant to talk to forty business associates of a friend on Thursday.

Knight is an exceptional speaker. More often than not, he talks without notes. He talks about the Olympics and about Indiana basketball. He even developed a routine to explain why he threw the chair.

"A lot of people have asked me about throwing that chair," he would begin, "and I've had to explain myself because my mother asked me about it. Well, if you want the truth, here's what happened. See, I had been up a lot during our last game against Illinois two nights before trying like I always do to give the officials whatever help I could. [*Laughter.*] Well, now we're playing Purdue, and I'm up, and I keep hearing this voice. Usually in Assembly Hall I don't really listen to all the people trying to give me advice, but this one voice kept piercing right through the crowd noise: 'Bob, Bob.' So, finally I looked over there and I see this little old woman, in fact, she reminded me a little bit of my mother.

"She said, 'Bob, Bob.' So I looked at her and I said, 'Ma'am, can I help you?' And she said, 'Now Bob, if you aren't going to sit on your chair the way you didn't sit on it the other night, these bleachers over here are very hard and I'd really like to use that chair.' Now, how can anyone get on me just because I threw that chair over there so she could sit on it? [*Gales of laughter.*] In fact, when I told my mother the story, she apologized for getting on me in the first place." (*Applause; Knight owns the audience.*)

Most places, Knight owns his audience. To start with, his very presence at most functions in Indiana is like a visit from above. Driving into a small town to give a speech, Knight is apt to encounter a dozen signs on the local main street reading, "Welcome Coach Knight." He enjoys himself during these speeches, even on nights when he is exhausted. One night he drove three hours through a driving rain to give a speech because he had promised an older friend he would be there. No one would have complained if he had canceled because of the weather.

Knight's speeches are funny, but also rousing. He usually finishes with some patriotic theme. "America, America, God shed his grace on thee," he said one night. "I can't think of eight words that mean more to me than those. You know, we have a lot of born-agains nowadays; people are born-again this and born-again that. Some of them mean it and a lot of them are phonies. But one thing I hope we'll never have is a born-again American. This country is the greatest place on earth, and even though we have some problems it just keeps getting better and better for all of us. Let's remember that." Usually, that brings the house down.

But Knight can also rip people in his speeches. The first time he ever addressed an Indiana alumni group he told the audience, "You know, I wish all alumni would be canonized. That way we coaches would only have to kiss your rings."

Last fall, during his annual speech to alumni in Chicago, someone asked Knight about Big Ten commissioner Wayne Duke, a longtime antagonist. "You know, if any of you someday are on the street and you see that Wayne Duke is about to get run over by a car, I would encourage you, I think, to try to save him. But not if it's in any way inconvenient for you to do so." Knight was delighted with himself for that shot. Duke was furious.

Mostly, though, Knight delights during his speeches. He is charming, signs every autograph, and has a kind word for almost everyone. He is especially good with kids. "Coach Knight," a little boy asked one night, "can I play for you at Indiana some day?"

"How old are you, son?"

"Eleven."

"Well, I'll do my best to last that long, but I can't make any promises."

Knight also gives an annual speech to the Indiana student body in October. Always, the auditorium is packed, with kids hanging on the rafters. Knight will talk for as long as the students want him to, opening the floor for questions when he is finished with his talk.

Student: "Coach, do you think it's fair to make athletes submit to drug testing?"

Knight: "If I were in charge, I'd drug test all you sons-of-bitches, not just the athletes."

Female student: "Coach, what do I have to do to become a basketball team manager?"

Knight: "Change your gender."

Knight's comments invariably draw some hoots and boos and offend some people. But for the most part, the students enjoy him. Much of that is because there is absolutely no bullshit in Knight's approach. He doesn't patronize them, speak down to them, or try to win them to his side. He just shows up and answers their questions. If some of them don't like the answers, that's life.

Knight went a step further with the students in the fall of '85, opening practice to them twice. A big crowd showed up each time, and when practice was over the first time, one student stood up as the players were leaving the floor and said, "Thanks, coach." "You're welcome," Knight answered, surprised at how much he had enjoyed the spectators. "Maybe we'll do it again." Sure enough, they did.

———

The first few weeks of practice were extremely hectic for Knight. He thought the six weeks before the opening game on November 30 against Kent State were crucial for this team because of the new players and the new roles many of the old players were being asked to fill. Each practice was crucial, and bad execution was agonizing for him.

But there was more. There was the speechmaking. And especially, there was the new emphasis on recruiting.

More than any other area, Knight had been forced to reevaluate his recruiting following 1985. The conclusion he reached was simple: he had done a poor job. Perhaps the assistants were to blame somewhat for not being more critical in their evaluations, but ultimately, recruiting is the head coach's job. He must decide who he wants and then decide what must be done to get them. If he chooses the wrong players or can't get the players he chooses, then something is wrong.

For Indiana, it was primarily a matter of choosing the wrong players. Because Indiana was Indiana and because Knight was Knight, the school was going to have an excellent chance of recruiting most of the players it went after, especially in the Midwest. A few players wouldn't want to play for Knight, and Knight wouldn't want some good players playing for him. But there would be a bevy of good players that Indiana could get.

Knight's recruiting approach, in six years as coach at West Point and fifteen at Indiana, has varied little. If he wants a player he tells him why; he tells him what his role can be if he comes to Indiana, and that if he does come to Indiana, it will be "the hardest place in the country to play." Very straightforward. You will go to class or you will not play. You will get yelled at. You will graduate. And you will become a better basketball player. It is, like the man himself, a black-and-white approach. If you like it, you'll sign right away. If you don't, you run right away.

Knight's lapse in recruiting in recent years had hurt the program. But now he was starting over. Crews, the number one recruiter for several years, was gone. In his place was Joby Wright. The new number two recruiter was Kohn Smith. Wright and Smith are about as different as two people can be. Wright, who was thirty-six, is black and from Mississippi, a huge man whose laugh could fill an entire room. He had been intensely recruited out of high school and had chosen Indiana from among the many bidders for his playing services. And that is what they had been: bidders. In Wright's senior year, Knight became the Indiana coach.

Everything changed. Suddenly, he was being ordered to go to class. Knight counseled him to work toward the degree he had virtually ignored for three years. After Wright had played pro ball for several years, he returned to Indiana at Knight's behest and earned both his undergraduate and master's degrees. In 1981, he became a graduate assistant coach, and in 1982, a full-time coach. He was now the senior assistant coach on the staff.

The players liked Wright because he spoke their language. He made them feel comfortable; it was his way of saying, "We're all the same." The players loved to tell the story about the night before a game in 1983 when Wright had decided to impart a few final words of wisdom. "Now don't be out chasin' no bitches tonight," Wright had said. "I guarantee you Coach ain't out chasin' no bitches. So why should you?" From that day forth, Indiana players constantly cautioned one another not to be out chasin' no bitches the night before a game. Once when Knight was trying to tell the players that they had better get to bed at a decent hour (Knight has never had a specific curfew), he told them, "If you boys think there's a trick you can try that I didn't pull, you're wrong. And if there is one, I guarantee you, Joby's tried it."

Kohn Smith could no more talk to the players in street language than he could talk to them in Swahili. He had arrived at Indiana the summer after the second national championship in 1981. He was thirty-three, a Mormon, married, with three children and a fourth one due. He had been raised in Utah and had become a successful high school coach in Idaho. He met Knight at a coaching clinic, and the two became summertime hunting and fishing partners. One reason Knight enjoyed Smith's company was that Smith was better than he was at both hunting and fishing. Knight always enjoyed competing with people who were tough to beat, regardless of the sport or setting. Smith was delighted when Knight offered him not just a college coaching job but a job at Indiana, the defending national champion. Smith's role with the players was that of a soother; when Knight blistered the paint off the locker room walls with his harsh words, he would often send Smith back to check the damage.

Most mornings when the coaches gathered to talk about the

day's practice plan, Knight would begin by saying, "Joby, did we recruit anybody today?" And Wright would shake his head and answer, "Well, Coach, we're hangin' in there."

These meetings took place in the coaches' locker room. The players' locker room sits on one side of Assembly Hall and that of the coaches on the other. This gives both players and coaches an oft-needed feeling of separation. The coaches' locker room was known to one and all as "the cave," partly because it was on the basement floor of the building, but more because of the long hours the coaches put in there.

The room was comfortable, but it often felt like a prison. This was where the coaching staff did most of its work. After games they would sit in the cave for hours going through the tape of the game. Knight would sit in his chair working the remote control while all the coaches sat around him. Everyone had pen and pad out to take notes. After a bad game, it might take hours to get through the tape because Knight would run back the poor plays so many times. Garl would go out and bring back huge quantities of food. No one ever went hungry at Indiana—sleepless, yes; hungry, no. There were times when the secretaries arrived the morning after a loss to find the coaches still in the cave, having not gone home yet. Wright, Smith, and Waltman were veterans of the long postgame sessions and were accustomed to them. Felling had some trouble adjusting; he occasionally nodded off to sleep while sitting on the couch as the tape ran on and on.

Wright and Smith were encouraged by Knight's attitude toward their recruiting reports. He was interested, even eager, and when Wright would suggest that Knight go to see a player practice, he was delighted when Knight willingly went. Early in December, Knight even flew up to Elkhart to watch a 6–10 high school sophomore named Sean Kemp practice. A sophomore; this was a breakthrough.

Knight needed to see players—lots of them, and often. If he didn't, emotional as he was in his evaluations of the players already at Indiana, he might see a kid once and decide he was better than anyone he had, simply because on that night *anyone* would seem better than the players he had. Indiana's recruiting thus far in the 1980s might best be summed up by the sad case of Delray Brooks.

Anyone who ever met Delray Brooks would put him on the list of the five nicest people they had ever known. He was generous, sweet-tempered, patient, funny, and everything you would want in a friend. He was, almost without question, the best-liked player on the Indiana team. He was as comfortable with the white players as he was with the other blacks; even on a team like Indiana's, where racial problems seemed almost nonexistent, this was unusual.

If Brooks had been just another guard trying to make it in college when he came to Indiana, he might have had a happy four years there. But Brooks was one of those high school kids built into a phenomenon by the time he was sixteen years old. He was almost 6-4 with long arms. He was mature beyond his years, and his size allowed him to dominate high school guards while playing at Rogers High School in Michigan City, Indiana.

By his junior year, everyone in the country was recruiting Brooks. When he visited Notre Dame to see the Irish play Indiana that year, Knight grabbed him before the game and told him, "Delray, we need you at Indiana. I expect to see you there." Brooks was thrilled. Bob Knight *needed* him.

That summer, Brooks was the big name at the Five-Star Basketball Camp—*the* basketball camp at the time—winning most of the awards. Knight had seen him play only once, during his junior year, a game in which Brooks played little because of foul trouble. And so, when the early signing date for high school seniors rolled around that November, Brooks chose Indiana. Knight was thrilled at the thought of Brooks and Alford in the same backcourt. It looked like a dream backcourt. Because of Brooks, he didn't even try to recruit Gary Grant, who went on to Michigan, or Troy Lewis, who landed at Purdue. Both would have been very interested in Indiana. Both turned out to be better players than Brooks.

Throughout the 1983–84 season, whenever Alford screwed up in practice Knight would tell him, "When Delray Brooks gets here next year, you'll never play. Your ass will be so far down the bench, no one will ever hear from you again."

These pronouncements hardly shook Alford. Knight's telling players that they would never play again was hardly unusual. His most famous pronouncement along those lines came in 1981 after a loss at Purdue. On the bus trip home, Knight walked back to where Isiah Thomas was sitting. "Isiah," Knight roared, "Next year we're bringing in Dan Dakich. He can do so many things on a basketball court that you can't do, it isn't even funny."

Comparing Dakich to Isiah Thomas was a little bit like comparing a horse and buggy to a jet. Older players constantly kidded Dakich about all the things he could do that Thomas couldn't: not jump, not run. . . .

When Brooks did arrive, his teammates were shocked. Not only had he been considered one of the three best high school players in the country the previous spring, he had been one of two high school players Knight had invited to the Olympic Trials. "I knew I was over my head pretty quickly," Brooks remembered. "First, they had me guard Johnny Dawkins. He made one move and was gone. Then, they had me guard Alvin Robertson. Same thing. I thought, 'Oh boy, Delray, you have a problem here.' "

Not being able to guard Dawkins or Robertson hardly made Brooks unusual. What shocked Brooks's new teammates was that he had trouble guarding *them.* "I had heard so much about him I didn't think I'd even be able to play with him," said Steve Eyl, who was in the same recruiting class. "When we played pickup ball, though, it was like no big deal to guard him. I couldn't understand it."

Neither could Knight. He had expected a taller version of Isiah Thomas, or at least someone who played like 1983 graduate Jim Thomas. He got neither. Brooks was not a good shooter—he had scored most of his high school points by getting inside against smaller players—was not a great jumper and had trouble playing man-to-man defense. He was cursed by his feet, which were big and slow. Brooks's body—long arms, bad feet—was built to play zone defense. Indiana played only man-to-man, and Brooks, though he tried mightily, simply got lost trying to make the cuts and switches necessary in man-to-man.

If Knight had seen Brooks play eight or ten times, he would have known these things about him before signing him. Instead, as they became more apparent with each passing practice, Knight became more and more depressed. He wanted desperately for Brooks to succeed at Indiana because he liked him so much. But as Brooks's sophomore season began this fall, Knight was convinced with each passing day that he would never find happiness playing at Indiana.

Brooks was the kind of person Knight looked for, but not the kind of player. To be successful at Indiana, you had to be both. That was why, even now, Knight still shied away from some players who were clearly good. A good example of this was Tion McCoy. Quick and spidery, McCoy was a 6-2 guard from Hammond. He played for Jack Gaber, one of Knight's former managers.

Knight and his assistants had visited McCoy's home early in the fall. The family had seemed interested, even eager, but after the visit, Knight heard secondhand that McCoy and his family were telling people that Gaber was trying to con McCoy into going to Indiana. Oklahoma or Maryland, they said, might be a better place for him. This kind of talk turned Knight off; he didn't like Billy Tubbs, the Oklahoma coach, as a person, and he couldn't imagine a good player choosing to play for Lefty Driesell at Maryland over him even though he did like Driesell personally.

When McCoy showed up at the first Sunday afternoon scrimmage of the season in late October, Knight told him exactly what he thought of him. "Why don't you go play at Oklahoma?" he said, his voice dripping with sarcasm. "The last time we played them they had Wayman Tisdale and a lot more talent than us, and we beat them by fifteen. Or Maryland would be great. The last time we played them they had Buck Williams and Albert King and we only beat them by thirty-five. You want to be a good player, Tion? Those are the places for you."

McCoy was apparently undaunted by this talk. A week later, Gaber called and said McCoy would like to come down for an official visit that weekend. Knight agreed, but told Gaber, "I have some problems with the way he's handled being recruited. I can't see us offering him a scholarship now. Maybe in the spring, but not now. Tell him that, and if he still wants to come down, that'll be fine."

McCoy still wanted to come. This intrigued Knight; if the kid was looking for the easy way out, it had been offered to him. Yet he still wanted to visit. That Sunday, during the scrimmage, Knight sat at the scorer's table with his arm around McCoy and talked to him about what he would expect of him if he came to Indiana; what he would have to work on. McCoy said he wanted to come. "Well, Tion, if you still want to come in the spring, we can talk," Knight said. "But right now, we don't have a scholarship to offer you, just like I told Jack on the phone."

Knight was being honest. At that moment Indiana had fifteen players on scholarship—the NCAA limit—and it had Morgan playing without a scholarship. Two scholarship players, Stew Robinson and Courtney Witte, would graduate in the spring. Two players, 6-11 junior college sophomore Dean Garrett and 6-6 Cincinnati high school senior David Minor, had already been offered and had accepted those two scholarships. Knight suspected that the situation might change by spring, but at that moment he had no scholarships. McCoy was welcome to wait, he said, but there would be no hard feelings if he didn't since Knight could not and would not promise him a scholarship.

A week later, McCoy announced that, after careful consideration, he had chosen Maryland over Indiana and Oklahoma. Reading this in the newspaper, Knight smiled. "Outrecruited again," he said. His gut had told him McCoy wasn't right for Indiana. What was important, though, was that he had done his homework on the player before making a decision one way or the other.

Putting down the paper, Knight looked at Wright. "Joby," he said, "did we recruit anybody today?"

"Coach," Wright answered, "we're hangin' in there." This year they were doing just that.

———

Knight had one other major responsibility as he prepared for the start of the season: Patrick Knight. On the day before practice started, Nancy Knight left Bloomington for a ten-week stay at Duke University. There, she would go through Duke's famed "rice diet," and return home in December thirty-five pounds lighter.

With his wife gone, Knight found himself a bachelor father for Patrick, who had turned fifteen in September. As things turned out, Knight enjoyed the experience—except for the inevitable rumors that cropped up with Nancy Knight away. They were wrong, scurrilous, in some cases cruel. Father and son learned to laugh when they heard them. One day, a friend of Pat Knight's asked him if the rumors about his father were true. "Oh, yeah,"

Pat Knight answered, "he brings a different girl home every Friday night." The only thing Knight was bringing home were tapes of that day's practice, some ice cream, and an occasional stray reporter. Their marriage was in trouble, and Knight filed for divorce after the end of the season, but it had nothing to do with the wild rumors.

Bob and Pat Knight were a true Odd Couple. If one wanted to imagine what the father had been like at fifteen, one needed only to look at Pat. He had shot up to 6-2 over the summer, a fact that disturbed his older brother, Tim, no end. Tim was twenty-one, a Stanford senior. He was stocky, built more like his mother than his father, and had never made it past six feet. When he returned home for Christmas vacation, Pat made a point of walking up to him whenever he could to point out the difference in height.

Pat's weight had not caught up with his height. He weighed 135 pounds—maybe—and had a typical teenage diet: soda for breakfast, McDonald's for lunch, dinner, and sometimes a late snack. His father tried to wean him of such things with about as much success as most fathers have.

Their relationship was interesting. Bob Knight's world was filled with people intimidated by him in one form or another. He was, almost always, the controller and dictator of his relationships. Things were done on his terms or they were not done at all. Few people—coaches, players, professors, writers—had any interest in incurring his wrath. But to Pat Knight, he was just dad, a guy who had a knack for locking his keys in his car or forgetting his garage door opener.

When Bob Knight ran his brand-new car through a flooded road one day and drowned its computer system, there were a lot of suppressed giggles at Assembly Hall. When Pat Knight heard what his father had done, he just looked at him and said, "Boy, are you stupid." He was right and his father knew it. He just glared at his son as if to say, "Who asked you?"

No one had. But you didn't need to ask Pat Knight for his opinion in order to hear it. Like his father, he was sharp-witted and sharp-tongued, bright and clever. He won most arguments with his father: "I want you in at 10 o'clock, not a minute later." "But I can't get a ride until 10:30." "Okay, be in by 10:45."

Inevitably, Pat would show up at 11:30 with some explanation. "Everyone else was hungry, so we had to stop to eat. I told them not to, but they made me."

Knight tried to get angry, but really couldn't. "The problem," he said one night, "is I like him too much and he knows it."

Being a single father wasn't always easy. When Pat got sick during the day at school, the single father had to go pick him up. Sometimes, if Pat needed a ride in the middle of practice, Knight would have one of the managers go get him, but more often than not he did the chauffeuring himself. He also spent as much time as he could working with Pat on his game.

Pat Knight, unlike his older brother, is a basketball player. He is a good shooter who, like his father, has a knack for seeing the game developing in front of him. He is an excellent passer for someone his age, and occasionally when he makes a good pass during a game, his father has to restrain his excitement. Pat Knight was a starting forward on the Bloomington North freshman team, and whenever he played Bob Knight would slip in, sit in as unobtrusive a spot as he could find and watch the game impassively. After the game he would wait until Pat asked for his opinion on his play before he gave it.

Softly, he would push every now and then. "You really should come in early and work on your foul shooting." But for the most part he left it up to Pat. If he was going to become a good player, it had to be because he wanted to, not because his father wanted him to. If twenty-four years as a coach had taught Bob Knight anything, it was the dangers of pushy parents. If Pat wanted help from his father, it would be there. But it would only be forthcoming if solicited.

Each day, Pat would call after his practice was over, looking for a ride. Each day, the father's side of the conversation sounded like this:

"Did you have a good practice? . . . Uh-huh. . . . Did you guard anybody? . . . Uh-huh. . . . Did you hit any shots? . . . Uh-huh. . . . Were you tough? . . . Uh-huh. . . . Patrick, how come you say yes to all my questions every day? No one is that good."

The coaches, listening to their boss, enjoyed the looseness that

Patrick brought out in his father. They thought it was healthy for him, especially if it kept him from getting upset after a bad practice.

———

There were bad practices. Some days the team would practice well for an hour, then get tired. Some days it would drill well and then scrimmage poorly. Practice started every day at about 3:30. The players would usually get to the gym at about 2:30 to get taped and to warm up. Their latest classes were over at 2:15.

Knight was kept apprised of the players' academic progress by the athletic department's academic supervisor Elizabeth (Buzz) Kurpius. If a player was struggling with a class, or cutting a class, or missing a session with a tutor, Kurpius would be informed. She would then pass the information on to Knight and to Waltman, the assistant coach responsible for monitoring the players' academic progress and making certain they were doing what they were supposed to.

Cutting class and cutting a tutor were inexcusable offenses at Indiana. Giomi had been dismissed because of a pattern of cut classes. If Kurpius sent Knight a notice about a missed class, the player was asked to explain his absence. Short of a hurricane or a flood, no excuse was accepted. The same was true of a missed tutor. The guilty player might have to run the steps after practice or, in the case of a tutoring session, might not be allowed to practice until he had seen the tutor.

Knight's toughness in this area was consistent with his approach throughout his coaching career. When he recruited a player he told him that he would have to go to class to play, and that he would be expected to graduate. Certainly, parents hearing this were bound to feel kindly toward Indiana, but Knight had the record to back up what he said: In fourteen years at Indiana only two players who had stayed four years had failed to graduate. One of them, Bob Wilkerson, had all the necessary credits but needed to fulfill a student teaching requirement. The three seniors on the '86 team—Morgan, Robinson, and Witte—were all on schedule for graduation in the spring.

Knight tells players that he doesn't think a player who cuts class can succeed as a basketball player in his program. Going to class requires a minimal amount of discipline, and if you don't have that, you probably don't have the discipline needed to learn Knight's system and flourish in it. "I have never had a good player who cut class," Knight often said. "I just don't think that kind of kid can play for me."

There might have been exceptions. But they didn't last long enough for Knight to find that out.

Once practice began, there was not a lot of free time for the players. They had classes, practices, tape sessions with the coaches, and study time. There was not a lot of party time. That was one reason why Knight had very few specific rules. There was no curfew at Indiana, even during the season. The players knew they were expected to stay out of bars during the season even if they weren't drinking, and they were told to exercise judgment about the hours they kept. With the schedule most of them had to follow, good judgment usually meant eating dinner after practice, doing some studying, and going to bed—exhausted. This was especially true of Alford, a business major, who was taking a special advanced course known as A-Core. The course was accelerated, and the professor didn't particularly like basketball players. Alford was struggling.

And this was still only October.

5.

November

November is the toughest month for any college basketball team. The excitement of starting practice on October 15 has worn off, and practice has become drudgery. There are no games to prepare for or get excited about. There is no crowd to provide electricity or support. There is just day after day of practice—the same faces, the same coaches, the same drills, the same teammates.

This is especially true at Indiana. Winter is closing in rapidly

The days are cold, sunless, and depressing. In 1985, it rained in Bloomington for twenty-seven of November's thirty days. It wasn't just a drizzle breaking up a sunny day but cold, steady, depressing rain. And for this team, the weather and the drudgery were only part of the difficulty. Right next to the cloud that dumped rain every day was an even darker cloud: the specter of last season. Each time practice went poorly, last season would come up. "If you guys think I was an awful sonofabitch last year, you haven't seen anything yet," Knight said angrily one day. "You boys better think about that."

They did. Constantly. Pushed by Knight, Alford had assumed the role of leader on this team. He received a good deal of help in this area from Stew Robinson, a senior and a natural leader. Often, Knight and the coaches would leave the players alone in the locker room to talk after a bad practice or a bad scrimmage. "I don't know about you guys," Alford said one day, "but I can't live through another season like the last one. We have got to start playing better."

Knight knew the team was working hard, and occasionally he would loosen up to show the players that he was aware of their effort. One day before practice Knight turned to Kreigh Smith and said, "Kreigh, what do you think we should work on today? I need a few ideas for practice."

This was in the locker room after the players had finished warming up. That is the routine each day: Knight walks out of his locker room and announces, "Let's go inside." Everyone retreats to the locker room, where Knight will brief them on that day's practice plan. He can talk for thirty seconds or for fifteen minutes, depending on the day and his mood.

Smith, a 6-7 sophomore from Tipton, Indiana, was one of Knight's favorite targets. He was a small-town kid who Knight thought had the potential to be as good as Randy Wittman. But Smith's concentration sometimes wandered, and Knight had gotten in the habit of calling him "Tipton." The reason: "I often wonder if he understands that our schedule is a little tougher than the one he played at Tipton High School."

In truth, Smith was a lot more savvy than Knight gave him credit for. One day in practice, Smith lost his man on defense.

The man he should have been guarding was Morgan, who had grown up in Anderson, Indiana.

"Tipton," Knight yelled, "who are you supposed to be guarding?"

"Anderson," Smith answered without batting an eye.

Knight paused, his face breaking into a grin. "That's pretty good, Tipton," he said, "but remember, there's only one goddamn comedian on this team."

Now, in the locker room, the comedian was asking Tipton for some ideas for practice. Smith knew he was being set up, but didn't have much choice but to go along. "I think we should work on conversion defense," he said, bringing up the area that had been bothering Knight lately, the team's inability to get back on defense.

"That's good, Kreigh," Knight said, still straight-faced. "I really want everybody to help with practice and I thought I would start with you, as one of the most in-depth thinkers on the team."

The other players were beginning to convulse with giggles.

"Conversion defense, okay," Knight continued. "What else?"

"The press," Smith answered. "I think we should work on the press."

"You know I've always said, you can beat a bad team with a press but not a good team. You still want to work on the press?"

"No."

"Now, Kreigh, don't let me intimidate you."

The whole room broke up. Knight was still smiling when he walked onto the floor. So were the players. In November, every light moment was greatly appreciated.

———

Such byplay was the exception, though, not the rule. Practice was, for the most part, all business. Time and again Knight reminded his players that basketball is not an easy game to play. "It is the toughest game in the world to play," he said one day. "There are no huddles, no time between pitches, no breaks. You have to be able to think on every possession. If you can't think, you can't play."

Not thinking, to Knight, was a cardinal sin. Players were going to miss jump shots, they were going to mishandle the ball, and they were going to throw bad passes. Knight almost never got on a player for missing a shot, unless the shot was a foolish one. But some things were unforgivable: not boxing out, not knowing where your man was on defense, not setting a proper screen. Those were mental errors caused by a lack of concentration. There was no excuse—none—for not concentrating.

Indiana's practices were never very long; usually they lasted about two hours. Knight didn't think the players could concentrate for much longer than that. During those two hours, though, there was no wasted motion. When the players needed a rest they got one—by shooting free throws.

By the time November started, everyone noticed a change in Knight. There were still explosions. There were moments when he would stop practice and say, "There is no way you can play basketball like this and beat anybody on our schedule. Not anybody. Not one of the twenty-eight games we play could you win. I couldn't make a schedule easy enough for you people to play."

But more often when he stopped play it was to instruct, to teach. That had been missing the previous season. Then, Knight had left more of the instruction up to the assistants while he sat on the sidelines with Bob Hammel or Ed Williams or Ralph Floyd or whoever happened to be at practice that day. But now, Knight coached aggressively every day. He knew that each player on the team had to be better on November 30 than he had been on October 15 if Indiana was to succeed this season. And so Knight worked as hard in preseason as he had in years.

The players were delighted. This was the Bob Knight they had come to Indiana to play for. His teaching methods were hardly gentle but that didn't matter; they didn't expect or want that. The players liked the assistant coaches and thought they were good teachers, but they had come to Indiana to learn from Knight. Each day he was out on the floor, demonstrating what he wanted done, taking them by the arm literally and by the hand figuratively to show them the proper way to execute.

Two players were getting special attention: Harris and Calloway. Each was about as good an athlete as Knight had ever recruited. Harris was two years older than Calloway, but Calloway was a quicker learner. Almost from the beginning, Knight assigned Dakich to work with Calloway whenever there was free time. It was unusual for Knight to single out a player this way, but he thought Dakich could help Calloway, especially since he had just graduated that past spring.

They were an odd duo. Calloway was a wonderful athlete who knew very little about playing the game. Dakich was the exact opposite—a nonathlete who knew lots about playing the game. If Dakich could put his knowledge into Calloway's body, Indiana would have an excellent basketball player.

Calloway was a willing pupil, but Harris was not as easy to deal with. Clearly, he was not used to being yelled at, and when he did get yelled at he tended to sulk. Knight loved Harris's athletic ability, and was relatively easy on him at first. But Harris's progress was slow. Some days he would dominate practice. On others he took bad shots and made mental mistakes. Also, the coaches could not understand how someone who could jump like Harris got so few rebounds in practice every day.

Harris and Jadlow, the two junior college players, were both adjusting to their new environment. Harris was quiet by nature and Jadlow wasn't very mature; this made life difficult for the two of them at times. Harris came across as stuck-up to some of his teammates, many of whom quickly grew tired of hearing Knight talk about what a great athlete Harris was. Their attitude was, "Great athlete, okay fine. But does that mean he doesn't get yelled at the way the rest of us do?"

There was one other group less than thrilled with Harris: the managers. At Indiana, managers play a crucial role in the day-to-day running of the team. Knight usually has a minimum of twelve. The senior managers, who are given scholarships if they have been managers since their freshman year, interview and select prospective managers each fall. Often, Knight's managers go into coaching, the best example being Chuck Swenson, now the number one assistant at Duke.

There were four senior managers on this team: Jim Kelly, Bill Himebrook, Jeff Stuckey, and Mark Sims. Harris met Kelly first, and proceeded to call every senior manager Jim. Eventually, the managers began calling one another Jim. Later in the season, the managers put together a takeoff on the Chicago Bears' "Super Bowl Shuffle." They called it "The Managers Shuffle," and it included a line that went, "Andre Harris, he can jump right over the rim but he calls all the managers by the name of Jim." Harris did eventually learn all four names, but still had trouble at times because other players would intentionally call Bill "Jim," or Mark "Jeff."

Through it all, Harris hung in, and before the season was over he began playing up to the potential that showed up in flashes during November. But it was not an easy process for the player, the coaches, or the managers.

———

The first break in the daily practice routine was looming. On November 9, the Czechoslovakian national team would come to town for an exhibition game. Teams are allowed to play one preseason exhibition game under NCAA rules, and Indiana usually played one seven days before the opener. But this year Knight had moved it up, partly because of the Czech tour schedule, partly because he thought an earlier break in the practice routine would be healthy.

By the beginning of the week, the coaches knew who would be in the starting lineup: Alford and Robinson at guard; Morgan, Harris, and Thomas up front. The only other serious candidate to start was Calloway, and Knight saw no reason to push him. Robinson was a senior, he should get the first chance.

The real decision that had to be made that week concerned redshirts. Once upon a time, Knight had been opposed to the redshirt concept; he didn't think a player should sit out a year unless he was injured. College was supposed to be a four-year experience, and extending it for a year just gave a player a potential excuse for cutting class and falling into bad habits.

But in 1983, Randy Wittman and Ted Kitchel both spent a fifth year at Indiana after sitting out a year because of injury. Each had the best season of his career—by far. That season changed Knight's thinking about redshirts. In fact, and this was hardly atypical, he had gone from opponent to all-out advocate, just as he later would with recruiting junior college players.

Any player who dressed for the Czech game would be ineligible to redshirt, unless he was injured before Indiana had played six games. Because of that, Knight was not going to dress anyone for the game he thought he might want to redshirt.

Oliphant was going to be redshirted, that much was certain.

The other candidates were the seven sophomores: Kreigh Smith, Brian Sloan, Joe Hillman, Steve Eyl, Todd Jadlow, Magnus Pelkowski, and Delray Brooks. Hillman, who had come to Indiana without a scholarship (he now had one) from a Los Angeles suburb, wanted to redshirt so that he would have two years of eligibility left after Alford graduated. Smith didn't want to redshirt, he wanted to play. Sloan was willing. Eyl, who had been a starter at the end of the previous season, was only a serious redshirt candidate on days when he didn't practice well. The same was true of Jadlow; his shooting touch in practice improved steadily, and by the time the season started he was actually a candidate to start.

The special cases were Pelkowski and Brooks. Pelkowski was a pet project of Knight's. He was a 6-foot-10, 230-pound Colombian who had first been brought to Knight's attention by Julio Salazar, the graduate assistant coach from Colombia. Knight thought Pelkowski had the potential to become a top-notch big man, but that he needed time. Normally, he would have redshirted him just as quickly as he had redshirted Oliphant, but there was a problem: before coming to Indiana, Pelkowski had taken some courses at a college in Colombia. The NCAA rules have what is known as a five-year clock, meaning that once a person enrolls in college he has up to five years to complete his eligibility unless he leaves for military duty or a church mission. If Pelkowski's clock had been started when he was enrolled in school in Colombia, he could not be redshirted. Knight believed that since he had only been a part-time student, those classes shouldn't be counted against him. Indiana was trying to get the Colombian school to send written confirmation that Pelkowski had only been a part-time student and that there had been no basketball program. Once that was in hand, Indiana would ask that Pelkowski be granted a fifth year by the NCAA and the Big Ten. In the meantime, Pelkowski would not dress for this game.

Brooks would. After long discussions, the coaches decided it would be better for everyone involved to throw Brooks in now and see if he could play. Their guess was that he probably couldn't, that he had too many physical deficiencies. But to ask him to sit out a year with no guarantee that he would play in the future wasn't fair.

"If he can't play and he wants to transfer, the sooner he finds out, the better off he'll be," Knight said. "I really wish the kid could be a star. I really do feel for him." Twenty-five years earlier, Bob Knight had gone to Ohio State with high hopes. Not the kind of hopes that Brooks had arrived at Indiana with, but high nonetheless. He spent most of his college career on the bench. Knight genuinely ached for the kids who gave him everything they had only to find that it wasn't enough.

———

Three days before the Czech game, Al McGuire came to town. Knight and McGuire had been friends for years. They were friendly adversaries when McGuire was at Marquette, and now, with McGuire at NBC, they helped each other out: It helped McGuire that Knight was always willing to cooperate with him, and it helped Knight that McGuire was always willing to stand up for him.

McGuire was taping a segment for his preseason special with Knight that evening, so he sat and watched practice. "It's not a very good team," he murmured halfway through.

Indeed, the Hoosiers were struggling that day. At one point, Knight took them all into the locker room for a verbal spanking. He was on everybody at one point or another. Robinson's defense was a big problem. "Stew, you look like a goddamn dog chasing a rabbit through a briar patch," he said. "I can't redshirt Hillman because of your defense." Thomas wasn't much better: "If you can't guard these guys, Daryl, what chance do you have against [Kentucky's] Kenny Walker?"

When the reds fell behind the whites during a scrimmage, Knight threw up his hands. "Coach yourselves," he told the reds in disgust. With Alford in charge, the reds went from an 18–10 deficit to a 26–24 lead. Knight, who had been silent, jumped on Kreigh Smith for losing Alford on defense.

"That was a short sabbatical," McGuire noted.

A moment later, Smith was gone. With most expletives deleted, this is what Knight told him as he left: "I'm tired of having to get on you every night. Sick and tired of it. Go take a shower, just get out and don't come back until I call you. This is just bullshit. You guys just won't push yourselves, will you? I've never seen a group that has more excuses for poor play than this one."

He sent them home a few minutes later. Walking into the locker room, he turned to McGuire and said, "I needed to get on them a little today."

The following day, Jim Thomas called Knight. He had been cut by the Indiana Pacers. Could Knight call some of his friends in the NBA to find out if anyone had any interest in him? Knight immediately put in several phone calls. Thomas was a 6-3 guard who had been very effective during his years at Indiana, but he wasn't big enough, quick enough, or a good enough shooter to be a legitimate NBA player. The fact that he had gotten in two full years was as much a tribute to the respect the pros have for Knight's players as anything else. Knight knew this, but still would do anything Thomas asked him to if he wanted to keep playing.

For all the grief he gives his players during their four years with him, Knight honestly believes he owes them something in return once they graduate. The day an Indiana player finishes his career, his relationship with Knight changes forever. Knight is still the dominant figure, still intimidating, still forceful. But now he is also your friend—not a friend you call to go have a beer, but a friend you call when you need help. Knight expects his ex-players to do that—wants them to do it, in fact. Loyalty is a huge word in his vocabulary. He expects it, and he returns it—no qualifiers. If you mess up, in all likelihood you are through. But if you don't mess up, you have a friend who will do just about anything you ask.

Knight's phone calls didn't produce much good news for Jim Thomas. "Come on down here, Jim, and let's talk," Knight told him. He was thinking that Thomas might want to go to graduate school. Thomas was thinking he might want to coach. Knight doesn't encourage his players to coach: "My father always wanted to know why someone had to go to college to become a coach," he often said. But if they wanted coaching, he would help them, and give them a job if they wanted it.

Thomas thanked Knight for his help and was about to hang up when his coach stopped him. "Jimmy," he said, "do you remember when you were six years old? You were a happy little kid then, weren't you? And you had never even heard of basketball then. Just think, if you never play basketball again, you can still be a happy person."

Knight's voice was soft as he spoke. He wanted Thomas to get the message, but he didn't want him hurt.

Just before practice that afternoon, Knight called Alford and Morgan aside. He wanted to talk to them about leadership. "Somebody besides me has to get on these people," he said. "I'm tired of having to do it all myself. Personally, I don't think the two of you could lead a whore into bed. But you're going to have to."

He turned to Alford. "Steve, you always talk about God. Well, I'm gonna tell you something, Steve, God is not going to provide any leadership on this basketball team. He couldn't care less if we win or not. He is not going to parachute in through the roof of this building and score when we need points. My father used to tell me that God helps those who help themselves. And, I'll tell you one more thing. No, let me ask you this. Do you really think that God is going to help a team that *I'm* coaching?"

Knight was not trying to be blasphemous; he had been raised in a Methodist home and had gone to church every Sunday with his mother and grandmother. But the spectre of organized religion made him uncomfortable, and he really did have a problem with athletes invoking God as their helper. Earlier that week, during a speech to the local Rotary Club, he had brought up the Texas A&M kicker who had made a field goal with time running out to beat SMU and then said that God had helped him kick the field goal. "Does this mean," Knight asked, "that God decided to screw SMU? God does not give a damn what goes on in athletics. Nor should he."

After Knight had finished his talk with Alford, Joby Wright couldn't help but tease his boss a little. "You know, Coach," he said, "I think you're probably paving Steve's way to heaven by persecuting him for being a born-again Christian."

"Joby," Knight answered, "there ain't no SOB who can't play defense that's going to heaven." And then he added with a smile, "God grant me patience—and goddammit, hurry up."

Thus endeth the day's sermon.

———

On Friday, twenty-four hours before the Czech game, the team had its first night practice. The game would be at 7:30 the next night, so a scrimmage was scheduled for that time on Friday to simulate game conditions.

Everyone was on time for the scrimmage—except Knight. He had been out hunting with Johnny Bench and another friend, and their brand-new hunting dog had run off. Distraught, Knight had zoomed to practice, hopped out of his car, and locked his keys in the car. He was on the phone getting the campus police to come over and get his car open at 7:30. Pat Knight would have a field day with this one.

The scrimmage started fifteen minutes late. The first half was textbook basketball; the reds dominated the whites, moving the ball well, executing better than they had since practice started. But at halftime, following Garl's orders, Alford was excused to ice his right foot. He had broken a bone in the foot two years earlier and occasionally it swelled up on him. As a precaution, Garl only wanted him to play a half.

Knight almost always defers to Garl's judgment on injuries. Sometimes he will ask Garl to have a doctor check something, but he trusts Garl completely. He doesn't believe in giving players painkilling shots, and although he will at times ask a player if he can play with an injury, he only does so if Garl tells him there's no risk in playing with the injury. There was no need to risk Alford in a scrimmage, especially since Knight wanted him ready for the game the next night.

But without Alford, the reds bogged down. A good shooter, one who is good at getting open, can hide a lot of weaknesses in an offense. Stripped of that shooter, the reds began turning the ball over, making bad passes. With the whites playing a zone, the reds struggled. Knight didn't even go in to talk to the players when the scrimmage was over. He had lost a dog, locked his keys in his car, and seen graphically just how dependent his team was going to be on Alford's offense.

It had not been a good day.

But the next day, although ugly and rainy, proved to be much better. Thanks largely to the weather, no one was in a particularly good mood when the players gathered for their pregame walk-through.

The walk-through was the beginning of Indiana's game-day ritual. Perhaps no coach in the history of basketball has ever believed more strongly in the walk-through. A walk-through is a rehearsal. One of the assistant coaches goes through the scouting report on the other team, showing the players where they will make their cuts on offense, what passes they will try to throw, where the ball is likely to go on inbounds plays. He will also go through Indiana's offense based on the defense the opponent is likely to play.

Knight honestly believes it is almost impossible to walk through too much. He believes that the more times the players see the plays developing in front of them, even in slow motion, the better off they will be.

The team usually meets after dinner the night before a game for a thirty-minute walk-through in their street clothes. Then, for a 7:30 home game, the team gathers in practice gear at about 3 P.M. the next day to go through everything again. Often, Knight will show the players an opponent running a particular play on tape, take them onto the floor to walk through, then return to the locker room to show another play on tape. Sometimes the team will go back and forth between the floor and the locker room six or seven times.

The players understand exactly what their coach is trying to accomplish. They also have trouble concentrating; by the sixth or seventh walk-through of an offense, boredom becomes a major factor.

Once the walk-through is over, Knight will talk to the team briefly. Usually, he will harp on a theme for that game. For the Czechs, the theme was, "November 9 to March 9." In other words, tonight is the beginning of a four-month season that ends on March 9. "Let's make sure that on March 9 we've met the goals we have on November 9," Knight said. "Let's get started in that direction tonight."

With that, he sent them to pregame meal.

The pregame meal is step two in the game-day ritual. At home, the team eats in the student union, in an elegant third-floor meeting room. Everyone, players and coaches, wears a coat and a tie—everyone except Knight, who usually arrives in slacks and a sweater. The players sit at a long table and eat spaghetti, hamburgers without rolls, scrambled eggs, pancakes, and ice cream. They drink orange juice or iced tea. The meal is always the same, home or away. Everyone gets vanilla ice cream—except Knight, who gets butter pecan.

Knight never sits down to eat at the pregame meal. His seat, at the head of the table, is always unoccupied. The players sit in the same seat at every meal. New players take whatever seats have been vacated by graduation; those become their seats for as long as they are at Indiana. If a player is injured and not at pregame meal, no one sits in his seat.

No one talks during the pregame meal, except to ask for something. Occasionally the assistant coaches sitting at the far end of the table will whisper among themselves, but for the most part the only sound heard is forks and knives clinking against one another. The mood is somber. The players are supposed to be concentrating on the job ahead of them.

Usually, Knight arrives at pregame at about the same time as the ice cream. He will sit in an anteroom and wait until the players are finished before coming in to give them another talk. The game theme is repeated. Reminders about how to play a particular team are given.

Knight didn't come to the pregame meal at all on this day. He left it to the assistant coaches. Wright and Smith both spoke, talking about how this was a chance to begin to wipe out the memories of last season. Once the coaches were finished, the players quickly left, leaving the coaches behind.

For the four assistant coaches, game day, any game day, was tense. The three holdover coaches all knew how difficult their lives would be after a loss or, in the case of a game like this one, after a poor performance. But the tension also produced a bond among the coaches. They were friends, though about as different as four men could be: one black and southern; one white and a westerner; one white and an easterner; the fourth, a white midwesterner. All were married with children, though Felling was divorced.

For Felling, the few months he had spent in Bloomington had

been a revelation already. He had known when he took the job that Knight would demand a lot of him, but, like the players Knight recruits, he could not possibly understand what he was getting into until he arrived. Felling and Knight were almost the same age, Felling the elder by nine months. They shared a passion for country music and basketball. But where Knight was consumed by basketball, Felling often felt the need to escape from it. Felling had quickly learned the first lesson of survival as an Indiana assistant: never think you've done enough. Usually, you haven't.

Felling had also learned quickly that when in Rome, one did as the Romans did. The expensive cowboy boots that had been his trademark in Lawrenceville were never seen in Bloomington. Knight didn't even like the curly perm Felling wore. Maybe it reminded him too much of Kentucky coach Eddie Sutton. The perm stayed, though; one small victory for mankind.

Felling had been quickly accepted by the other three coaches, partly because he was needed, but mostly because he had an endearing personality. Felling almost never took anything seriously, which at Indiana was a breath of fresh air. "I just like to laugh," he often said, although he was careful to control that urge when the head coach was in a serious mood. Whenever Knight addressed Felling by using one of his favorite words—cocksucker—Felling would look at him very seriously and say, "Well, coach, I'm tryin' to quit." And whenever anyone accused Felling of anything, be it a passion for the opposite sex or a poor choice of sport coat, Felling would just shake his head and say, "Well, I resent it, but I can't deny it."

The players accepted him quickly because of this self-deprecating manner, and by the time the Czech game was played, Felling was one of the boys.

While all the boys—players and assistant coaches—went off to prepare for that night's game, Knight returned to his locker room for a pregame steam. This too was a ritual, especially this year, when Knight was making a concerted effort to lose weight. He had not enjoyed the descriptions of his pot belly the previous season and had worked hard to lose weight. He had gotten to as low as 217—twenty-five pounds less than he had weighed the previous March, but as the season approached his weight inched higher. It was 221 an hour before game time, following a solid hour of steam. "I've got to be 215 for the opener," Knight said. "That's my goal."

It would be a tough goal for Knight to reach because he was a prodigious eater. He could put away monumental amounts of food when he was enjoying himself, and the only thing that kept him from truly getting fat was that he didn't drink. Knight had never liked the taste of beer and never touched hard liquor. Occasionally he would drink a white wine spritzer, but usually would switch after one drink to iced tea or ginger ale, or some awful concoction like orange juice and 7-Up or Coke and tea. Later in the season, when the team was going well, Knight would break down after a game and have a sangria, but even then, if he drank two glasses it was a lot.

Even though this was just an exhibition game, it was approached in Indiana like the real thing. More than 15,000 seats were sold in 17,259 seat Assembly Hall, remarkable on a rainy November night when the game was being televised statewide. But that is the way Indiana is about basketball, especially basketball at I.U. Every game Indiana plays is televised. If it isn't on some kind of national TV or Big Ten hookup, it's televised statewide by WTTV-TV.

While the gym was slowly filling up, the players, dressed now in their white game uniforms, waited in the locker room. The assistants circled the room, softly whispering reminders about getting back on defense, about pushing the ball up the floor, about fundamentals. Some players sat on their chairs in front of their lockers, others stood passing a ball back and forth. There was chatter, but no real talk. Mostly, they filled time waiting for Knight to walk in for a final pregame talk.

About one hour before tipoff, Knight dressed. He put on slacks, a golf shirt, and a golf sweater. After the Purdue game the previous season, Knight had abandoned sport coats. The plaid jackets that had become his trademark had disappeared from his wardrobe. This season, to feel relaxed and comfortable, he planned to dress in a relaxed and comfortable outfit for games.

Once dressed, Knight ducked out the side door of his locker room and circled the building through back hallways to reach the players' locker room. He took a game program from one of the managers and stopped in a small dressing room adjacent to the locker room. Five minutes later, he walked into the locker room and all noise ceased: the balls stopped bouncing, the chatter halted.

Indiana's locker room is large and comfortable. It is carpeted in red with various signs and sayings posted on the walls around the room. "Victory favors the team making the fewest mistakes," is Knight's favorite. There are two doors to the locker room. The one Knight comes through leads to a private hallway that includes the graduate assistants' office, a tape room, and the training room. Near that door is a poster that lists the team's offensive and defensive goals for each game—and how it did in the previous game.

On the far side of the room is another poster, which, like the goals poster, is kept up to date by the managers. It contains pictures, statistics, scouting reports, and newspaper stories on the next opponent. Reading the stories and the scouting report, one would think every Indiana opponent is the Celtics.

In that same corner sits the television set that is used to show tapes. When tapes are being shown, the players bring their orange plastic chairs up from their lockers and sit in a semicircle around the TV. The door on that side of the locker room leads to a public hallway and the floor. The locker closest to that door is Alford's— a coincidence, since players inherit empty lockers the way they inherit empty chairs at pregame meal, but a coincidence that often causes a logjam near the doorway when reporters are in the room because so many of them congregate around Alford.

On the back wall of each locker are the names and numbers of players who dressed in that locker while playing for Knight. You must graduate to have your name and number posted in your locker when you leave. Transfers don't make it. In all, there are nineteen lockers in the room, so there is always a little extra space.

On the far side of the room from where Alford sits is a white marking board. When Knight walks into the room on game night, he has tucked his game program into his back belt. He walks to the marking board and lists the last name and the number of each of the opponent's starters. The names are already familiar to the players: they have heard them in scouting reports, seen them on tape, and talked about them during walk-throughs.

Game night is the only time that Knight talks to his players when they don't have notebooks in their laps. At all other times, each player has a red hardcover spiral notebook. Knight sees no reason why his players shouldn't take notes when he talks, the same way they take notes in a history or an English class. "The only difference is that in those classes they have a textbook they can go back and use. With me, there's no textbook."

When Knight talks about a game, an opponent, a defense, or a theme, the players take notes. They can write whatever they want in their notebooks, and they can write as much or as little as they want. Usually they are very careful to write down only serious thoughts and not doodle or put down anything snide or funny—not because they're graded or checked on, but because over the years Knight has occasionally picked up a notebook and leafed through it.

Now, though, the notebooks are put away. The information written in them is supposed to be in the players' heads at this point. Next to the name of each opponent, Knight writes the first name of the Indiana player who will guard him. He will then go through details again: a reminder if a player is lefthanded or if he likes to shot fake and drive. Then, a final word, usually going back to the game theme. On this night it was simple: "Let's just play basketball as well as we can play. Think. Think. Think. Remember, this is the start, only a beginning, but let's get off to a good start and go from there."

They did not get off to a good start. The first two minutes were a disaster. Alford let his man get by him twice and was unceremoniously yanked by Knight. As Calloway reported in and Alford came out with Knight barking in his ear, scattered boos wafted down from the fans. These were memories of last year, and the new season was not yet two minutes old. They missed their first seven free throws and fell behind by as many as seven points.

But Daryl Thomas was using his quickness inside to destroy

the bigger, slower Czech centers. He got them in foul trouble, scored consistently, and, eventually, the Hoosiers began to play the way they were capable. Alford came back midway through the half, and with 5:45 left Brooks stole a pass and fed Alford for a layup. Indiana led for the first time, 23–22. They built the lead from there and had it to eight by halftime.

That was fortunate. Knight had been extremely upset through much of the half. During one time-out he slammed his clipboard so hard that the sound reverberated around the building. This was not unusual; Garl came to each game equipped with two clipboards. Once, in an earlier year, the game had ended with Knight drawing plays on the top half of the second clipboard because that was all that was left.

There were no hysterics at the break this time. Knight felt his team gaining command. He knew it had been nervous early because of the crowd. Harris had already become a favorite with two impressive blocked shots. Thomas was playing well. "Let's put them away quickly," Knight said at the half. "Let's jump on them and get a big lead. Don't let them get back in this thing."

They didn't. A Harris dunk really got the crowd wound up and built the lead to 55–43. The lead eventually was more than 20, and the final score was 94–74. No contest. Still, there were moments. When Morgan threw a foolish pass, Knight screamed in his face during the next time-out. The two were literally nose to nose, one giving, the other taking. Did Morgan resent this treatment? Did he think it unfair? "I was thinking," he said later, "that I had screwed up again."

The screwups were balanced, though, by the potential that showed in flashes. Alford finished with twenty-three points; Harris had sixteen and nine rebounds. Thomas also had sixteen. It was, after less than four weeks of practice, a good beginning. Knight knew this. He also knew there was a lot more to do before this team could beat Notre Dames and Kentuckys. But they were not that far off. As the players congratulated one another after Knight had reminded them one more time, "November 9 to March 9, keep that in mind," they had little idea that they were about to enter the most difficult three weeks of the season. Over the next twenty days, they would have one day off. They would practice twenty-four times, look at endless hours of tape, and receive absolute hell from their coach.

After that, if they survived, they would play their first game.

6.

Three Long Weeks

When Knight makes life difficult for his players, which is often, it is not always because he is unhappy with them. He believes that the tougher he makes things for his team in practice, the tougher they will be in games. He points often to Indiana's remarkable road record in the Big Ten as evidence that this philosophy is effective. "I want them to start the season having faced their toughest times," he says. "I feel like if they can handle me, they can probably handle any crowd on the road or any kind of adversity that may come up in a game."

But there are also times when Knight simply gets furious and reams his team because he is furious. The three-week period between the Czech game and the opening game against Kent State had moments when Knight ripped his team as part of the master plan. It also had moments when he simply ripped his team. Either way, there were not a lot of laughs in Assembly Hall during this period.

The players got a hint that the last three weeks of preseason were not going to be much fun on the Wednesday after the Czech game. The Monday and Tuesday practices had been prickly, but not wild. Knight had snapped at people on several occasions, but it was mostly in the name of teaching. When Harris reached lazily for a pass with one hand on Monday, Knight crackled at him, "Andre, there is no room for one-handed basketball on this team. If God had wanted you to play this game with one hand you would have an arm growing out of your ass."

A few moments later, when Robinson made a good defensive play, Knight again stopped practice. "Stew," he said, "do you know what a good play that was? See, those assholes watching the game don't know what a good play that was. But I do. When I see that, I think, 'God, that Stew Robinson is a great defensive player.' I mean really great. Do you think, Stew, that I ever think that?"

Robinson shook his head no. "Not very goddamn often I don't," Knight went on. "But that was a great play."

Always pushing, always testing, always wanting more.

On Wednesday, though, the testing and the pushing became an explosion. This one was real. And, as often happens, the on-court explosion had a little to do with poor play and a lot to do with something that had happened earlier off the court.

At lunchtime that day, Knight went to a local radio station to tape a commercial. The arrangements had been made for Knight to go in, do the commercial, and leave. Knight arrived shortly after noon. In the lobby, he asked someone where he was to go to tape the commercial. Someone told him downstairs.

As Knight turned to walk in that direction, a young man with long hair, dressed rather sloppily in a T-shirt and blue jeans, arrived in the lobby. He was carrying a chair. He put the chair down in the middle of the lobby and announced, "Okay, I brought the chair." Knight was confused. He thought he had been told to go downstairs. He started to walk that way, and the young man followed. "I guess no one's going to laugh at my joke," he said.

At this point, Knight understood what was going on. He turned on the jokester. "You know, I'm here to do some business, that's all," he said. "I really don't need any trouble from someone I don't know."

"Sorry you don't have a sense of humor," the young man said, stalking away.

Knight's reaction was justified. If he had a dollar for every chair joke he had heard since the previous February 23 he could have bought and sold General Motors and IBM. But instead of laughing it off as the ravings of an idiot, Knight seethed. Later in the day he would remember what Ed Williams often told him: "Bob, you have to learn to let things go." But that would be later.

After taping the commercial, Knight was back in the lobby. The chair wielder was across the lobby, having no interest in another meeting with Knight. But Knight was not about to let the incident die. He walked across the lobby. "Listen," he began, "I want to tell you a few things."

He never got started, though, because his adversary looked up and said, "Look, I'm sorry I did it, okay? But I don't have to listen to you," and walked off.

Now Knight was furious. "Who runs this station?" he demanded. A woman in the lobby identified herself as the wife of station owner Roland Johnson. The two of them went outside to talk. Knight told Mrs. Johnson that he was insulted by what had happened. Mrs. Johnson agreed with Knight and apologized. "If I were running the station, that kid would be fired," Knight said. "Have your husband call me at my office when he gets back."

Knight was relating the story to his assistants an hour later when Roland Johnson called. Knight went through the story again. Mr. Johnson apologized again. Not good enough. "I think that kid should come out here and apologize to me in person," Knight said. Mr. Johnson didn't think that was a good idea. Why stir up potential trouble? The young man had been spoken to and had been told he was wrong and had agreed he had been wrong.

Not good enough. "If you can't get one of your employees to come out here and render a simple apology," Knight said, "then I don't see any reason to do any further business with your radio station."

End of conversation. Knight was not blackmailing or threatening. He was angry, and he meant exactly what he said. When he walked on the floor to start practice a few moments later, he was still upset by what had happened. The assistants knew that what came next was almost inevitable.

If the team had been sharp and crisp that day, Knight might have forgotten the radio station for at least a couple of hours. But they weren't. They were, in fact, a little sluggish. They were scheduled to fly to Fort Wayne the next night to play an intrasquad game in the Fort Wayne Coliseum. Maybe they were looking ahead to that; maybe it was just the way the stars and the moon were aligned. In any case, practice lasted less than an hour.

It ended when Kreigh Smith, who had the misfortune of flashing enough potential at times that he had become a favorite target, threw a silly pass. "That's it," Knight roared. "I've seen all I want to see of this crap. If you people are only going to demand enough of yourself that you end up playing on a horseshit team then the hell with you. Go take a shower. I've seen as much of this crap as I can take for one day."

He stalked off. The players and the assistants went to the locker room. Everyone talked a little. It was the same stuff: we have to work harder, concentrate better. Knight burst into the room. "There was no effort to get better out there at all. You guys don't listen and you don't think. It's the same bullshit as last year. Boys, you are just not good enough to play like this and be any good in the Big Ten."

He left. They sat and looked at each other for a while. Finally, the assistants softly suggested that everyone go back on the floor for some individual work. In his locker room Knight had stripped and was heading for the steam room to try to cool off.

"I can't go through another year like last year," he said. "And right now, we just aren't very good." There were no mind games today. The frustration, starting at lunchtime and extending into the evening, was quite genuine.

———

The next day the entire Indiana entourage flew to Fort Wayne. Sixteen players, five coaches, Ralph Floyd, Ed Williams, team cardiologist Larry Rink, Tim Garl, Bob Hammel, and John Flynn made the trip. Flynn was a newspaperman Knight had known since his days as a junior varsity coach at Cuyahoga Falls High School. That had been Knight's first job after graduation from Ohio State, and he and Flynn had remained friends long after Knight had gone on to Army and then Indiana. Flynn was living in Bloomington while waiting to receive word on a job application in Memphis, and he came to practice almost every day.

He was a bright, sharp-tongued man who had known Knight long enough that he was not intimidated by him. Flynn enjoyed Knight and Knight enjoyed Flynn. Knight found Flynn's intellect challenging. And Flynn, while recognizing Knight's flaws, was devoted to him. "Bob Knight is an asshole," Flynn said one night, "but he knows it and tries like hell to make up for it."

Both Indiana University Foundation planes were used for this trip: the big plane, which had twenty seats, and the brand-new little plane, which had eight. Indiana always travels by charter. The team will usually fly to a game site the evening before a game; the rest of the entourage, which for regular season games usually includes team doctor Brad Bomba, Floyd, sports information director Kit Klinglehoffer, radio play-by-play men Don Fischer and Max Skirvin, and TV play-by-play men John Laskowski and Chuck Marlowe, will arrive on the afternoon of the game. The big plane group always includes Knight, Garl, Hammel, anywhere from one to four assistant coaches (the recruiters usually meet the team the next day), and the players.

This trip was a chance to give Indiana's fans in the northern part of the state a chance to see the team live. The Fort Wayne Coliseum was completely sold out, a crowd of 9,200 packed into the place to see a preseason scrimmage. Outside the building, tickets were being scalped for up to $25. This was a measure of how deep-seated the feeling about Indiana basketball is throughout the state. Neither Purdue nor Notre Dame could guarantee anything approaching a sellout for an off-campus game, much less for an intrasquad scrimmage. In Fort Wayne, tickets for the scrimmage were sold out within hours of going on sale.

Knight revels in the popularity of the team and the school. This was the kind of night he enjoyed. These fans were less jaded than the ones in Bloomington. To them, the mere presence of the Hoosiers was an honor, so they weren't about to do any second-guessing. At the airport, a police escort met the team bus and Knight was assigned a personal bodyguard from the local sheriff's department for the evening to protect him from the crush of adoring fans in the hallways of the Coliseum.

Despite the lively crowd, the team did not play very well. The most notable exception was Alford, who made three straight steals at one point in the second half, prompting Knight to call him over. "Have you been reading books on how to play defense?" he asked. Alford giggled. From Knight, this was a compliment.

Few other compliments were passed around. Knight was particularly unhappy with Thomas and Harris for their inside play and told them so in the locker room when the scrimmage was over. It was not until the next day, after looking at the tape of the scrimmage, that Knight became genuinely upset. The tape showed sloppy play, missed passes, bad rebounding position. Knight had planned to give the team Friday off except for a brief meeting and to practice only briefly on Saturday afternoon. After he saw the tape, he changed his plans. He wanted to practice Friday afternoon.

The players, expecting the day off after arriving home from Fort Wayne after midnight, were sluggish. Knight knew this, and he knew they were tired, but he believed they had reached a point where they had to learn to play tired. During the season, they were going to have to deal with that at times, and now was as good a time as any to emphasize it. So, halfway through the Friday practice, he threw them all out and told them, "We'll see you all in here at six o'clock tomorrow morning."

Six in the morning?

Early morning practices were the oldest form of punishment in the book for most coaches. But not for Knight. He had never gone in for the standard forms of punishment—early practices, running wind sprints, four- or five-hour practices. Only on a couple of occasions during twenty-one years as a head coach had he resorted to such methods. But he was resorting to it now.

The players understood. They weren't happy about it, but they also didn't find it unfair. This was a crucial time, and they hadn't been sharp for a week, not since the Czech game. Sharpness was a lot to ask four weeks into practice with two weeks left until the first game, but these players were used to being asked for a lot.

They dragged themselves out of bed and made it to practice at six the next morning. The first hour was a nightmare. Knight was so angry he even ordered several wind sprints. He was going to make them work when they were tired even if it killed all of them. Finally, play picked up. The offense began moving the ball. By the time they left the floor at 8 A.M. Knight felt better. But not satisfied. "Be back at noon," he ordered.

They went for another ninety minutes at noon. Play was brisk, mistakes were few. No one wanted to even think about the consequences of a poor practice. There was still a lot of time left in the weekend. No one relished the thought of spending Saturday night in Assembly Hall. Knight had made his point: if you want to rest, you have to earn it, even when you're tired. When he let them go that afternoon, he told them to be back to scrimmage at 4:30 the next day—all except Alford and Robinson, who were told to be at the airport at 9:15 the next morning to fly to Chicago for the annual Big Ten media day.

Knight would boycott the meeting for the second year in a row. The year before he had skipped it to protest the Big Ten's failure to do anything about conference teams (read: Illinois) that were cheating (in his view) in recruiting. For that act, Knight had been censured by the league. For that censure, Knight was boycotting again. But he told no one of this plan. "I'll see you in the morning," he told Alford and Robinson.

They were there the next morning. Knight was not. Alford tried to study on the plane. "I am definitely going to flunk A-Core," he groaned between yawns. Alford and Robinson made it back to Bloomington just in time for the Sunday scrimmage. It had been a long week. The next two weeks would be worse.

The team didn't make it through practice on Monday or Tuesday. On Monday, Knight sent them home early, telling them again to return at 6 A.M. But that one didn't stick; after talking to the coaches, he changed his mind. Having them come in at that hour on a weekend was one thing, but having them come in that early when they had to be in class was another. Practice would be at the regular time on Tuesday.

On Tuesday, mistakes by Thomas, Morgan, and Calloway led to the team's third mass kickout in less than a week. "You know something, Daryl, if I were you I wouldn't come to practice," Knight said. "I'd just not even bother because why show up and be a shitty player? There's no point."

A moment later, when Harris tried to save a ball from going out of bounds, Thomas and Morgan, the two players closest to him, neglected to yell directions at him. That was it. "How much patience do you expect me to have? I won't tax myself any more. Everybody out."

Into the locker room they went. A few minutes later, Knight followed. Everyone expected an explosion. There was none. More often than not, Knight is a very good reader of his team's mood.

He had been on them almost without letup since the Monday after the Czech game. He knew this was going to be a delicate team. It was not that experienced, not that deep, and not big or strong physically. There were going to be times, if they were to succeed in any way, that Knight would have to suppress the side of him that wanted to rage at incompetence; there were going to be times, later in the year, when he couldn't suppress that side, but now, with the record 0–0, he could.

"You know, every single one of you is a good kid," Knight began. "I know, we all know, that you try to do everything we ask you to do. I know it isn't easy all the time. In fact, sometimes it's just about f—— impossible. But you have got to try. You have got to play through being tired.

"You new people, ask the other players how hard it is to play in the Big Ten. Ask them how tough every game is. We don't have any gimme games on our schedule. Not one. There is not one game we play that you people can win just by showing up. Some are harder than others, but bad play, stupid play, nonthinking play will get you beat on any night. I guarantee it."

Knight paused to look around the room. He looked into the faces of the players. His voice was soft. "You know, there is no way I would have [Michigan State guard] Scott Skiles on this team. We don't want kids like him here. [Skiles had been arrested three times.] We want kids like you. But Scott Skiles is tougher than every single one of you. Toughness, boys, wins basketball games. Intelligence wins basketball games. Thinking wins basketball games. Just running around in circles and not thinking loses them.

"We work too hard, you work too hard to go through another season like last year. Every one of us suffered last year. I know I did and I know you did, too. I know you don't want to lose. But I also know that you can't win playing like this. You just can't. You're not good enough. We've had some teams here that were talented enough to win most nights even when they didn't play their best. You people simply are not that good. You are not great athletes, except for Harris. You are not great shooters, except for Alford. You are small. To win, you have to be smarter and tougher every single day than the other guys. And you aren't going to be smarter and tougher by some magic formula when the games start. You have to come to practice every day and work on it.

"Now, do you think you are ready to go out there again and work the way we have to work? If you aren't, tell me and we'll call it a day. Don't come back out on that floor unless you are really ready to play."

He walked out the door. No one said a word. For a moment, everyone just looked at each other. Then Alford got up and followed Knight back to the floor. Fifteen players followed.

For the rest of that night and the three days after that, they practiced better than they had all year, perhaps better than they had in two years. One sentiment seemed to run through the entire team: Just when you think the man has lost control he turns around and proves he's a genius all over again.

On the morning of November 23, Knight gathered all seven coaches and Garl in the coaches' locker room to talk about a starting lineup. Everyone agreed on four names: Alford, Thomas, Harris, and Morgan. The fifth spot was a tossup among Calloway, Robinson, and Jadlow. Knight never voted. He just left the names on the board and went to watch the Indiana-Purdue football game. The season was seven days away.

———

That evening, Knight had as much fun as he had had in years. Jim Crews was to begin his college coaching career at Evansville that night, and Knight had been planning for several weeks to surprise him by showing up at the game with a group of Crews's former teammates, friends, and coaches.

This was, for all intents and purposes, a reunion. Steve Green, John Laskowski, Steve Ahlfeld, Steve Downing, and Tom Abernethy had played with Crews. Kohn Smith, Royce Waltman, and Julio Salazar had coached with him. Tim (Doak) Walker had been a manager all four years Crews had played at Indiana. Dan Dakich had been recruited by him.

The group that flew to Evansville that night was a mix of the generations that had grown up during the Knight era at Indiana. Sitting in his customary seat at the front of the plane, facing toward the rear, Knight was in a buoyant mood as everyone swapped old stories. The players from the '75–76 era, who had not been on an Indiana team plane in years, were shocked when they boarded.

"You mean," Green said in a stunned voice, "there's no partition between him [Knight] and the players?" On the old plane, Knight and the assistants had sat in a partitioned-off front area of the plane. Even though Knight often came stomping back to tell the players what he thought after a loss, there was at least some small separation. On this plane, there not only was no separation, but Knight sat facing the players.

Plane stories are a large part of Knight lore. One of the more popular ones came after a loss at Michigan in 1980. Indiana had lost by a point on a forty-foot shot at the buzzer. One person who did not play in that game was Steve Risley, one of the seniors on the 1981 championship team. Risley was in the doghouse. When the initial shock of the loss had worn off, Risley sat in the locker room thinking, "What a terrible loss. But at least he can't yell at *me* on the plane going home since I didn't play."

The team rode in silence to the airport. As they boarded the plane, Risley saw several bags of McDonald's food sitting up front. "Perfect," he thought, "I'll just curl up in back, eat my McDonald's, and stay out of the way."

It never happened that way. First, Knight grabbed the McDonald's bags and threw them onto the tarmac. No Big Macs for Risley. Then, as soon as the plane was airborne, Knight charged out of his seat and headed straight for Risley. "Risley, if we could afford to play you in games like this we wouldn't be losing. The reason we lost this game was *you*. It was *your* fault." Knight never yelled at anyone else the whole trip. For two days he didn't let Risley practice. The next night, he started him. Of course, Risley then played the best game of his career.

There would be no yelling on this trip. Just story-telling. As the plane landed in Evansville, Knight yelled, "Doak, the bus better be here." Walker was thirty-one years old and a successful businessman, but to Knight he would always be a manager. Managers were in charge of making sure a bus met the team plane on the road. The bus was there. At the game, Knight sent Walker (who else?) to the locker room to tell Crews his old friends would be watching.

When Walker relayed this news to Crews and he looked up to

where Knight and company were sitting, Crews shook his head. "Jesus," he said, "we've got a horseshit team." But Crews was slightly choked up when the public address announcer told the fans that Knight and Crews's old teammates were in the building. Evansville was bad, but Kentucky State was worse, and Evansville won the game, 50–48. After the game, when the hugs and the congratulations were over, Knight took Crews aside. He had been taking notes during the game, and he wanted to tell Crews what he needed to work on with his team.

When the plane landed back in Bloomington, Knight said to everyone, "That was a really nice thing you all did going down tonight. I know it meant a lot to Jimmy." It also meant a lot to Knight.

———

The four-day honeymoon that had started with Knight's quiet locker-room talk on Tuesday came to a screeching halt on the cold, rainy Sunday when Knight destroyed Thomas in front of the whole team.

Knight was up most of that night. He had already decided to talk to Thomas alone because he knew that he had gone too far during the screaming session in the locker room. What is extraordinary about Knight is how sensitive he can seem within hours of being so brutally insensitive. He knew as he began that last week of preseason that another week of screaming was not what the team needed. Lots and lots of work, yes. Screaming, no. That was why he skipped the Monday morning practice.

Knight arrived at Assembly Hall shortly before noon. The assistants had run the morning practice, and when it was over, Robinson, speaking for the players, had thanked them for sticking with them at a time when Knight was down on them.

This was not going to be an easy week. The campus was virtually empty because of Thanksgiving break. Since there were no classes, Knight saw the week as an opportunity to get extra work done. Knight didn't think of practice as "practice" unless the players had their ankles taped and there was an actual practice plan to be followed. So he saw no reason not to bring the players in for a morning session that might consist of some drills and some work looking at tape. For the players this meant a week of getting up early for drills and tape, going to lunch, coming back for practice, going to dinner, and then returning home to an empty dorm or apartment building. With the weather still cold and dreary, it was not a week that anyone looked forward to.

It was, in fact, fair to say that the players looked at school breaks as a mixed blessing at best. While it meant a chance to get away from the pressures of school, it inevitably increased the pressures put on them as basketball players. With no classes or study time to worry about, Knight wanted them concentrating on basketball full-time. That could be both wearing and, depending on his mood, depressing.

This week was both. Although Knight had spent much of his rage during the Sunday night tirade, he was noticeably uptight when he returned for practice Monday afternoon. He did not want to get on Thomas again until he had talked to him alone in private, which he would not do until the next morning, so instead he picked on Calloway.

Knight thought Calloway was going to be a great player. One reason he thought that was the ability Calloway had already displayed to deal with Knight's temperament. Knight doesn't often pick on freshmen because they are just that—freshmen. He knows they are feeling their way, learning the system, learning about going to college. During the course of the entire season, Knight would get on Oliphant no more than three times and each time it was a very minor outburst, almost kidding.

But Calloway was different. He was a precocious talent, and therefore someone Knight felt had to contribute right away for the team to be successful. Calloway had played at Withrow High School in Cincinnati, and in his junior and senior years Withrow had a losing record. Knight reminded him of that often.

On Monday afternoon, when Knight thought Calloway was a step slow, he jumped all over him. "Ricky, how many games did Withrow win last year?" he asked. "Ten? With you the best player in the Midwest the team was still lousy. Why do you think that was so? Do you think maybe it was because you didn't play hard enough?

"Believe me, Ricky, you can't not play hard and play well at this level. You think Withrow could play in the Big Ten? Do you think you have some kind of special talent? Well, if you do, you're wrong. There are five thousand players in college basketball with your talent. The only way you're going to beat them is by playing harder and smarter than they do. And this, Ricky, doesn't get it done."

With that he banished Calloway to the white team. A few plays later, noticing Calloway had taken a break, he exploded again. "You don't want to play, Ricky, that's fine. Go take a shower."

Calloway had been baptized. As he departed, Knight, his anger still escalating, told Dakich to take him across the way to the field house. "Make him run, Dakich," he said. "We'll turn him into a track man." Thirty seconds later Knight changed his mind and sent a manager after Dakich and Calloway. When Calloway returned Knight told him to get back in—with the white team— "and don't even think about trying to come out."

During this whole interlude Knight's voice never got much louder than it gets when he is making a teaching point. This was what players and coaches over the years had come to call "BK theater." Knight was performing. Calloway had committed no real crime; Knight knew that, and Calloway knew that. Calloway was a player who was going to play a lot this season. Knight wanted him to know that being a good player, one looked to for production, carried with it a good deal of responsibility.

This was a basic Knight mind game. Any player who had taken a freshman psychology course understood exactly what he was doing. But it went beyond that for one rather simple reason: fear. "After you've been yelled at by him once," Calloway said later, "you tell yourself to try never to get yelled at again. Of course, you do get yelled at. But that doesn't mean you don't try to avoid it at all costs."

This was Knight's basic coaching philosophy. Beyond all the talk about his complexity, his fundamental approach to motivation has never changed: fear is his number one weapon. He believes that if the players are afraid of getting screamed at or of landing in the doghouse, they will play better. And, if they fear him more than the opponent, they are likely to play better.

Most of the time this worked—as time and Knight's record proved. But occasionally it backfired. When the team wasn't going well, fear often caused the players to play scared, and no team plays well when it plays scared.

But now, with the season a few days away, Knight had the fear level about where he wanted it. The next morning, after he finished his talk with Thomas, he called Alford, Harris, and Calloway in. "You three," he said bluntly, "are our three best players. You are going to have to carry a lot of the load if we're going to win this season."

He turned to Alford. "Steve, do you remember last year when I told you that you weren't playing hard and you didn't believe me?" Alford nodded. "Was I right?" Alford nodded again. "Tell these guys."

Knight had pressed the exact right button. Alford, after a summer off, had come to the conclusion that Knight was right last winter about his not playing hard. Alford was self-critical by nature, not given to copping out. In spite of the emotional ups and downs that were always going to be part of his relationship with Knight, his respect for Knight's basketball judgments almost never wavered.

He explained that morning to Harris and Calloway how easy it was to convince yourself you were playing hard. "If you're a good player, you can still make good plays but you won't make near as many as you should," Alford said. "You've got to keep going even when you think you're tired. That's been our problem this fall. We get tired and we just figure, 'Well, we're tired, Coach will understand.' When the games start, he's not going to understand. And he shouldn't."

Alford had delivered just the speech his coach wanted, unrehearsed and uncoached. Two months later, Calloway would remember Alford's little talk clearly because he had been thinking all through fall practice, "I am playing hard, why does he keep saying I'm not?"

The long week dragged on. Hillman went down with a knee injury. No one knew it at the time, but he wouldn't play for two months. Pelkowski caught an elbow in the eye from Jadlow and couldn't practice. Todd Meier took a shot in the kidney and couldn't practice for two days. Jadlow was out for two days with strep throat.

That wasn't all. Alford and Harris both got kneed, and although they didn't miss any practice they were hobbling. By Wednesday, Felling was convinced the team needed a rest and told Knight so. They had been in uniform twice Monday, twice Tuesday, and twice Wednesday, and each day they had looked at tape after the morning workout. On Thanksgiving morning, they were all in at 10 A.M. to walk through Kent State. The start of the season was now forty-eight hours away. Knight was itchy. Time and again he asked the coaches. "Are we any good? Are we all right? Who do you think we should start?"

They practiced again on Thanksgiving afternoon. Finally, all the players and coaches—without Knight—went to an I.U. professor's house for Thanksgiving dinner. Most of them gave thanks that preseason was one day away from being over.

The next day, a carbon copy of the rainy, dreary days of the entire week, they practiced twice and then came back after dinner for one last walk-through in street clothes—their fifth walk-through for Kent State. They had been told how dangerous this team could be. They had been reminded that two years earlier, opening the season against Miami of Ohio, a team from Kent State's league, they had shown up flat and lost.

It was not until after the last practice Friday night that Knight decided on a lineup. Alford, Morgan, Harris, and Thomas had been a lock. The fifth spot had been up for grabs among Jadlow, Calloway, and Robinson. Jadlow's throat had set him back enough to eliminate him. Then, Friday afternoon, Calloway lost his man twice on defense. "Ricky," Knight yelled, "we're sitting in there trying to decide whether to start you and you practice like this. That's just bullshit. We can't beat anybody with that kind of play."

Knight wasn't really unhappy. He wanted to give Robinson, the senior, the first chance. Calloway's mistakes had given him the chance to do that while reminding Calloway he had better be ready to play. That was fine with Knight. Finally, shortly before 8 P.M. he sent them home. "Get a good night's sleep," he said. "We'll see you here at 9:15." The game was at 2 P.M.

As the players headed out into the rain, too tired to do anything but go home and sleep, Knight returned to his locker room with the coaches. He had two questions: "You think we'll draw a good crowd?" No one knew the answer. "Do you think we're ready to beat anybody?" No one knew the answer to that one either.

7.

The Season Begins

The last day of November may have been the ugliest day of a truly ugly month. As the team gathered in the morning, the skies were still dark, the clouds seemed to hang on the roof of the building, and the fog was so thick that one could barely make out the far side of the adjacent football stadium.

Knight arrived in a snappish mood. He was annoyed because Alford had been quoted in one of the newspapers as saying Indiana would be a quicker team this season. "Steve, just let those assholes figure that kind of stuff out for themselves, okay?" "Those assholes" was about the nicest reference to the media that Knight ever made in front of the players.

The team walked into the locker room that morning to find a message in red letters awaiting them: "Miami (Ohio) 63 . . . I.U. 57." Knight believes in these little messages. This was the first of many he would deliver during the season. Murry Bartow, because he had the neatest handwriting on the coaching staff, became the designated message writer.

After the team had gone through one last walk-through of Kent State, Knight brought athletic director Ralph Floyd in to talk to the players. Knight did this for two reasons: one, he had a standing policy of giving the players another voice to listen to on occasion, but two, and more important, he knew Floyd enjoyed it.

Floyd had very little to do with the running of the Indiana basketball program. Knight has a clause in his contract that gave him final say in all basketball-related matters, but even if he didn't, Floyd would have deferred to him. When Floyd's wife died in the summer of 1984, Knight spent hours and hours with him nursing

Floyd through his grief. "I don't think I would have survived without Bob Knight," Floyd often told people.

Floyd was as gentle as Knight was volatile. If Knight wanted something for the basketball program and needed Floyd's help, he got it. Their relationship was in many ways a prototype of Knight's relationships with most people: their loyalty to one another was absolute. And, even though Floyd was twenty years older than Knight, and in this case was his titular boss, he almost always deferred to the younger man. But on this morning, Knight deferred to him.

When Floyd was finished, Knight sent the players to pregame meal. He and Floyd then drove crosstown to watch Pat Knight play in a tournament. Pat Knight, who had been fighting the flu, did not play well. "We're starting a new program tonight," Knight said after Pat's game. "He doesn't take care of himself. He's going to be in bed at nine every night." This program had little chance of surviving the weekend, as Pat Knight was sure to talk himself free.

Knight would normally have shown up at the end of the pregame meal on a day like this one if Pat hadn't been playing. Even at ten in the morning, they would eat spaghetti, pancakes, hamburgers, and eggs. On each plate as the players silently sat down to eat was a three-by-five card. On it was written the same message they had seen in the locker room: Miami (Ohio) 63 . . . I.U. 57.

If the players hadn't figured this one out by now, they were not likely to anytime soon. Only Kohn Smith spoke at the pregame meal. He reminded them one more time about how tough every game was going to be. "Don't lie down now," he said. "Don't get sleepy."

Knight was anything but sleepy. When he came back from Pat's game, Harold Martin was waiting for him in the locker room. Harold Martin is one of those little-known stories in Bob Knight's life. He lives fifty miles from Lexington, Kentucky, and was a lifelong Kentucky fan. But in 1977, he spotted Knight trying unsuccessfully to buy a ticket to the Kentucky state high school championships. Martin had extra tickets. He walked up to Knight, introduced himself, and offered Knight two tickets. He would take no money for them because he respected Knight too much to take money from him.

Shortly after that, Martin got a letter from Knight, inviting him to Bloomington for a game anytime and adding, "If you need a place to stay up here, you are more than welcome to stay at the house." The friendship built from there. Martin came up whenever he could get away from his job at a Coca-Cola bottling plant and stayed with Knight. He became a rabid Indiana fan. He was a quiet little man who had learned to read Knight's moods. Knight called him Adolph, after legendary Kentucky coach Adolph Rupp.

Martin had a problem. The work force at the Coca-Cola plant where he worked was being cut back. He had enough seniority that he wouldn't be laid off, but he was going to be asked to drive fifty miles each way daily to work at another plant. Martin wanted Knight's advice. How should he deal with these people? He didn't think it was fair to ask him to do all that driving, especially for less money than he was already making. On the other hand, having worked for the company for more than twenty years, he didn't have that many outside options available.

Knight considered all this for a moment. "Quit your job, Adolph," he said finally.

Martin was stunned. "Coach, I can't afford to do that."

"Sure you can," Knight said. "You can come up here and work for me. I could use some help running my camp, keeping all my speaking engagements straight, all that stuff. I mean, I could really use your help. Listen, just think about it. If they give you a hard time down there, you know you have this as an option. If you want to stay with them, well, I understand that too."

With that Knight went off to take his steam. Harold Martin looked relieved, which was exactly what Knight wanted. Knight came out of the steam an hour later and weighed in at 222. "Too much," he grumbled.

A few minutes later, dressed in an Evansville basketball sweater that Crews had sent him earlier in the fall, Knight made his way through the catacombs of the building to the players' locker room. As usual, he was thinking out loud as he walked. "I hope we can play well," he said for perhaps the hundredth time that week. "But I haven't got very much faith in this team."

Why not?

"Past history."

The tension in the locker room was genuine. All the reminders about Miami, all the memories of last season, not to mention the memories of the forty-eight practices that had led to this afternoon, had combined to create a sense of dread. Indiana would play this game not to lose. That wasn't the atmosphere Knight wanted but against an opponent like Kent State it was almost unavoidable. Knight would never make light of an opponent's ability. He thought if the players didn't think he respected an opponent, they wouldn't respect it. And, he believed, that would almost guarantee a disastrous performance. So Knight went the other way. As the players sat in the locker room that day, they half believed that when they ran onto the court, Larry Bird and Julius Erving would be wearing Kent State uniforms.

"This is what we've been working for since October 15th," he told the players. "Everyone in here knows what he has to do for us to be successful." Knight turned to Alford. "This team had no leadership last season. If that happens again, you are going to be the one I come looking for. Understand that from the beginning."

Then, talking to the team again, Knight said, "You cannot just walk out on that floor and think you are going to play well because you're Indiana. It doesn't work that way. We had a team that sat in here last year ranked number 4 in the country, and they were so fatheaded and fatassed that they were no more number 4 in the country than Kohn, Joby, Royce, Tim, and I would be.

"You have to go out there understanding how hard it is to play this game well. If you don't understand that, you're gonna get beat. It's as simple as that. You walk on that floor today and you are privileged just to be here. Only two schools in the country have won two national championships in the last twenty-five years and this is one of them. There have been countless great players who have sat in this locker room and now you're sitting here. They went out to play just like you people are going out here to play today.

"The most interested person in this whole arena today in terms of how you people compete and how hard you play and how intelligently you play is gonna be me. Let's go."

Shortly after 2 P.M., with a crowd about 1,000 below capacity in the building, the season finally began. It took thirteen seconds for Kent State to score. It took three minutes for Robinson to miss a box out; it took about one half-second for Knight to leap from his seat screaming, "Stew, that's yours," as Robinson went by. It took seven minutes for Indiana to gain control of the game. Daryl Thomas, who six days earlier had been deemed totally incapable of playing, swooped into the passing lane, grabbed the ball, and went the length of the court for a dunk. Indiana had the lead at 17–9 and Knight was on his feet, clapping his hands. Knight's handclap is often imitated around the Indiana locker room. He turns his hands perpendicular to one another and brings them together almost like two cymbals. He almost never claps more than once and the clap is usually the capper to a rousing "Let's get 'em," or an equally rousing "What the hell is wrong with you?" By midseason, Murry Bartow was doing Knight's clap every time he stood up on the bench without realizing it. It was both distinctive and addictive.

Thomas's steal put the Hoosiers in command, and they didn't really give up that command for the rest of the half. Robinson got yanked after Kent State guard Mike Roberts beat him on a drive to the basket. Brooks subbed for him. Calloway came off the bench and hit his first six shots. In the press box, Hammel, feeling comfortable as the lead built to fourteen points, cracked, "I wonder if anyone has ever gone an entire career without missing a shot?"

Sitting near Hammel during an Indiana game was worth the price of admission in itself. Hammel had missed exactly two games in Knight's fifteen seasons at Indiana. Although he had not graduated from the school, he was about as loyal to it as any alumnus could be. This was especially true in the case of his relationship with Knight.

They were an interesting couple, Knight and Hammel. The writer was four years older than the coach and was as gentle as the coach was vitriolic. Even though other writers knew how close the two were, Hammel was rarely disparaged for this relationship in a business where that kind of relationship is always frowned upon.

Part of the reason for their tolerance was the simple understanding that no sports editor in Bloomington could survive if he was ever cut off from the Indiana basketball team. If you can't cover that which interests your readers more than anything else, you aren't going to be valuable to the paper for very long. And everyone who knows Knight at all knows that one is not allowed to be neutral in a relationship with him. You are either for us or against us. Hammel, whose sympathies were bound to lie with Indiana and Knight in most cases anyway, had made the decision years ago that he was with Knight.

The other reason few people disparaged Hammel was Hammel. Not only was his basketball knowledge respected, but he was generally considered a true gentleman in a business often sorely lacking in them. Some hometown writers allow their prejudices to affect what they write about other teams. Hammel never did that. He wasn't about to attack Knight, but he didn't run around attacking other people unfairly either.

Hammel is a good newspaper man. He is one of those people who can write the entire paper—his prolificness is legendary—lay it out and write all the headlines if necessary. It bothered him sometimes that he wasn't as objective as he should be. In fact, he had been angry with himself the previous season when someone had written him a letter about his column on the chair throw, commenting, "It read like a legal brief prepared on behalf of the defendant."

"Probably," Hammel said much later, not without chagrin, "he was right."

Hammel's friendship with Knight was quite real—on both sides. Knight respected Hammel's knowledge of the game and would often solicit his opinions. Only rarely did Hammel disagree with Knight—partly because they generally thought alike, partly because disagreeing with him was usually a waste of time. It had to be very important and Hammel had to be quite certain he was right and Knight was wrong before Hammel would actively disagree with Knight's position on something.

Because he was very much a part of the inner circle, Hammel had as much stake in the outcome of the games as the players and coaches. If Indiana lost or played poorly, he was going to be subjected to late-night phone calls and a depressed and angry companion. Hammel didn't want that any more than Alford,

Daryl Thomas, or Tim Garl did. His face during games was a mask of indifference, but when something went wrong, he would very quietly agonize: "Oh no, oh goodness no, Jiminy Christmas, no. Oh no, I don't think I want that." He never called Indiana "we," and he never changed expression. But in tight situations he got very quiet and noticeably nervous. Usually with good reason.

On this day, the half ended poorly. Leading 52–38, Indiana gave up the last two baskets of the half, a huge sin since Knight had fifteen minutes to vent his anger about this regression. First, though, Knight stopped the officials at center court to tell them what a lousy job they were doing. This was not a good sign. Knight was still finishing the one-year probation that had accompanied his suspension after the chair-throwing incident, and getting upset after twenty minutes of the first game with a ten-point lead was not an encouraging signal to those hoping Knight would cool his act this season.

The first halftime was not encouraging, either. Even with the lead, Knight was not happy. Once the game started, Kent State had ceased being the Celtics. Now they were just the goddamn Golden Flashes from the goddamn Mid-American Conference, not capable, probably, of beating anyone in the Big Ten. And here it was halftime, and the lead, which could have been sixteen or eighteen, was only ten.

He blistered Harris and Jadlow. "This is not f—— junior college," he told them. "You guys have something go wrong and you sulk and pout. That doesn't go over very big with me. Jadlow, you are just flopping around out there on the boards like a great white whale. You let them get five rebounds that you had your hands on."

Knight's distress was very real—not because he thought this game was in serious jeopardy, but because he was looking ahead to a week that included games against Notre Dame and Kentucky, with Louisville not long after that. "We got outrebounded 17–9," he said. "Do you know what it's going to be like rebounding against Louisville if you get outrebounded by this team? You'll never see the basketball.

"They've scrapped and fought and played hard, and we've whined and bitched. Robinson, you get beat twice in the first four minutes. Brooks, you are two plays behind all the time. We gave up forty-two points—forty-two points!"

Like the pregame ritual, halftime was almost always the same: Knight would come in and talk to the players, telling them what he thought of the first half—in this case not much. Then he and the coaches would retreat to the private hallway just outside the door, where they would review the first half and make decisions about the second. Felling, as the junior man on the staff, was in charge of knowing how much time was left before the second half started. Generally, Knight would ask him three or four times—sometimes more—how much time was left. Waltman was responsible for knowing the time-out situation, and Smith was responsible for knowing who on both teams was in foul trouble.

The coaches' pow-wows consisted, more often than not, of Knight's analysis of the first half. His commentary on different players was often brutal. Today, Brooks, who had only played briefly, and Robinson were his targets. "They cannot play, simple as that," he said to the coaches, using a phrase he would use to describe every player on the team at some point before the season was over. "Robinson can't see anything and Brooks can't think out there."

The coaches listened. Often they agreed with Knight's assessments. Almost as often, they knew he was being too harsh, reacting emotionally in an emotional situation. They were not likely, however, to interrupt and say, "Coach, you're probably being a little too emotional."

What was important was to get through the complaining and decide what to do in the second half. Knight has been through this so many times that he seems to know just how long he can afford to let off steam before he has to start making decisions. This day was easy. He wanted to make two changes: "Let's set our defense up at the top of the key. They're just too quick for us to get out and try to guard them." This admission disturbed Knight because he hated nothing more than having to play containment defense. Second, he wanted to start Calloway over Robinson. That made sense; Calloway had six field goals, Robinson none.

Once the coaches finish their initial meeting, they return to the locker room to tell the players what changes will be made. Sometimes Knight will diagram a play or a defense he wants to use. Almost always, he will reinforce his initial comments. Then the coaches will go back to the hallway once more. "Anything else?" Knight will ask. An idea might be discussed, or everyone might just look at each other and shrug.

The second meeting produced shrugs. There were four minutes left. Knight was calmer now, but as the coaches turned to go back into the locker room for a final word, Knight slumped against the wall in the hallway. "I'm just not sure," he said softly, "I can take another year of this. I'm really not sure I can take it."

Back inside for a final word, Knight was upbeat again. "You've done some good things offensively. You've found people, you've run good plays. You've had some good moments in the first twenty minutes. Let's go out now and play twenty good minutes."

With those words ringing in their ears, they proceeded to play horribly for six minutes. A Roberts jumper with 14:07 left in the game drew Kent to within one, 55–54. Assembly Hall, which is not very loud at best, was like a morgue. Knight had already called one time-out. He would not call another. "Oh my," was Hammel's murmured comment. If this game were to get away, it would be, as Hammel often put it, "a major disaster."

But it didn't happen. Calloway made a textbook cut and Harris found him for a layup. Thomas stole an inbounds pass and Alford swished a twenty-footer while he was being fouled. His free throw made it 60–54. Kent got a bucket, but Indiana scored the next eleven points, the last of them coming on a gorgeous pass off the fast break from Alford to Calloway.

The 16–2 run took less than four minutes. The rest of the game was academic, Indiana coasting, 89–73. As the band played "Indiana," Knight walked off the floor, shoulders hunched, head down. He almost always walks off the floor this way, even when he is happy. This time though, he wasn't happy.

The locker room would not have been much quieter if Kent State had won the game. "You just played a team that played so much harder and smarter than you, it's not even funny," Knight told them. "You didn't play smart, you weren't where you were supposed to be. This team has a long, long way to go. You struggled like hell to beat a team that last year finished 17–13 and lost its two leading scorers. You don't scrap, you don't see things. You got little chance of winning. This team was probably one of the five weakest we'll play on our twenty-eight-game schedule. Harris, you and Jadlow gave us nothing. This is not junior college, boys. It's a different ball game."

When he was finished, Knight asked Hillman and Smith to come into the hallway. "I can't redshirt you two," he told them. "I need you to play this year. We just haven't got enough players without you. I'm sorry."

Smith, who had no desire to be redshirted, was delighted. Hillman, still injured, wasn't sure if the decision would stick. "We'll see what happens," he said.

Mentally, Knight had decided he needed Hillman and Smith in place of Robinson and Brooks. They were deep in the doghouse. Twenty-four hours earlier, Knight had called Brooks aside in practice to tell him how pleased he was with the way he had worked and the way he had progressed. He had honestly believed what he had said then, and he honestly believed what he was saying now.

After they showered, he blistered them one more time. Only three players had pleased him: Alford, Thomas, and Calloway. "Do you know how different it's going to be for you people trying to play Kentucky and Notre Dame? They're so much better than these teams, it's not even funny. If you got outrebounded by these people do you know what Darrell Walker is going to do to you?"

Knight meant Kentucky All-American Kenny Walker, but he had a mental block and continually referred to him as Darrell Walker, a former All-American at Arkansas who now played for the New York Knicks. "Be back here at six o'clock," Knight finally told them. "We'll go through the film. We've got no time to waste because I guarantee you we aren't ready to play Notre Dame this way."

The players dismissed, Knight began his postgame ritual. It began, always, in the small room off the locker room. He retreated there with Ed Williams, Ralph Floyd, and any other close friends who might be at the game. Occasionally one of the coaches joined the group. Often, Knight sent for Hammel. Then he repeated what he had already said to the coaches. In this case it was more on Brooks, more on Robinson. "It's so disappointing," Knight said, "to sit there and not see them play the way we want them playing."

Everyone nodded. Kit Klingelhoffer, the long-time sports information director (SID), came in. Knight looked at him. "Are they ready?" Klingelhoffer nodded.

Klingelhoffer was another person who had long ago adjusted to Life With Knight. He had as difficult a job as any SID in the country because he had to deal with a coach who said no far more than he said yes, who was apt to become upset at any moment, who might blow up at him at any second.

Klingelhoffer, like everyone else who had been at Indiana for any extended period, had been through Knight purgatory. One season Knight had not spoken to him. Another season Knight had not spoken to the press after games, instead speaking only to Klingelhoffer, who would then type up Knight's quotes. Most writers that season took to reporting what Knight "reportedly said" after games, since none of them actually heard him say anything.

Knight had come a long way in his press relations over the years. He almost never ducked a postgame press conference, and the Indiana locker room was almost always open to the press following games. In fact, in a league full of paranoid coaches, many of whom never allowed writers in their locker rooms, Knight was now viewed as not uncooperative by most in the media. At times he was downright entertaining, and he was almost always quotable. Knight still viewed most of the media with disdain, but he had learned not to go off the wall every time someone criticized him, and he had also learned to stay calm through most of his press conferences.

Klingelhoffer never said anything when he came to get Knight after a game. Years of experience had taught him that when Knight was ready, he was ready. Not before. Usually, though, Knight was ready when Klingelhoffer came in because he was just as happy to get the postgame press conference over with.

Knight almost never told the press exactly what he thought, but that hardly made him unusual; few college coaches tell the press what they really think after a game. If the play of Brooks, Robinson, Harris, and Jadlow disturbed him, the media never knew. Knight talked at length about Daryl Thomas, Steve Alford, and Rick Calloway. He lauded Kent State for playing hard. He said he saw a lot of things that he had liked. All of this was true; it was just incomplete.

Press conference over, Knight drove crosstown to tape his weekly TV show. The assistant coaches began to go through the tape of the Kent State game. Waltman and Salazar were on their way back from Notre Dame, where they had flown for Notre Dame's game that afternoon against Butler. Waltman had gone to the game to put together a scouting report, while Salazar had checked into a local hotel to tape the game off a local telecast.

As Knight drove away from Assembly Hall, his mind was totally focused on Notre Dame. The Kent State game existed now only as a tool to get ready for Notre Dame. "We'll beat Notre Dame," he said. "In fact, I think we can pound them. They don't play very good defense and this game was absolutely perfect for us in terms of preparation. Now we'll have their attention the next three days. They won't get bigheaded because they've blown somebody out."

Knight had a faraway look in his eye as he drove as if he was seeing the game in front of him. "The best defense to play against them would be a two-three zone. That way [David] Rivers can't penetrate. Make them play a halfcourt game and they're not that good."

Knight was not likely to put in a zone defense in three days after twenty-one years of coaching man-to-man. But he would set up his man-to-man to pinch inside so hard that Notre Dame would feel as if it was playing against a zone. "The only thing that worries me," he said pulling the car into the TV station, "is time. I wish we had more than three days to get ready."

Although his assistants prepare two or three games ahead, looking at and preparing tape, Knight never begins to think specifically about an opponent until that is the next game. In six weeks of preseason practice he had often talked in the abstract to the team about Notre Dame, Kentucky, and Louisville, the three truly tough December games on the schedule, but was never specific. Now, Knight and his players would walk, talk, eat, and sleep Notre Dame for three days.

Knight's TV show was always an adventure. He taped it after Saturday games for airing on Sunday afternoon. Sometimes this meant a taping session at three in the morning after returning from a night road game. The host was Chuck Marlowe, a gentle, sweet-tempered man who had learned over the years to let Knight run the show. If Knight was in a bad mood, Marlowe made the questions as soft as possible. If Knight was in a good mood, Marlowe just got out of the way because Knight was apt to say or do anything.

That fact had been best illustrated in 1981 when Knight had brought a jackass wearing a Purdue hat to the show. He had introduced the jackass as "someone who is here to represent Purdue's point of view." Naturally, the show caused an uproar, especially among Purdue people. Knight was so pleased with himself that he wanted to bring the jackass back for the Indiana basketball banquet, which is televised statewide. Ed Williams, who knew better than anyone Knight's penchant for pushing a good thing too far, had called Nancy Knight to ask if there was anyone who could talk Knight out of repeating the jackass act. "Only Pete Newell or Fred Taylor," Nancy Knight told him.

Williams called Newell and Taylor and asked them to convince Knight not to do this. Indiana had just won the national championship and Knight was riding high. Why try to get the last word when he had already had the last word? Newell and Taylor called Knight, and for once, he went along with sound advice. But he still shook his head when he told the story and said, "Boy, would it have been great to do that."

Knight's show is different from other coaches' shows. There are never any features or interviews with the players. The taped highlights are limited. Mostly, Knight just talks. This can be dull, but given the quality of most other coaches' shows, it would still be above average. More often than not, it is quite entertaining, especially if Knight wants to get something off his chest. Marlowe has done the show for fourteen years. He has gray hair. People joke that he's only twenty-nine years old, but looks the way he does because he has hosted Knight's show for so long.

Knight was subdued during the show, wanting to get it done so he could get back to work on Notre Dame. By the time he returned to Assembly Hall, Waltman and Salazar were back and the coaches were almost all the way through the Kent State tape. "Well," Knight said to Waltman, "can we beat the Irish?"

"I think so," Waltman said, "if we control the tempo and keep them off the boards."

"See?" Knight said, starting to get excited. "I think we can pound them."

But it would not be easy. Knight made that clear to the players that night as they went through the tape. There is nothing that Indiana players like less than going through tape—especially after a game that Knight is not pleased with. At its very best, going through tape is drudge work. At its very worst, it is a nightmare.

Knight rarely stops the tape to show a good play. More often, he focuses on the mistakes, and seeing them again may make him angrier than he was when the play happened in the game. Later in the season, Steve Green was visiting the day before a game, and he was sitting quietly in the back while the coaches took the players through a tape.

Seeing the sleepy looks on the players' faces, Joby Wright decided a fresh voice might aid the cause. "Steve, when you were a player, what did you want to accomplish when the team went through tapes?"

Green, half dozing himself, stammered for a moment. Finally, his voice rich with sincerity, he said, "Well, Joby, I always tried to look at it as a good chance to learn something that would help me be a better player."

Wright beamed at that answer. A few moments later, leaving the locker room, Green was laughing at himself. "I didn't know what the hell to say," he said. "That was the first time I ever sat through a tape session without getting my ass chewed out."

That was what players remembered most about tape sessions. If it wasn't boring it was because you were getting yelled at. The post–Kent State session was fairly mild; even though he hadn't been completely satisfied with the game, it had been a victory. Knight's mind was now completely focused on Notre Dame.

He didn't need to pump Notre Dame up to the players the way he had to pump up Kent State. They knew that Notre Dame had beaten them the year before and would come into the game ranked tenth in the nation. In fact, knowing all this, Knight took a very different tack. He wanted to be certain his players knew they could win. Before Kent State, he had to remind them that they could lose. Now, he would spend the next three days telling them repeatedly that Notre Dame was beatable.

"This game will be there for you," he said. "But only if you do exactly what we tell you to do the next three days."

Shortly before 9 P.M.—just about twelve hours after they had arrived that morning—Knight sent them home.

"Well, boys," Knight said to the coaches after the players had left, "we're one and twenty-seven." This was Knight's way of tracking the team's record: one game played, twenty-seven to go.

———

The next three days were just as tough as Knight had promised, but no one seemed to mind. The drudgery of preseason was over. The opponent was someone worth getting excited about. Everyone was sharp, including the coaches. Knight is never better than in the days before a big game. He forgets about mind games. Often, he forgets his temper because there is no time for a blowup. He may speak emphatically when a mistake is made, but there is almost never a tantrum.

"With some teams you can afford to get mad and throw everybody out," Knight said during preseason. "It gives them some rest and, perhaps more important, it gives you some rest because you get tired of practice, too. But we can't have that with this team. This team isn't good enough that we can waste time. It has to work every day to get better."

Even with that awareness, Knight had tossed them all several times during preseason. But not now. There was no need now because the players were as psyched for this game as the coach was. No extra motivation would be needed.

They practiced for more than two hours on Sunday afternoon and came back that night to go through drills and some tape.

Knight reminded them again and again that if they didn't beat themselves, they would beat Notre Dame. November was over. It was December 1. As the players left practice that night, it was snowing.

Knight ignored his tapes that night in order to watch Duke play Kansas in the final of the Big Apple–NIT. Knight rarely watches basketball for recreation, but Mike Krzyzewski was Duke's coach. Knight may be closer to Krzyzewski than to any of his other former players or coaches. Krzyzewski was one of his first recruits at Army, a player who personified Army's style of play in those days. He wasn't a good shooter and he wasn't quick, but he would run through a wall to win a game.

Late in Krzyzewski's junior season, with Army struggling to get an NIT bid—that was the goal at Army each year back when the postseason NIT still meant something—Krzyzewski's father died suddenly, of a heart attack. Knight flew to Chicago for three days to be with Mike and his mother, leaving the team in the hands of his assistant coaches. Krzyzewski never forgot the gesture, mostly because of what it meant to his mother. "He just sat around the kitchen for hours, telling her stories, keeping her mind occupied. It was as if nothing else mattered to him right then other than helping my mom and me."

After Krzyzewski completed his Army duty, he coached in 1975 at Indiana before, on Knight's recommendation, he became the coach at West Point. Five years later, after another Knight recommendation, he became the Duke coach. This was a quantum leap for a thirty-three-year-old. For three years, Duke struggled, and there were cries for Krzyzewski's head. But now, after two straight twenty-win seasons, Duke was ranked in the top five nationally and was playing Kansas for a prestigious tournament championship. A victory would mark the first time Duke had ever won a national tournament of any kind.

Watching this game was difficult for Knight. Watching any game he cares about is tough for him. Often, he simply won't watch. This time, he watched. When Duke switched to a zone defense at one juncture Knight moaned. "Michael, what are you doing?" Kansas scored twice against the zone. Duke abandoned it. Knight nodded. "Hope you learned your lesson, Mike."

In the game's deciding moments, Knight was almost as tense as he might be during an Indiana game. "We need a basket here," he announced at one point. Duke got the basket and won the game. Knight was delighted. "That is really great for Mike," he said. "Boy, that's great."

The next morning, Knight called Krzyzewski. "Mike," he said, "how did you guys do last night?"

Krzyzewski had only about four hours sleep and wasn't thinking that clearly, so he didn't recognize a put-on when he heard it. "We won," he answered.

"You did? That's nice. Was that the championship game or the consolation?"

Still biting all the way, Krzyzewski answered, "Championship."

"Oh, who did you beat in the semis?" Knight had watched that game, too.

"St. John's. Coach, don't you get a newspaper out there?"

"I've been kind of busy, Michael. Oh, by the way, I'm glad your goddamn zone didn't work."

Finally, Krzyzewski realized he was being put on. "Proves I'm Polish," he said later. Knight, having had his joke, then told Krzyzewski how proud of him he was.

That afternoon, I.U. president John Ryan came to practice. Normally Ryan gives the team a preseason talk, but he had been away the week before. Ryan sat with Hammel through almost the entire practice. "Steve," Knight yelled at one point when Alford wasn't in shooting position on time, "you can't stand there like a f—— statue. That's what they've got in the harbor in New York—a f—— statue. I don't need that bullshit in here." And when Harris took a horrendous shot, Knight told him, "Andre, that was the worst goddamn shot anyone has taken in here since October 15. Jesus Christ could not have made that shot."

Ryan never blinked. He had been hearing his coach talk this way for years. "I don't use that kind of language myself," Ryan would say later. "It is not one of Bob's characteristics that I admire. But it is part of Bob. If I take all the good things that are part of Bob, I suppose I have to take the not-so-good things, too."

Ryan does occasionally let Knight know that his language doesn't delight him. That evening, when Knight finished his lengthy, lavish introduction of Ryan to the players, Ryan stepped forward and began by saying, "Thanks for making my speech for me, Bob."

"Oh no, Dr. Ryan," Knight answered, "I couldn't do that. You use all kinds of words I never use."

"No, Bob," Ryan said, "you use all kind of words that *I* never use."

The players broke up. So did Knight. Score one for the president. Ryan then gave his annual speech. Winning and losing was not as important as representing the university well. "That's why," Ryan said, "when I come in here after games, whether it is after a win or a loss, I always just say 'Thank you' to each one of you. Because I have always felt that you represent the university well."

The players nodded. They were glad Ryan told them this because the older players had been wondering about that for years. When Ryan was finished, Knight gave the players an hour for dinner, brought them back, and walked them through Notre Dame one more time. Everyone, including the coaches, was a little bleary-eyed by now. "Get a good night's sleep," Knight said, and then he went off to do his weekly radio show.

Knight's radio show, broadcast every Monday night during the season, is, much like his TV show, an adventure. The host is Don Fischer, who has done play-by-play of Indiana's basketball games for thirteen years. Fischer is as good at what he does as anyone in the business. He is a consummate play-by-play man, and, like Hammel, like the coaches, like Klinglehoffer, he has long ago learned the ins and outs of the care and feeding of Bob Knight.

Knight usually does the show sitting behind his desk in his office. He never gives his full attention to the show for the whole hour. Most often, he opens his mail during the show. Occasionally, he looks at tape. It used to be a call-in show, but the repetitive questions and an occasional less-than-supportive call changed that. Now listeners are urged to write letters asking questions. Fischer reads them and Knight answers them. Sometimes.

Knight usually bombards Fischer with sarcasm, and Fischer,

like any good straight man, just lets it roll right off him. On one night, Fischer made the mistake of phrasing a question this way: "Coach, talk about Iowa's press."

"Don," Knight answered, "is that an order?"

"No, Coach, a request."

"Just checking, Don."

During this show, as Fischer was asking Knight about the Big Ten's new supervisor of officials, Bob Wortman, Knight broke in. "Don, I hate to interrupt, but I just found an ad in this catalogue for a grouse gun that I think I might order. What do you think, Don?"

"Sounds like a great idea to me, coach."

It went that way almost every week. The better Knight's mood, the less likely Fischer was to get straight answers. The less straight Knight's answers, the more entertaining the show—at least for those who knew Knight well. For most of the listeners, the show probably bordered on unintelligible at times.

The same was true of Knight's pregame radio show. This only lasted ten minutes and consisted of Fischer's asking Knight several basic questions about the upcoming ballgame. Sometimes Knight answered them. Often, he ignored them. Almost always—unless he was depressed or uptight—he made Fischer go through half a dozen takes before he would do the show in a manner that could be played on the air. Knight almost always asked Fischer to select a starting lineup. "Whatever you think is best, Coach," Fischer would answer.

"Don, I can't tell you how much your faith in me means to me, especially going into a big game like this one."

For Knight, the shows were, more often than not, a way to entertain Knight. For this, Knight was paid handsomely, some- where in the neighborhood of $40–50,000 a year. The ratings were good, people bought the advertising, and Knight had fun. The real hero of the shows, though, was Fischer, who one way or the other got the pregame show and the Monday night show on the air. Sometimes this was not nearly as easy a task as it may seem to their listeners, and no one knew that better than Knight. Behind Fischer's back he told anyone who would listen that Fischer was "the best there is in the business." He said the same things about Hammel. Good things come to those who stand by Bob Knight.

———

The sun actually made an appearance the next day, a welcome sight if not necessarily an omen. Notre Dame showed up to shoot at 11 A.M., and as they did, Knight sat in the bleachers with Digger Phelps. If their fans had seen the two coaches this way, relaxed and friendly less than nine hours before the game was to start, they might have been shocked. But Knight and Phelps are friends. They have known each other for twenty years, having first met at a summer clinic in Pennsylvania when Phelps was a graduate assistant coach at his alma mater, Rider College, and Knight was an assistant at Army.

During his six years as head coach at Army, Knight often thought the Notre Dame job was the one he would like to have. He even went so far as to call the Reverend Edmund P. Joyce, the Notre Dame vice-president who hired coaches, to tell him that he would be interested in the job should Johnny Dee ever leave.

In 1971, Knight heard from a friend associated with Notre Dame that Dee was thinking of retiring. He was looking around at the time, having decided that six years at West Point was enough. At the Final Four that year in Houston, Indiana approached him about becoming the coach there. Dee still had not announced that he was leaving. There were rumors, but nothing concrete. Knight took the Indiana job.

Two weeks later, Dee announced his retirement. Phelps, one year younger than Knight, had just completed a spectacular 26–3 season at Fordham, taking a dormant program playing in a bandbox gym in the Bronx and quickly turning it into an electrifying, brilliant team. One of Fordham's victories had been over Notre Dame before a sellout crowd at Madison Square Garden. Phelps and Fordham had pumped new life into New York City basketball, and Joyce, who had once received a letter from Phelps telling him that he dreamed of someday coaching at Notre Dame, noticed. So did Roger Valdiserri, an assistant athletic director at Notre Dame who wielded considerable influence because he was widely considered one of the brightest and most charming men in college sports. Valdiserri urged Joyce to hire Phelps, and Joyce took that advice.

And so it was that Knight, then thirty, and Phelps, then twenty-nine, migrated to the Midwest from the New York City area at the same time. They had met once as head coaches during Phelps's year at Fordham, and Fordham had won a close game. Near the end, Phelps had walked down to shake Knight's hand. "I have to do this now, Bob," he said, "because when the game's over, they're going to carry me off." Sure enough, the Fordham fans carried Phelps off the court.

One year later, Knight and Indiana destroyed Phelps and Notre Dame, 94–29. Phelps thought Knight twisted the knife a little hard in that game because he was upset about what had happened the year before. Not so, Knight insisted. But he remembered the handshake as clearly as Phelps.

They had since become good friends. Much of this was because both were controversial and outspoken. Knight won games and championships, and outraged people with his acts and words; Phelps won games, though few championships, and outraged people with his words. Both were considered arrogant, Phelps especially so. Knight often told him, "I'm the only friend you've got in coaching." Phelps didn't argue.

They had advanced, rockily, into coaching middle age, their hair now graying, each now an elder statesman of sorts. The previous year when Knight had boycotted the Big Ten meetings in November to protest the cheating he thought was going on in the league, he asked Phelps before their game against one another to defend him at the press conference after the game. Phelps not only did that but endorsed Knight's actions. They now saw themselves as the Don Quixotes of college basketball, tilting against the windmill of rampant cheating.

They sat in the bleachers swapping stories, comfortable after twenty years of friendship. Knight was 8–4 against Phelps and Notre Dame. Phelps could live with that and still feel close to Knight. Had the record been reversed, it might have been hard for Knight to feel so comfortable. That was the major difference between the two men: Phelps coached basketball; Knight lived it.

Knight left Phelps to go to lunch with his coaches. Most days Knight eats lunch at the same place: the Southside Cafe, better known as Smitty's. Smitty has sold the cafe twice and twice has bought it back after the new owners failed to make a go of it. It is a small luncheonette, and Knight has been eating there almost since the day he first got to Indiana.

He and the coaches eat in the room marked very clearly, "Executive Dining Room," which in reality is a storeroom filled with boxes. In the middle of the room is a small table. This is where Knight and his group eat every day—after Knight has burrowed through the kitchen, checking on the home-made soups and pies being cooked.

Lunch was no different on this day than any other game day. The closer a game gets, the more apprehensive Knight becomes. Watching Notre Dame shoot that morning, he had been surprised by their size, not so much their height as their bulk. "They'll get us in foul trouble," he kept saying. "I'm just not sure we have the talent to beat good teams. And this is a good team. Their size really shocked me. I didn't remember them being that big."

The players came in at three o'clock for the final walk-through. Knight wanted nothing overlooked. Seven times he showed the players something Notre Dame did on the tape in the locker room and then marched them to the floor to go through it. The players must have been dizzy by the time Knight was through. Even after he had finally sent them to pregame, Knight fretted. "Is there anything else?" he kept asking the coaches. "Are we all right?"

The pregame meal was even quieter than normal. For this game, Knight would give the pregame talk. "You know, before this season is over, you boys are going to play against a lot of assholes," he said. "You're gonna play a lot of people that I don't have much use or respect for. That is not the case tonight. Notre Dame is a lot like us. They do things the right way and they play good basketball. This game will be the biggest game in the country tonight. That's why you came to Indiana—not to play games like this but to win them."

Knight liked the "biggest game in the country tonight" theme. It was one he had used often over the years. It was effective. The players enjoyed the notion that their game was somehow more important than others. It pumped them up. That was exactly what Knight had in mind.

Knight had just finished his pregame steam—"We go into the ring at 221," he announced—when Ralph Floyd came into the locker room. There was a problem. Two conferences, the Missouri

Valley and the Atlantic Coast, had assigned officiating crews to the game. For years, Notre Dame and Indiana had used Big Ten officials when they played, but Phelps had balked at using them this year. Knight, after all his disputes with Big Ten officials, didn't mind the change, and the two coaches had agreed on neutral officials. But there had been a communications screwup somewhere and both leagues had sent crews. There were six officials in the building ready to work. The contract had called for Missouri Valley officials. Apparently, the problem was with the ACC.

Knight put out a call for Phelps, who came to Knight's locker room. With Phelps present, Knight called Fred Barakat, the supervisor of ACC officials, to see what had happened. Barakat wasn't certain. Knight and Phelps agreed that they would use the Missouri Valley officials and that the two schools would chip in to pay the ACC officials if need be.

Throughout this discussion, with the pregame noise of the band and the fans echoing just outside the door, Knight sat in his chair naked. Phelps was wearing a gorgeous blue pinstriped suit, a red tie, and a matching red handkerchief in his pocket. He looked like he had stepped right out of *Gentleman's Quarterly*. What Knight looked like isn't really describable. But there they were, one hour before tipoff, Phelps looking like a fashion model, Knight naked. Somehow, it seemed exactly right.

Knight finally got dressed after Phelps left, and made his way to the players' locker room. The place was crowded. In addition to the players and the regulars, some nonregulars who were Knight buddies were in attendance. This was a big game. Among them was the Reverend James Higgins, one of Indiana's chaplains. In spite of Knight's nonreligious approach to things, he and Higgins were friends even though Knight had once been forced to calm Higgins down during a game when Higgins started getting on the officials.

"My first game at Army, I had someone say the Lord's Prayer," Knight recalled. "As we were walking out of the locker room, our trainer turned to me and said, 'Coach, that Lord's Prayer thing just isn't you.' I said, 'Thanks for telling me, I didn't really think it was either.' " That was the last time anyone prayed in Knight's locker room. At least openly.

When Knight walked in, as always, the room went silent. The

tension was palpable. Knight started to turn to the board to write down the starters' names but then he spotted Higgins.

"Padre," he said warmly, "how's the God business?"

While hands around the room were clapped over mouths to stifle giggles, Higgins, never missing a beat, replied, "About the same as the coaching business, Bob."

Knight, back now turned to Higgins as he wrote down the starters' names, nodded his head. "That's what I was afraid you were going to say."

Even as the teams warmed up, Knight sat in the locker room, wondering if there was anything else he could do. Was he forgetting anything? He called the coaches into the hallway. "What would you guys think if we opened the game in a two-three zone? Just to show it to them even if it was just for one possession."

Knight was serious. The coaches looked stricken. There was silence for a moment. Finally, Felling spoke. "I'd hate to give them an easy two," he said. Kohn Smith jumped in. "Coach, we've never used gimmicks here before."

That was enough for Knight. "Yeah, you're right," he said. "Why start now?" And yet, the idea clearly intrigued him. If nothing else, it would have shocked Phelps right out of his pinstripes. But this game meant too much to play around with anything new—even for just one possession.

There was no need for a pep talk for this game. Alford was so ready he couldn't sit still. He jiggled his legs nonstop as Knight went through matchups one last time. Even the crowd, so dead on Saturday, was excited. Indiana crowds are not normally very loud. Because Assembly Hall was built with close to 17,000 theater seats, fans tend to get comfortable during a game. That comfort doesn't often lend itself to jumping up and down and creating havoc. But when Alford scored the game's first basket on a seventeen-foot jumper, the place exploded.

Knight's plan against Notre Dame was simple: make the Irish shoot jump shots all night and don't let them run. David Rivers, Notre Dame's extraordinary sophomore point guard, was a gamebreaker in the open floor but rather ordinary in a halfcourt game. The man assigned to keep Rivers under control was Morgan. He had strict orders to play off him, not let him penetrate. That was Rivers's game—penetration.

Morgan followed his orders perfectly. Rivers kept yoyoing the ball up and down while going nowhere. He had scored twenty-three points the year before against Indiana while Alford had been held to six. Indiana needed a big game from Alford. The first jump shot was a good sign.

But less than a minute later, Alford caught an elbow in the chest. As small as he is, weighing just 160, Alford is vulnerable in a physical game. He was having trouble breathing, and he missed his next three shots. Still, the Hoosiers led early, by as much as 22–13 with 8:23 left.

But Notre Dame, an experienced team with four seniors playing, came back after a Phelps time-out. A Rivers jumper closed the gap to 25–23 with six minutes left. Knight was off the bench, clapping, trying to get his team to hold together. It was exactly at this point in many games a year ago that Indiana had fallen apart: midway in the first half at Notre Dame last year they had led 22–15; by halftime, Notre Dame led 45–30. Knight was afraid of a repeat performance.

But Alford was not about to let that happen. During the last four minutes of the half, he took over. Two free throws. Then a double-pump jumper. A quick pass from Todd Meier that led to a layup. An eighteen-footer. Then another one, this one from the baseline. In all, Alford scored ten straight Indiana points, and by halftime the lead was up to 41–31. Alford had sixteen points. Suddenly, all the preseason work, all the screaming and yelling and torment, was paying off. A ten-point lead.

But it was only halftime. Alford was still having trouble breathing, and Garl worked on him throughout the halftime break. Thomas and Harris were both in foul trouble—just as Knight had feared—with three each. Thomas's third had really irked Knight because he had swung an elbow after grabbing a rebound and been called. "Stupid, Daryl, just plain stupid," Knight said. Thomas couldn't argue.

With Thomas and Harris in foul trouble, Meier and Steve Eyl had come off the bench and played well. They had held their own on the boards and that had allowed Alford to have his little binge. But twenty minutes was a long time to play, especially against an explosive team.

"Now you can see what can happen if you play the way we

want you to," Knight said during the break. "You're halfway there, boys, but now comes the tough half. They will come back at you, I promise you that. There's no way this is going to be easy. But keep doing what we've been doing and we're gonna be okay."

Knight's eyes were alight as he spoke. He had looked tired so often during the fall, but now he looked energized. Just seeing his team play basketball this way seemed to pump life into him. If sitting on the bench and watching the team play poorly against Kent State depressed him—and most assuredly it did—then seeing his team play well pumped life into him.

"I still coach," he had said before the season started, "because there is nothing that gives me more pleasure than seeing our system work. If good kids like Alford and Thomas and Calloway and Morgan and Robinson can come here, go to class, graduate, and play the game well enough to compete with anybody, then it's all worthwhile to me. I want people to understand that our way is the best way to play."

More than anything, Knight had been torn up the previous season because he believed that the team's failures would be seen as an indictment of his system, that people would say he had lost it somewhere, that discipline and toughness couldn't overcome sheer talent anymore. He wanted this team to succeed to prove that last season had been an aberration, not a turning point. A loss to Notre Dame at home would have people pointing again to last season. Knight couldn't bear the thought.

The second half, as Knight predicted, was a struggle. Briefly, it looked as if Indiana would turn the game into a blowout. Alford was still sizzling. He drove the baseline for a basket, then made a pretty steal and fed Calloway for a dunk. A moment later he knocked in a twenty-footer for his twentieth point. Indiana led 49–33 and Phelps called time.

"I knew before the game they would be pumped up and I knew they were capable of beating us," he said later. "But I never expected to be down sixteen."

They didn't stay down sixteen. Thomas picked up his fourth foul setting an illegal screen, a problem that would plague him and the offense throughout the season. Harris picked up his fourth a moment later. Notre Dame clawed back. Rivers hit a jumper. Ken Barlow, an Indianapolis kid whom Knight had recruited and lost, hit twice. Harris committed his fifth foul with 9:08 left when he lost control of a rebound to Donald Royal. Royal laid the ball in just as Harris fouled him.

If Harris had grabbed the rebound, Indiana could have had the ball and a fifteen-point lead. Instead, the lead was cut to twelve, Harris was gone, and Notre Dame had a big boost. Forty seconds later, Thomas committed number five. This was the scenario Knight had feared: playing a big, strong team with his two best big men fouled out. With the lead at ten, Knight sent Robinson in, wanting a smaller ballhandling lineup in the game. Rivers promptly burned Robinson and Knight threw up his hands in despair.

The lead was down to eight when Calloway picked up his fourth foul with 7:07 left. A moment later, Alford missed a short jumper in the lane and Notre Dame freshman Mark Stevenson hit one at the other end to cut the lead to 67–61. There was still 6:15 to go. Disaster loomed. "Oh my, this would be terrible," murmured Hammel, thinking of the sixteen-point lead. The building was almost quiet. Alford was tired. Thomas and Harris were gone. Calloway had four fouls. Robinson had one foot in the doghouse. Who would score?

Morgan. He drove the left side, pulled up from ten feet, and with no hesitation at all shot the ball softly over Stevenson. A miss and the lead could be four with an eternity to play.

Swish. Explosion. It was 69–61. Rivers hit one free throw a moment later but here came Morgan again, breaking the press and scoring. 71–62. Rivers missed, Morgan grabbed the rebound and was fouled. He made just one, but the crisis had passed. The lead was ten and the clock was under five minutes. Notre Dame was finished. Indiana's last points of the game, appropriately, came on a Morgan dunk after Eyl had broken the Notre Dame press with a lovely pass. The final was 82–67. Knight and Phelps hugged at midcourt. For Phelps, it was a loss. For Knight, a moment of vindication. Take note, world: The System still works.

They were celebrating even before Knight walked through the door. They knew there would be no critiques tonight and no complaints. "Is there any better feeling than this?" Knight asked.

"You boys should be proud of yourselves. I'm damn proud of you. You beat a very good basketball team and I mean you really beat 'em. Steve Eyl, Todd Meier, you gave us exactly what we needed coming off the bench. You were terrific. Daryl, Andre, you've got to avoid silly fouls—you see that, don't you? Steve Alford, you hung in and did what you had to do? And Winston, dammit Winston, what am I gonna do with you. You see how good you can be when you think out there? Do you?"

Morgan nodded. Knight looked at him for a moment, trying very hard to keep a straight face. He couldn't. The whole room broke up. Knight walked out to join his friends and leave his players to their celebration. He knew they were entitled.

No one deserved to be part of the celebration more than Morgan. No one had been through more land mines and lived to tell about it than Morgan. He had come to Indiana from Anderson wanting to follow in the footsteps of Bobby Wilkerson, the brilliant defensive guard on the 1976 championship team. Like anyone else in the state, Morgan knew all the Knight stories. But he was not highly recruited, largely because he was barely 6-4 and played center, and so when Knight told him he'd like to have him at Indiana, Morgan jumped at the chance.

That spring, Knight was the speaker at Morgan's banquet. At the end of his speech, Knight called Morgan up to the podium. "He took a dollar out and laid it on a plate," Morgan remembered. "He told me to take it because it was the last thing he'd ever give me for free."

Morgan had come to understand the truth of those words the hard way. His first two years he had been a Knight favorite because he was tough and willing to work hard. But an injury suffered during the summer in Korea had forced him to sit out his junior season. When he came back in the fall of 1984, he was not the same hungry player and his relationship with Knight was not the same.

Knight suspected that being away from basketball had changed Morgan. He had hung out with "the wrong crowd," and he seemed more interested in having a good time than in being a good player. Secondhand, Knight heard stories that backed up his instincts. He rode Morgan hard, giving him a spot in the doghouse right next to Giomi. When Morgan played horribly in the loss at Ohio State, Knight banned him from the plane ride home. Morgan played a total of fifty-eight seconds in the last eleven games of the 1984–85 season, getting in only when Knight didn't have a healthy body available to finish a game. Knight made it clear that he didn't want Morgan back even though he had an extra year of eligibility because of the injury. But Knight had softened on Morgan, partly because of his kindness that night to Jim Crews, partly because he honestly thought Morgan was a good kid who had done a bad thing rather than a bad kid. And through it all, Morgan had never lost his sense of humor. He and Stew Robinson, who had been high school teammates in Anderson, Indiana, were known as Daddy Rap (Morgan) and Rap Junior (Robinson) because they spent a lot of time rapping, much of it with or about members of the opposite sex. Whenever someone asked Daddy Rap how he thought he was doing, Daddy Rap inevitably would shake his head and say, "Can't call it." That became the team's credo: "How's Coach Knight's mood today?" "Can't call it."

Tonight, Daddy Rap could call it. After being told all fall that he was on the verge of extinction, Morgan had taken full advantage of his last chance. He was a hero again when he had thought that part of his life was over. "I never thought I'd get to be part of something like this again," he said that night. "I can't remember the last time I was this happy."

Neither could Knight.

———

Knight didn't celebrate very long, though. While the players went off to party—"We can worry about Kentucky tomorrow," Alford said—Knight and the coaches began to worry about Kentucky. As soon as Knight had finished his press conference and had seen all the well-wishers, he turned to his staff and said, "Well, let's go figure out how to beat Kentucky."

He was on a high. He knew—*knew*—they could beat Kentucky. Waltman had gone to see Kentucky play that evening, and Knight was itching to see the tape. When Waltman returned at 12:30 A.M., the coaches were spread around the locker room, well fed but exhausted. They had been through the Notre Dame tape. Knight wanted Wright to take Morgan aside the next day to

remind him that this game was "just a start." He wanted a tape
made to show Thomas and Harris how they committed their silly
fouls. He wanted Alford to work briefly the next day driving the
ball to the basket against big men since he had missed a couple
of shots in the lane.

When Waltman walked in, Knight's first words were, "You got
the tape?" Waltman nodded. "Pop it in there." And so they went
back to work. Knight likes to work late on the night of a game
because, win or lose, he is too wound up to sleep. Rather than
waste time trying to sleep, he works. The assistants know that
on a game night their work is often just beginning when the game
ends. The only real question is what the atmosphere will be like
as the hours stretch on toward morning. On this winter morning,
it was buoyant.

It was after 2 A.M. when they stopped. The writing board was
filled with things to work on. Practice would be light the next
day. Knight was going on a recruiting trip. As Knight walked to
his car, a light snow falling, he looked back at the now-empty
building.

"I can't tell you," he said, "just how good that felt tonight."

He didn't have to.

8.

Poster Boy

The joyride lasted forty-eight hours. The team practiced only
briefly on Wednesday, and Knight had flown to Elkhart to watch
Sean Kemp, a 6-10 sophomore, practice. In a sense, this gave
everyone a day off. When Knight is absent, everyone relaxes a
little. More often than not, Knight is tense, and he creates tension
around him. When he takes a day off, he knows he is giving
everyone—including himself—a chance to take a deep breath.

Thursday he was back and his mood was cheerful. In the locker
room before practice, Knight joked with several players who had

taken to wearing gray shorts underneath their red practice shorts. "Why do you guys do that?" Knight asked innocently.

There was silence. Finally, Robinson, often the spokesman in situations where no one else wants to say anything, answered. "They're more comfortable than the red shorts."

"Comfortable *where?*" Knight said pointedly, knowing the answer. Everyone was giggling by now. "It helps, you know," Robinson stammered, "jock itch."

"Oh," Knight said as if learning something brand-new. "Pretty smart doing that then, huh?" He turned towards Kreigh Smith. "Smith, do you wear them because of jock itch or because you saw the other guys doing it?"

He didn't wait for Smith's answer. They left the locker room in a light, happy mood. It didn't last. Waiting on the floor was Chuck Crabb, the athletic department's promotions director. In Crabb's hand was a calendar. It had been put together by a sorority to raise money for a camp the sorority sponsored during the summertime for handicapped girls. The calendar was a takeoff on the now-familiar calendars put out around the country that feature attractive women. This one featured attractive men. Mr. February was Steve Alford.

Crabb was pale as he and Knight talked in one corner of the gym while the players were warming up. Alford was even more pale when Knight, his voice cutting the air like a knife, yelled, "*Steve!*" The other players tried not to look as Alford trotted over to Crabb and Knight.

By posing for the calendar, Alford had broken an NCAA rule. It had never occurred to him when the women from the sorority approached him about posing; he received no money, and the women putting the calendar together would make no money. Alford posed in a sport coat, a shirt open at the top, and slacks. It was hardly a risqué pose. The picture had been taken in the fall in Assembly Hall, the session lasting all of about ten minutes.

None of that would matter to the NCAA. The NCAA has proved itself time and again to be a body incapable of policing collegiate athletics. Players are given cars, money, horses, condos, women, you name it, and the NCAA almost never proves anything. Many of the powers in college football and college basketball cheat. Most exploit their athletes and have embarrassing graduation—or non-graduation—rates.

Because it is unable— or unwilling—to successfully prosecute the big-time cheaters, the NCAA often goes after the so-called little guys. Schools like American University and Akron University find themselves being treated like felons by the NCAA. That fall, the NCAA had penalized American because one of its assistant coaches had participated in a pickup game in September. According to the NCAA, the coach's presence in the pickup game constituted an illegal off-season practice.

If there has ever been a college basketball program that follows NCAA rules to the letter, it is Indiana. Knight has often made his alumni unhappy because he allows them so little contact with the players but the less alumni contact, Knight figures, the less tempted the alumni will be to try to break any rules. Knight is so rules-conscious that he would not allow Winston Morgan to eat training meals with the team. Only scholarship players were allowed to eat at the training table, and Morgan wasn't on scholarship. No one outside the team even knew that Morgan wasn't on scholarship, and it would have been easy for Knight to bend this rule, but he wouldn't even consider it.

But now, Alford had broken a rule. Scholarship athletes at NCAA schools aren't allowed to pose for any picture or film made by anyone outside the athletic department. This rule didn't prevent athletic departments from selling posters of its athletes, but it did prevent businessmen from using college athletes to sell their products. Alford could not pose for a local department store or a shoe store or whatever; he understood that, but he hadn't understood that the ban extended to something like this.

Crabb had seen a mention of the calendar in the student newspaper that morning and, panicked, immediately got a copy of it. As soon as he saw Mr. February, he knew he had a problem. As Knight, Alford, and Crabb talked, the women who had put the calendar together were sitting upstairs in Crabb's office.

For the better part of the next two hours, Knight, Crabb, and Alford were in and out of practice. Knight's mood had quickly changed to black. Alford was in for a couple plays, then out. He and Knight were gone for thirty minutes, then back. Serious negotiations were going on. Sales of the calendar had been suspended as soon as Crabb told the sorority there was a problem. But the question was what to do next. They *had* been on sale. There was also the question of blame: Alford said he had told the sorority to make certain there was no problem with his posing. The women claimed Alford had made no such request. They argued this back and forth for a while before Knight, privately, told Alford it really didn't matter.

"*Their* eligibility wasn't at stake, Steve." he said. "Yours was. You should have checked it out yourself."

Knight was right. Alford had made a mistake. There was really only one thing to do: call the NCAA and tell the people there what had happened. Given the nature of the "crime," and given Indiana's track record over the years, there was a good chance— or so it would seem—that the NCAA would let Alford off with a letter of reprimand. They had done this before when minor infractions had been inadvertently committed, writing a letter to the athlete and the school that said, basically, "Don't do this again." This had happened, most notably, two years earlier when an Ohio State quarterback named Mike Tomczak had posed in a magazine ad for a local clothing store. He had received no money for doing the ad and the NCAA had let him off with a letter of reprimand.

Knight called the NCAA Enforcement Office himself as soon as practice was over and explained what had happened. He got the answer he had been hoping for: "They say," he reported back to the waiting coaches, "that we should be all right."

This was after practice. This was after Alford had explained what happened to his teammates, who sat and listened in silence. This was after Knight had told Alford in front of the team that he had been selfish.

But now it seemed the crisis had passed. Under NCAA rules, a player involved in something like this calendar, provided he receives no money, can be suspended for up to three games. With the game at Kentucky two days away, losing Alford for even one game was unthinkable. Knight was angry with Alford because he had been careless. But he was also relieved after his conversation with the NCAA.

It was after seven o'clock before Knight felt comfortable that the Alford situation had been resolved. Pat Knight had a game at 7:30. Knight jumped in his car and drove to Bloomington North High School. He walked into the gym just as the ball was being thrown up to start the game. The other team won the tip and, just as Knight was taking his seat, he looked up to see North setting up in a zone defense.

"Can you believe after the day I've just had that I walk in here and have to watch my son playing *zone?*" He smiled. The crisis had been averted. He could live with watching Patrick play zone defense—at least for one night.

———

But the crisis had not been averted. Shortly after lunch the next day, the NCAA called back. The infractions committee's initial ruling was that Alford would be suspended for one game. All the mitigating circumstances, not to mention the fact that Indiana had turned itself in, apparently didn't matter. Nor did the precedent set in the case of Tomczak. "The rule wasn't as widely publicized back then," was the explanation. "Now, everyone knows it."

Only Alford hadn't known it. Knight was, in a word, enraged: enraged at the NCAA, enraged at Alford, enraged at the sorority, enraged at life. He also had a decision to make. The suspension could be appealed. If it was, Alford could play at Kentucky and continue playing until the committee met formally to hear his appeal on December 23. But if the committee decided then that a three-game suspension was merited, which was possible, Alford would have to sit out the next three games. The third of those games would be the Big Ten opener against defending league champion Michigan. Given a choice between losing Alford for Michigan or Kentucky, Knight would choose Kentucky.

In all likelihood, if Alford had appealed, he would have ended up with a one-game suspension and would have missed only a game against Idaho. But the mere possibility, even if slight, of losing him for the Michigan game made appealing look unappealing. There may have been one other factor, although Knight never mentioned it: If the NCAA was going to put its foot in its mouth by making Alford an example this way, what better way to emphasize its selective enforcement than having Alford sit out the Kentucky game?

The irony was delicious. Kentucky was one of the most penalized schools in NCAA history. It was one of two schools that had had an entire schedule canceled. In late October, *The Lexington Herald-Leader*, in a Pulitzer Prize–winning series of stories, revealed in detail a protracted pattern of payoffs received by Kentucky players during the thirteen-year coaching tenure of Joe B. Hall. Already, the NCAA was dragging its feet in following up on the newspaper's revelations, whining that it couldn't get the twenty-six ex-players who had been quoted on the record to repeat what they had said. What a scenario: Kentucky, bastion of cheating, facing Indiana, bastion of honesty, and who had the NCAA suspended? Indiana's best player.

To Knight this irony was more infuriating than delicious. "For Alford not to play when all their kids are playing kills me," he said. "There are kids on that team right now who have gotten more crap from alumni than any players in the country. I suppose [star forward] Kenny Walker's never gotten anything. Anyone who believes that is either stupid or blind."

Knight was also influenced in making his decision by his anger at Alford. To him, especially now, Alford had gotten himself in trouble by acting as if he was above the law. Later, Knight would soften on the issue, coming to understand that Alford was a good kid who had been careless. Nothing more, nothing less. But on that frigid Friday, Knight was angry enough to want Alford punished. Sitting out the Kentucky game would certainly be a major punishment.

The bottom line, though, was getting the whole dreary incident over with. If Indiana appealed, the question would hang over the team for the next seventeen days and Knight didn't need that. And if by some chance the suspension was extended, it would become a complete disaster. This way, one game would be sacrificed and then it would be over.

Knight was not conceding the game by any means. Even after he made the decision to keep Alford out of the Kentucky game, he still honestly thought his team could win if the players held together and played smart. Practice that day was as intense as any day since October 15. Alford did not practice. He sat alone in the locker room.

There was no way practice was going to be without incident. The only question was who would cause the explosion. It turned out to be Kreigh Smith. His crime was not fighting through a screen properly. Knight, sitting at the far end of the court with Hammel, came out of his chair screaming. The chair went flying. It sailed through the air and landed—miraculously—on its feet, a good thirty feet from where Knight had been sitting. Knight wasn't even looking when the chair landed, but everyone else was. Looks of fear were replaced by looks of amazement when the chair landed on its feet. Knight had to walk so far to get to Smith that he was almost out of steam by the time he arrived. He yelled, and Smith listened. But everyone was still staring at the chair.

This happened every once in a while. Once, Knight had kicked a ball high into the air in disgust and the ball had come down right into a garbage can. Another time he had punted a ball and it had bounced off the head of one of his hunting buddies sitting up in the stands. At all times, everyone kept a straight face when these things happened. Only later did they laugh about them.

When Knight was finished yelling at Smith, he returned to his chair, which had been put back in its place by a manager. After practice, he was succinct: "We are not going down to Kentucky to lose. We are not going down just to go down. If we play with our heads and our hearts, there is absolutely no reason why we can't win this game. We can give them a lot of trouble with some of the things we do with or without Alford. Let's get dressed and get down there."

Knight left the players to dress for the trip and returned to his locker room. Indiana had put out a release earlier in the afternoon announcing Alford's suspension. Wayne Embry, a close friend of Knight's who was a vice-president of the Indiana Pacers, called to find out what had happened. So did Quinn Buckner, who was playing for the Pacers. The team had the day off Saturday. Would Knight like Buckner to come to the game? "Quinn, that would be great," Knight said. "You can fly down from here tomorrow afternoon with Ralph [Floyd]."

Knight told Buckner and Embry what had happened, expressing

disgust with Alford, the sorority, and the NCAA. "I'm not even going to take the little sonofabitch on the trip," he told both men. "Screw him."

But Knight never told Alford he wasn't making the trip. Alford knew he wasn't playing, but didn't know whether Knight wanted him to accompany the team to Lexington. Not wanting to venture anywhere near the coaches' locker room, Alford went to the graduate assistants for advice. Dakich, who knew Knight best, told Alford he had to get on the bus.

"If he wants you there and you aren't, it's irreparable and you're in bigger trouble than you are now," Dakich said. "If he doesn't want you there and you are there, then he just leaves you on the bus. You have to go unless someone tells you different."

No one told Alford different. Knight thought he had told Alford, but he had only told Buckner and Embry. The bus rolled silently through the darkness to the airport. Always, the Indiana bus is quiet. Knight sits in the front seat, occasionally calling an assistant coach or Hammel up next to him to talk. There was no talk at all on this trip.

Alford always sits in the very back of the bus and, naturally, is the last one to get off. The players always get off before the coaches, Garl, Hammel, and anyone else along on a trip. This gives them a chance to grab luggage and equipment and move it from bus to plane and, later, plane to bus. As Alford went past him, Knight sat up straight in his seat as if someone had stuck a rod in his back. Alford never put a foot on the tarmac.

"Alford!" Alford stopped. "What the f— do you think you're doing? Get back in here. Didn't you hear me tell you that you weren't making the trip?"

"No sir."

"Well then you must be f—— deaf. Can't you do anything right?" And so on.

By the time Knight boarded the plane, everyone else was in their seats. Alford was left sitting forlornly on the bus. Knight was dressed in a red sport coat, slacks, and a shirt and tie. Everyone who travels with Indiana wears a jacket and tie. Even though he had abandoned this look for games and almost never wore a tie to speaking engagements, Knight still dressed to travel.

The ride was brief, but when the plane arrived in Lexington, the bus was not waiting. While Garl went off in search of it, everyone just sat and looked at one another blankly. The bus had gone to the wrong end of the airport. By the time Garl found it and got it to the plane, everyone was shivering since the engines and the heat had been shut off.

The bus was loaded quickly. But as the bus pulled away, manager Jim Kelly had a stricken look on his face. "The VCR got left home," he whispered to Felling. "We [the four senior managers] must have forgotten to pack it."

Just then Knight came back to tell Felling he wanted the VCR set up as soon as the bus reached the hotel so the players could look at tapes of Kentucky after they had eaten dinner. "Coach," Felling said in the same tone one might use when confessing to a murder, "the VCR didn't get packed. It's not here."

"It's my fault, Coach," Kelly broke in, a brave man willing to die with his boots on.

Knight stared for a moment. "*What?*" he said. "It's not here?" Felling and Kelly shook their heads. Knight didn't say another word. He walked back to the front of the bus, sat down and stared out the window. By the time the bus reached the hotel, a plan had been hatched: the managers would be sent out to rent a VCR and Murry Bartow would be called in Bloomington and told to drive Indiana's VCR and the remaining tapes—some had made it on the plane, some had not—down to Lexington.

Solution or not, it was clear that Murphy's Law had taken charge of this trip. It was also clear that Knight was not going to be any fun to live with during the next twenty-four hours. That evening, Harold Martin joined the coaches for dinner. An hour later, when Knight was going through a tape with the team on the rented VCR, Martin coughed. "If you can't be quiet, you can just leave," Knight snapped. Martin left.

Knight wanted to walk through Kentucky's offense after the tape session. But the only room large enough for a walk-through was being used. Probably by someone named Murphy. Knight gave the team a brief talk and left. Felling lingered, hoping to loosen things up a little. Knight charged back into the room. "If

I wanted you to talk to them, I'd tell you to talk to them," he yelled after pulling Felling into the hallway.

An hour later, Felling's phone rang. It was Knight. "I'm sorry I snapped," he said. "Come on down. Let's talk about this game a little." It was one o'clock in the morning.

———

Alford almost played in the game.

When the team went to practice at Rupp Arena in the morning, Cawood Ledford was waiting for Knight. Ledford has been Kentucky's radio play-by-play man for about 100 years. He is a legend throughout the state, a man linked as closely to Kentucky basketball as anyone short of Adolph Rupp.

Ledford had known Knight for years, had even done some postseason games with him on radio. Ledford always interviews the opposing coach for the pregame show. Knight knew Ledford would be waiting, and he sat down with him to tape the pregame interview.

Halfway through the interview Ledford asked Knight about the Kentucky-Indiana rivalry. "These games are special, aren't they?" Ledford asked innocently.

Knight couldn't resist. "You know, Cawood, with all the crap that has gone on down here over the years with recruiting and all, these games are not nearly as special to me as you might think."

Zap. Take that, Kentucky.

Driving back to the hotel after practice, Knight was thinking aloud. "It's just not right for Steve not to play in this game," he said. "I've got a mind to have him fly down here and play him. There's no way the NCAA will suspend him for more than one game. Public opinion would bury them if they did."

Hammel said nothing. Back in the hotel, Knight called Pete Newell. Knight listens to Newell more than to anyone else in the world. Their relationship is coach-protégé, father-son, big brother–little brother. Knight believes that no coach did more to change basketball than Newell did during his years at the University of California at Berkeley. He respects him totally. After most games, Knight will call Newell, who lives in San Francisco, to brief him on the game and ask him what he thinks should be worked on. Now, he wanted to know if Alford should play.

"I might just say screw the NCAA," he told Newell. "How can Steve not play and Walker can play? That just isn't right and you know it."

Newell knew it, but he counseled Knight not to change his mind, reminding Knight of the reasons he had decided to go this way in the first place: getting the incident over with, and not gambling on the Michigan game. The NCAA could not be counted on to react logically. Don't take the chance. Don't do anything because you are angry.

Knight also called Alford's parents. They had been bombarded by phone calls from the media, and Knight wanted to cheer them up. "Steve made a mistake. But it doesn't make him a bad kid."

Knight knew that Newell was right about not playing Alford. But it still pained him to take the floor that night without him. He had Buckner talk to the team before the game. "It doesn't matter who plays," Buckner said. "It doesn't matter if it's me or Steve Alford or you. The system works. The rules work. Play that way and you win the game."

The Kentucky fans were lying in wait. Many of them had listened to Knight's comments on the pregame show, and that, added to their general dislike for someone who had beaten them often over the years, brought out the worst in them. There were the usual obscenities and catcalls about the false rumors that had been spread since Nancy Knight had been away at Duke. The crowd was, in a word, ugly.

The game was not. Indiana played its guts out. Calloway, playing his first college road game, was brilliant. The Hoosiers did the two things Knight had said they had to do to stay in the game: handle the Kentucky press and rebound. It is easy to say, but Indiana almost certainly would have won the game if Alford had played. The one thing the team lacked on this night was someone to shoot the ball over the Kentucky zone with consistency.

It was 32–32 at halftime. The screaming crowd seemed not to bother the Hoosiers. If they could handle the forty-eight practices from October 15 to November 30, they could certainly handle 24,000 fans. There were mistakes. But Kentucky couldn't hold a seven-point lead, and it was even at intermission.

"You have now made this a twenty-minute basketball game," Knight told them at halftime. "But you have to play smarter to win the game. We are still making mistakes on defense. Play hard and smart. You tell me now that we aren't capable of playing with anybody. Don't mope, don't feel sorry, don't feel hurt. Feel like, 'Goddammit, we're gonna win a basketball game.'

"The easy twenty minutes is over. This is the hard twenty minutes. Don't let the effort you've made go down the drain with sloppy effort early. Let's be smart and get it down to the last three minutes where we can win the game with our guts and our hearts. Don't go out there now *thinking* you're ready to play. Go out there *knowing* you're ready."

They were ready. Each time Kentucky took a lead, Indiana answered. Thomas and Jadlow were doing a good job on Walker inside. Walker and Kentucky coach Eddie Sutton were crying to the officials for help, but weren't getting it. Later, Sutton would accuse Indiana of "thuggery in the pivot," a comment that would infuriate Knight.

A Calloway layup off a pretty pass from Robinson tied the game for the tenth time at 42–42. Sutton called time. "Twelve minutes," Knight said in the huddle over the din. "You've taken it from a forty-minute game to a twelve-minute game. Hang with it now, don't make mistakes, and we'll be fine."

But they were getting tired. Without Alford, there were no easy baskets. Every possession was work. Kentucky reeled off nine straight points to lead 51–42. The crowd was berserk. Knight called time. His voice in the huddle was almost matter-of-fact. "Just be patient," he said. "There's lots of time. Don't get rattled. There is nothing to be rattled about."

They listened. They came back. Robinson hit from outside. Thomas hit two free throws. Smith came off the bench to hit a bomb. It was 57–54, Kentucky, with 2:20 to go. The crowd was nervous. This couldn't happen. Indiana couldn't win at Rupp Arena without Alford. The teams exchanged baskets. It was 59–56. Ninety seconds to go.

Kentucky wanted to go inside to Walker. Guard Ed Davender penetrated and looked for Walker. Harris poked the ball loose. Robinson came out of the scramble with it. He and Harris burst downcourt with only Kentucky guard Roger Harden back. Robinson, on the left side, glanced at Harris, a step behind him. If he passed, Harris might dunk. He also might lose the ball or charge into Harden. Better, thought Robinson, to go straight to the hoop. He did. Harden had only one play: turn, plant his feet, and try to take the charge.

Robinson soared. He and Harden collided and went down together in a heap. The ball went in the basket, and 24,000 pairs of eyes were on referee Tom Rucker, who had blown his whistle as soon as the two players made contact. Rucker is a Big Ten official. He was working the game with two officials from the Southeastern Conference—Kentucky's conference. Like most coaches, Knight hates "split crews." He had asked Sutton the previous spring to get neutral officials for the game. Sutton said after the game that he had forgotten. That was why Rucker was there. Rucker was one of Knight's least favorite Big Ten officials, which is saying quite a bit, given Knight's general feeling about Big Ten officials.

Now, as Robinson and Harden untangled, as both benches stood, Rucker came out from under the basket, his hand behind his head, giving the call for charging. Not only had he called the foul on Robinson, he had ruled that the contact had come before the shot, meaning the basket didn't count. If Rucker had called Harden for a blocking foul, the score would have been 59–58 and Robinson would have gone to the foul line with a chance to tie the game. It could have been a tie game with one minute left and all the pressure on the home team. It would have been exactly the situation Knight had wanted before the game began.

But Rucker wasn't going to give it to him. Once, twice for good measure, he pointed towards Kentucky's basket to indicate it was Kentucky's ball. The crowd screamed. Knight, hands on hips, just stared at Rucker. When you spend a career getting on officials, there are going to be moments when one of them turns on you and says, in effect, "Take that." This was Tom Rucker's moment.

Much later that night, the game tape would show that Harden had still been moving when the contact was made. Rucker had missed the call. But he hadn't had the benefit of the tape. He had a split second to make the call. He could side with one man he didn't particularly like or he could side with 24,000 fans. Did he consciously think of any of that? Almost certainly not. But the tape showed his call was wrong.

That call was the ballgame. Kentucky ran the clock down to thirty seconds before Harden drove the baseline for a layup. Harden was a mouthy kid from Indiana who had earlier in the week "guaranteed" that Kentucky would beat Indiana. Having him score the basket that nailed the game for Kentucky was like being spit on when you've already been flattened.

It ended 63–58. Knight shook hands briefly with Sutton and sprinted for the locker room. He was inconsolable. His team had given him everything he could have asked of it—except a victory. But that was the only thing he had come for. He had almost no voice left as he went through their mistakes in the locker room.

"The problem is you aren't hurt enough," he said. "You're sitting here satisfied because you played a good game. All I want to do is go into a room somewhere and cry. I could just cry. Boys, there's no such thing as a moral victory. The game was there to win and we lost. If you just followed the rules, we would have won. Instead, those cheating sonsofbitches won."

He was standing in front of the blackboard where earlier he had written the lineups. He looked at his players. They looked at him. Knight turned his head back to the board and, not so lightly, hit his head against the board. "All I want to do is go somewhere and cry." He was close to tears.

Ten minutes later, Knight walked into the hallway, calm and clear-eyed, to go to the interview room. Sutton, having just finished there, was walking past. Earlier in the week, Sutton had been quoted as saying that Knight had advised him not to take the Arkansas job in the mid-1970s. Knight remembered telling Sutton that he thought Arkansas was a terrific job. Knight was annoyed that Sutton, in his view, had twisted the story.

Sutton saw Knight, and came over to offer a final word of consolation after a taut ballgame. Knight cut him off. "Eddie, didn't I ask you to get neutral officials when we talked last spring?"

"I don't really remember, Bobby, I suppose you might have. I don't pay much attention to that sort of thing."

"Well I do. And I wanted neutral officials." Knight was walking away now.

Sutton dropped the charm school routine. "If you wanted neutral officials, Bob, why didn't you get 'em yourself?"

Knight stopped short. The hallway was empty because the media was waiting inside the interview room. He and Sutton were about fifteen feet apart. Knight turned and glared at Sutton. "*You* were the home team, Eddie. That means *you* get the officials. And when I ask you to get neutral officials and you agree, I think I have every right to think I'll get neutral officials."

Knight didn't wait for Sutton to respond to this comment. He turned and walked into the interview room. Sutton waved his hand in the air as if to say, "The hell with you." Fortunately, Knight didn't see the gesture.

The interview was brief. Knight had told the players that if they were asked about Alford's absence, they should answer simply, "I have no interest in talking about Alford." Knight was almost as succinct: "I would like to think that the NCAA would have given some consideration to our past record. A rule was broken. They have to live with what they did. But I accept responsibility. We didn't have a good enough checking system."

That was it. Knight could not have been more diplomatic if he had been briefed by Henry Kissinger.

The plane trip was predictable. Brooks and Smith were out of the doghouse; Morgan and Robinson were in. So was Eyl, who had made a crucial defensive mistake, and Harris, who had once again gotten into foul trouble. Maybe Kreigh Smith should start. Maybe Brooks should start. The last statement brought Kohn Smith out of his doze.

"I don't know about that," he said.

It was after midnight when the bus pulled up to Assembly Hall. "It bothers me," Knight said, "that Alford's not here to see his teammates. That disappoints me."

He reviewed the game for the players. They had done some good things, but not enough. "Kentucky will win twenty-five games this year and they were laying right there for you to beat tonight. I'm proud of you for going down there and believing you could win the game. But you have to understand why you came up short tonight. Alford had not one goddamn thing to do with our losing that game. Right here in this room we've got all the talent I need to win. We didn't need Alford to win tonight. Don't feel sorry, don't feel down. We just kicked a golden opportunity away tonight.

"We'll be in here at eleven o'clock in the morning."

The players went home. The coaches went to the cave. It was after 4 A.M. when they finally went home. The record was 2–1. It had already been a long season.

9.

No Reason to Lose to Anyone

Kansas State was next. This was a game that truly scared Knight. His team had played two emotionally draining games and now faced an opponent that everyone—including the players—would expect to beat without much trouble. Kansas State had talent. Not great talent, but good talent, certainly good enough to beat Indiana if the Hoosiers were flat. And there was good reason to believe they would be flat.

Knight began hammering on this theme Sunday morning. "This team will be better than Kentucky," he said. "I mean that. They are good athletes and they aren't spoiled assholes like Kentucky. To them, this will be a monumentally big game. You're going to spend the next two days getting patted on the ass, being told how well you played at Kentucky, all that crap.

"Let me tell you something, boys. If you expect to be any kind of basketball team this year, you have to win this game. This game is the most important one we'll play this month. I know you'll be up to play Notre Dame and Kentucky and Louisville. But you have to get up to play these people, too. If you don't, I guarantee you'll get knocked right on your ass."

Knight wasn't exaggerating. The problem was that the players, the experienced ones anyway, had heard this speech before. For a coach, deciding what to tell your players about an opponent is never easy. If you play Kent State and say, "Hey, we should beat these guys easily," then you take a chance on overconfidence. But if time and again you tell your team that the Kent States of the world are great teams, then when you tell your team that Kansas State is good—and it is good—you run the risk that the players will nod and think, "Yeah sure, Coach, they're better than Kentucky. Right."

Kansas State was not better than Kentucky. But in basketball, timing always plays a role in the outcome of a game. To Kansas State, this game was as emotional as Notre Dame and Kentucky had been to Indiana. Knight understood that. He worked the players twice on Sunday, emphasizing fundamentals.

"We gave away twenty points last night because we didn't help on defense," he said repeatedly. "Twenty points. If we follow the rules, we're ahead 65–52 with five minutes left and we win easily. Boys, *no one plays this game well.* If you follow our rules, we're going to beat all these teams. You people just don't understand that you have to sweat blood out here to play. We haven't had anyone here since Wittman, Kitchel, and those kids played who was willing to do that."

Knight and his rules. One former player once said whimsically of Knight, "He's not a man, he's a set of rules."

Written on a blackboard, the rules for playing basketball Knight-style are easy. Executing them is not. "Help-side defense" is a perfect example of this. The rule is simple: If you see an opponent on the other side of the court beat his man going to the basket, you must leave your man and help. The "help side" is the side opposite where the ball is, because that's where one can get to the basket in time to help if someone is beaten.

To play good help-side defense, the move must become instinctive. A player can't see a teammate lose his man and think, "Should I help?" He must react automatically, or he will be too late. Some players have this instinct, some acquire it from hours and hours of practice, but others never acquire it. Harris was having particular trouble with this because he was still thinking rather than reacting. By the time he was through thinking, he would arrive just in time to commit a foul. Eyl had done the same thing against Kentucky. This kind of mistake drove Knight insane, especially when he saw it on tape. To him, it was as fundamental as boxing out on a rebound. But players are taught to box out from the very first day they play basketball. Unless they play in a Knight-type system, they aren't taught about help-side defense.

For a smart player, Knight's system isn't difficult to learn. But it requires thinking, and it requires reacting differently on almost every possession at both ends of the floor. On offense, all five players have to read the defense, not just the point guard. If one player makes the wrong cut, or sets the wrong screen, or fails to screen, the whole play breaks down. The same is true on defense: if one player fails to help, or fails to make a switch, or fails to get in a passing lane, the whole defense collapses.

Knight now found himself coaching a team that was very willing, but often not able, to execute what he wanted. If he had never coached a team that was willing *and* able, this might not have bothered him so much. But he had been spoiled. He kept thinking back to the mid-1970s. But this was the mid '80s. Quinn Buckner and Scott May were nowhere in sight, and Kansas State would be a very tough game.

What was most surprising about the two days following the Kentucky game—other than the fact that the sun came out on Monday—was that Knight never once berated Alford. Knight not carrying a grudge is a little bit like George Burns not carrying a cigar. It is inevitable, just as inevitable, as Knight might put it, "as the sun coming up in the east."

In fact, even though Knight repeatedly told the players on Sunday and Monday how tough this game would be, he was almost loose—by his standards. As the team walked to the field house on Monday night for its final walk-through—Kansas State was using Assembly Hall—Knight noticed Calloway and Felling walking together.

"Hey, Ricky," Knight shouted, "you ever see a white guy with an Afro before?"

Calloway elbowed Felling. "He got you with that one, Coach."

As Knight went through the Kansas State personnel one final time, he looked at the players and said, "What kind of a team do you want to be? That's the question. You've got to come up with the answer."

In the locker room, after the players had gone home, Knight

worried once more. "I wonder," he said, "how Alford will play."

Knight knew that Alford had been the subject of nationwide sympathy the last three days. Almost no one agreed with the NCAA's decision to suspend Alford; Knight was glad of that, and he agreed with the sentiment. He was furious with the NCAA. But he was also angry with Alford, and he was afraid Alford might end up feeling like a martyr. That may have been the reason for his tirade the next afternoon. Or maybe he had just been holding back for seventy-two hours and could do so no longer.

The players arrived at three for their final walk-through. Before they could get started, Knight took off on Alford.

"Alford, you really cost us that game on Saturday and I want you to know that I really resent it. I can't forget it. I'm just out of patience with you. What you did was stupid. It wasn't a mistake, it was just plain stupid. You've been told and f—— told and f—— retold, and you screwed up and cost us a game. I really have trouble forgetting that. This is a habit with you. You don't listen, whether it's defense or playing hard or this. I don't know about anyone else in here but I resent it and it pisses me off. Because of you we lost to a chickenshit f—— operation. I won't forget that."

Knight never forgets. The message to Alford was clear: you owe us one. The message to the others was just as clear: forget what I said Saturday, Alford *did* have lots to do with the loss. The others had been granted absolution for the sin of losing to Kentucky. Alford still had some time left in purgatory.

Shortly after Knight's diatribe, Henry Iba walked into the gym. He was in town for the week to visit Knight and spend some time with the team that he had gotten to know as Knight's guest on their summer world tour. At eighty-one, Iba was still alert, could still tell a good story, and still liked to put down a Kahlua or two late at night.

Knight sat with Iba in the locker room before the game, recounting the previous week in rich detail from the Notre Dame victory through the calendar fiasco to the Rucker call on Robinson. He stood up to demonstrate how Harden had turned into Robinson.

"I saw it on television," Iba said. "I thought it was too bad."

No one argued. Knight went off to take his steam. "He's a good boy," Iba said. "I just wish losing didn't hurt him so darn much." He left to go talk to the players. When Iba was gone, Knight sent for Chuck Crabb, who did the public address announcements. He wanted Iba introduced to the crowd, and he wanted him introduced in a specific way. "The most legendary figure in the history of basketball," Knight told Crabb. Knight wrote most of Crabb's introductions when his friends came to town.

Kreigh Smith would start. The coaches had decided this on Sunday, but Smith didn't find out until just before pregame meal. This was a prime example of how quickly things can change at Indiana: Smith had been a redshirt candidate before the Kent State game ten days earlier, and now he was a starter.

But as he warmed up before the game, Smith felt something pop in his knee. Bomba took a look at it. Could be nothing, he told Garl. Or it could be a serious injury. Garl reported to Knight inside the locker room. Knight rolled his eyes in disgust. "Can he play?"

"I don't know."

When the team came back inside, Knight took Smith into the hall. "Are you okay? Are you certain?" Smith would have answered yes if his leg had been broken. He wanted desperately to play. As it turned out, it didn't matter whether he played or not. X-rays would later show a tear in the cartilage, Smith would need an operation, and he would end up as a redshirt anyway—a medical redshirt because of an injury. He played that night. He felt pain, but not unbearable pain, so he kept playing.

Unfortunately, Smith's teammates all played as if *they* had bad knees. Knight's fears had been legitimate. Indiana was flat, Kansas State wasn't. The Wildcats had a twenty-four-year-old Army veteran named Norris Coleman on their team. Late in the season, Coleman, who is 6-8, would be ruled ineligible by the NCAA because of poor grades in high school, but on December 10 he was eligible and Andre Harris couldn't guard him. By halftime he had seventeen points, and Morgan had escaped the bench to try to guard him. He wasn't doing much better than Harris, and Kansas State led 39–32.

The sound the players heard in the locker room was the roof, about to cave in on them. Knight was raging one moment, resigned the next. "It's your team," he said. "Your goddamn team. You wanna be horseshit, that's fine with me. I won't fight it. There's no communication out there, no enthusiasm, nothing. You did exactly what I told you you would do. You went around and got patted on the back and everyone told you that you were great at Kentucky. Everyone felt sorry for Alford. *Alford f—— up.*

"I might as well have stood in here the last three days and talked to empty lockers because I would have gotten as much response. Andre, you are afraid of Coleman. You can't play like that for us. You people sit in here and figure out what to do the second half."

He walked into the hall, turned, and came right back in. "When are you people going to get this crap out of your system? I really believe that we're gonna be terrible until we get rid of all you people. This just defies my ability to comprehend anything."

In the hallway, Knight looked at the coaches and said, "I'd have bet the goddamn farm that this would happen tonight. Now, what should we do?"

They talked about benching Harris. No, give him another chance. Morgan would have to start for Smith. They needed his defense. They had been outrebounded 18–13. Calloway had finally played like a freshman. He had been awful. "Ricky doesn't have it tonight," Knight said. "Maybe we should try Brooks or Robinson."

"I think Ricky will come around," Felling said. Knight said nothing. But he stuck with Calloway.

Knight had little more to say before they went back out except this: "If you don't get yourselves together and understand that this team can kick your ass, you'll be down twenty in no time. And if that happens, we're all gonna be in big trouble."

They were down ten quickly. But Alford, who had only gotten off three shots, began to take over. He hit from twenty feet, then he set Thomas up inside for a three-point play. A moment later he pulled down a rebound and went the length of the court to cut the margin to 50–47. The dead crowd suddenly revived. Calloway cut it to one with 12:49 still remaining on a soft jumper from the corner. But Coleman hit twice, both times over Jadlow, who had come in for Harris early in the half.

Indiana got back to within one, Kansas State built the lead back to five. Three times, the Wildcats scored on the very cut Knight had warned about constantly before the game. But Thomas was coming on inside. He hit another three-point play, then got fouled and made two free throws. They hung close. Finally, Calloway pulled down a missed Morgan free throw, seemingly jumping over everyone in the building, and put the shot back. Indiana led 70–69 with 4:01 left. A moment later, Coleman proved human when he missed the front end of a one-and-one. Calloway drove the lane, got fouled, and made both foul shots. The lead was three. Kansas State never got any closer. The bullet had been dodged.

The heroes were Alford, Thomas, Calloway, and Felling—Felling had probably kept Calloway in the game, and he had responded with sixteen points, most of them in the crunch. Knight was still angry about the first half, but relieved about the result, and delighted with the comeback.

"You got in a hole because you had a terrible mental attitude," he said. "That should never happen. But last year you would have quit and lost the game. You did a hell of a job coming back. Daryl, you really did a great job, and Todd Jadlow, you came off the bench and did the job when we had to have it on Coleman. You hung in and scrapped. That's good. But remember, this was a lucky escape."

The players knew. As the coaches went through the tapes late into the night, the players went to the nearby Big Wheel Restaurant for their late dinner. Pat Knight, as always, went along. And, as always, Pat Knight was loose, joking, having a good time. Harris, knowing he was in the doghouse now, finally snapped.

"What are you laughing about so much?" he yelled at Pat Knight.

"The way you play," Pat Knight answered.

Winston Morgan almost gagged. No one else said a word. The team was now four and twenty-four.

In truth, they had come through the first tough stretch of the season in excellent shape. The wins over Notre Dame and Kansas State were gratifying, the loss to Kentucky frustrating but understandable. Most important, everyone could see that this team had potential. It could be what Knight wanted most from one of his teams: "Hard to beat."

The weekend would bring to town the annual Indiana Classic, better known to the players as two absolute lock victories. Indiana never lost in the Classic. The Hoosiers had won every game they had played in it for thirteen years, and with Louisiana Tech, Texas Tech, and Alcorn State making up the field, that wasn't likely to change this year.

Naturally, Knight was worried.

There was no reason to be. Indiana would win both games easily, beating Louisiana Tech Friday and Texas Tech in the final on Saturday. The weekend was hectic for Knight more because he was playing host to two dozen people than for any other reason. The Classic was more a social event than a basketball event. Friends of Knight's came from far and wide each year for this weekend, figuring they would have much more fun coming to see two easy wins than coming to see a possible loss.

Iba had arrived Tuesday. By Friday afternoon about ten of Knight's friends from Orrville were in town, including Dr. Donald Boop, Knight's boyhood neighbor and one of his many older-brother figures. Eddie Gottlieb, an old friend, had flown in from Florida. Mickey Corcoran, one of Knight's coaching gurus, had come in from New Jersey. And Tim Knight was home for Christmas vacation.

Knight's problems that weekend had little to do with his team. It performed well in both games. But he did have problems.

On Friday, he and Corcoran were driving a brand-new car Knight had just acquired when they came across a road that had been flooded by two days of downpours. Knight tried to slog on through. No luck. The car stalled. For a moment, Knight thought he was stuck and would have to swim out. Finally, the car limped through the water, but then died. The computer system had been drowned. Knight had to knock on a stranger's door to call for help. Needless to say, everyone who had gathered for the weekend had a field day with that story.

Friday night, after the easy victory over Louisiana Tech, Knight walked onto the floor at halftime of the second game to do a radio show. Three Big Ten officials were working that game. One of them was Tom Rucker. When Knight had finished the interview, he found himself seated fifteen feet behind where the officials were standing, waiting for the second half to begin.

"Hey, Rucker," Knight yelled, "Have you figured out the difference between a block and a charge yet?"

All three officials smiled at Knight's reference to the Kentucky game. "You think I'm kidding, don't you," Knight continued, now standing and walking towards Rucker. "Why don't you do everybody a favor and just quit? You make everyone in the game look bad."

The gym was almost empty, most of the fans having gone home after the Indiana game, and Knight's words seemed to echo. He was past Rucker now, but looked back to get in a few more swipes. "It's not funny, Rucker, the only thing funny about it is that you're a goddamn joke."

Back in his locker room, Knight smiled. "I really nailed him." The last word—again. Knight and Rucker would meet again before the season was over. Knight knew that. But . . .

Indiana annihilated Texas Tech in the final, breaking the game open after a sloppy first half that nonetheless produced a nine-point lead. But before the game could end, Knight's sense of honor got him into trouble.

Knight had been unhappy with the officials throughout the tournament. They were Mid-American Conference officials, and he hadn't been pleased with them from the start. During most of the Texas Tech game, he practically begged for a technical foul. The officials, clearly intimidated, never gave him one. But with 4:06 left in the game and Indiana leading 69–47, the officials gave one to poor Gerald Meyers, the Texas Tech coach.

Knight was distressed and embarrassed. Meyers had not said or done half the things Knight had done and now, trailing by twenty-two points, he was given a technical—in Indiana's tournament. First, Knight ordered Alford, who had automatically gone up to shoot the technical fouls, to back off. Instead, he had Steve Eyl, far and away Indiana's worst foul shooter, take the shots. He missed both.

One minute later, Jadlow was called for a routine foul. Knight stormed onto the court, running to the opposite foul line, acting berserk. He was going to get a technical if it was the last thing he ever did. For his efforts, he received two technicals. The crowd hooted. To them, Knight was going berserk with a twenty-point lead in a game that was already over.

Knight was doing what he thought was right. He felt obligated to get a technical and he knew that as long as he stayed in the coaching box—the area right in front of the bench—he wasn't going to get one. He had already called one official "a chickenshit mother——" and not received one. By charging onto the court, Knight gave the officials no choice. He had done this before in a similar situation. It was the right thing to do in his mind. He wanted everyone to know that the officials were *awful*.

Knight also knew that most people would not see the incident this way. They would see it as another example of Knight going over the edge. In this case, they would be completely wrong. Knight knew just what he was doing. Even so, he hated behaving this way in front of Iba. When he walked into the coaches' locker room after the game, Iba was waiting. "Coach, I just feel so bad about what happened, . . ." Knight began.

"Don't say another word," Iba said, holding a hand up to brake Knight. "I know what you were doing, Bob. You did just fine."

Knight sighed and sat down heavily. When he is depressed about something he looks about 100 years old. That was the way he looked now. "I really don't want these things to happen," he said, thinking out loud again. 'I keep telling myself not to let them get to me and then they do. I mean it's our tournament, the game is over, and the gutless sonofabitch calls a technical on Gerald. It just isn't right."

Knight was still bothered by the incident when he walked into the post-tournament party. All his buddies from Orrville were there along with the coaches from Indiana and the other three schools. This was an annual event. One person who had looked forward to the party was Murry Bartow—until he had mentioned to Knight how much his wife was looking forward to the party. That was when Bartow learned that his wife shouldn't be looking forward to the party, since no women need apply. Men only.

"I'm taking her a doggy bag," Bartow said glumly, shoving some barbequed ribs onto a plate.

Knight's sexism is no secret. In fact, he often wears it like a badge of honor. The women in his life have very defined roles: Nancy Knight has been a wife in the most traditional sense— mother, cook, housekeeper, fan of the husband's basketball team. Knight has two secretaries whom he treats with great respect at all times. As secretaries. Buzz Kurpius, the academic counselor for the players, is someone Knight feels comfortable with and often tells jokes to.

One day in practice Knight used the word "piece." "You know what a piece is, don't you, Buzz?" Knight said. "All women do."

This was Knight's way of treating Kurpius as a near equal. But most women didn't merit such treatment. Knight was always polite to them, curbed his language around them, and had little use for them in a social setting. When he wanted to relax, he wanted to be around men. He didn't feel he could be himself with women around.

Mike Krzyzewski, who had three daughters, often thought it would have been very healthy for Knight to have had a daughter. His sons were not so sure. "I think if I had come out a girl he would have shoved me back inside," Pat Knight often said.

An exaggeration. Maybe.

Knight didn't stay at the party that long. The team was now 5–1. But Louisville was next. The game would be tough enough— especially at Louisville—under ideal circumstances. But the players were beginning their one-week exam period on Monday. This meant shortened practices, players arriving late and leaving early, and a generally distracted atmosphere. Knight blamed himself for this. "I never should schedule a game like this, especially on the road, during exams," he said on his radio show Monday night, a rare public admission of a mistake. "We'll just go down there and do the best we can."

Louisville, as it was to prove in March by winning the national championship, had as much talent as anyone in the country. No one, including Knight, quite understood how Denny Crum managed to amass so much talent year in and year out. But he and Crum had always had a good relationship if not a close one. They even ate dinner together the night before the game.

The road atmosphere in Louisville could not have been more

different than Kentucky. Before the game, Knight and Alford were presented with plaques from the school as a tribute to their Olympic involvement. Knight received a standing ovation, a marked contrast to the ugliness of Lexington.

Coaching a game in old Freedom Hall took Knight back a lot of years. As a sophomore at Ohio State he had played one of his best games in the NCAA regional semifinals against Western Kentucky. "I still remember [Coach] Fred Taylor putting his arm around me after we beat Kentucky in the final and saying, 'Bobby, we wouldn't be here right now if not for you,'" Knight said. That was 1960. Five years later, as a rookie coach at Army, he brought his team to Freedom Hall to play Louisville. "Got hammered 84–56," Knight said, remembering the exact score as he almost always did.

On the morning of the game Knight and Hammel walked from the hotel into the arena for the game-day shootaround. The walk was only about half a mile, but the temperature was about zero and the winds made it feel even colder. Knight never blinked. He is an inveterate walker, regardless of temperature on the road. And when Knight walks, Hammel walks. It isn't a matter of choice. Knight says, "Come on, Hamso, let's go," and they are off.

Knight and Hammel spend so much time together on road trips that the players over the years have taken to calling Hammel "the shadow." What the players don't know is that this is more Knight's idea than Hammel's. Knight doesn't like spending time alone, and over the years he has become extremely comfortable with Hammel. He trusts him, and Hammel knows his moods well enough that if Knight doesn't say a word during an hour-long walk, Hammel knows to stay silent. When Knight feels like talking, he will talk.

On this frigid morning, Knight was in a nostalgic mood. "Hamso, do you realize I made this exact same walk on a game morning twenty years ago?" he said. "I haven't come very far since then, have I?"

Because Knight calls Hammel "Hamso," everyone else in the Indiana party calls him that, too. Everyone else in the world calls him Bob, but on the Indiana basketball team there is only one Bob—the one everybody calls Coach.

When Knight coached at Army, he was known to one and all in the East as Bobby. His mother calls him Bobby. Most of the people in Orrville still call him Bobby, and Fred Taylor calls him Bobby. But Knight has always signed his name Bob and identified himself as Bob. When he first arrived at Indiana, Hammel asked him which he preferred in print. Knight said it didn't matter to him. "Well, then, let's go with Bob," Hammel said, "because I hated being called Bobby as a kid." That was fine with Knight. That is what he is called throughout the Midwest—Bob. But he answers to Bobby just as easily. The only person who ever refers to him as Robert is his wife.

The game that night was markedly different from the one Knight had coached in twenty years earlier. Once again, Indiana proved that it could compete with very good teams. The game was much like the Kentucky game, close all the way. Neither team led by more than four points during the first half. Harris was a different player—hanging in with the Louisville leapers on the boards, playing with intelligence. But Daryl Thomas, who had scored twenty-nine points against Texas Tech and really looked to be coming into his own, was having trouble. At halftime he had four points, zero rebounds, and three fouls. Harris also had three fouls, but when he came out with 1:38 left, Knight walked down the bench and put his arm around him. "Keep your head up, you're doing a hell of a job."

It was the first time that Harris had earned praise since the Czech game. At halftime it was 34–32, Indiana, after Alford shocked everyone by missing a free throw with four seconds left. Still, Knight was pleased. Standing in the shower room that he and the coaches used for their meeting, he said firmly, "There's no doubt in my mind that we can play with anybody."

They played with Louisville until the final seconds. In the end, the foul trouble that plagued Harris and Thomas did them in. And at the finish Louisville guard Milt Wagner, a fifth-year player who had been out the entire 1985 season with a broken foot, found his missing shooting touch. He finished the game with twenty-two points—five less than Alford—but made seven of eight free throws down the stretch. The last two came with Louisville leading 62–61 and ten seconds left.

Knight called time to try to rattle Wagner and to set up a play in case he missed. "I think he's going to miss," he told the players, "and we're going to hit a shot and win the game."

Wagner didn't miss. Louisville won 65–63. But the point had been made. Playing an excellent team on the road, the chance had been there. Knight was encouraged. There was no crying, no gnashing of teeth. They had played well and so had Louisville. Games like this were excellent preparation for the Big Ten. "We've got Iowa State in three days," Knight said. "Let's not have a repeat of Kansas State."

When Klingelhoffer came to get Knight for the press conference, the players were almost dressed. Crum had taken a long time. "I can't go," Knight said. "I've got to get these kids home. Some of them have exams in the morning. Explain that to them." Klingelhoffer asked Knight for a couple of comments about the game he could take back. Knight gave them to him.

While Klingelhoffer went to type these quotes, he sent his assistant, Eric Ruden, to tell Louisville SID Kenny Klein that Knight wouldn't be coming to the press conference because the players had to get home for exams in the morning. Klein then announced only that Knight would not be coming to the press conference.

Knight had done himself in again. His reason for skipping the press conference was legitimate. But even so, if he had taken ten minutes to go in and answer a few questions, it would have made little difference to the players and would have avoided any problems. Even if his explanation had been properly relayed through channels, the fact remained that because of his past, Knight was always going to be guilty until proved innocent in the eyes of most reporters. Was this fair? No. But it was the same way Knight viewed most reporters.

The newspaper reports the next day said that Knight had refused to attend the postgame press conference. Technically, this was accurate, though incomplete. When Knight saw this reference in a game story in *The Indianapolis Star*, he exploded. He called Klingelhoffer down to the locker room. Klingelhoffer explained what had happened. Knight was, to put it mildly, unhappy with Klingelhoffer. "I get enough crap from those people without this kind of thing happening," he said. "Jesus Christ, is that fair, Kit?"

Klingelhoffer escaped. Knight walked into the bathroom. For a moment there was silence. Then he began kicking the bathroom stall. He stormed back into the room, kicked the phone sitting on the floor and the garbage can in the corner. "I just can't take it anymore," he yelled.

To Knight, this was a classic case of being unfairly made out as a villain. This is an image Knight has appeared to court for years but, in fact, he hates it. He hadn't been upset after the game; he had been pleased with the way the team had played. But now, it looked to the public like old Bobby was sulking over a loss again. He blamed Klingelhoffer, and he blamed the *Star* reporter, Bill Benner. But Benner hadn't reported the incident any differently than other writers, Knight had seen only his story.

Once, Knight probably would have stayed angry over such an incident for several days. But he has come a long way in letting go of incidents that involve the media. Losses he cannot let go of, but he has consciously worked at caring less about what is said and written about him. He still gets angry, as the Louisville incident illustrates, and will brood at times about what he sees as mistreatment, but on a scale of one to ten he has improved from a solid one to perhaps a five over the years.

That is progress. Because of that progress, the two days of practice between Louisville and Iowa State were brisk, sharp, and almost temper-free. The players were still in exams on Thursday and Friday, and Knight didn't want to add any pressure. Because of the exam schedule, he worried that they might be flat for Iowa State, a good team that had already beaten Iowa and Michigan State earlier in the month. Iowa State was coached by Johnny Orr, a longtime Knight buddy. Knight had respected Orr when he coached at Michigan, and he thought Orr had his most talented team in six years at Iowa State.

Knight was correct, as Iowa State would prove by reaching the NCAA round of sixteen, but if truth be told he had absolutely no reason to worry about this game. With exams over Friday, the players were scheduled to go home to see their families after the game on Saturday—unless they played poorly and put Knight in such a bad mood that he decided not to send them home. Or, he might decide to bring them back on Christmas Eve—that had happened in the past. The players wanted none of this. They wanted to win and go home. When they walked into pregame meal on Saturday morning, a message was waiting on their plates: "You have to earn this Christmas present." Knight knew how to appeal to basic desires.

The score was 17–4 before Iowa State knew what had happened. By halftime it was 44–26. Knight started Robinson on Iowa State's star guard Jeff Hornacek, ordering him to stay with Hornacek all over the floor, not to switch, not to look for help. He wanted Robinson to use his quickness to deny Hornacek the basketball. This was an ideal assignment for Robinson because he only had to concentrate on one thing: Hornacek.

Hornacek was one for six at halftime, and not a factor. Nothing changed in the second half. Iowa State crept briefly to within fourteen, but Thomas (thirty-one points) and Alford (twenty-four) pounded away, and the lead grew to 74–49 with 7:54 to play. Indiana was making a good team look helpless. Even with Calloway and Harris shooting a combined five for fifteen, Iowa State had no chance. The only hitches in the whole act came late. Jadlow got careless with a couple of rebounds, allowing Iowa State to get to within seventeen. Knight called time to berate Jadlow for careless play. And in the final minute, someone in the stands noticed that Harris had his uniform shirt hanging out. "Tuck your shirt in, Andre," he yelled. Harris reached for the shirt as everyone laughed. Knight did not. He sent Brooks over to tell Harris to get the damn shirt in. He did.

The final was 86–65. Merry Christmas.

As the players charged into the locker room, Royce Waltman looked at the other coaches and said, "Now that's the way to strike a blow for liberty." That's exactly what they had done. They had four days of liberty. Normally, Knight would have asked them to be back Christmas morning because they had a game on December 27. But he was so pleased he gave them the morning off, meaning most of them could spend it with their families.

"Come back ready to go, though," he warned. "When we get back, Michigan will only be a week away." Michigan. The Big Ten. The players knew they had better enjoy Christmas while they could.

Knight was almost obsessed with Michigan. The Wolverines had won the Big Ten championship in a runaway the year before, winning their last fifteen league games. One of their losses had been in the opener, at Ann Arbor, when Indiana destroyed them by twenty-five points. That had been before the collapse at Indiana. Now, Michigan had everyone back from that team and was a heavy favorite to win the league again.

But Michigan was more than just the league favorite. The Wolverines were coached by Bill Frieder, a longtime Orr assistant coach who had been given the job in 1980 when Orr left for Iowa State. Once, Knight and Frieder had been friends. Frieder was one of those young coaches who looked up to Knight, asked him for advice, and treated him like one of the game's statesmen.

In 1981, just prior to the start of the national championship game, Frieder had gone to the locker room to wish Knight luck. A photographer had taken a picture of them standing together in the hallway outside the locker room. For Frieder's fortieth birthday, Knight had the picture laminated and signed it, "To Bill, who no doubt will be on the other side of this picture (playing for the national championship) some day soon." Frieder was so proud of the picture he hung it right next to the desk in his office.

In January 1983, when Indiana blew Michigan out in Bloomington, Knight went into the Michigan locker room to tell the players that if they stuck to what they were doing and listened to Coach Frieder, they would be a fine team someday. That freshman group was now the senior nucleus of the current team.

It all changed between Frieder and Knight in 1984. The day before an Indiana-Michigan game in Ann Arbor, Frieder came to see Knight at practice. He had a problem. The local writer in Ann Arbor was really on his case about changing lineups. The writer maintained that Frieder was indecisive and this was proof. Would Knight talk to him?

This was quite a favor to ask, especially the day before a game. But Knight almost never says no to a friend, and Frieder was a friend. When the writer came to see Knight after practice, Knight said to him, "Tell me, do you think I'm a good coach?"

"I think you're the best."

"Well, let me tell you something. There probably isn't a coach in America who changes lineups more than me. It doesn't mean you're indecisive. It means you're still looking for a combination that works. That's what Bill is doing here."

The next day, the writer's column was, more or less, an apology to Frieder for questioning him. If Bob Knight said it was right, then it was right.

That day during the game, Knight got entangled in a messy argument with the officials near the end of the first half. He was given a technical. He continued screaming. As he did, he heard Frieder a few feet away yelling, "Give him another technical!" When the half ended, Knight went after Frieder in the runway leading to the locker rooms. He was enraged. Knight doesn't think any coach should get involved in another coach's argument. But for Frieder to do this one day after he had asked for—and received—the kind of favor Knight had done for him was inexcusable. In no uncertain terms, Knight told Frieder just that.

Frieder maintains that he didn't realize Knight had been given a technical and he was trying to tell the officials that what Knight was saying merited one. Either way, he was involved when Knight thought he had no right to be involved. As far as Knight was concerned, that was the end of the friendship. Apologies were a waste of time. Frieder took down the picture next to his desk. "I didn't think Bob would want me to have it there," he said.

Two years later, Frieder regretted the incident and still hoped that someday Knight would forgive him. It would, at the very least, take a while.

Before Michigan came to town there was the little matter of playing the post-Christmas Hoosier Classic. This was a four-year-old Indianapolis version of the Indiana Classic. Because I.U. is so popular that it can sell 15,000 seats in Indianapolis regardless of the opponent, this tournament had been invented. It meant Indiana never had to play away at Christmas, and all the revenues from the two tournaments were profit because expenses in Bloomington were zero and in Indianapolis near zero.

The opposition in this tournament would be Idaho, Mississippi State, and San Jose State. Even Knight had to concede that Indiana would be hard-pressed to lose to any of these teams. Because of this, Knight did something that no one could ever remember him doing in the past: he looked beyond an opponent. The Christmas day practice and the two the following day were spiced with constant talk about Michigan.

"I am not interested in beating Idaho or San Jose State or Mississippi State," Knight said during practice. "I'm interested in beating Michigan."

Hammel, hearing this, was shocked. So was Tim Knight. Neither could ever remember hearing Knight talk to his team about a game before it was the next game on the schedule. "I worry," Hammel said, "about putting so much into one game."

They didn't put much into the Idaho game. Perhaps the first half of this game was proof of the Knight theory that you have to build up every opponent. Indiana was sloppy, sleepy, not into the game. A 5-9 guard for Idaho named Chris Carey hit his first five shots. Idaho actually led, 25–23, with 4:49 left in the half before Indiana came back to lead 37–33 at the break.

"I am so depressed I don't even want to talk," Knight told the players. "I'm through fighting you kids. I can't do it anymore." Then he cleared the locker room: assistant coaches, doctors, trainers, managers. For four minutes it was just Knight and the players. He said nothing he hadn't said before but the message was clear—and loud.

Knight stalked onto the floor still angry. He called Crabb over to the bench. One of Crabb's jobs is to supervise Indiana's cheerleaders. "This crowd is dead, absolutely dead," Knight told Crabb. "I don't want these people [the cheerleaders] out here just to be seen. I want them doing something. I want them to get these people in the damn game. If they don't do it, they won't be here tomorrow night."

Crabb understood. He also understood that the world's greatest cheerleaders would have had trouble getting a response to the first half that had just been played. But he wasn't about to point that out to Knight.

Fortunately for Crabb, the cheerleaders, and everyone else inside the city limits, the players responded to their halftime whipping. After six more minutes of struggle they scored ten straight points to turn a 47–41 lead into a 57–41 lead in a two-minute stretch. The lead just kept building from there and the final was 87–57.

Calloway, who had struggled before Christmas, had twenty-six points, and Alford had twenty-four. But the real hero was Delray Brooks, who came off the bench to spark everyone. Brooks had only four points, but he had seven assists and outhustled everyone on the floor. He earned himself a start with his play and got a standing ovation at the end of the game. The second-half margin was 50–24. Everyone breathed a deep sigh of relief.

The opponent in the final would be Mississippi State. Knight worried about their quickness, but there was no need. It was 46–22 by halftime, and the final was 74–43. Brooks and Jadlow both got starts. Jadlow finished with ten points and eight rebounds and had Knight raving about his toughness.

The whole day was a high for Knight. That afternoon, he and Kohn Smith walked across the street from the hotel to a Bob Evans restaurant. Knight loves to eat in Bob Evans. Whenever Indiana stays in a hotel near a Bob Evans, Knight is apt to eat there three times a day, the last time usually at two or three in the morning. Many a Knight diet has gone aglimmering at Bob Evans over apple pie and ice cream in the wee hours on the morning of a game.

Knight was sipping an iced tea when a boy of about twelve gingerly approached him. Behind him were two older men; one appeared to be his older brother, the other his father. Knight is eminently approachable in these situations, patient and polite. He always signs an autograph when asked politely.

The young man's name was Garland Loper. Shyly, he explained that his father and older brother were deaf-mutes and would like to meet Coach Knight. Garland was the family spokesman. When the other two wanted to say something they signed it to him and he spoke it to the world. Knight was completely charmed by Garland Loper. He talked for several minutes to the three Lopers, gave them his autograph, and asked Garland for his address. When Knight returned to school, he had Indiana shirts, brochures, and an autographed team picture sent to the Lopers. Then he called and invited the whole family to come to a game.

"Sometimes," he said softly, leaving the restaurant, "you see what it really means to have guts."

Several hours later, Landon Turner wheeled himself into the Indiana locker room. Turner had graduated the previous spring, and Knight had helped get him a job working in minority counseling at the Indiana-Indianapolis campus. Turner said hello all around the room. When Knight walked in, he looked at the gaudy sneakers Turner was wearing. They were Air-Jordans, the Michael Jordan–sponsored shoe that had become the rage among kids.

"Where did you get those?"

"Mike Jordan sent them to me. . . . Airmail."

"Yeah, well they make you look like a fag."

A moment later, after the team had gone out to warm up and the locker room was virtually empty, Knight walked over to shake hands with Turner. "Your grip, Landon, it's really getting stronger." Turner beamed. The two men talked for several minutes, Knight's arm around Turner the whole time. As they left the locker room, Knight asked Turner if he was coming to Bloomington for the Michigan game. "I'm going to try, Coach," Turner said.

They had reached the door now. People were milling around outside, finding their way to seats. Knight changed his tone as soon as they were outside. "You better get your fat ass down there or you're going to be in trouble. You got it?"

Turner grinned. "I got it, Coach."

He wheeled off to find his seat. Knight went off to watch his team rout Mississippi State. When it was over, there wasn't much he could say. "I don't think we can play much better than that," he told the coaches. "They've done just about everything we've asked of them so far."

So far. One year ago the record had been 8–2 going into Big Ten play. Now, it was 8–2. There had been hope then. There was hope now. But there was also a hint of fear. No one could even bear the thought of déjà vu. In three days, 1985 would be over. If 1986 was anything like 1985 had been, there might not be a 1987.

10.

Déjà Vu

The day after the Mississippi State game was about as close to a day off as Knight gives the team during the season. They met for about thirty minutes to go over Michigan's personnel, but that was all. The next day, Monday, would begin a four-day period that would burn with intensity. Classes did not start for another two weeks, so Knight expected his players to think nothing but basketball.

It is impossible to overstate how much Knight wanted to beat Michigan. He wanted this game to send a message to the basketball world that Indiana was most definitely back. Notre Dame had offered a clue, and the near misses at Kentucky and Louisville might have caught some people's eyes. But to beat Michigan, the top-heavy favorite in a conference where Indiana had been picked anywhere from third to fifth in preseason, would most certainly get the attention of basketball people.

What's more, the game was at home. In Knight's first thirteen years at Indiana, the Hoosiers had compiled a record of 99–12 in Big Ten games played at Assembly Hall. In 1985, they went 3–6, losing their last four home games. This was unacceptable to Knight. Now, the Big Ten season would open with home games against Michigan and Michigan State—both teams that had won at Indiana the previous season. Knight wanted to get things back to normal quickly, and he felt that to have any chance to win the Big Ten, Indiana had to win these two games.

They practiced twice on Monday and twice on Tuesday, New Year's Eve. Knight was in a barely controlled fury in each workout. On Monday morning he told them they had practiced well, were doing just what they had to, and were going to win the game. On Monday afternoon, he threw them out. On Tuesday morning, he told them that this was the first game he had ever gone into as a coach believing his team had no chance to win. On Tuesday afternoon, he told them if they just played hard Michigan would fold down the stretch.

Up and down he went, the team bouncing along with him.

Someone made a good play and he knew Michigan was going to lose. Someone made a bad play and he couldn't see any point to even showing up for the game on Thursday.

Knight was so intense about the game that he even made a plea to the fans on his TV show, pointing out that the students were still away and their support, their noise, would be badly needed on Thursday. He was distressed because there were still some tickets left. He wanted a sellout, day after New Year's or not.

The only time Knight took a break from coaching, looking at tape, or asking the assistants over and over, "Do we have any chance?" was to watch football. When Army beat Illinois in the Peach Bowl on New Year's Eve, Knight was delighted. "It just proves," he said, "that God does watch football games sometimes."

It was on New Year's Day that Knight put his game face firmly into place. There was only one practice that day, in the afternoon, but it was a war. When the white team spurted for a few minutes, Knight was furious. "Reds, you are getting eaten alive by the white team. You play like this tomorrow, it's gonna be 20–25 points and you'll never be in the f—— ballgame."

This was normal day-before-a-big-game stuff. Everyone understood. Everyone knew how much Knight wanted to beat Michigan. If it had stayed that way until the end of practice, everyone would have gone home feeling good, feeling ready. But then the simmering antagonism between Knight and Alford, that feeling of rivalry that seems to exist just below the surface in their relationship, exploded in everyone's face.

It started when Knight decided that Alford had not picked up quickly enough on defense. "Goddamn it, Alford, how many times do I have to tell you about finding your man on conversion?" Knight said. "How many f—— times?"

What Knight had not seen—what he would see later on tape—was that Alford had been accidentally bumped going down the floor by Daryl Thomas. He had been with his man until Thomas sent him flying. Alford started to explain. "I don't want to hear it," Knight broke in. "I don't want to hear your excuses. I'm sick of them."

Knight threw his most withering glare at Alford. To everyone's surprise, including Knight's, Alford glared right back—if only for a moment. That was enough, though. From that point on, Alford could do nothing right. Indiana players are not supposed to glare back.

The only Knight player who had ever made a habit of glaring back at Knight was Ted Kitchel. Now, Knight grudgingly admitted that Kitchel was one of the toughest, most stubborn players he had ever coached. Then, he made Kitchel's life miserable. Players still told the story about the postgame tirade that Knight had ended by glaring right at Kitchel. Kitchel glared right back. The two of them had stood there glaring for what seemed like an hour while everyone else just sat and watched them.

Alford was a little bit like Kitchel. Not as openly stubborn or rebellious, but like Kitchel, he had a definite love-hate relationship with Knight. "I can't tell you how important my relationship with him is to me," Kitchel said of Knight. "It makes me feel like I'm special just because I had a chance to play for him. I still care what he thinks of me. Probably too much, but I do. And yet, he makes me feel uncomfortable when I'm around him, and I can vividly remember times when I hated him. Really hated him."

The one that most people remembered most had happened in 1983. Knight had just finished blistering the team, telling them how awful they were, how they would probably never win another game. Finished, Knight stalked out the door. Or so Kitchel thought. What Knight had done was walk around the corner to the door where he could not be seen and stopped.

Thinking Knight was gone, Kitchel turned to the team and said, "Just ignore him. He's full of shit. We aren't nearly that bad."

With that, Knight roared around the corner. He grabbed Kitchel's red notebook and tore it up, throwing the pages all over the locker room. Kitchel, he vowed, would never play again, he would suffer for this. Kitchel just sat and stared at Knight. For two days he didn't practice and when he did practice again, Knight chased him up and down the court kicking him in the rear end, yelling, "Move, Kitchel, move!"

Several weeks later, Kitchel, who had undergone back surgery as a freshman and then come back to lead Indiana in scoring as a junior and senior, played what turned out to be his last game.

It was at Iowa. His back had been getting worse and worse, and he had soaked it almost the entire night just so he could walk on the floor.

"I played five minutes and I could barely walk, much less run," Kitchel remembered. "I had to come out. That night he [Knight] came to see me. 'I know how hard you tried, Ted,' he said. 'You gave this team everything you had and I want you to know I know that and appreciate it.'

"It was as if he knew it was over and he didn't have to get all over me anymore. He had done what he had to do."

Someday, Knight would tell Alford how much he appreciated how hard he had tried. But not on New Year's Day, 1986. He picked on Alford and picked on him and finally, when Alford shot him another look, he threw him out. "You go take a shower," he screamed. "And if you ever give me another rotten look like that you'll never f—— play here again."

Alford left. The last thing the team needed twenty-four hours before playing Michigan was a Knight-Alford feud. Or for Alford to miss any practice time. Knight realized the latter. Five minutes after bouncing Alford, he went into the locker room after him. His angry words could be heard from the floor. Both reappeared a few minutes later. Alford made it to the end of practice without further incident, but the focus had shifted: On a day when the team truly needed to feel like a team, everyone was wondering what would happen next between the coach and his best player.

Knight would not have been Knight if the end of practice had marked the end of the incident. He called Alford outside the locker room after dismissing the rest of the team for the evening. "I want to tell you just how mad I was at you after that Kentucky game," he began. The Kentucky game was now twenty-four days ago. No matter. Knight was still getting the last word.

———

As always, even amidst the feuds and the blowups, Knight had done a superb job of getting his team ready to play a big game. He even had the crowd—a sellout finally—ready to play. They were louder and more into the game than at any time all season.

During the afternoon walk-through, Knight kept reminding the players that Michigan was going to come in overconfident. "We're

going to have a hell of an opportunity, because they're going to
come in here fatheaded," he said. "They haven't played anybody
tough to play in a month. We will be tough to play."

Knight casually mentioned during the walk-through that he
had noticed on the tape that Alford had been knocked flying by
Thomas on the play that had started the flareup the previous day.
It was as close to an apology as Knight was going to come with
Alford.

Everything Knight wanted was there. The players were wound
tight. "I've never seen us like this in a walk-through," Kreigh
Smith said to Joe Hillman. "We're going to win this game."

They began as if they intended to win by fifty points. It was
8–0 Indiana before the game was three minutes old, and Frieder
had to call time. The place was rocking. Alford shook his fist at
the crowd in his excitement after a Michigan turnover. Harris
began the game with a thunderous dunk off a gorgeous pass from
Morgan. Calloway hit twice. Harris hit again. Michigan couldn't
find the basket.

All was right with the world.

But it didn't last. Poised and experienced, Michigan methodi-
cally came back. It outscored Indiana 11–2 to take the lead, and
just kept building the lead. Indiana couldn't keep Michigan from
getting the ball inside. Alford was being blanketed by Michigan
guard Gary Grant. The frustration quickly built inside Knight's
head. It was last year all over again. During a time-out he screamed
at Calloway. "You can beat all the f—— Mississippi States in the
world with your bullshit but you can't beat anybody any good
with it. Get in the game or get the hell out."

Dakich grabbed Calloway leaving the huddle to soothe him.
The game was ten minutes old and things were getting out of
hand. A moment later, Thomas was called for charging by London
Bradley, perhaps Knight's least favorite official. It was Bradley
who had made the call that had led to the chair throw. Knight
certainly hadn't forgotten. Neither had Bradley.

When Bradley called Thomas for charging, Knight was off the
bench, yelling at him. A few seconds later, when Thomas missed
a shot inside, Knight was certain he had been fouled. Bradley, on
the play, made no call. "You stupid sonofabitch, can't you see
anything?" Knight railed.

Bradley could certainly hear. He stopped and nailed Knight with a technical. The score was already 23–14. After the technical, it was 25–14. It could have become a complete disaster at that point, but Michigan, on a 25–6 run, finally cooled, and Indiana limped to the locker room trailing 35–27 at halftime.

There were no tantrums at halftime. Knight was angry, but not hysterical. Thomas (zero rebounds) had backed down from Michigan center Roy Tarpley. Alford had taken bad shots. Calloway had forgotten what he was supposed to do. "You are going to play teams like this for eighteen straight games," Knight said. "You can't play like this and beat anybody."

They decided to try Jadlow on Tarpley to start the second half and Robinson in Morgan's place. They wanted Robinson's quickness and Jadlow's size. Harris had played well, but Jadlow's extra height and bulk were needed against Tarpley.

It took less than three minutes to get the lead down to 39–37. It took Michigan another three minutes to punch the margin back up to 50–39. It was almost as if the Wolverines were toying with them: let them get close, then pull away again. The lead was 56–44 when Alford finally got going. He hit from twenty feet to cut it to ten. He hit again to cut it to eight. Calloway hit twice. Alford made a steal and fed Morgan for a layup and suddenly it was 60–56 with more than six minutes left to play.

Richard Rellford hit one free throw to make it 61–56. Alford promptly bombed again. It was 61–58. The crowd was berserk. But Michigan was not going to fold. Grant hit from the baseline. Alford answered. Butch Wade hit two foul shots. Alford answered again. Alford now had twelve points in six minutes. Michigan still led 65–62.

"Defensive possession," Knight screamed. "One time on defense." But they couldn't. Rellford, a nonshooter, hit a ten-footer. There were still more than three minutes left. Steve Eyl, playing for the fouled-out Thomas, flashed open inside. His layup rolled around the rim. Harris went up as if to tip the ball, but pulled back. The ball rolled in to cut the lead to three again.

But no. Charging into the lane came London Bradley, waving his arms. Harris, Bradley said, had touched the ball on the rim. Harris had not touched the ball, in fact, he hadn't come close to touching it. The official with the best view of the play, Phil Bova, had watched the play and turned to run downcourt. Bradley had made a horrendous call, and one had to wonder if at least subconsciously—like Tom Rucker at Kentucky—he hadn't been saying, "Take that, you sonofabitch."

Knight had to be physically restrained by Wright and Bomba. "Grab me, Brad," he said, "because if you don't, I'll hit the sonofabitch." They grabbed him.

Bradley's call ended Indiana's chances. The Hoosiers never got closer than four after that call. Would they have won if he had not made that call? Probably not. Michigan had taken every shot Indiana had thrown and never looked shaken. But there was no telling Knight that later on.

The locker room was a morgue. Knight didn't scream, but he railed. Daryl Thomas had somehow played the entire game without getting a rebound. "You might as well not have even shown up tonight," he told Thomas. Alford's first-half fist-shaking rankled. "What kind of bullshit was that, Alford? You can take that bullshit and go straight back to New Castle High School. We don't need that kind of crap here.

"Boys, is this going to be last year all over again? Are we ever going to win a game that means something again?"

The sense of dread hung heavy in the locker room. Five straight losses at home in the Big Ten. Five. Hammel's concern about putting too much emphasis on one game now loomed as reality. The coaches' tape session was stormy, Knight getting up and leaving several times to walk off his frustration. Finally, just after 2 A.M., they went to the Big Wheel to eat. Knight never said a word until he stood up to leave.

He looked at his four assistants, each of them bleary-eyed with exhaustion. "I waited nine f—— months to play this game," he said. "Nine months. I can't tell you how sick of basketball I am right now. If I never see another basketball game in my life, that will be just fine."

———

By noon the next morning, Knight wasn't the only one feeling that way. The day after at Indiana is always a nightmare. Knight has seen the tape and then seen the mistakes in his sleep—or nonsleep—all night. Losing a Big Ten game at Indiana is, in the

The young mentor: Bob Knight, in his first year at Indiana, chats with Adolph Rupp before Indiana's 90-89 double-overtime win at Kentucky in December 1971. (*Dave Repp photo*)

The 1986 Knight, with athletic director Ralph Floyd at his feet, watches practice. (*Dave Repp photo*)

The assistants in the cave: from left, assistant coaches Joby Wright and Royce Waltman, Bob Hammel of the *Bloomington Herald-Telephone,* and assistants Kohn Smith and Ron Felling. (*Dave Repp photo*)

Knight and Hammel at practice. (*Dave Repp photo*)

Teaching, teaching, and more teaching: Knight brings home a point to Courtney Witte, Daryl Thomas, and Winston Morgan. (*Dave Repp photo*)

The 1985-86 Indiana University basketball team: (*Bottom row*) Todd Meier, Courtney Witte, Stew Robinson, Winston Morgan, Steve Alford, Kreigh Smith, Joe Hillman, Delray Brooks. (*Top row*) Jeff Oliphant, Magnus Pelkowski, Ricky Calloway, Steve Eyl, Daryl Thomas, Todd Jadlow, Andre Harris, Brian Sloan.

Steve Alford driving against Kansas State. (*Dave Repp photo*)

Daryl Thomas works on his defense against Magnus Pelkowski in practice. (*Dave Repp photo*)

Winston Morgan gets in position for a rebound against Wisconsin. (*Dave Repp photo*)

Andre Harris skies to reject a Notre Dame shot. (*Dave Repp photo*)

Daryl Thomas grabs a rebound against Purdue, as Alford (12) and Harris look on. (*Dave Repp photo*)

A critical element of Knight's preparation is the pregame walk-through. From left: Courtney Witte (watching), Kreigh Smith, Steve Eyl, Stew Robinson (at back, watching), Jeff Oliphant, Steve Alford (back to camera), Todd Meier, and Magnus Pelkowski. (*Dave Repp photo*)

Ricky Calloway with Knight on the sidelines at Assembly Hall.
(*Dave Repp photo*)

"Will we ever win another game?" (*Dave Repp photo*)

words of manager Jim Kelly, "like having someone die, only worse. Much worse."

Knight cannot stand to lose. Not in the way that most competitors cannot stand to lose; it goes far beyond that. It tears him apart emotionally, largely because he somehow equates losing a basketball game with his self-worth. He seems to believe that people will think less of him if his team doesn't play well. Because he is a man whose emotions know no perspective, losing is like death to him—to steal a line from football coach George Allen. He doesn't merely brood over it, he rages at it. Everyone is to blame: the players, the coaches, the system, and anyone else who happens to wander into view.

Exactly why Knight is so destroyed by defeat isn't easy to understand. Certainly, part of it stems from his competitiveness. Knight competes at everything he does, every day, and enjoys the fact that he wins most of the time. But even though he will rationalize the loss and seemingly not blame himself, always, ultimately, he blames himself. Somewhere, he failed. That failure may have taken place four years earlier when he failed to recruit a certain player or did recruit another one. It may have taken place with thirty seconds to go when he made an incorrect substitution. Somewhere, somehow, he failed. Somehow, that failure is just that—*failure*—and it tears at Knight's gut. It leaves him angry, frustrated, and unable—or at least unwilling—to deal with the world on civil terms for hours, perhaps days, sometimes weeks, depending on the dimensions of the defeat.

Intellectually, Knight knows he is a good coach and that one loss, or even one losing season, won't change that. And he knows that people will not stop respecting his coaching ability. But emotionally, he seems to believe that everyone else will see the score with Indiana on the short end and laugh and point and think, *"Bob Knight failed."* In truth, few people give any basketball game or any basketball coach even that much thought. But Knight doesn't see that. Defeat somehow takes a giant chip out of his self-esteem. It makes him miserable, and in turn all those around him miserable.

The players were in at 11 A.M. to look at the Michigan tape. That lasted about thirty minutes. Everyone was guilty. Harris was more guilty. Alford was most guilty of all. Knight finally stalked out of the room after asking Alford, "Will you ever, just once, take a charge?" He was back ten seconds later. "You guys sit here for a while and if you still want to have a team, then you come and tell us."

These were the days the players hated most. These were the times that had caused earlier generations to refer to Assembly Hall as "Monroe County Jail." That was what it felt like. The locker room was a cell and the building was a prison. There was no escape. They sat looking at each other. What was there to say? It had all been said. But they had to play the coach's game. So Alford, Morgan, and Robinson walked to the coaches' locker room to tell Knight that, yes, they still wanted to have a team. One wonders what would happen someday if the captains walked in and told Knight, "You're right, coach, it's hopeless, let's cancel the season."

Knight looked at the three players. It was Alford he was most angry with. He had harped on the fist-shaking and had decided after watching the tape that Alford wasn't guarding anybody again. So when the players reported that they wanted to play, Knight said simply, "Yeah, but Steve doesn't guard anybody."

Robinson came to the rescue. "That may be so, Coach," he said. "But the rest of us didn't do much guarding, either." That saved Alford—at least for the moment. Knight decided he would grant the request to continue the season.

In fact, Indiana had not played a bad game. It had shot 66 percent, including a remarkable nineteen of twenty-five in the second half. Michigan had just been a little bit better. Knight knew this, and to some extent was already blaming the officials for the loss. But he couldn't let it go. Every mistake seemed to dance in his mind's eye. Officials or no officials, good shooting or no good shooting, *they had lost. At home. To a coach he didn't like.*

Practice that evening was the longest of the season—two and one-half hours. Michigan State would be in Sunday. There could be no question about winning that game. Before the players even went on the floor, Knight had written on the board, "99–12; 3–7." The first number was Indiana's record at home from 1971 to 1984 in Big Ten play. The second was the last two seasons, the

Michigan game tacked on. "Doesn't that make you people feel sick?" he said.

After they worked, Waltman went through the Michigan State personnel. All the assistant coaches knew the players were tired and discouraged, because *they* were tired and discouraged. Waltman is ordinarily the most low-key member of the coaching staff. He is quiet most of the time, but a man blessed with a keen wit and an intensity that he usually keeps inside. Normally, his scouting reports are straightforward, to the point. But he wanted the players to be ready Sunday. And the key to beating Michigan State was stopping Scott Skiles.

Skiles was the classic dead-end kid, a stocky little guard, described by his coach Jud Heathcote as "a fat little white kid." Three times in little more than a year he had been arrested: once for cocaine possession, twice for driving under the influence. Knight, who was friendly with Heathcote, was shocked that Heathcote let him remain on the team. Because Skiles had a reputation for getting into trouble in high school, Knight hadn't recruited him even though he was from Indiana. Skiles had responded by helping Michigan State beat Indiana four times in six tries, including two of three at Indiana. Waltman wanted to be sure that amidst all the putdowns of Skiles the players remembered how good a player he was.

"We've made a big thing here the last few years about what an asshole he is," Waltman said. "He probably is, but if you don't respect him as a person, you better respect him as a player. Don't just write him off as that jerk from Plymouth because he's come in here a couple times and stuck it up our ass. The way to get him is to respect him as a player first and then stick it up his ass."

They went out for a walk-through after that. Everyone was dragging by the time they left the floor at eight o'clock. "Back at eleven," Knight told them.

They were back at eleven in the morning, on the floor at 11:05, and back in the locker room at 11:13. It took Knight that long to blow up at Harris for going after a rebound with one hand. "Coach," Harris said, "I couldn't get it with two hands, all I could do was tip it."

"Oh really, Andre," Knight answered. "Well, that's all I want to see of that crap this morning." Into the locker room they went. The assistants stayed on the floor, under orders, while Knight went inside. Five minutes later, everyone was back again.

Knight cooled off after that. He went back to teaching and encouraging. He seemed to have caught himself, at least for a moment, just when things seemed about to spin out of control. It didn't last. Alford was caught standing on defense. "Put on a white shirt, Steve, you be Skiles. Maybe you can help us that way." That started the Steve Alford show again. It was still going on when Calloway came down hard on his left ankle and didn't get up. Garl helped him off. It was a sprain. Shortly before one, Knight sent them home. "Be back here at five, taped and ready to go," he said. Then he went hunting.

A second practice the day before a game, especially an afternoon game, was almost unheard of. The players had practiced twice Monday, twice Tuesday, and once Wednesday; they had played Michigan on Thursday, looked at tape for two hours and practiced and walked through for almost three on Friday, and practiced for almost two on Saturday.

It was probably too much. The best thing would have been a brief walk-through in the evening and a good night's sleep, but Knight was still hurting because of the Michigan loss. The coaches knew this, but knew it was futile to try to change his thinking. "He just can't let go, can he?" Felling said to the others.

The hunting seemed to help Knight's mood. "We aren't going to practice that long," he told the players, as if to tell them things were about to get better. "Ricky, how's your ankle? Better? Good. If you weren't so damn clumsy you wouldn't get hurt."

Garl had already told him that Calloway shouldn't practice that night, but could play in the game. Knight was relieved.

The practice was clumsy. Pelkowski went down early, holding his ankle. Two sprains in one day. Thomas caught an elbow in the jaw and came out briefly. They had been going at it for about forty minutes when Knight walked over to Kohn Smith. "Think we've done enough?" he said.

"Absolutely," said Smith, wanting to get everyone home as soon as possible.

"Couple more plays," said Knight.

Two plays later, Thomas went up for a rebound. No one touched him, but the minute he hit the ground he let out a shriek of pain. Somehow, his foot had twisted under him as he landed. He was in agony, howling in pain as he writhed on the floor. Knight stood rooted to the spot where he stood, his face pale. He turned his back for a moment as if he thought when he turned back he would see Thomas standing again. He didn't. "Go to the other end," he told the other players who stood staring at Thomas. "Shoot some free throws."

Thomas was still rolling on the floor, screaming, "Oh no, oh no." He was convinced he had broken his ankle. When Garl tried to take his sneaker off, Thomas panicked, cried, "No, no, don't take it off." Knight walked over to Thomas and put his hand on his shoulder. "Calm down, Daryl," he said and stood there until Garl called for Wright and Smith to help Thomas into the training room.

"Let's go inside," he said to the others.

The mood was now funereal. The anger had gone out of Knight. Already, he was mentally kicking himself for the second practice, for staying on the floor too long. "Okay," he said calmly, "we don't know if Daryl can play or not. But you really practiced well tonight."

Thomas was going to the hospital for X-rays. Clearly, he would not play the next day. "I'll bet it's broken," said Joe Hillman, voicing everyone's thoughts.

Knight had committed to flying to Muncie that night to see a high school game. He told the assistants to wait until Thomas came back from the hospital. "Make sure he's okay," Knight said, knowing Thomas would be in a cast of some kind and scared. He went into the snowy night looking about 100 years old.

The ankle was badly sprained. Prognosis: ten days to two weeks, minimum. That meant Thomas would miss at least three games: Michigan State, Northwestern, and Wisconsin. The goal, immediately, was to get him back playing in eleven days against Ohio State.

Jadlow would start in his place at center. Suddenly, a game that had looked tough but eminently winnable had become a struggle. All of this wounded Knight. He knew, deep down, that he had made a mistake by refusing to let go of the Michigan loss. Injuries are freaks, nothing more, but the more time you practice, the more chance there is for those freaks to occur. That Thomas's injury was the third sprained ankle of the day was testimony to how flukish such things are. But that it happened at a moment when the players should either have been listening to Knight talk or eating dinner was something Knight had to deal with.

Worst of all, the way the injury happened reminded everyone of last year. Team loses, coach overreacts, team goes further downhill. Knight seemed to be fighting a psychological war with himself: one part of his brain was telling him to take it easy, to be patient, to understand that the players were giving him everything they had. The other part was running amok, screaming at the indignity of defeat, pointing out every error on the tape and saying, "Everyone around me is failing but I'm not." One minute Knight was saying the team had played horribly against Michigan, the next he was saying the officials had stolen the game. One minute he was saying Michigan was as good as any team in the country, the next he was saying they weren't a very good team at all.

Knight was still dueling with himself Sunday morning when the players came in for walk-through. He began softly. "We have to play without Daryl today, boys, and that's not going to be easy because Daryl has really worked hard to make himself a much better player this year. But you other guys: Jadlow, Todd Meier, Whopper [Courtney Witte's nickname among the players was Whopper, and Knight had picked it up and started using it] are perfectly capable of stepping in and doing what Daryl has been doing.

"As a basketball team, we face different challenges. Thursday, our challenge was to beat a talented team and we failed. We're 0–1 with challenges this year." He hardened for a moment. "In fact, it's been so goddamn long since we met a challenge I can't remember the last one."

Soft again: "During the American Revolution Thomas Payne once said, 'These are the times that try men's souls.' Well, maybe. Maybe today we're going to be tried—challenged—twice. First, there is the challenge of bouncing back from a poor performance. We haven't met that challenge around here in a long time.

"Then there is the challenge of playing without Daryl in a game we simply have to have. I can't tell you how much we need to win this game. We need to respond to that challenge. Now, we can do that, go out and play like hell, or we can just use it as another excuse and go out and get our ass beat again."

He hardened again. "Challenges, boys. We have been absolutely destroyed by every challenge, every obstacle we've faced in the last two years. You have an excuse to lose today. If that's what you want, you have an excuse."

It was not so much an excuse as a fact: Indiana was not the same without Thomas. Without Thomas, Michigan State's too-small center, 6-6 Carlton Valentine, was suddenly an effective player. None of Thomas's subs had his quickness, and that was what Valentine had: quickness. All day long, he would get angles inside on Jadlow, Meier, and Eyl. For one day, he was an All-American, scoring twenty-one points—eighteen above his average. It never could have happened with Thomas playing.

The sight of Thomas on crutches seemed to send the Indiana crowd—which was 2,000 shy of a sellout after Thursday's disappointment—into a state of depression. In the locker room, before Knight came in for his final talk, Stew Robinson shook his head and muttered, "This whole place is like a morgue."

It only got worse. The first half was tight, Morgan doing a good job on Skiles by denying him the basketball, but Valentine and Larry Polec were hurting Indiana inside. Harris was struggling and Jadlow just wasn't quick enough to compete with the Spartans on the inside. A couple of silly plays near the end of the half and Michigan State led at intermission, 39–37.

The angry side of Knight was in control at halftime. Morgan, Calloway, and Alford had each made a foolish play that stuck in his mind. Morgan had hustled after a loose ball and thrown it back inbounds blind to a waiting Polec for an easy layup. "A goddamn sixth grader would know better than to make that play," Knight told Morgan. "Right off the top of my head, I can think of those three plays that cost us six points. It's like starting the game behind 6–0.

"When are you people going to start giving the effort necessary against these Big Ten teams? When? How long does this go on?"

He stalked into the hall, his shoulders sagging to his knees. "I can't take this anymore," he told the assistants. "I just can't take it. It makes me sick. You guys think of something."

It took Knight about three minutes to gather himself. They would change the lineup, play Eyl for Harris. Should they try Jadlow again? Yes, Knight said, because he had the best chance to score. "Boys," Knight told the players before they went back out, "now we're going to find out what kind of a team we've got here."

Those words seemed to hang in the air during the first five minutes of the second half. It was sheer disaster. Jadlow threw a stupid pass on the first possession and got yanked. Morgan threw a bad pass and Knight called time, yanked him, and slammed his clipboard in disgust. Calloway missed a short jumper. Skiles rebounded and went the length of the floor to make it 48–39. Eyl lost a rebound and he was pulled for Harris. Eight seconds later, Harris lost his man inside, fouled him, and found himself right back on the bench as Witte went in for him. It was standing room only in the doghouse, the crowd was booing, and Michigan State led 57–42.

Delray Brooks, who had not played one minute against Michigan, got a chance. He got screened for a Skiles bucket. Knight's voice could be heard all over Assembly Hall: "Delray, you have absolutely no idea what is going on out there."

It looked as if no one had any idea what was going on. But Indiana didn't quit. Alford made a steal and fed Robinson for a basket. He hit a jumper and then Calloway hit one. The lead was down to nine. The crowd came back into the game. Michigan State was a little rattled. Morgan stole the ball from Skiles. Valentine missed a layup. Alford hit two foul shots to make it 61–54.

They kept chipping away. A Robinson layup made it 66–64 with 4:32 left. Indiana had outscored Michigan State 20–7. The game turned. But Skiles stuck his nose back in, hit a tough baseline jumper, and Valentine rebounded a Polec miss. It was 70–65. Alford bombed to cut it to three. Valentine walked. Alford faked a jump shot, spun into the lane, and hit a soft bank shot from ten feet as he was being fouled. The free throw tied the game at seventy. There was 1:42 left. Indiana had come all the way back.

Challenges. Obstacles. Times that try men's souls. They were right there.

Polec tried a jump shot. It was no good. Valentine and Calloway went up for the rebound. Eric Harmon, one of the few Big Ten officials Knight truly liked, blew his whistle. Foul, Calloway. The contact had been minimal, but it had looked like Calloway had committed the foul. Once again, the tape would convince the coaches they had been jobbed. But at that moment everyone in the building, including Knight, thought Calloway had fouled.

Valentine calmly made both free throws with 1:10 left. This time, Alford couldn't get open. Robinson shot with the forty-five-second clock running out. Short. Valentine rebounded and fed Polec. He was fouled and made both shots. 74–70. Alford had one last jumper left to make it 74–72. They immediately fouled Darryl Johnson, who had played horribly (one of eight). Johnson made the first to get the lead to three. That was enough. Alford missed, Polec rebounded, and it was over, 77–74, Michigan State.

Déjà vu. They were reliving the nightmare. They were 0–2 in the Big Ten, both losses at home. "Don't even hang your heads," Knight said angrily. "Don't bother, because you don't care. Don't even try to tell me you care. Every time you make a mistake you just nod your head. I told you at the half about those six points that we gave them. Ricky, you foul on the rebound with the score tied. Jesus. Harris and Jadlow, I've never had more disappointing people here in my life. You two haven't contributed two ounces to what we're trying to do. You don't improve or change from one day to the next.

"Boys, I want to tell you how long a season you're in for if you don't compete any harder than that." He paused. His voice was almost choked now. "I never thought I would see the day when Indiana basketball was in the state it's in right now."

They went home dreading what was to come. The assistant coaches were genuinely frightened about what might happen next. Wright, Waltman, and Smith had talked before the season about the need to stick up for the players when Knight got down on them. The previous season had turned into a circus, with players going from forty minutes to zero minutes and back again. All those elements were there again. Players were being yanked for mistakes. Knight was an emotional yo-yo.

The tape session was brutal. Knight would run a playback, get disgusted, and walk out of the room. Once, he walked back in, sat down, grabbed Waltman's coffee mug, hurled it against the wall, and stormed out again. It was Wright who spoke first after he was gone. "Guys, we have got to stick with these kids. We've got to tell him that we know they've got a long way to go, but we can't give up on them. This is all we got. This is the hand we've been dealt. We just can't quit on Andre Harris now."

For Wright, Harris was a special project. He was the kind of athlete Wright believed Indiana had to recruit to win. If Harris washed out, it might be a long time before Knight was willing to take a risk on a good athlete/bad student again. The other coaches, who had not been nearly as happy with Harris in preseason as Knight had been, understood this. They had been nervous when Harris had been handed stardom before playing a game because they saw his deficiencies. But now they knew Wright was correct. He could not simply be washed down the drain after two games.

"What bothers me," Waltman said to Wright, "is the rebounding. You can miss shots, okay. But a leaper like him should be able to rebound. He hasn't."

"You're right," Wright said. "But what else have we got?"

The others nodded assent. They had to stand up for the players before the circus started again. This was easier said than done when Knight was in this mood. Knight returned. The tape began again. "Look at this, will you look at this shit?" Knight kept saying. "We cannot play with these people. We just can't."

Silence. Finally, Wright, his voice barely a whisper, spoke. "Coach, I know we've got problems with these kids right now. But I really think it's important that we keep working to try to make them better. We've only played twelve games. I'm discouraged too, we all are, but until those other kids get here next year, we've got to try to make these guys play better."

"I know that, Joby, but Jesus, why are they so dumb?"

"Coach, I don't know. I know they aren't any damn rocket scientists, but I really think they'll get better."

Knight slumped in his chair. "Why don't you guys go home. I want to be alone for a while."

They walked out. "That was good," Kohn Smith told Wright. "That's what we have to do."

"Yeah, that's true," Waltman said, "but will we get through tomorrow?"

"Tomorrow?" Felling said, "It's only eight o'clock. At least one of us will be back here tonight."

It was Felling. Knight called him thirty minutes later. "You got anything [tape] on Northwestern?" That was Felling's signal to go back to work. He walked in and put on a Northwestern tape. "I don't want to look at that crap," Knight said. He wanted to talk. They sat and talked until after midnight. Felling went home wondering, like Waltman, if they would make it through the next day.

11.

Will We Ever Catch Another Fish?

This crisis was real. The players hadn't been given a time to come in the next day. All they could do was wait by the telephone. Knight was still depressed when he came in the next morning but at least he wasn't wild and screaming. "Maybe," he said to Kohn Smith, "you and I ought to just go hunting."

Even though he had the flu, Smith thought that was a terrific idea. He and Knight would hunt while the other assistants met with the players. Then they would all go through tape that night. Knight's willingness to go hunting showed that he knew he needed to stay in control of the situation. Northwestern and Wisconsin were the league's two weakest teams. Without Thomas, though, neither game looked like a lock, especially on the road. The team was on the brink of complete chaos. Hunting was the best thing Knight could do for himself and for the players that afternoon.

The players came in shortly after Knight and Smith left. Waltman, Felling, and Wright each spoke to them. What did they think was wrong? Did they understand why Coach was so upset? "It's not so much this mistake or that mistake," Waltman said.

"It's competing. You guys have got to understand that if Coach is nothing else, he's a competitor. And he likes to think that there's enough of him in you that you'll be just as competitive as he is. Right now, he doesn't think you are and that's killing him."

They went around the room, asking each player how he felt. Some gave stock answers. Others admitted being uptight, nervous. Maybe even scared to make a mistake.

"How many of you," Waltman asked, "worry about making a mistake because you're going to get yelled at by Coach?"

For a moment, no one moved. Finally, Calloway put his hand up. Soon, sixteen hands were up. "Do you feel that way, Steve?" Wright said, turning to Alford, the player least likely to be bothered by yelling.

Alford folded his arms. "Well," he said. "It's not a feeling. It's reality."

That broke the tension. They all laughed, including the coaches, because it was so true. "Look, I think I know what you're feeling right now," Waltman said. "I think we all got to know each other pretty well overseas and we all know what's facing us. But everyone has got to stick together. Someone makes a mistake, pick him up, help him out. Don't get down on each other. Everyone in here is trying like hell. Coach may not always know that, but you guys do. So stick together."

Everyone nodded. Everyone felt better. But what would happen that night?

In the meantime, there was another problem. Delray Brooks's mother had called Wright that day. Delray, she said, was terribly unhappy. He had played zero minutes against Michigan and four against Michigan State after starting against Mississippi State. What was going on? Would he ever play? Maybe he should transfer.

This didn't come as a shock to Wright or any of the coaches. Brooks's transferring had been discussed. But the timing, smack in the middle of a major crisis, wasn't great. Wright told Knight about the phone call before he met with the players that night. "We'll deal with it after the meeting," Knight said.

The hunting trip had saved the day, perhaps the season. Knight was firm as they went through the tape, often emphatic, occasionally angry, but there were no hysterics, no profane tirades. He even found some positive things to say, some kind words for Todd Meier—who had played zero minutes against Michigan State— and for Stew Robinson, who had missed the last vital shot.

"I want to tell you people about Todd and about Stew," he said. "I'm not sure anyone in here gives us more than Todd does. He's got bad knees, so bad he maybe shouldn't even be playing. I looked down the bench at him at the end of the game, he's got tears rolling down his cheeks—and he didn't even play.

"Andre, I looked at you and you were no more into the game than someone sitting in a home for the mentally ill in Northern Indiana. We've got guys like Todd rooting like hell for you, and when it's your turn to root, you just sulk. I think there are people here in this room who resent that."

Knight paused. "If any of you disagree with my assessment, say so. I'll respect the hell out of you for standing up and disagreeing." Knight waited. No one said a word. He went on.

"I want to tell you something else, Andre, you too, Todd Jadlow. Stew has been here four years. He's helped us win some big games. He's started, he's come off the bench, he's not played at all. He had no idea Sunday how much he would play, if at all, and there was no one more into the game than he was. If we had fifteen guys like that, this team would be a lot different than it is."

More than anything, Knight was philosophical. "You know, I tell you all the time that basketball is thinking and playing smart and working hard. You hear that so much from me you probably stop hearing it after a while. But I was thinking this morning about Scott May. I can remember Scott May coming in here on Sundays, his one day off, and working for two hours on not walking with the basketball. He ended up a two-time All-American and player of the year as a senior. And I'll tell you something, he didn't have any more athletic ability than a lot of you do. But he wanted to compete so much, he made himself better.

"See, boys, basketball should be your favorite class. Because what basketball has done for teams here in the past is taught those kids how to compete. That's a great thing to learn. I guarantee you we've had players who have sat in the classroom with people who had 3.7 cums, who they no way should have been able to compete with after college, and have gone on and done much better than those kids did.

"Why? Because they knew how to compete. They knew how to stay after something. They knew how to get knocked down and get up. Those other guys, 3.7 and all, some of them couldn't sell handwarmers to eskimos. But until this team, or the last two teams, we always had players who wanted to play and wanted to compete. I feel like with you guys that you are *required* to play. And I hate using that word—required."

The lights were off in the locker room, the tape machine was frozen right behind where Knight stood. He hadn't raised his voice once, but he certainly had everyone's attention. "Let me take a wild guess at something here," Knight went on. "On Christmas night, all of you had dinner at Dr. Rink's house. I would imagine that Mrs. Rink spent the better part of three days cooking that dinner for you. What did you, as a team, do to thank her for dinner? Tell me. Did you all kick in a dollar to send her some roses? Did anybody write a thank-you note? Anybody? Speak up, anyone who did anything to thank Mrs. Rink."

He looked around the room. No one looked back. He turned to Alford. "Steve, why do you think I was able to ask that question with absolute and complete confidence that no one had done anything?"

"Because we're selfish."

"Exactly. And that is reflected in the way you play basketball. The most selfish thing in the world is only worrying about guarding your man or only worrying about boxing out your man. If Winston helps me when I lose my man, you better believe I'm going to try like hell to help on his man when he needs it. But you don't do that. You just worry about yourselves. And as long as you do that, you'll continue to play selfish basketball, you'll continue to make the mistakes that cost us this game and you won't be able to beat anybody. Think about it."

This time, when Knight left his players alone, they did have something to think about. As the coaches followed Knight out of the locker room, Kohn Smith said softly, "Now *that* was coaching."

The next morning, Mrs. Larry Rink received two dozen roses, courtesy of the Indiana basketball team.

Delray Brooks's name was on the card that went with the flowers. It was his last act as an Indiana basketball player.

Knight met with Brooks after the team meeting on Monday to ask him if he was as miserable as his parents said he was. Brooks said he wasn't miserable, but confused. He wanted to play more. Knight understood. He had spent three years in college wanting to play more. He had almost quit the team several times each year only to be talked out of it by friends.

He understood Brooks's frustration, but just as Fred Taylor couldn't guarantee young Bobby Knight more playing time, Coach Bob Knight could make no guarantees to Brooks. "I think you should talk to your parents and make a firm decision on what you want to do," Knight told Brooks. "If you want to leave, I understand. If you want to stay, I'll do everything I can to help you improve."

Knight suspected Brooks would opt to leave. Brooks was such a gentle person that he would never think of questioning his playing time even if it was bothering him. But his parents were not that gentle. Like any parents, they thought their son should be playing all the time. When a high school star from a small town goes to college and doesn't play, it is hard on the player. But it may be even tougher on the parents who are back home being asked all the time why their son isn't playing.

Brooks talked to his parents again that night. They decided that he should find a school where he would have a chance to play. That did not appear to be Indiana. The next morning, Brooks told Knight his decision. He was leaving Indiana. Knight told him that if he wanted to come back to Indiana for graduate school or ever needed any help, not to hesitate to call. Brooks thanked him and told him, "Coach, I know I tried hard and so did you. Thank you."

Knight sat staring into space for a long time after Brooks had left the cave. "I doubt," he finally said, "if we've ever had a nicer kid here than Delray Brooks."

The first practice that Brooks missed may have been the most brutal of the season. Knight had given them philosophy on Monday night. Tuesday morning he gave them hell. Almost every tough drill, those used almost exclusively in preseason, was part of the practice. When Knight caught a gasping Harris bent over with his hands on his knees, he jumped him.

"Dammit, you're not that tired. I don't want to see anybody with their hands on their knees. You boys have got to learn some toughness."

Harris, of all the players on the team, had a legitimate excuse for fatigue. Six years earlier, when a player named Glen Grunwald had been having terrible fatigue problems during games, Bomba had called Dr. Rink to see if he could run some tests and figure out the problem. Rink's tests showed, among other things, that Grunwald had a smaller lung capacity than anyone on the team, far smaller than average capacity for a normal man his height (6-9), much less someone trying to play basketball.

From that time on, Rink had tested every Indiana player every year for lung capacity. Harris had the weakest lung capacity on the team since Grunwald. Part of his problem in games was that he started lunging at the ball when he got tired. A practice like this was simply too much for him. During a one-on-one drill, Harris died completely. He just stopped. Fortunately for everyone, Knight was looking the other way at the time.

The practice could have been a disaster. Knight was at his most snappish, angry from the start. Perhaps he was still upset about Brooks. Or perhaps he wanted to make a point. Twice, he ran them into the locker room and screamed at them. He exploded at Dakich for allegedly running a drill incorrectly. He yelled at the coaches for not being tough enough on the players. For one hour it was boot camp again.

But it didn't last. A pat on the back here, a compliment there. And finally, "Better, boys, that's a lot better."

He still wasn't happy. But he wasn't berserk, either.

More than anything that week, Knight was searching. He felt like a researcher who had checked every book in existence on a subject without finding any answers. How could he get this team to play better? How could he end the two-season streak of 7–13 in the Big Ten and 3–8 at home? Those numbers were incomprehensible to him. Yet they kept piling up and he, Bob Knight, Supercoach, didn't seem to have any solutions.

He looked at tape. He asked the coaches over and over what they thought. He called Pete Newell and Fred Taylor. He lay awake in bed thinking, thinking, thinking. There had to be a way out of this. He had always found a way before. Why not now? What hadn't he tried? He had tried everything: anger, threats, pleading. Philosophy, quotations. Long drills, short drills, different lineups. Everything.

Almost everything. Knight sat up almost all night that Tuesday going over and over in his mind the last two seasons. Finally, he decided there was one approach he hadn't tried. In fact, it was an approach that no one had ever thought of—ever. Anywhere.

The players arrived for a ten o'clock practice the next morning a little tired. They had thrown Brooks a going-away party at his apartment the evening before, sending out for pizza and then sitting around together reminiscing. It was hard for them to see Brooks leave because they liked him so much, but they understood.

When the players walked onto the floor, their coach was standing under one basket holding a fishing rod. "Boys, the biggest problem you have as basketball players is that you don't see," Knight told them. "I am now going to show you why basketball is just like fishing. Because if you don't see what's going on around you as a fisherman, you'll never catch a fish. The same thing is true in basketball.

"You can have the very best equipment. You can have a great rod, like this one. You can have the right bait. You can have great-looking clothes. But if you can't see a rock in front of you when you cast your rod, you'll be in trouble. If you can't see a tree over your shoulder, you'll be in trouble. If you don't know what to look for in a stream, you'll never catch a fish.

"The same is true in basketball. You can be a great leaper. You can be a great shooter. You can be quick. You can be all those things. But if you don't *see* what is going on in front of you or behind you or around you, if you don't know what to look for, you can't play basketball."

For almost an hour, Knight stomped around the gym floor, casting his rod over and over, talking about fishing. He told stories about catching fish when others claimed there were no fish. At one point, he began tromping around the gym screaming, "Kohn, where are the fish, Kohn? I don't see any damn fish here. Why can't I *see* the fish? Where are they? Boys, if you don't look, you can't see."

As Knight stalked around in endless circles, the players broke up. It was the first good laugh the team had had since New Year's. The fishing analogies were wild, but they made sense. It was a different way of saying the same thing. Knight made his points at great length, but everyone listened and everyone enjoyed it. No one got yelled at. There was no tape droning on and on. And the sight of their coach stamping around acting as if he couldn't find any fish was a story that would certainly be told and retold for years to come.

When it was over, Knight, exhausted, retreated to the cave. The coaches were left to go through tape with the players. Knight has a habit when he is pensive—which is often—of looking at friends in mid-conversation and saying very seriously, "Do you think we'll ever win another game?" All his friends repeat this to one another at times. But from that day forth, the question changed to, "Do you think we'll ever catch another fish?"

The next fish was Northwestern. Hardly Moby-Dick, but this team had to start somewhere.

———

That afternoon, Knight decided it was time for a new point guard to play, one who could show the players how to pass the basketball. The point guard's name was Bob Knight.

This is a tactic Knight tries about six times a year. He is an excellent passer because he sees the floor so clearly. Almost always, he will make several good passes, and almost always he will keep playing until he is breathing very hard and has to take himself out.

One of Knight's first passes was stolen by Jadlow. The rest he converted. Finished, he walked over to where Hammel was sitting and said with a huge smile, "Hamso, am I or am I not the world's best forty-five-year-old passer?"

What the world's best forty-five-year-old passer didn't know was that most of the players were not about to intercept his passes. In fact, Jadlow received a stern talking-to after practice for his lone interception. To make their point to a wayward player in this area, older players always invoked the Dakich story.

It was 1982. Dakich was an eager freshman who was getting a pretty good chunk of playing time. The team was practicing at Minnesota the day before a game there and Knight was angry with the offense, so he inserted himself. Dakich, all intensity playing on the white team, figured that his coach would want nothing less than all-out play from him, even if the man he was guarding was his coach.

On Knight's first play, Dakich stole the ball from him—clean. "Sonofabitch," Knight said, and he threw the ball at Dakich, catching him square on the nose. Dakich shook that off and went back into his stance. Knight made another move, and Dakich went for the ball again. He got it again—only this time he fouled Knight, slapping his wrist. *Wham.* Dakich's face collided with the basketball again. "Don't you ever f—— foul me!" the coach screamed. Dakich was dizzy by now, half wanting to fight Knight, half wanting to cry. Instead, he kept playing. And learned his lesson—the hard way. Jadlow had been lucky.

———

They flew to Evanston after practice and Knight, the coaches, Garl, and Hammel went to dinner. Everything with Knight is ritual. Every road trip is the same: leave after practice, check into the hotel, send the players to dinner, go out to dinner, meet with the players, look at tape with the coaches, go to sleep.

Knight was in a reflective mood that night at dinner, feeling almost relaxed after a week full of tension. He talked at length about Brooks, wondering aloud if leaving was the best thing for him—hoping it was. Earlier, before sending the team to dinner, Knight spoke to the team about Brooks for the first time since he had left. "I think we all feel badly that he's gone," Knight said. "But do any of you think he ever would have become a really good player here?"

No one answered. "He was just absolutely the wrong kind of player for us," Knight said at dinner. "He's not a ballhandler, and Alford needs someone to handle the ball. I told him not to leave just because his parents wanted him to, but that's what I think he did. I told him that he should only leave if he felt he had to go somewhere that he knew he would play a lot. I really don't know where that is."

Knight rambled. He questioned his handling of the Michigan game, wondering if it had been his fault that London Bradley had not only given him a technical but had made the horrid goaltending call against Harris. "I did everything but call the guy a nigger," Knight said. "People are human. If I were a referee I would tell a guy, 'I'm not gonna call a technical, I'm just gonna throw your ass out.' "

Finally, he returned to his favorite subject: the team. "I enjoyed December with this team as much as I ever have. I thought we were playing as well as we possibly could have. I just can't stand not being competitive. In 1983, if Kitchel hadn't been hurt, we could have made the Final Four. In '84, we weren't that good, but we almost sneaked in anyway. That makes it all worthwhile. Last year, though, we had no chance. Now, it's the same thing this year. That's discouraging."

Practice the next morning was not encouraging. Jadlow, fighting the flu, had a rotten practice. Knight decided to start Eyl in his place. Daryl Thomas was at home, having his ankle worked on in the hope that he could play next week. Knight was concerned about this game. He had tried every trick he knew to get the team out of its doldrums, but without Thomas, he just wasn't sure what would happen. Northwestern, as it turned out, would have a horrid season, one in which the players stopped playing hard because they sensed—correctly—that their coach, Rich Falk, was a lame duck. But early in January, Knight knew none of this.

Just before pregame meal that afternoon, he got some news that picked up his spirits immensely. The Big Ten and the NCAA had ruled that Pelkowski was eligible to redshirt, that the courses he had taken in Colombia didn't count against his five-year clock. "Goddamn, that's the first big win we've had in two years," Knight said. "That's just great. Really great. I think with that extra year he can really be a good player. Don't you, guys?"

The coaches nodded eagerly. Pelkowski, they knew, was a project. He had potential, but whether he could overcome his lack of natural instincts was a question. Knight often talked about how hard it was for foreign players to learn the game because they weren't weaned on it like American kids. That was why, he believed, Uwe Blab had never become a great player. But he seemed to block that sentiment from his mind when talking about Pelkowski.

"You know, he might be our second-best shooter," Knight rambled on. Nobody stopped him. They were just glad to see him happy.

Knight stayed happy that evening. Whether it was the long talk on Monday night, the brutal practice on Tuesday, or the fishing lesson on Wednesday, something worked. Indiana led 8–2 after four minutes, 28–14 after twelve, 48–26 at halftime, and never let Northwestern into the game at all. The final was 102–65, an extraordinary margin against anyone, especially on the road, especially without Thomas. The Hoosiers shot 64 percent. Calloway had twenty points, Alford nineteen, Harris fifteen, and Robinson fourteen. Everyone played well. Everyone contributed.

The Northwestern students, who showed up with signs that said "Give Bobby Knight the chair" and "Extradite Bobby Knight," had little to say after halftime. The only not-so-great moment came with seven minutes left, when Northwestern "cut" a 70–42 lead to 76–53. Knight called time and screamed for a solid minute. "You've outscored them by one goddamn point since halftime. That's just the same shit we've been doing for two years. Now goddamn it, let's play."

They played. They outscored Northwestern 26–12 the rest of the way and Knight, fighting the flu like everyone else, walked off the floor coughing but happy. The postgame celebration lasted until the team was on the bus. "You did a hell of a job tonight," he told the players. "But start thinking about Wisconsin right now. If we don't get that game, we're right back where we started. It just makes me sick to think about that Michigan State game when I see how we played tonight."

Back up front, he shook his head and said softly, "I wonder if there was anything we could have done different against Michigan State."

Wisconsin would not be a walkover. Knight knew that. The

Badgers were not very good, but they weren't awful, and, historically, they played well at home against Indiana. Knight always felt a little bit strange going to Madison because he had almost become Wisconsin's coach in 1969. He had interviewed, been offered the job, and had virtually accepted it. He had gone home on a Wednesday to discuss it with his wife and with friends, and had told Wisconsin he would fly out Friday to finalize the deal.

But in the forty-eight-hour interim, two things happened: first, the story leaked in the Madison paper that Knight was the coach. Then, on Friday morning, Knight woke up at 6 A.M. and called Bo Schembechler. Once, Schembechler had interviewed for the football job at Wisconsin. "Don't take it," Schembechler counseled. "It's not the job for you. It will try your patience too much." Knight never got on the plane to go back to Madison.

Madison is the prettiest town in the Big Ten. The only trouble with it is that it's usually buried under several feet of snow in the winter. Indiana got lucky this time. After a week of snow and subzero temperatures, Madison was in the midst of a heat wave, with temperatures climbing toward forty. Friday was bright and sunny, and Knight and Hammel went for a long walk through town. Knight even did his good deed for the week, stopping to give a young woman whose car was stuck in a snowdrift a push free.

Good weather or not, Knight shouldn't have been out. He was coughing and having trouble breathing, and he wasn't the only one. Alford was now sick, and most of the team was fighting the flu in one form or another. With only nine players available, stamina was a major concern. "We gotta win this game and get the hell home and get some rest," Knight said late Friday night. Then he insisted on going looking for some ice cream.

Saturday dawned bright and cold. The game was at 1 P.M., so pregame was at 9 A.M. Spaghetti at 9 A.M. is a sickening sight. Everyone was still a little bleary-eyed as the bus rolled towards the ancient Wisconsin field house. When the bus reached the back parking lot, the driver found his pathway into it blocked. On one side of the entrance sat a car. On the other was a roadblock. There was a man in the car. "Can't park here," the man told the bus driver.

"This is the Indiana team," the driver told him.

"Doesn't matter, can't park here."

Knight, who had been half listening to the conversation, jumped up at this remark. "Listen, do you want to have a game here today or not?" he said.

The security man, who clearly had no clue, simply repeated his line about the bus not being able to park. "What the hell is wrong with you?" Knight said, beginning to get angry. "Don't you understand, we're playing in this goddamn game."

"I don't care. I can't move the barrier."

By now everyone was half standing in his seat. Was Madison about to become San Juan II? Knight was off the bus. "Well, if you can't move the barrier, I sure can." He picked up the barrier and threw it out of the way. The security guard glared at him. But there still was not enough room for the bus to pass. The bus driver got off the bus. Mr. Security was on his car radio, asking for either instructions or reinforcements. "Look, pal," the driver said, "you better move your car before he moves it for you."

The guard glanced at Knight. "Okay, I'll move, but this isn't supposed to happen."

Everyone got back on the bus. The players, relieved first, then giggling, sat down. The bus pulled up to the players' entrance without further incident.

There was, naturally, an aftermath. Several Wisconsin players had been walking by on their way to the field house when the incident took place. By the time Indiana got into the building, the word being spread was that Knight had thrown the barrier at the security guard. Fortunately, Knight didn't know this. The gross exaggeration would have made him crazy.

The game almost took care of that. As at Northwestern, Indiana came out blazing. Alford was unstoppable. Harris was superb inside. Todd Meier, starting at center, played solid defense and rebounded well. After fifteen minutes, it was 38–18. Another blowaway. Perfect.

But the Hoosiers were tired. Harris was having trouble breathing. It was 40–20 with 3:24 to go. During a TV time-out Knight implored the players to hang in until halftime. "Suck it up for three minutes and we'll be okay," he said.

But they couldn't. Alford turned the ball over. Harris missed. Robinson, who was playing with a pulled hamstring, turned it over. Wisconsin began to hit. Finally, with twenty-five seconds left, Mike Heineman, a hard-nosed kid from Connersville, Indiana, whom Knight truly regretted not recruiting, got past Eyl for a bucket that cut the margin to 42–28. Alford missed at the buzzer.

Knight was wild at halftime. He trashed Eyl first, then Morgan. "The game was over boys, over. We have a twenty-two point lead [actually twenty] and then you guys just collapse and let them get back in the game. Jesus Christ. Morgan, you've been here five years and you are still giving us nothing but terrible, terrible basketball. We cannot play you. Eyl, if one of my assistants ever recruits a player like you again, I'll fire him. How can you let Heineman beat you on that play? How?"

Knight was hysterical because he honestly believed his team had little left physically for the second half. He wanted to lead by twenty because he thought with a twenty-point lead, Indiana might win by about five. Now, it was just a fourteen-point lead.

Quickly, though, the Hoosiers upped the margin to 46–28. Everyone breathed a sigh of relief. But Wisconsin chipped back. Time after time the Badgers punched the ball inside. Harris was tired. Meier's knees hurt. Jadlow was struggling. They got to within 52–42 with almost fourteen minutes to play. The lead stayed right there for the next eight minutes. Every time Wisconsin looked ready to make a run, Alford would answer.

If anyone had ever questioned Alford's grit, this game was definitive proof of just how truly tough he is. Alford's throat hurt so much he could barely swallow. He was running a fever and he was having trouble breathing just sitting still, much less running up and down the court. But time after time, when the Wisconsin crowd started to rock the old building, Alford would quiet them. He swished a twenty-footer with 6:05 left to make it 70–59. That was his thirty-sixth point.

But ninety seconds later, Wisconsin had the lead down to 70–63. They were dogging Alford's every step now. Robinson was open. He missed. The rebound rolled loose. Heineman flew out of bounds and tried to throw the ball back in off of Morgan's leg. But Morgan saw the play coming and he jumped high in the air. The ball went right between his legs and on one bounce to Harris, who was wide open for a layup since everyone had been watching Heineman and Morgan. That made it 72–63 with 3:45 to go. If Morgan had not been so alert, Wisconsin would have had a chance to cut the lead to five. Instead, Rick Olson missed a shot, Calloway hit a jumper from the baseline to up the lead back to eleven, and it was over. Indiana had survived.

"I can't ever remember a game being so hard," Knight said when it was over. His sweater was soaked, but he was relieved and happy. "Andre, you made a great play when they had it down to seven," he said. In truth, the great play had been made by Morgan. But nobody cared. They were 2–2 in the Big Ten. They had caught two fish—not big ones, but at this stage, no one was about to throw them back.

_____**12.**

"If We Can Just Get into Position to Get into Position"

For the next two weeks, the players heard over and over again about positioning. But not positioning on defense or under the boards.

"We are now 2–2 in the Big Ten," Knight told them Sunday, writing it on the board in the locker room. "We have three home games coming up—Ohio State, Purdue, Illinois. We have now put ourselves into a position where, if we can win these three games, we'll be in position to be a factor in the Big Ten race."

Getting into position to get into position. But to get into position to get into position, Knight continued, they would have to beat Ohio State. "We just cannot lose any more games at home, boys. We cannot lose to these people."

Beating these people would not be easy. To begin with, a quirk in the schedule had turned what would ordinarily be a Thursday game into a Wednesday game. The previous summer, Ohio State had been offered the chance to play a game that Saturday on national TV. They asked if Indiana would mind playing a day earlier. In August, that had seemed just fine, but now, with Daryl Thomas's ankle literally a day-to-day proposition, that extra twenty-four hours could be the difference between his being a factor and not even being able to play.

Thomas had responded well to the injury. He knew that Knight thought he had a low threshold of pain, and he knew Knight didn't think he was very tough. He wanted to prove to Knight that he was wrong. The initial pain had been so excruciating that Thomas was convinced he had broken the ankle. He was relieved when it turned out to be a bad sprain, but knew that meant Knight would expect him to come back quickly. Garl's prognosis had been ten days to two weeks. Ohio State would be exactly ten days after the injury.

The only person under as much pressure as Thomas was Garl. Knight put a lot of faith in Garl, especially when it came to trusting his judgment on whether someone could play or not. Garl was much more than the team trainer. He was the team's travel agent; he was in charge of setting up training meals and pregame meals; he was in charge of expense accounts and giving expense advances to the coaches. He was probably the one person on the team who was genuinely plugged in to both the coaches and the players.

Garl was a little guy, only slightly more than 5-6. On a basketball team, that fact was going to be pointed out to him more than just occasionally. This was especially true on the road, where Knight left Garl essentially in charge of everything but game preparation. When Garl started barking orders, as he often did, players, coaches, and managers would respond by calling him "Little Napoleon" or "Der Führer." Garl took the ribbing well, although occasionally he admitted that being short "really pisses me off." About the only time he reacted badly to kidding about his height was when it came from Waltman, who was perhaps an inch taller than he was.

This week, no one was kidding Garl about his height. He was too busy working on Thomas's ankle until all hours of the night trying to get the swelling down. By Monday, Thomas was able to shoot the ball at a separate basket while the team practiced. "I don't think he's going to be able to move laterally by Wednesday very well," Garl told Knight.

"Can he play?"

"He can play, but I don't think he can guard anybody."

"You let me worry about that."

That was fine with Garl. Knight was about as keen and as honed in for this game as he had been all season, perhaps in a couple of seasons. He was sick of losing at home to Big Ten teams. He was sick that Indiana had lost twice to his alma mater the previous season. He was tired of only beating weaklings in the Big Ten. He wanted no distractions this week.

Naturally, one showed up. On Monday afternoon a young Japanese man appeared at Assembly Hall with a letter. In English, the letter explained that the young man was a Japanese basketball coach who thought Knight was a coaching genius. He had flown to the U.S. hoping to watch Knight coach for a month so he could learn from him. He spoke no English.

Knight was stunned that the young coach had simply shown up on his doorstep this way. He couldn't communicate with him because he spoke no Japanese. But he had an idea. He called a professor who had come to Indiana from Japan. The professor had a teenage son who spoke Japanese. How would he feel about acting as interpreter? No problem. So, for the next few weeks, the young Japanese coach and the American-born teenager sat at practice each day, with the professor's son interpreting what Knight was saying to the team. Or at least most of it. By the time the young coach went home in February he not only had dozens of pages of notes and diagrams, he had a basketball autographed by the entire team and several Indiana shirts and sweaters to show to his friends.

Having done his bit for international relations, Knight turned to the problem of Ohio State. Other than a healthy Thomas, he believed the key to this game would be Winston Morgan. Ohio State's two best players were 7-foot center Brad Sellers and 6-5 guard Dennis Hopson. Sellers was going to be a problem because of his size; there was little that could be done about that. But if Hopson, averaging twenty-two points a game, could be controlled, Ohio State would not have its inside-outside balance.

Morgan, at 6-4, was the one Indiana player with the quickness and the size to have a reasonable chance to guard Hopson. Knight had been extremely happy with Morgan for most of the season. He had even tried to get Morgan put back on scholarship when Brooks left, but was told that the NCAA would not allow that at midseason. Brooks had announced on Monday that he would transfer to Providence College. Knight was pleased about that; Providence was rebuilding and played a lot of zone. Brooks would have a chance there.

But Morgan was a much more immediate concern. Knight had been angry with him after the Wisconsin game, and the Monday and Tuesday practices were often a five-year review of that long-running show, "The Screwups of Winston Morgan." "If that's the kind of crap you're going to give us Wednesday, Winston, don't even bother practicing because you're wasting everyone's time. I just don't want to see any of that garbage like I saw up at Wisconsin."

Walking away, Knight said to the coaches, "I just hope God takes note of the fact that I coached Winston Morgan for five years." But if God was handing out points for that relationship, Morgan would have a few of his own to collect.

On Tuesday, Thomas practiced a little. He moved awkwardly and was wearing a special light cast to protect the ankle. He would play; the question was how much.

While Knight was worrying about Thomas and screaming at Morgan, Quinn Buckner was wondering about his future. Buckner was in his tenth year in the NBA. After leaving Indiana in 1976, he had captained the U.S. Olympic team that summer and then gone on to a solid pro career in Milwaukee, Boston, and now Indianapolis. The Pacers had brought him in that summer hoping that at thirty-one he could give a young team some leadership, and because they knew his name still carried weight in the state of Indiana.

But Buckner and Coach George Irvine had never hit it off. Irvine, a nervous, chain-smoking man, seemed to see Buckner more as a potential threat to his authority than anything else. On a team that would finish the season 26–56, Irvine was uncomfortable with anyone around who might be viewed by management as potential coaching material. Buckner, articulate, savvy, and a natural leader, was certainly coaching material.

He had played little under Irvine even as the team struggled, constantly losing leads late in the game. Now, with Clark Kellogg about to come off the injured list, Buckner knew Irvine had to cut somebody. "I was sitting at dinner with my wife and all of a sudden it hit me," he said. "I said to her, 'I think I'm gone.' "

The next morning, Irvine called him in for a meeting. Buckner's instincts had been correct; he was being placed on waivers. Little-used and thirty-one, Buckner knew that his being waived was probably the end of his NBA career. Buckner was much too bright and much too well set up financially to be crushed, but it still hurt. It hurt his ego, and it hurt to have Irvine almost try to make him a scapegoat for a lousy team. When Buckner got home that morning he called Knight.

This was Wednesday. Knight had just gone through a morning walk-through with the team. "Why don't you come down here for the game tonight?" he asked Buckner.

Buckner wasn't sure. He thought maybe he would just like to stay home with his family and give himself a little time to feel sorry for himself. "Quinn," Knight said, "it would mean a lot to me." End of discussion. Buckner called Tom Abernethy and asked for a ride to the game.

Knight had Thomas do some extra work with Pelkowski and Brian Sloan after the three o'clock walk-through. He wanted him to try catching the ball in the low post, turning, and shooting. Normally, this was Thomas's favorite move. Now, he looked uncomfortable wheeling to make the move.

The theme for this game was simple: January 15. "Let's remember January 15," Knight said at the pregame meal, "as a beginning. As the beginning of us becoming the kind of basketball team we want to be. It won't be easy. It will be hard. I promise you that. But this is an opportunity for this team. Let's make this a night when we do something to someone rather than having someone do something to us."

With that, he went off to his pregame steam. He had stopped announcing his weight in mid-December, and the suspicion was it was creeping back toward 230.

Buckner and Abernethy walked in shortly after 6:30. Knight, lying on the couch, pointed them to chairs immediately. "I need you guys tonight," he said briskly, acting as if Buckner's waiver had never happened. "Quinn, you gotta talk to Morgan. Take him in the hall and tell him, 'You owe this f—— operation a lot and tonight you start paying it back.' Tommy, I want you to talk to the inside guys about not committing stupid fouls."

They both nodded and got up to leave for the players' locker room. "Don't screw this up now," Knight said. "Quinn, I'm holding you responsible for Morgan's defense on Hopson."

"He'll guard him," Buckner said. "Don't worry about it."

Knight had already given Crabb his marching orders. After the teams were introduced, Knight wanted Abernethy and Buckner introduced. Both were sitting on the Indiana bench. Abernethy had been through this before, since he was a regular at home games. But Buckner, because of his pro career, had not been to a game in Assembly Hall since graduation.

Buckner's introduction was lavish. ". . . Captain of the 1976 national championship team, captain of the 1976 gold-medal-winning U.S. Olympic team . . . one of Indiana's all-time greats . . ." They were standing and cheering before Crabb even said Buckner's name. Buckner didn't know what to do. He finally settled for a wave. They were still cheering him when he sat down next to Knight.

The first half was almost perfect. Morgan was making life miserable for Hopson. Thomas was holding his own inside. By halftime he had eight points and seven rebounds. Alford was merely Alford with seventeen points. At halftime, Indiana led 39–30, and the only noticeable chink was a running feud Knight had started early in the game with official Darwin Brown.

That chink became a problem right away in the second half. On the opening possession, Alford, going up to shoot, appeared to get fouled. There was no call. A moment later, after Ohio State's Clarence McGee scored to make it 39–32, Knight was still screaming at Brown about his not calling a foul on the previous play. Brown, who had warned Knight in the first half, nailed him with a technical.

The timing could not have been worse. Not only did Ohio State get two points from the two free throws, but it got the basketball back from Indiana. When Hopson hit from twenty feet for his sixth point of the game, the lead had gone from nine to three in less than a minute.

Knight was so furious that he called Ralph Floyd from the stands and sent him to press row to tell the new Big Ten supervisor of officials, Bob Wortman, that Brown was incompetent. Wortman didn't necessarily disagree, but that wasn't going to change this game. "Brown," Knight yelled, getting in the Last Word, "why don't you do everyone a favor and quit?"

Brown did Knight a favor and didn't give him a second technical.

But the first technical had brought Ohio State close. It stayed close, but couldn't seem to catch up. The lead went down to two, then popped back up to eight. Indiana had a chance to go up ten, but Thomas turned the ball over and committed his fourth foul. A disastrous possession. Hopson promptly posted Morgan and hit to make it 54–48.

But that was Hopson's last basket. With Buckner giving him private counseling sessions at each time-out, Morgan was hanging right with him. The problem was Sellers. He was too big and too quick to be stopped when he chose to play. Against Indiana, he wanted to play. Time and again he jumped over people for rebounds or shots. He would score twenty-nine points and get sixteen rebounds before the game was over.

But Indiana was hanging on. A baseline jumper by Alford with 5:15 left made it 62–56. It took Indiana three minutes to score again. By then it was 62–60, and only the defense was keeping the Hoosiers alive. Alford hit a short pop to make it 64–60 with 2:10 to go. Sellers answered to make it 64–62. With 1:30 left, Calloway was called for a charge. Ohio State had a chance to tie. "This," Hammel said, "is as big a possession as I've seen in a long time."

Hopson drove and beat Morgan. Morgan fouled him before he shot. It would be one-and-one with 1:10 left. Hopson missed! But Sellers jumped over everyone and rebounded. He flipped the ball outside and went into the low post. Thomas was practically clinging to him. Sellers spun to try to get position. The whistle blew. Foul. Thomas's fifth? No. It was an illegal screen on Sellers. "Good call," Sellers said later. "He caught me. Thomas wouldn't give up. He showed guts."

There was still a full minute left, meaning Indiana would have to take a shot before the forty-five-second clock ran out. But Ohio State guard Curtis Wilson foolishly fouled Alford going for a steal. Since Ohio State had not yet committed seven fouls in the second half, Alford didn't get to shoot free throws. But the forty-five-second clock recycled, and with thirty-seven seconds left, Indiana now did not have to shoot the ball again.

Ohio State had to foul and did, Gerry Francis slapping at the ball as soon as Calloway caught the inbounds pass. So Calloway went to the line. One year ago, he had been playing for a bad high school team. Now, he stood in suddenly quiet Assembly Hall trying to be a hero for Indiana University. No problem. Calloway made both shots to make it 66–62.

Wilson partially atoned for his foul on Alford with a drive down the middle. That made it 66–64 with twenty-three seconds left. Ohio State needed a steal or it would have to foul. It almost got a steal on the inbounds when Morgan couldn't find anyone open. He called time—just in time—before a five-second violation could be called. The second time he did exactly what Knight wanted: he inbounded the ball to Alford.

Alford was fouled immediately with fifteen seconds to go. Alford on the foul line with a game on the line is exactly what Knight would ask for in any close game. Not only does he hit 90 percent of his foul shots, but the pressure of the endgame almost always brings out the best in him. He calmly made both shots. It was 68–64. Sellers tried one last shot. It rimmed out. Thomas rebounded, passed to Alford and, seconds later, it was over. Indiana had the victory it had to have. It was now in position to get into position. Or something.

The joy in the locker room was unrestrained. It had been a difficult, draining game. But it had been the kind of game that one year ago would have beaten Indiana. Tonight, Indiana had overcome everything thrown at it: Sellers's size, Thomas's injury, Knight's foolish technical.

Knight was subdued when he walked into the locker room. Subdued, but happy. He was carrying a basketball, the game ball. Without a word, Knight flipped the ball to Alford.

"Hey, that was a great effort, boys," Knight said. "It really was. I'm sorry I dug you a hole at the start of the second half. I'm proud of all of you. Daryl, you couldn't have done that a year ago. I guess you stitched up that vaginal orifice, huh? You went out and you dealt with the pain and you hung in there the whole game. You should feel really proud of what you just did. Ricky, I had absolutely no doubt about you sticking those two free throws—none. If you had had to guard somebody, I might have been worried, but not free throws. Hey, that was just a hell of a win, boys. A hell of a win."

Knight paused and looked around the room. When he started talking again, his tone was soft, and as he went on, each sentence became tougher and tougher to get out because his throat was choked with emotion.

"You know, I've been coaching here fifteen years. We've had a hell of a lot of big games in that time. I talk to you people about leadership and I talk to you about what it means to play basketball at Indiana. And I talk to you about the guys who have played here before you. Their names are in your lockers all around this room.

"We talk to you when we recruit you about how special it is to come to Indiana. And we talk to you about how special it is after you're gone, because you've been a part of it. Tonight, Quinn and Tommy came down for the game. Let me tell you about Quinn. Quinn just got put on waivers today by the f—— Indiana Pacers. He's down here to see you people play tonight. He's in here in the locker room with you, working his ass off. He's trying to keep me in control on the bench, he's just, I don't know when I've ever seen someone show a more selfless approach to something than this kid did tonight."

Knight was barely audible now. "Fifteen years, all the wins we've had here, we've never given a game ball to anybody. Let's give this one to Quinn, what do you say?" Knight was crying by the time he finished and so was everyone else in the room. Alford handed the ball to Buckner as the players burst into cheers and whistles. Knight just turned and walked out of the room, wiping his eyes. Buckner was wiping his.

When Buckner talked about the scene later, he would laugh and say, "I would have broken down completely if not for that damn pedestal I'm supposed to be on." Some of the players were yelling, "Speech," but Buckner waved them off. He was no more capable of talking at that moment than Knight was.

Knight wasn't quite finished with the Indiana Pacers. After he had put himself back together, he went into the interview room. He talked about the game and how pleased he was with Thomas. And then he talked again about Buckner and how much it meant to him to have Buckner come to the game that night.

"Buckner contributes so much to any team that understands basketball," Knight said. "He gets everybody to play better. It's a damn shame in a state like this that loves good basketball that we have a professional organization up in Indianapolis that so clearly doesn't understand anything about the game."

When Knight returned to the locker room he told Buckner what he had said. Buckner smiled. "Thank you," he said.

By blasting the Pacers, Knight, naturally, started a flap. The Pacers' beat writer, David Benner, blasted Knight in a column in *The Indianapolis Star* three days later. Knight, Benner wrote, had no more right to criticize the Pacers than the Pacers had the right to criticize Knight. What's more, teams were not exactly lining up to grab Buckner, so apparently all twenty-three NBA teams didn't understand much about basketball.

Others agreed with Knight's analysis. The Pacers were a horrid team, so they were easy to knock. Their record at the time of Knight's speech was the worst in the league, 10–30.

But what people didn't understand was that Knight would have said the exact same thing if the Pacers had been 30–10. To him, it wasn't a question of won-lost record or statistics or Buckner's age or anything else. One of his own had been wounded, hurt. Knight was going to attack those who had hurt him. As Mike Krzyzewski once put it, "Bob Knight is the guy in the military who jumps on the grenade to save everyone else without giving it a second thought."

If Buckner needed a grenade jumped on, Knight was there.

———

The Ohio State victory was crucial not only because it put Indiana into position to get into position, but because it came just before an eight-day break in the schedule. Each team in the Big Ten has two weeks during the season when it only plays one conference game. For Indiana, it is always the two weeks that it plays Ohio State because Ohio State is Indiana's "travel partner."

This means that they play the same opponents each week. When Indiana plays at Michigan on Thursday, Ohio State plays at Michigan State. Then they trade opponents for the weekend. It works that way throughout the league. The week you play your travel partner, you only play once.

Most coaches use those weeks to schedule a nonconference game that might interest one of the TV networks. Knight was the only major coach in the country who refused to do this. Indiana didn't need TV exposure or TV revenue. Knight wanted no nonconference games to distract his or the team's attention once conference play began.

That meant a week off for Indiana. A loss would have meant misery for the players. But with the victory, it meant rest. Not for Knight, though. The eight days between the Ohio State game and the Purdue game were just about as hectic as any period during the season for him.

He made two recruiting trips. One was to South Carolina to see a player named Rodney Taylor who wanted to come to Indiana. Knight wasn't sure about him as a player, although he was sure about him as a person. Remembering where that kind of thinking had gotten him, Knight was approaching Taylor cautiously. The other trip was to Kansas to see a junior college guard named Keith Smart. Smart, on the surface, was everything Knight didn't want: he wore lots of gold chains and oozed cockiness. But he was an athlete, a swift, penetrating leaper.

Two years earlier, Knight would have written Smart off right away and gone after Taylor hard. Now, he withheld final judgment on both.

When he got back to town, Knight's mind was on recruiting. He and the coaches sat down in the cave and put the names of every player they had recruited since 1980 on the board. Then they put a mark by every name: a check for players who should have been recruited, an X for those who shouldn't have, a dash for players who were borderline. There were very few checks and lots of X's.

Knight also used the break to catch up on his mail. It is almost impossible to comprehend how much mail Knight receives. His secretary, Mary Ann Davis, goes through it to try to weed out the cranks and things that she can take care of, like requests for autographed pictures of the team. Knight answers everything else himself, including notes from fans that may say as little as, "Great win last week." Sometimes, Knight brings his mail on the road with him and goes through it in the locker room before a game.

One letter Knight wrote this weekend was to Isiah Thomas. He had been reading in the newspapers that Thomas was so depressed by the poor play of the Detroit Pistons, his NBA team, that he was actually considering retiring at the age of twenty-five. Of all the truly gifted players Knight had coached, his relationship with Thomas had easily been the most stormy.

It had started even before Thomas arrived in Indiana. Knight and Thomas's brother had staged a shouting match in Thomas's living room during a recruiting visit. Knight had left the house convinced he had lost Thomas. "I always thought if he made the decision himself, Isiah would come to Indiana," Knight said. "But I really wondered if he could withstand the pressure from people in the family like his brother."

Thomas withstood the pressure. He turned down his hometown school, DePaul, and his homestate school, Illinois, and chose Indiana. From day one, he and Knight were antagonists. Thomas was so good that Knight really couldn't use his usual threats of "You'll never play a goddamn minute" and the like on him. Thomas knew he would play. What's more, Thomas was like Knight: a rebel, not one to back down from authority. One Sunday afternoon when Knight was thirty minutes late for a team meeting—a not infrequent occurrence—Thomas turned to his teammates and said, "Come on, let's get out of here, we've waited long enough." Thomas was two steps from the door with the others behind him when the managers spotted Knight and the coaches coming. Everyone scrambled madly for their seats. But it was that close.

Thomas was a wonderful freshman and an extraordinary sophomore. He was the lynchpin in the 1981 championship drive, and when the season was over, Knight was fairly certain Thomas would turn pro. He did, and was quickly a star with Detroit. The usual closeness between Knight and his ex-players never grew between Knight and Thomas even though Thomas came back to Bloomington for summer school.

In the summer of 1983, a Fort Wayne sports club that gave an annual award to the Indiana Man of the Year in athletics approached Knight and asked if Thomas would be willing to accept the award from them that summer at their annual dinner. This was a delicate situation. The club had never named a black before, and Knight knew they wanted Thomas because they were under pressure to choose one. Knight asked Thomas how he felt about accepting the award, telling him he would understand if Thomas didn't want to accept it, but that if he did want it, Knight would go up with him to Fort Wayne and present it to him at the dinner.

Thomas agreed. But the night was a disaster. Before Thomas got his award, an earlier speaker made a couple of racial jokes. Knight, furious but not wanting Thomas to respond, whispered to him before he got up to speak, "You let me take care of that. If you want to get on someone, get on me."

Thomas did just that. Speaking to a crowd filled with middle-aged men and women, Thomas talked about some of the things he had learned at Indiana from Coach Knight. In particular, Knight's profane vocabulary, which he then lauched into, leaving almost nothing to the imagination. Knight was horrified. So was the crowd. The next day, when he realized what he had done, so was Thomas. He apologized, verbally and in writing, several times over.

But Knight was not about to forgive him. The next afternoon when Knight went into the field house, he found Thomas playing a pickup game. Angrily, he threw Thomas out, something he had the right to do since he was renting the field house for his camp that week. Thomas tried briefly to explain, but Knight wanted no explanations. Their relationship went into a deep, deep freeze. It thawed slightly the next summer when Thomas played in a couple of the pre-Olympic exhibition games. But player and coach were still miles apart.

Knight felt saddened when he read of Thomas's depression. He had never thought Thomas a bad kid, in fact he thought he was a good one. And so, he sat down and wrote Thomas a letter, encouraging him, telling him not to give up on the game, the team, or himself. Weeks later, Thomas would ask Joby Wright during a phone conversation to please tell Coach Knight how much the letter had meant to him.

As an avid reader, Knight often saw things in the newspaper that intrigued him. Weeks earlier, he had read a story about a twelve-year-old boy who was a dwarf. In the story, the boy talked about how much he loved Indiana basketball and how he dreamed of seeing Indiana play in person some day.

Knight immediately got in touch with the family. Would they please be his guests at a game some time in the future? The family was delighted. When the boy's father called back, he asked for six tickets to the Purdue game. Knight's secretary who was handling the request, Barbara-Jean McElroy, was flabbergasted. Getting six tickets for Purdue was a little bit like coming up with six Super Bowl tickets an hour before kickoff. But McElroy said she would do her best.

Unlike some coaches, Knight does not have access to unlimited tickets for each game. This is because he doesn't want them—too big a headache. He told McElroy to do the best she could. The best she could do was four tickets, which was actually quite remarkable. But when McElroy called the family back, the father was adamant. He had invited friends to the game. He couldn't call them back now and say they couldn't come. McElroy didn't know what to do. She called down to the cave where Knight was getting ready for practice. This was Wednesday, the day before the game. Knight was telling Hammel about his concern over Andre Harris's continued lack of improvement—a frequent theme of late—when McElroy called nearly hysterical.

Knight asked for the phone number and called the boy's father himself. Politely, he explained how difficult it was to get tickets for the Purdue game, how his staff had really had to search to find four, and how this way, the boy, his mother and father, and a friend could still attend the game.

The man remained adamant. He insisted he had been promised six tickets. Indiana—Knight—was reneging on a promise. Knight was aghast. He was also furious. "Now you just listen to me for a minute," he said. "You berated my secretary, which you had no right to do, and you are acting as if these tickets are owed you. We don't owe you anything. All I wanted was for your son to come to an Indiana game. I really don't give a damn if you go and I certainly don't give a damn about some friends of yours.

Don't you know how much trouble we went to just to get four tickets?"

Apparently not. The man continued shouting. He and his family would just withdraw their future support for Indiana basketball. "Well, that's just fine," Knight yelled. "I don't want your support, Indiana doesn't want your support, and our players don't want your support." He slammed the phone.

For a moment, Knight just sat silently in his chair. Then he turned to Hammel. "Why do I even bother?" he said. "Why try to be nice to people? I wish everybody could have my job for a week."

He stood up and shook his head. "I hate this job, I really hate it." His voice was rising. Finally, he turned towards the door and pounded his fist against it. "Jesus Christ, Jesus Christ. I just can't believe it." He slammed the door on his way out.

Nothing frustrated Knight more—short of failure by his team to help on defense—than being put in the role of the heavy. He had wanted to do something nice. This was not unusual. Quietly, Knight did a good deal of charity work and was always picking out people to write or call or send things to. Now he had wanted to help a little boy and he ended up in a shouting match with an adult. The last thing he wanted was a shouting match with anyone, especially twenty-four hours before Purdue.

Hammel knew this. An hour later he volunteered to call the man back. "Let's start over," Hammel began the conversation. A compromise was reached: the family would get six tickets for the Minnesota game. Still, Knight had been scarred—again.

The other distraction that week was a brief, almost amusing one. Like everyone else, Knight had followed the adventures of Tito Horford with great amusement. Horford was a 7-foot-2-inch stud center, the kind everyone wants desperately. He had been recruited by every bandit school in the country. First, he had signed with Houston, but the NCAA had ruled that out because Houston had broken rules in recruiting him. Then he landed briefly at LSU, fleeing in the face of another NCAA investigation. He had talked to Kentucky and Louisville, who had said thanks but no thanks, knowing the NCAA posse was only a step behind Horford.

Hearing and reading this, Knight had an idea. If there was one program that could recruit Horford without getting into trouble with the NCAA, it was Indiana. If Horford came to Indiana, it would give him instant credibility. Maybe the kid wasn't for sale, as everyone thought, after all. Knight toyed with the idea. A 7-2 center would be a boon. If Horford couldn't do the work academically, so be it. He would be told he would have to enroll and pass his classes for a semester before he could play.

That weekend, Knight decided it was worth a try. He called a friend, who was a lawyer, and talked to him about contacting Horford. He didn't want Horford offered even so much as a visit, but he wanted the scenario explained to him. If Horford was interested, a visit would be arranged. It was a tantalizing idea. But that weekend Horford visited Miami of Florida. Early that week, he enrolled there. End of the adventure.

"Would we have shocked the world or what?" Knight asked the coaches, amused at the very thought of the ultimate bandit recruit signing to play at Indiana.

While all this was going on, there was also the little matter of playing Purdue. This game would be at least as tough as Ohio State had been, perhaps tougher. Purdue was playing very well and was tied for first place in the Big Ten with a 5–1 record. Indiana was 3–2.

Practice on Monday and Tuesday was tense. Knight continued to be angry with Harris. "You know, I'm sick and tired of losing to these sonsofbitches," he said at one point. "But I guarantee you if you boys aren't ready for their competitiveness, they'll come in here and thump you. Andre, I'm so sick and tired of your pouting, I can't tell you. Just play the game, son. Go after it."

When practice was over—this was Tuesday—Knight sent Wright to talk to Harris. "Either he needs a personality transplant or I do," Knight said.

After they had gone through their last walk-through on Wednesday evening, Knight asked the players how they wanted to play this game. "Should we just try to contain them or should we go after them defensively?"

There was only one way for the players to answer this question: go after them. An Indiana player would no sooner vote to play containment defense than he would suggest a two-three zone. Knight knew this, but he wanted the players to tell him.

"I really think," he told the coaches that night, "that we're really ready to go. I hope I'm not fooling myself."

Game day was by far the prettiest seen in Bloomington in months. It was sunny, breezy, and warm, the temperature pushing towards fifty. Knight's mood was good when he and the coaches went to Smitty's, and they lingered over lunch as if knowing that once it was over there was serious work to be done.

The game was about as difficult as one could imagine. The intensity level on both sides was high from the start. Purdue coach Gene Keady was guaranteed to do two things every season: dress worse than any coach in the country and produce a team that played as hard as any in the country. When Keady's center, Melvin McCants, picked up his third foul early, Keady took off his jacket and hurled it into the stands behind the bench. If Knight had tossed the jacket, it would have made headlines. Keady just looked better without the jacket on.

Alford caught a knee on the thigh early, but he never left the game. At halftime it was 34–34. "They're just hanging on," Knight told his team. "We make a couple plays early and we're gonna be just fine."

But the first play that mattered wasn't made by Indiana. On the first possession of the half, Purdue's Doug Lee nailed Calloway with a knee and Calloway crumpled. He had to be helped off. Calloway had scored twelve first-half points, high for both teams. His absence was crucial.

It became one of those games where every possession is painful because it is so important. The tension was almost unbearable. Hammel was almost silent the entire second half. Neither team led by more than two points for the first nine minutes until a Harris tip-in made it 54–50 Indiana with eleven minutes to go. But Purdue came back. A jumper by Troy Lewis, the same Troy Lewis Indiana passed up because of Delray Brooks, put Purdue up 57–56 with 9:30 remaining.

The lead continued to seesaw. Harris fouled out with 6:30 left. Thomas, still not 100 percent on his ankle, was gone a minute later. McCants's two foul shots made it 66–62, Purdue. The situation could hardly be more grim: Harris and Thomas had fouled out. Calloway couldn't play. Todd Meier and Steve Eyl were playing the inside positions now. They should have been overmatched.

Purdue went to a box-and-one, four men playing zone, one hounding Alford. Keady was willing to let anyone but Alford shoot the ball. When Morgan tossed a brick with 4:20 to go and Lee nailed a twenty-footer, it was 69–64. The crowd was completely silent. Hammel just shook his head. Knight stood in front of the bench, his sweater rolled up, his hands on his hips. He didn't say anything, either. What was left to say?

Thirty seconds later, Alford turned the ball over, and with 3:30 left it was Purdue's game. The Boilermakers had a five-point lead, they had the basketball, and Indiana's entire starting front line was out of the game.

What happened next was nothing short of miraculous. During the last four minutes of regulation, Purdue did not score again. Meier made a steal that led to one Alford free throw. When he missed the second shot, Meier rebounded. He fed Stew Robinson, who missed. But Eyl got the rebound and put it back and suddenly it was 69–67. Meier and Eyl—overmatched—had made it a ballgame. A moment later, Alford put his 6-1, 160-pound body in the path of 6-9, 215-pound Melvin McCants and did what Knight swore he never did—he took a charge. He made both foul shots to tie the game at 69–69.

No one scored the rest of regulation. Alford got the last shot, but his twenty-five-footer bounced off the rim. In the overtime, Purdue scored first, taking a 70–69 lead when Jeff Arnold made one of two free throws with 4:33 left. Amazingly, that was Purdue's last point of the game. But Indiana couldn't score either. Alford missed. Eyl turned the ball over. Eyl missed the front end of a one-and-one. Finally, with 1:52 left, Alford scored his twenty-seventh point on a baseline jumper. It was 71–70.

That was the final score. But the game wasn't secure until Purdue's Mack Gadis had missed a short jumper in the lane and Meier somehow got the rebound. In nineteen minutes, Meier got seven rebounds. The last was his biggest. The deed was done. Indiana had held Purdue to one point in nine minutes and somehow had won a game that it had absolutely no right to win.

"Miracle at Coogan's Bluff," Knight said much later that night. Before that, though, Knight had to meet with the press. He never said a word about the game. Instead, he talked about what a beautiful day it had been and how he had gone fishing and had sat thinking how unimportant basketball truly was. He went on in that vein for several minutes, holding his audience spellbound. Finally he said, "I'd like to answer your questions, but I have to go plan another fishing trip for tomorrow," and walked out.

Exactly why Knight pulled this routine only Knight knows for certain. But he enjoyed it greatly. In fact, he grabbed several friends in the hallway before walking in, saying, "Watch this." For the first time all season, the locker room was not open to the press. "When you leave, tell those assholes you can't talk," Knight told the players. "Don't tell them I said you couldn't talk. Just tell them . . . Oh, tell them I said you couldn't talk."

Why?

"Just a little victory for me," Knight said. "Why not?"

———

Once again, the schedule wasn't doing Indiana any favors. The Illinois game would be at 1 P.M. on Saturday because of national television, meaning the players had just thirty-six hours to recuperate from Purdue. It had probably been the most physical—not to mention emotional—game of the season. Knight knew there was no sense even trying to practice on Friday. He wasn't feeling very good himself; his head was stuffed and he was again having trouble breathing.

The person suffering the most that day, though, was Harris. He had shot four for eleven against Purdue and committed a foolish fifth foul. Harris was now occupying the penthouse suite in the Knight doghouse; Jadlow had an apartment down the hall. Looking at the Purdue tape, Knight had commented to the coaches, "We didn't get any bargain with these junior college players."

Those words stung Joby Wright, who was holding out hope that Knight would overlook Keith Smart's gold chains and try to sign him. Wright had probably spent more time with Harris since October 15 than he had spent with his wife. When Knight yelled, Wright soothed, cajoled, and pleaded. Harris listened, but often, Wright was convinced, he didn't hear. Harris, like Alford the year before, honestly believed he was working hard and trying to improve.

But he wasn't. Instead of using his athletic ability to full advantage, Harris made silly plays. He had a terrible habit of catching the ball near the basket and instead of just jumping over people as he was capable of doing, he would spin and shoot a fallaway jump shot—one that almost inevitably missed. He was still lunging on defense—a major sin—and because he was not an instinctive defensive player he often arrived one step late to help, usually just in time to commit a foul.

What made the situation even tougher for Harris and Jadlow was that they had not yet gained complete acceptance from their teammates. Each of them was different from the others: Harris was quiet, and often came across as aloof. This had been especially true early when the players grew sick of hearing Knight tell Harris day after day what a great athlete he was.

Now, with Todd Meier, who couldn't jump over the foul line, moved ahead of Harris in the pecking order, some of the players couldn't help but giggle a little about how short-lived Knight's love affair with junior college players had been. But at the same time, looking at the now forlorn Harris and Jadlow, they empathized. After all, each of them had been there, too.

The worst thing for the players about playing at 1 P.M. on Saturday was getting up at 8 A.M. to go look at spaghetti an hour later. They were sore and tired, but they were ready to play this game. Illinois had hammered Indiana three straight times, including the infamous "benching" game the previous season. Knight believed that Illinois had as much talent as anyone in the country, but he also believed the Illini could be beaten because they weren't well coached. That was why three straight losses, each of them decisive, galled him.

The players had extra incentive for this game. The Super Bowl was the next afternoon at 5:15. Most of the players, being from the Midwest, either were or had become avid Chicago Bears fans. They wanted very much to see the game. A loss to Illinois would diminish greatly their chances of doing so.

The coaches knew this. They also wanted to see the game. "If we lose," Felling asked during pregame, "do you think we can still watch the Super Bowl?"

"I would imagine," Waltman answered wryly, "that one of our three practices tomorrow would be during the Super Bowl."

Felling was still learning.

John Batts, a hunting guide from Montana who was just one of Knight's many friends in town for the game, was keeping Knight company after his pregame steam. There were no coaches around, so Knight asked Batts his favorite question: "What do you think, John, will we ever win another game?"

"Sure you will," Batts said. "You're going to win today."

"I don't know," Knight said. "I don't know if we can handle the brilliance of Lou Henson."

They handled it. The game was no different from the Ohio State or Purdue games, a brutal, every-possession-is-life-and-death affair. Illinois looked overwhelming early. Center Ken Norman was dominating the inside. Alford was having trouble getting shots against cat-quick Illinois guard Bruce Douglas. And Calloway simply couldn't move on his knee. He was one for five at halftime and only played five minutes in the second half.

But with Illinois leading 33–22 and the afternoon beginning to look grim, Stew Robinson rode in on his white horse to save the Hoosiers. He forced Douglas into a turnover and then made two foul shots. He hit a fifteen-footer. He made another foul shot and then he stole two straight passes and scored both times. He scored nine points in four minutes and Indiana scored the last twelve points of the half to lead—amazingly—34–33 at intermission.

There was one small incident just before halftime. The final point of the half was scored by Alford on a free throw with two seconds left. He had been fouled with the score tied and went to the line to shoot two free throws. It had become a tradition at Assembly Hall during Alford's three years to talk him through his foul shots. Alford had a ritual: He stepped to the line, wiped his hands on his socks and then his shorts, and took the ball from the referee. He dribbled three times, then shot. The crowd followed this ritual, chanting, "Socks, shorts, 1-2-3 . . . Swish." They had done it hundreds of times and Alford almost always responded with a swish.

But this time he missed the first shot. Knight was furious. Not with Alford—with the crowd. As soon as Alford missed, Knight began gesturing across the floor and yelling at the crowd to be quiet. This was not unique. In fact, two nights earlier, Knight had ordered Crabbe to quiet the crowd when they had chanted, "Bullshit," after a couple of calls went against Indiana. His exact words to Crabbe had been, "You tell those sonsofbitches to cut that shit out!"

After Alford made the second shot and time ran out, Knight stalked across the floor to the Indiana cheerleaders. "I better not hear any more of that goddamn crap in the second half when our players are shooting free throws," he yelled. "I'm holding you people responsible for that. Jesus Christ, that one point can cost us a ballgame because of that bullshit!"

As Knight turned towards the locker room, he spotted two cheerleaders' megaphones in his path. He kicked them out of the way. Naturally, the TV cameras picked all this up. Later, Knight would learn that he had clipped one of the cheerleaders on the leg with one of the megaphones. He called the girl and asked her to come to his office. He apologized for the accident. "If I had known that the megaphone had hit you, I would have stopped right then and said something," Knight said.

Stunned by this outpouring, the girl answered, "Thank you, coach, I appreciate that."

Knight looked at her again and said, "But do you understand why I did it?"

Sure, she understood. Alford missed a free throw, why not kick a megaphone?

As it turned out, Knight was just getting his leg warmed up. The second half was no different from the first. With twelve minutes left, an Anthony Welch jumper gave Illinois a 54–48 lead. A moment later, Harris missed a lob pass from Morgan. Knight screamed for a foul. No call. Then, Alford missed and appeared to be pushed. Knight turned and slammed his foot into his chair.

He turned around just in time to see Thomas block a Winters shot, leading to a Robinson bucket. But fifteen seconds later, Robinson was called for a touch foul near midcourt. That was more than Knight could bear. He picked up his chair—uh-oh— and slammed it down—whew. There was a TV time-out and Knight called official Randy Drury over. He pleaded his case.

Illinois was getting away with murder inside. Drury nodded and walked off. On TV, CBS colorman Billy Packer was saying that Drury should have given Knight a technical. Knight sent Alford over to continue the argument. As Alford was talking, Drury looked at Knight, who demonstrated how he thought Illinois was throwing elbows inside. When Knight swung his elbow, Drury blew his whistle. Technical—Knight's fifth of the season.

While Tony Wysinger made one of the two shots to make the score 55–50, Knight walked into the hallway, partly to talk to Floyd, telling him that he wanted to see Wortman when the game was over, and partly to calm down. Knight came back in time to see Norman called for walking—a makeup call—and Alford hit a twenty-footer to cut the margin to three.

Except for tossing a cup of water over his shoulder into the stands, Knight was relatively calm the rest of the afternoon. His team was superb. This was Daryl Thomas's day. His ankle seemed forgotten. Time and again he established position in the low post, caught the ball, and then used his quickness to get inside for a shot. He cut the margin to 62–60 with 4:38 left with just that kind of move.

Then Harris, who had missed several shots inside, tipped in a Robinson miss—the ball hit the rim three times and then bounced through—to tie the game. Illinois's Glynn Blackwell was called for steps and Thomas went inside again. He was fouled and made both shots. It was 64–62, Indiana. Douglas tied it. Alford untied it with 1:40 left. Then, a bad break. Harris made a great play, jumping out to partially block Welch's jumper. But the loose ball went right to Norman, who was fouled as he made a layup. It was 67–66, Illinois. No problem. Alford found Thomas inside, he was fouled and coolly made both shots to make it 68–67. Welch missed, Robinson rebounded. Indiana held, Alford was fouled. Thirty-one seconds left.

The fans had a new chant for Alford's free throws: "Shhhhhhhh." Amazingly, Alford again made only one of two. It was 69–67 and Illinois could tie. But Douglas missed and there was Winston Morgan going over all the Illinois big men for the rebound and getting fouled with seventeen seconds to go. Henson called time to let Morgan think about the one-and-one he had to shoot.

Morgan thought about it. "I thought, this is my time," he said later. He was right. Swish. Swish. It was over. Bad ankles, bad knees, bad thighs, kicked megaphones, and all, Indiana had won.

The joy in the locker room was unbridled. They had played about as well as they could have. Thomas had finished with thirty points, playing all forty minutes. "Do you know what you've done, Daryl?" Knight said gleefully. "You've gone from being a pussy to being a tiger. A goddamn tiger!" They cheered Thomas. They cheered Robinson, who had sparked them in the first half and finished with thirteen points, five assists, and four rebounds. They slapped one another silly. The locker room was jammed: among the visitors were Steve Green, Steve Alhfeld, Tom Abernerthy, and a slew of Knight's cronies from back in Orrville.

Finally, when they were quiet, Knight wanted to make plans for Sunday's meeting. "How about if we meet in here at 5:30?" There was silence. The Super Bowl started at 5:15. Would someone tell him? After all, they had won the damn game. The next voice belonged to Donald Boop, the Orrville dentist. "Super Bowl starts at 5:15," he said softly.

Knight whirled and glared at Boop as if Boop was a Russian MiG violating the airspace in his locker room. "You running this team now, Boop?" But he couldn't hold the glare; his face was breaking into a broad grin. "Okay, boys, since Boop wants to watch the Super Bowl, how about 4:30?"

That was just fine with everybody, and the day now had four heroes: Thomas, Robinson, Morgan, and Boop.

———

Celebrations don't last long at Indiana. There isn't time; as soon as a Purdue is beaten, Illinois is waiting. Beat Illinois, and games at Iowa and Minnesota loom. "You beat as talented a team as you can find anywhere," Knight said after the Illinois victory. "You could play the NCAA final and not meet a better collection of players. Enjoy that. Take ten or fifteen minutes. Then start thinking about Iowa."

That was almost exactly how much time the coaches took. The players had a little bit longer, but by the time they arrived for their Sunday afternoon meeting, the giddiness of Saturday had been forgotten. It was a grim, snowy day and the streets were devoid of traffic, everyone staying inside to watch the Super Bowl.

Knight couldn't have cared less about the Super Bowl. He predicted that the Patriots would win—"short passes, they'll eat them up with short passes,"—and showed up fifteen minutes late for the 4:30 meeting. This was no upset. Knight often made the players wait. What he didn't understand was how tough that was on them. No one really wanted to start telling a joke or clowning around because no one knew when the door was going to swing open and when it did what kind of mood the coach who walked through it would be in.

Knight's mood was far less buoyant than it had been twenty-four hours earlier. He was upset because *The Indianapolis Star* had run a front-page picture of him slamming the chair. John Ryan had been contacted by the Associated Press: Would there be any action taken against Knight, Ryan was asked, for his behavior on Saturday? No comment, Ryan had responded.

Knight couldn't understand why his behavior on Saturday was newsworthy. "I haven't seen anybody write one word or run one picture on Keady throwing his coat here the other night," he said. "If I had done that it would have been on the front page."

Undoubtedly. Once again, Knight had to live with being guilty until proved innocent. If Keady had ever thrown a chair, his every act during a game would be monitored by TV, by camera, and by reporters. If Keady was one of the game's most outspoken and controversial figures, his behavior would be newsworthy at all times. Was that fair? No. Was that life? Yes.

"I can't think of a business more dishonest in this country than newspapers," Knight said, once again keeping matters totally in perspective.

Knight only kept the team for thirty minutes, going over Iowa's personnel. But he told Calloway he wanted him to do some extra shooting because he had obviously been bothered by the knee brace he had worn the day before. "How come you told Tim Garl before the game that the knee didn't bother you, and then you told Hammel after the game that it was bothering you?" Knight asked Calloway while he was shooting.

"I told them both that it was a little sore," Calloway said. "I said the same thing to both of them."

"Ricky," Knight continued, "is everyone from Withrow High School just a little bit of a pussy?"

Calloway laughed. He had learned quickly to shrug off most Knight insults. Dakich, who had taken more than his fair share in four years as a player, deserved credit for that.

While Calloway shot and everyone else watched the Super Bowl (Bears 44, Patriots 10, no short passes to be found), Alford shot free throws. He had missed one against Ohio State, one against Purdue, and two against Illinois. This constituted a major slump. He shot 300 that evening, making 290.

The coaches wanted to go watch the Super Bowl, too. But the boss wanted to sit around and chat, talk about how pleased he was with the way the team was playing, and discuss the Minnesota situation. The day before, Minnesota coach Jim Dutcher had resigned in the wake of three arrests of Minnesota players in Madison that Friday. All three players had been charged with sexual assault. Minnesota had forfeited that day's game to Northwestern and was considering canceling the rest of its schedule. Indiana was scheduled to play there the following Saturday.

"Boy, it'd be great if we could just go to Iowa, play, and come home and have a week off," Knight said. "But it can't happen. They have to play. You just can't say that a school of 40,000 can't field a basketball team because it loses three scholarship players. You have to play. We'll play."

Knight was correct. The next morning Minnesota announced that it would play with the five scholarship players it had left on the team and several walk-ons from the football team.

Knight was more upset that morning by something else in the paper. Having gotten a no comment from John Ryan, the AP had called Ralph Floyd for a comment on Knight's Saturday behavior. Floyd had been asked whether the university was contemplating any action against Knight. "No," Floyd had answered, "not at this time."

The last four words had been like waving a red flag in the face of a bull. Knight charged to Floyd's office demanding to know what the hell Floyd had been talking about. Nothing. Floyd had been talking in nonspeak and had nonspoken four words that meant nothing. Indiana wasn't about to discipline Knight, but

Knight was angry with Floyd for not handling the situation better.

"I really get screwed," Knight said that day, "because I don't kiss the press's ass. People, even people that know me like Ralph, just can't understand until they've been through it what it feels like to have gnomes like that go after you. The vast majority of people read that and think, 'Oh, so Knight's acting like an asshole again.'

"I know I'm not an asshole. I know how I am with people and how I treat people day to day, and then I have to hear about people coming up to my kid and saying, 'Well, I see your dad had another tantrum.' "

Like so many public figures, Knight hurt most when his public persona invaded his private life. That, more than any gnomes or anything Ralph Floyd said or didn't say, bothered him.

For the most part, though, this was as laid-back a week as Knight had spent all season. His team had won five in a row. It was playing good, hard-nosed basketball. It was winning close games again. The crisis of the first week of Big Ten play had been weathered. Knight's mood was so good that he began checking on reports he had been hearing about a player named Damon Bailey.

Damon Bailey was an eighth grader. He would enroll in college in the fall of 1990, the same fall that Knight would turn fifty. Knight had heard he was a gifted young guard, a player already turning heads even at the age of fourteen. With his team playing well and coaching fun again, Knight was interested in Damon Bailey. Maybe, he told Hammel, they should drive down to Shawswicke (about thirty miles south of Bloomington) and look at this kid. Maybe next week.

This week was a travel week. The toughest trip Indiana makes all winter is the one to Iowa and Minnesota. The flights are the longest, often the bumpiest, and the weather is almost always brutally cold. When Knight had considered the CBS job in 1981 he had told a friend that one reason he was thinking about it was that "I'm not sure how many more times I want to go back to Iowa City, Iowa, in January."

The temperature had been below zero for a full week just prior to Indiana's arriving in Iowa City, but it shot all the way up into the teens on game day. Knight had worked the team lightly all week. He had done little on Monday. "I'm exhausted," he said. "If I feel lousy, the players must feel worse." The workouts Tuesday and Wednesday had also been brief. Beating Iowa was simple: beat their press and you beat the Hawkeyes. Don't beat it and they will beat you.

Knight knew this would be a wound-up crowd. On local TV, the game promo screamed, "Come see the Hawkeyes face the team that everyone loves to hate, Bobby Knight and the Indiana Hoosiers." And the local paper had a long story on Knight's bench behavior. It began this way: "Put away your chairs and your children, Bobby Knight is coming to town." Lou Henson was quoted in the story as saying, "He gets away with more on the bench than anyone." Bob Wortman was quoted as saying, "We can't allow behavior like that to continue."

Fortunately, Knight didn't see the paper that day. His pregame mood was sanguine. He talked during his pregame radio show about how this team was beginning to remind him of the 1984 team, the one that had been expected to do almost nothing and that had come within one basket of the Final Four. Knight was as relaxed as anyone could remember him on a game day.

The Era of Good Feeling ended quickly. This time, the Iowa press beat Indiana. On the first possession of the game, Calloway walked. He had four turnovers in the first four minutes. The Hoosiers, who had committed fourteen turnovers in two full games, had eleven by halftime. It was 6–0, Iowa. Then it was 22–8, Iowa. Knight called time and ripped them. They scored six straight points to make it 22–14, but Iowa guard Andre Banks was having one of those nights where, going inside consistently, he was unstoppable. His backcourt mate, Jeff Moe, another kid from Indiana, was lights-out from outside. They combined to build the lead back to 36–19. Alford had a shot blocked by Banks. That almost never happened. Iowa scored on nine straight possessions. By halftime it was 44–28.

Knight was shocked. He had expected a tough game, but never this. In seventeen games, Indiana, even in its four losses, had never been this far behind. It had been in every game until the end, but now it was getting blown out by— in Knight's opinion— a team it should be able to play with.

"Did you not listen when we told you this team was quick?"
he said. "Did you hear anything we said all week? Jesus Christ,
boys, we're getting hammered. I mean hammered. This game is
over—we've lost. There's almost no reason to play the goddamn
second half."

They played the second half, but it really didn't matter. Iowa
built the lead to as much as 67–45. Knight sat Thomas and Alford
for the last ten minutes because he could see no point in playing
them. Indiana made a late charge to make the final score a respectable 79–69, but it was no contest. For the first time all season,
Indiana had been embarrassed.

One year ago, Knight almost undoubtedly would have gone off
after such a game. He would have called them names, questioned
their manhood, and gone on and on. But not this time. He knew
they had given him everything they had to win five straight
games, and he also knew that a letdown had been almost inevitable. Was he happy about it? No.

"I worked to get you ready to play this game and you went
out and got played off your feet from the beginning," he told the
players. "I think you all owe me an apology for that. You were
not ready for what this team threw at you. You should be very
disappointed in yourselves. You just went out to play rather than
going out and playing to win. You owe everyone concerned with
Indiana basketball an apology."

But that was all. Until they got to the plane. By then, the
frustration was starting to fester. "Boys," Knight said as they
waited to take off, "we're going to find out what kind of people
you are on Saturday. Saturday will determine what kind of a team
this is.

"Steve [Alford], if you were feeling sick again, you did us all
a disservice by not coming to me and telling me you were too
sick to play. You and Stew both owe us a hell of a game Saturday.
Stew, you were just terrible. Do you realize that no team in the
Big Ten other than Northwestern has been as far behind in a
game as we were tonight?"

He sat down to let them think about that a little. Felling was
seated across from him. "This game was almost impossible for
them psychologically," Knight said softly. "They had won five
they had to win and Iowa was coming off a bad loss to Wisconsin.

We would have to have been very good to win tonight and we were bad."

Reasonable. Rational. But a moment later, as the plane started to taxi, Knight began running down botched plays. He was midway through a description of a Steve Eyl defensive error when the plane suddenly, frighteningly, skidded. It slid almost off the runway and stopped. Fortunately, it had not built up much speed.

For a moment no one moved. No one said anything, including Knight. The pilots pulled the plane back onto the runway, taxied again, and took off without incident. The plane was well above the clouds before Knight started talking again. "Like I was saying about Eyl . . ."

———

It was after midnight when the plane landed—without further incident—in Minneapolis. Before they even left the airport they heard some bad news: Minnesota, with its five remaining players, had beaten Ohio State. The Gophers were not going to roll over and die. Saturday's game would probably be difficult.

As soon as the bus arrived at the hotel, the players ate and then trooped wearily up to Knight's room to look at the game tape.

A session like this one was not apt to accomplish much. Everyone was exhausted, including Knight. For the players, this session was punishment: play poorly and you have to listen to the coach ramble on about your mistakes until all hours of the morning. Of course, Knight didn't see it that way. After a loss, his mind focused on how much work had to be done. To him, everything that had gone before was wiped out. All he could see was that night.

"I can't remember an Indiana team being worse prepared than you people were tonight," he said as the tape droned on. "Stew, you were no more into the game mentally than a dead man. You are simply incapable of putting two good games together. The way we played this game there is not one team in the Big Ten we could have beaten. I can't believe that you could work as hard as you work and then go out on the court and play like that. I just cannot understand it.

"If you play like this against Minnesota you'll get your ass beat. They came up with a great performance against Ohio State, and they'll do the same thing against us Saturday. Everyone says they only have five guys, well, hell, it only takes five to play the goddamn game. We lose this game, boys, and we're right back to last year. Right back. You better be ready to go to work tomorrow.''

They went to bed with those final words in their ears: *last year.* Every time the players heard those words they shuddered a little. Saturday's game would bring them to the midway point of the Big Ten season. They did not want to live through a second half anything like 1985.

It snowed from the moment Indiana's plane touched down early Friday morning right through the moment it took off late Saturday in Minneapolis. The streets seemed empty. The hotel was empty. It was like being in a ghost town. Knight and Hammel went for not one but two walks on Friday, Knight alternating between understanding that the Iowa game was almost inevitable and worrying that the team was going to sink to that level and stay there.

Hammel had learned to just listen to these monologues. He knew that Knight wasn't looking for input as much as he was looking for a sounding board. But when Knight switched subjects, even for a minute, Hammel would often jump in quickly and try to steer the conversation away from Indiana basketball. It was as if this was a chance to give Knight a mental coffee break. If someone didn't change the subject, Knight was apt to go on for hours wondering if his team would ever win another game.

Today's coffee break subject was Joe Lapchick, the old St. John's coach who had been one of Knight's early coaching mentors. Knight had been talking about dealing with criticism when he thought about something Lapchick had told him.

"Right after I got the job as the coach at West Point I went to Lapchick's house in Yonkers to tell him about it," Knight remembered. "He looked at me and said, 'Do you care what people think of you?'

"I said, 'Not really.'

"And he said, 'Good, because if you want to be liked, don't coach.' "

Knight laughed remembering the line. Hammel kept him on

Lapchick and Knight kept reminiscing. "The first time I met him was when Tates (Locke) took me to one of those New York writers' lunches in the city. Joe took me by the arm and introduced me to everyone in the room. Made me feel really important.

"Later that year, I went on a scouting trip to the Midwest to see St. John's play DePaul and Marquette. I was scouting St. John's because we were getting ready to play them. Lapchick insisted that I travel with them everywhere, eat with them, do everything with them. Of course we ended up beating them.

"After he retired (in 1965) he would come to the Garden whenever we played. When I would walk onto the court he would look at me and put his hand under his chin and push it up. He always said to me, 'Keep your nose in the air. Be arrogant. Walk with kings.'

"He's the reason I have so few rules on my team. He told me not to make any rules because that way if a bad kid screws up you get rid of him. If a good kid screws up you do what you have to do and let it go at that. Rules just get you in trouble."

Knight's voice softened as the memories of Lapchick kept coming back to him. "I was in my car driving to a basketball camp in the Poconos in August of 1970 when I heard that he had died. It was exactly three weeks after my dad died. I had a scrapbook in the back seat of my car that Joe had put together about the betting scandals of the 1950s. He made every one of his players read it and then sign it each year.

"I went back to the city for the funeral. Just after I got there, Mrs. Lapchick took me aside into another room. She told me she wanted to be alone for a minute because she wanted to tell me something. She said to me, 'You know, you never played for Joe, but you should know you were always one of his favorite boys.' When we won the NIT in 1979, I had her come out to center court with me to accept the trophy."

Knight's eyes glistened. The Iowa loss seemed far, far away. At least for a few minutes.

———

Whether it was the passing of twenty-four hours, the nonstop snow, or the huge Italian dinner Knight ate on Friday night with a coterie of local friends, his mood on Saturday morning was 180 degrees different from that of Friday.

Knight awoke early on Saturday and wanted to look again at the Iowa tape. Knight will often look at the tape of a loss five or six times. Usually, he can figure out exactly what went wrong the first time through, but he looks again and again anyway. Saturday morning, Knight couldn't find the tape. Manager Jim Kelly had accidentally put it into his pocket and forgotten it was there.

"Kelly," Knight asked after breakfast, "knowing my *relative* lack of patience, do you think I would be upset if I wanted to look at a tape and my Irish manager had it in his trench-coat pocket?"

"Maybe a little," Kelly answered, not certain what was coming next.

"Well, Kelly," Knight said, putting his arm around him, "that's where you and I differ. I'm not at all upset. You have to learn to understand human frailties. People make mistakes. Learn some benevolence towards your fellow man—like me."

The coaches, listening to this speech, broke up. "If we can just win this one," Waltman said to Felling, "we could be all right." He paused. "Why does it seem like I say that every game day?"

Knight was back to talking about positioning at the morning walk-through. Positioning and opportunities. "We told you at Northwestern and Wisconsin that you had to play your best basketball to get back into position. We told you before Ohio State, Purdue, and Illinois that these were opportunities. You took advantage, something last year's team never did. But now, after Iowa, we're back to needing wins to create opportunities. We've got this game tonight and then Wisconsin and Northwestern next week. We need those three games to have more opportunities— for the conference, for the NCAAs. But you have to start setting that up tonight. There is no cushion, no margin for error. Now, goddamn it, let's play the way we can."

Before they got on the bus to go back to the hotel, Knight took Andre Harris aside. He knew Harris was struggling and getting down on himself. He also knew that Harris was thinking Knight had given up on him. Not so, Knight told him. "It isn't that we don't think you're contributing, Andre. It's just that we think you have the potential to contribute so much more if you'll just try to do what we're telling you."

Harris nodded. But no one was really certain how much he

really heard. That morning at breakfast he had called Jim Kelly "Bill." That had sent the players into gales of giggles. It wasn't that anyone disliked Harris. He was just different. He and Jadlow were both different. And right now, both were struggling—on and off the court.

Harris struggled again that night. But he was not alone. All of Knight's pregame fears became reality quickly. The crowd was wild from the start. This was, after all, the ultimate underdog story: team decimated by scandal holding together and handling opponents they should have no chance against. Williams Arena, the ancient Minnesota field house, was chaotic from the first minute of the game.

Because of that, Knight desperately wanted his team to get a good start. "Let's take this crowd right out of the game," he said in the locker room. "There is no way we can allow playing us to be anything like playing Ohio State was for these people. Let's jump on them and get things going our way right away."

It didn't happen that way. Calloway and Alford were shooting well, but that was it. No one else could buy a basket. Indiana wanted a quick pace. It didn't get it. Minnesota controlled the boards and the pace. At halftime, it was 33–29 Minnesota, and the Gophers had scored twelve of their points by rebounding their own misses and putting them back for baskets.

The players, understanding that they were facing a potential disaster, were snappish with one another. Alford yelled at Morgan for missing a box-out. Robinson was on Harris, who failed to score the entire half. But most of all, when they got to the locker room, Knight was on everyone.

"Last year all over again, boys," he said. "We told you and told you that this game would be tough. Did you not believe us? You didn't believe us when we told you Iowa would be quick. Did you think this team would just die for you? What's your excuse going to be this time? Huh? I am sick and tired of hearing excuses for this team.

"We've done all we can do. We've given you an offense and a defense. That's all we can do. The rest has to come from you. Daryl, do you want to play? Because if you don't, tell me and I'll put Todd [Meier] into the game. If you aren't tough enough to play, we'll play someone else. Stew, playing you right now is like playing four on five. You haven't pass-faked yet in this game. Winston, son, you've got to box out. You people have given them twelve points not boxing out. Twelve. It's like we started the game behind 12–0."

And so on. The conclusion: "The next five minutes are more important than any you have played all season. Now, we'll find out just what kind of team you boys want to be."

If that had been the case, Indiana's season would have been over. The first five minutes were a calamity. Minnesota kept punching the ball inside. Their 7-1 center John Shasky got position on Thomas three straight times, turned, and easily shot over him. His last basket in the series, a soft ten-footer from the baseline, put Minnesota up 44–33.

Knight called time. No holding back now, he blasted them. He called them quitters, accused them of giving up. "I can't do anything for you if you aren't tough enough not to quit when you get behind."

Everyone was guilty—especially Thomas. Knight yanked him from the game, and when the time-out was over, he was still screaming. "If you don't want to play, then don't go in the f—— game, Daryl. Same old shit with you."

In the meantime, Calloway threw away another pass. Minnesota could go up thirteen. But Ray Gaffney missed an open jump shot. Suddenly, remarkably, Indiana revived. Alford hit from the baseline. Calloway made a steal and Morgan scored. Minnesota called a quick time-out. It didn't matter. Knight asked Thomas if he wanted to play. Thomas said yes.

Quickly, Alford made a steal and Calloway scored. It was 44–39. Marc Wilson missed for Minnesota, Morgan rebounded and threw a long pass to Calloway, whose layup rolled in as he was fouled. The free throw made it 44–42. Another Minnesota miss and Thomas scored inside to tie the game at 44–44. It had taken less than four minutes, an 11–0 run. It may have been, to coin a phrase, the most important four minutes of the season.

Minnesota hung on for a while, leading again at 49–48 with ten minutes to play, but fatigue was finally catching up. A Thomas follow-up gave Indiana the lead at 50–49. Alford hit a jumper to make it 52–49. Wilson made a foul shot to cut it to 52–50, but that was Minnesota's last gasp. It did not score a single point during the next 7:07. Even though Indiana only produced six points during that period, it was enough. The Hoosiers had outlasted the game Gophers. The final was 62–54. Minnesota had scored ten points during the last fifteen minutes.

Victory cures a lot of ills. Knight had reason to be disturbed by the first twenty-five minutes, but they had come back and won the game and that was what mattered. "You played terrible defense for twenty-five minutes to get in a hole," Knight said. "But you did an excellent job the last fifteen minutes to get out of it. Last year we couldn't have done that.

"Daryl, when you went back in, you played. Goddamn it, Daryl, you're tougher than all these guys. They can't guard you, Daryl. If they block a shot, fine. Just shoot it again. Keep going after it no matter what, okay?"

Thomas nodded. Everyone was relieved. With Wisconsin and Northwestern at home coming up, there was an excellent chance that they would be 8–3 in league play and 16–5 overall with four weeks left in the season. After winning seven and fifteen, respectively, all of last season, that wasn't bad. Morgan, though, was disturbed at some of the sniping. "We can't be getting on each other," he said after Knight had left. "Damn, we got enough to worry about without getting on each other."

No one answered. But everyone agreed.

It was three o'clock by the time the plane reached home. Knight talked to the coaches all the way home about how tired he was of not being able to attack teams defensively. "We haven't been able to play defense the way I want to for three years now," he said. "Yet, somehow, we've won fifty-five games. I guess that's pretty good. But boy, does it tire me out."

Everyone was tired. And sick. Felling had the flu and Calloway, Morgan, and Alford were so sick that Garl insisted they stay in bed on Sunday and Monday. Their illness, however, was a relatively minor concern. Once again, a week that should have been easy for Knight was going to be full of land mines. And, as always, before the week was over, everyone was going to feel as if they had stepped on a couple of them.

13

You Can't Go Home Again

The tribulations began right away on Monday morning. Academic supervisor Buzz Kurpius informed Knight that there was a problem with Andre Harris: since the semester had started two weeks ago, Harris had not been going to class—at all.

Skipping class was not a bright thing to do under any circumstances, but for Harris, the timing could not have been worse. His first-semester grades, with tutoring help and the Dakich chauffeuring service to get him where he had to be each morning, had been a little bit better than C's. That wasn't bad, but it certainly wasn't enough to retire on. Now, during a period when he was playing poorly—he finished the Minnesota game with two points and one rebound—he also wasn't going to class.

A year earlier, Harris might have been gone. That had been Mike Giomi's fate. But Knight had a little more patience this season—and a better team. That may have saved Harris. Barely. "He thinks I'm picking on him," Knight said after telling Harris he was benched indefinitely. "He's really going to think I'm picking on him when he flunks out and I don't petition to get him readmitted."

Three players were sick. Another was deep in the doghouse. Nothing made Knight more uptight than a week with two games that looked easy and could end up tough. But there was more.

There was Ohio State.

Ohio State had not been as lucky at Minnesota as Indiana had. It had not escaped the way the Hoosiers did. And, as it turned out, that humiliation was the last straw. Eldon Miller, who had coached there for nine years, was called in Monday and told he was gone at season's end. The athletic director, Rick Bay, wanted Miller to announce he was resigning. No way. Miller told the press he had been fired.

Many names would be linked to the job. But one name came up right away: Robert Montgomery Knight. After all, it seemed reasonable: if Ohio State wanted to shake up its program, who better than Knight? Bring the alumnus home—regardless of the cost. What the public didn't know was that even though Knight was still friendly with many of his old teammates and close to his Ohio State coach, Fred Taylor, that period of his life was one he would just as soon keep behind him.

In fact, Knight's four years at Ohio State may have been the only time in his life that he had not been a star, not been in control. Knight was used to being the boss. He had almost always gotten his way in life—except for those four years in college.

———

He was born October 25, 1940, the first and only child of Carroll and Hazel Knight. His father, known to one and all as Pat, was a railroad man who had grown up on an Oklahoma farm and moved east as a young man, stopping in Orrville because it was a crossroads of the railroads in those post–World War I days. There, he met Hazel Henthorne, a schoolteacher who lived in Akron but taught in Orrville. Shy, Pat Knight had a friend ask her for a date. She said no. He tried again. She said yes. They were married in 1934. He was thirty-seven, she was thirty-one. Six years later, much to her surprise, Hazel Knight discovered that the cold she thought she had was slightly more than that.

One can almost imagine Bouncing Baby Bobby crashing into the world, gray eyes flashing, looking around the delivery room of the hospital and saying, "Bet you sonsofbitches weren't expecting me." It is the kind of scene the adult Knight would have loved.

The world young Bobby grew up in was not your ordinary household. Pat Knight had a severe hearing problem, so father-son communication was often unspoken. There was a closeness between the two, though, much of it coming through hunting and fishing, something Pat Knight taught his son at an early age. Around Orrville, Pat Knight was viewed as a tough, stubborn, uncommonly honest man. To this day, when Bob Knight wants to make a point about how honest a person is, he compares him to his father. They may not have been as close as many fathers and sons, but Bobby revered his father, respected his authority, and learned quickly never to question it.

Bobby's best friend as a little boy, even as a teenager, was his grandmother. Sarah Henthorne had come to live with her daughter and son-in-law three years before Bobby was born and became the person the little boy turned to most often. "When Bobby would get in trouble, he would come home and tell his grandmother," Hazel Knight remembers. "He'd always make her promise not to tell me, then he would tell her and ask her what she thought."

What she thought, for the most part, was that her grandson was the most wonderful little boy in the world. Early on it was apparent that this was not an ordinary child: He was uncommonly bright, made A's in school with little trouble, and was always a good athlete. He even did well in the second grade when his teacher was Hazel Knight.

He played Little League baseball and was always a good hitter. Before long, he was introduced to basketball by a man named Dave Knight (no relation). Bobby was in the sixth grade when Dave Knight took him to the gym to show him this new sport. "Always stay between your man and the basket," Dave Knight told him. And so, on the first day he played basketball, Bobby Knight learned his first lesson about playing defense.

He grew quickly and became a star athlete. By the time he was in eighth grade he was 6-1 and he was averaging twenty-nine points per game playing twenty-four-minute junior high school games. He was also good at football and baseball, but basketball was his obsession. They still tell stories about Bobby and his basketball, how he would carry or dribble it the half mile to school every morning; how he would stay in the park shooting until 2 A.M. when the weather was warm—the man who ran the park taught him how to turn the lights on and off—and how he would leave windows in the high school propped open so he could sneak in and shoot on winter weekends. Knight was so sophisticated that he figured out the best window to go through was the one leading to the music room because the room was set up like a little theater and the last row was only a short jump down from the window.

As a freshman at Orrville High School, he was on the varsity basketball team. This was unusual, and some of the parents of older boys not on the varsity were resentful. Kathy Harmon (then Kathy Halder), who was the star of the girls' basketball team, remembers the resentment and how Bobby would pretend it didn't bother him. "Except for losing games, he never liked to admit that anything bothered him," she says. 'But he was sensitive. He always seemed to hear everything people said about him."

What they said about him was not that different from what they say about him now. He was a superb student, never making lower than a B throughout high school, and he should have been chosen for the National Honor Society at the end of his sophomore year, but the teachers wouldn't nominate him because of his behavior. He had a bad temper. In Bobby's sophomore yearbook, Kathy Halder wrote, "To the English brain . . ." at the start; she finished by writing, "watch the temper."

The temper came more from father than from mother—at least according to mother. But it also came, undoubtedly, from growing up in an environment where he was always the star and the center of attention. Bobby grew up as the only child, for all intents and purposes, of not one but two women. His mother didn't drive a car, so his grandmother drove him everywhere. When it was time to learn to drive, his grandmother taught him.

In school, he was also a star—an excellent student and athlete. He was always close to his coaches, especially Bill Shunkwiler, the Orrville football coach, and Jack Graham, his basketball coach until senior year. While other boys might spend time with one another talking about girls, Bobby spent time with his coaches talking about how to get better. "He was always asking questions," Shunkwiler said. "You gave him an answer, it produced another question. He's always been that way. He can never know enough about a subject."

Both coaches were strict disciplinarians. No one got on the Orrville football team's bus without a coat and tie on. Today, no one gets on the Indiana basketball team bus without a coat and tie on. Shunkwiler believed greatly in using film to show players how to do things. No coach in the world makes more use of videotape today than Knight.

When Knight was a sophomore in high school, his parents built a home on North Vine Street, right down the street from the Orrville Power Plant. Hazel Knight still lives in that house. It is a small but comfortable one-story home, and Bobby slept in the sitting room. Shortly after the Knights moved in, Donald and Pauline Boop moved next door.

Don Boop was a dentist who had been wounded twice in World War II and then gone to dental school after the war was over. He was eighteen years older than Bobby when the two met, but they became fast friends. Every day when Bobby came home from practice—whatever the sport—he would stop at the Boops for a soda (Hazel Knight allowed no pop and no booze in her home). Boop was a sports fanatic, and in young Bobby he found someone to talk to, to encourage, and, on occasion, to drive down to Cleveland with when the Red Sox were in town to watch the great Ted Williams play.

By the time he was a senior. Bobby had grown to 6-4, although he was still slender at about 180 pounds. He was handsome with his short-cropped brown hair, the dimple in his left cheek, and the easy smile that lit up his face when he was happy. There were plenty of girls who wanted to date him, among them a junior named Nancy Falk. But most of Bobby's time was tied up with one sport or another. Often, he would take Halder to a basketball game and bring along a young friend named Bobby Weltlich, who was four years younger than he was. Later, Weltlich, now the coach at Texas, would be an assistant coach under Knight, first at West Point and then at Indiana.

He was an excellent shooter, even though he had a funny-looking jump shot. Instead of releasing the ball from right over his head, Knight would almost push it out of his hand from shoulder level. His college coach, Fred Taylor, believes he patterned the shot after an Ohio State player named Jamie Freeman. Others, including Shunkwiler, think he began shooting that way when he broke his foot as a junior and kept shoting while he had a walking cast on. In fact, Knight shot so much then that he drove his doctors crazy because he kept breaking casts.

Whatever the reason, the strange-looking shot stayed with Knight throughout college. The question in 1958, though, was where to go to college. He could go to a small school and almost undoubtedly be a starter and probably a star. Or he could go to a big time school like Cincinnati or Ohio State and take his chances there. In those days, scouting wasn't nearly as sophisticated as it is now. To get the big-time college coaches to consider Knight, Boop sent films of him to Cincinnati and Ohio State.

Senior year had not turned out the way Knight had hoped. He

had been the leading scorer for Orrville as both a sophomore and a junior, but the team hadn't been very good, winning just five games his junior year. That was disappointing. But what devastated Knight was the decision by Graham to leave Orrville for the chance to become a principal at another school. Knight was crushed. He felt deserted. He felt worse when the new coach turned out to be a man named Bob Gobin, who wasn't so much a coach as a recreation director. Gobin believed the games were played strictly for fun and everyone should have a chance to play. If Knight scored five straight baskets, Gobin would take him out, thinking it was time to give someone else a chance to play.

Knight was the star and the captain, and one night when a teammate was hurt and Gobin didn't call time to get him out of the game, Knight finally called time himself. Coach and player argued. The coach didn't think the player should act as if he knew more about the game than the coach. The player, in no uncertain terms, told the coach he *did* know more about the game than the coach.

"Bobby was right, he did know more basketball than Gobin," Boop says now, remembering the incident. "But at that point, Gobin didn't much care. As far as he was concerned, Bobby was off the team."

The following day, Pat Knight, Bobby Knight, and Boop huddled at Boop's house. If Bobby was not reinstated, his chances of getting a college scholarship would drop considerably. Scouts not only couldn't see him play, but they would view him as a troublemaker. Something had to be done. Finally, it was decided that Bobby and Boop would go to see Gobin. They did. After a long go-round, a compromise was struck: Knight would sit out a one-game suspension and Gobin would try a little harder to win games. The team finished strong, making the state playoffs for the first time in years, and Bobby Knight averaged twenty-four points a game. Still, the year with Gobin left a bad taste in his mouth.

In the spring, Knight and Boop drove the state visiting colleges. Boop, who had done undergraduate work at Cincinnati, would have been happy to see Knight go there. But when Knight went to a picnic thrown by incoming Ohio State coach Fred Taylor for recruits, he was sold on Ohio State. At the picnic that day were

John Havlicek, Jerry Lucas, Mel Noell, Gary Gearhart, and Knight. All Ohio kids. They would become one of the greatest recruiting classes in the history of college basketball. Knight was a bit leery about whether he could play with the group, but finally chose Ohio State.

He graduated eighth in a class of eighty from Orrville High School, was selected the best male athlete in school, and made big headlines in the local paper when he chose Ohio State. He left Orrville a local hero, off to give the town a big name 100 miles away in Columbus. Little did he know that the most frustrating four years of his life were about to begin.

As a student, Bob Knight enjoyed his four years at Ohio State. He was a voracious reader and an avid questioner, just as he is today. As a basketball player, he was miserable. There were a lot of places in the country where Knight could have played a lot of basketball. He was a good shooter. He was tough, hard-nosed, and smart. Most places, that would have been enough.

But Fred Taylor had put together a remarkable program in his brief tenure. Ironically, Knight was a weak defensive player, because he lacked quickness. "He was," Taylor says today, "a hacker. Bobby got in foul trouble a lot."

As a result, Knight was never much more than a spot player. He started some games as a junior and a few more as a senior, but always ended up back on the bench. He played on great teams. In 1960, when Knight was a sophomore, Ohio State won the national championship, led by Knight's classmates Lucas, Havlicek, and Noell. The next two seasons, the Buckeyes reached the national championship game again only to lose to Cincinnati.

Being on a winning team wasn't enough for Knight. Not playing destroyed him. Boop remembers numerous phone calls over the years from a distraught Knight. He and Taylor would fight, and Knight would want to transfer or quit or just come home. "Bobby hated not playing," Taylor said. "Which is exactly what you want. You want kids who want to compete, and that's just what Bobby was. But he was very blunt about thinking he should play more, and there were times when that was difficult for me and for him."

Knight was often in trouble. Once, on a trip to New York, he stole a bottle of wine just to show off and got caught. Knight was always showing off. He told his teammates that he had been part of a notorious motorcycle gang back in Orrville and earned the nickname "Dragon." His relationship with Taylor was always borderline, sometimes testy.

"Bobby was—and is—a character," Taylor said. "I remember in 1960 when we beat Western Kentucky in the regional semifinal, we broke open a close game in the last few minutes. I really thought our conditioning was the difference in that game and I told the players that when it was over. Bobby had played well that night. He came off the bench and hit a couple of key buckets from outside when it was still close.

"When I made this comment about conditioning, Bobby pipes up and says, 'I guess this means we're going to be doing that goddamn driving line (conditioning) drill again next year.' Everyone cracked up. It was a good line. But in truth, it wasn't Bobby's place as a sophomore reserve to say that. He never saw it that way, though."

Knight, like many players, never quite understood why he didn't play more. Knight still remembers one game where he came off the bench midway in the first half and played very well. He went into the locker room at halftime certain he would start the second half. "I was sitting on a training table when I heard Fred say, 'Okay, we'll start with the same lineup that started the game,' " Knight said twenty-five years later. "I'll never forget that because I was so crushed."

To this day if a Knight player comes in during the first half and outplays the starter, he starts the second half. Always.

Off the court Knight did quite well in college. School was always easy for him—unlike basketball. He began as a physical education major, but switched to history because PE bored him. He never had to work very hard and didn't, cruising through with a B average. If he had worked as hard at his classes as he did at basketball, he undoubtedly would have been Phi Beta Kappa. But classes were not his passion.

Knight talks now about considering a career in law or teaching. But his high school friend Kathy Harmon remembers him telling her when they were high school juniors that he wanted to be a coach. "He wrote an autobiography," she said. "He wrote in it that he wanted someday to coach the NCAA champions."

That didn't change in college. In Ohio State's 1960 media guide, Knight is described as a sophomore who aspires to be a college coach someday.

It was after Knight's freshman year that he began dating Nancy Falk. She still remembers his walking up to her at the swimming pool where she was lifeguarding on the day after her graduation from high school and saying, "Well, now that you're grown up would you like to go out?" That began a courtship that lasted through college and continued until they were married after Knight had gone to Army as an assistant to Tates Locke.

After Knight's sophomore year his grandmother died. He came home from picking up groceries to find her in her favorite chair—asleep, he first thought. Her death crushed him. "For at least a year," Hazel Knight remembered, "he would not talk about her and wouldn't let anyone else mention her. It hurt too much to even hear her name."

Knight's senior year was perhaps his most frustrating because he began the season as a starter and ended it playing very little. His best statistics were as a sophomore, when he averaged four points a game and had his career high—fifteen points—in a game against Delaware. It was a disappointing finish, and when Knight graduated he and Taylor were anything but close.

Knight got a job at Cuyahoga Falls High School in the eastern part of the state coaching junior varsity basketball and teaching freshman history. He worked there for a man named Harold Andreas. Andreas was about ten years older than Taylor, and he understood the frustrations of both the coach and the player. He encouraged Knight to mend the relationship. Knight respected Andreas enough to listen to what he was saying.

That winter he went to a clinic that Taylor was holding. He sat quietly in the stands listening until Taylor spotted him and asked him to come down and help him with the drills he was demonstrating. Shortly after that, Knight wrote Taylor a letter saying, among other things, "I think every player should have to be a coach before he is allowed to play." He was telling the coach that he understood. Taylor understood, too.

That spring, Taylor heard that West Point was looking for an assistant basketball coach. He and Knight had already talked about the possibility of Knight going to UCLA the following season to do some graduate work and to be a part-time assistant under John Wooden. But with Vietnam heating up there was a good chance Knight would be drafted. If that was going to happen anyway, perhaps Knight should volunteer and become the number one assistant at West Point under George Hunter. Knight thought that was a good idea.

There was nearly a hitch. Hunter got fired. Knight had already volunteered for the Army. Fortunately, Tates Locke, Hunter's replacement, agreed to honor the commitment that he had made to Knight. Two years later, Locke left West Point to become the coach at Miami of Ohio. The new West Point coach was Bob Knight, who would not turn twenty-five until ten days after his first practice that fall. He was the youngest Division I coach in the country, and he quickly became a star. His teams were extraordinary because of their defensive tenacity and consistently stayed right with—and often beat—teams with far more talent. Army was not allowed to recruit anyone over 6-6, but that didn't seem to matter to Knight. He found players willing to play his style and quickly built a reputation as one of the hot young coaches around.

He also earned an enduring nickname when one of his guards, Jim Oxley, a good shooter who played in the backcourt with Mike Krzyzewski, began calling him "the mentor." All of Knight's assistants have called him "the mentor" ever since. Tim Garl sometimes shortens it to "the ments."

His temper drew a great deal of attention, too. The New York media quickly nicknamed him "Bobby T." He was often crazed on the bench, kicking chairs, throwing coats, and generally wreaking havoc. But he won more games than anyone had ever won at Army, reached the NIT four times in six years, never once lost to archrival Navy, and had schools lining up to offer him jobs. The one he finally took was Indiana. It was in the Big Ten, it was near home, and it had a great basketball tradition.

In his second season, Indiana reached the Final Four. In his fourth season, Indiana won thirty-one games before losing in the regional final to Kentucky, a defeat that Knight still broods over. The next year there were no defeats, just thirty-two straight victories and the national championship. Indiana won the final

86–68 even though Bobby Wilkerson suffered a concussion in the first half. Walking out of the Spectrum in Philadelphia that night, an excited Hammel said to Knight, "Bob, you did it, you won the national championship!"

Knight turned to Hammel and said simply, "Shoulda been two." The memory of 1975 invaded his thoughts even at that moment.

That same spring, Fred Taylor was forced out as coach at Ohio State. Knight never forgave the school. Taylor had become, along with Pete Newell, Clair Bee, Joe Lapchick, and Henry Iba, one of the older coaches who Knight believed could do no wrong. Now his alma mater was pushing Taylor aside. Knight never forgot.

In the fall of 1985, Ohio State organized a weekend to celebrate the twenty-fifth anniversary of the 1960 national championship team. All the players and coaches from that team were invited back to be honored. Knight refused to go because he was still angry about what had happened to Fred Taylor. It was Taylor who called him and asked him to change his mind.

"Don't even ask, Fred, you know I won't come," Knight said.

Taylor went. The rest of the team went. Knight stayed away. They sent him the ice bucket, complete with a plaque and team pictures that were presented to each member of the team. Knight mailed it to Boop. "Doc," he wrote, "I want you to have this because if it were not for you I never would have gone to Ohio State and played on this team."

Knight certainly carried some pleasant memories from that team and those days. But his overall feeling toward Ohio State was anything but warm. He had absolutely no interest in the Ohio State job. But when Miller was fired and the rumors began flying, few people understood this. Including the members of the Indiana basketball team.

———

Ohio State was the least of Knight's concerns that week. He was wondering if Harris was going to make it at Indiana. He was also thinking that Jadlow might transfer at season's end. That would certainly put a damper on the junior college experiment.

More than that, he was concerned with the two games that week. On the surface they were walkovers. Indiana had beaten both Wisconsin and Northwestern on the road without Daryl

Thomas. But Knight worried that the players would be thinking just that, and with everyone fighting the flu, Knight was uptight.

This week's villains—outside of Harris—were the guards. Knight was convinced that Morgan and Robinson just couldn't play anymore. They had been heroes against Illinois but had quickly become goats at Iowa when they failed to handle Iowa's press. They weren't much better at Minnesota. But what really hurt them was Damon Bailey.

Bailey was the eighth-grade wunderkind from Shawswicke. The Monday after Minnesota, Knight and Hammel drove down to see him play. Knight's presence in the tiny junior high school gym caused something of a sensation. But Knight didn't even notice. He came back like a love-struck teenager, starry-eyed over what he had seen.

"Damon Bailey," Knight told the coaches on Tuesday, "is better than any guard we have right now. I don't mean potentially better, I mean better today."

When Knight spoke of guards, he wasn't talking about Alford. He thought of Alford less as a guard than as a shooter. To Knight, a guard was a creator. Damon Bailey, Knight seemed to think, was the Creator.

The coaches were, to put it mildly, skeptical. They knew that this was Knight's way, that he was bound to exaggerate. They cornered Hammel and tried to find out what he really thought. "He's pretty good," was all Hammel would say. In the meantime, Knight had invited Bailey and his family to Saturday's game against Northwestern.

Every time poor Morgan or Robinson screwed up in practice, Knight seemed about ready to put in a phone call to the NCAA to find out if eighth graders could be made eligible. Short of that, he put Hillman in the lineup one day. "Joe, I know you can't play in the games and I know your knee still hurts, but this is for me. I'm just sick of this horseshit guard play. I can't watch it anymore."

In the meantime, Morgan and Robinson suffered. They would survive, though. That's what Morgan and Robinson were—survivors. They had played together in high school and had come to Indiana one year apart only to end up in the same class because of Morgan's injury. They were the two funniest players on the team, the suppliers of most of the nicknames.

This was not a team full of lively nicknames. Courtney Witte was "Whopper," partly because he was a fan of former NBA player Billy Paultz, and partly because he resembled the somewhat portly Paultz in both build and (lack of) quickness. Andre Harris had become "Grace" because of his Grace Jones haircut. Daryl Thomas was "D Train," usually shortened to "Train." Alford was "Fred," which was short for "Alfred," a nickname Dakich had put on him the year before. Among the players, Knight was often referred to as "the big man."

Robinson had a knack for keeping things loose. More than anyone around he could make Knight laugh. His timing could not have been better the night before the Wisconsin game. Practice had once again been tight. When the players returned for the evening walk-through, Robinson walked into the locker room wearing a T-shirt that said "Puerto Rico" on it.

The other players were stunned. "Are you crazy?" Joe Hillman asked.

"Only one I got clean," Robinson said.

When Kohn Smith saw the shirt he did a double take. "Oh boy, Stew, are you in trouble." Everyone was beginning to convulse in giggles by now. Smith went outside to join Knight and the other coaches who were on their way in. "Stew is going to try to hide his shirt from you," Smith said grinning.

Knight walked in the door and before he even turned the corner he was yelling, "*Stew!*"

"Right here," came Robinson's voice in reply.

Knight walked around the partition. Robinson was holding his notebook up to hide the shirt. Knight walked over and pulled the notebook down. He looked at Robinson. Robinson looked at him. Calmly, Knight took the shirt by the collar and with both hands ripped it right in half. One side said "Puerto," the other side said "Rico."

"Stew," Knight said, "that's exactly the way we left Puerto Rico." He was fighting a losing battle with a huge grin. The players were falling off their chairs. As they went outside, Knight disappeared. A moment later he came back carrying a shirt to replace the one he had ripped. The team formed a circle around Robinson as he tried it on. It was a shirt left over from the Olympics, one Knight had been given right after the Russians announced their boycott. It read: "Let The Russians Play With Themselves."

"I like that one better, Stew, don't you?" Knight said.

"Absolutely," Robinson said. "It's not ripped."

It was as loose a night-before walk-through as the team had had all season.

If they had come out the next night and blown Wisconsin back to Madison, the loose atmosphere might have prevailed for a few days. But in spite of Knight's warnings that the crowd would be dead (it was), that Wisconsin would be ready to play (it was), and that the game would not be a walkover (it wasn't), the Hoosiers just weren't ready to play at their peak. Maybe Knight was a little bit to blame for this. For all his talk during the week about treating this game the same as Illinois or Purdue, he was not wound up the way he would have been on game day for one of those schools. He was even late for pregame meal because he was giving pro golfer and friend Fuzzy Zoeller a tour of the campus.

There were warnings. At pregame meal the players' note for the day read: "Wisconsin 69, Iowa 63; Iowa 79, Indiana 69 . . . And it wasn't that close!"

The players ate their spaghetti in silence.

Father Higgins was in the locker room prior to the game. His presence reminded everyone of Knight's now-famous "God business" line before the Notre Dame game. Now, when Knight walked in and saw Higgins, he thought about the horrid weather outside.

"Padre," he asked, "can God see through the rain?"

"It was hard for anyone to see coming down from Indy," Higgins answered.

Knight was writing the lineups on the board. "You know," he said, "I worry about you people. If we had a Methodist in here, we wouldn't have any problems. . . . Right, Stew?"

"Right."

Loose, everyone was loose. Then they went out and played atrociously. Todd Meier started in place of the benched Andre Harris, who would play exactly four minutes. After the game, when Knight was asked what Harris's problem was, he answered simply, "Not going to class is Harris's problem."

Just before the tipoff, Knight called Rick Olson, Wisconsin's only senior starter, over to the bench. This was the continuation of a tradition. Each season, when Indiana plays its last game against a Big Ten opponent, Knight will call the seniors over before the game begins. He tells them briefly how much he has enjoyed competing against them, wishes them luck, and shakes hands. Occasionally, the sight of Knight waving them over will confuse a player. Later in the season, when Knight waved Illinois's Scott Meents over for his valedictory, Meents walked away from him. That was too bad. Even in the darkest moments of 1985, Knight had stuck to this tradition.

Olson was clearly delighted by Knight's gesture. Then he went about the business of trying to whip Knight's team. He came a lot closer than Knight might have anticipated. Indiana led early, 14–10, after a Robinson steal had set up two Morgan free throws. But Wisconsin came back, tying the game at 16–16, then taking the lead on an Olson jumper a moment later. The lead seesawed until the last minute when Wisconsin center Gregg Steinhaus twice beat Indiana players to rebounds. He was fouled each time and made all four free throws, the last two with three seconds left, giving Wisconsin a 34–31 halftime lead.

Relatively speaking, Knight had not yet gone berserk at halftime. He had not quit his job, threatened to start a whole new team, or told them he wasn't going to bother coaching them anymore. But now he was disgusted.

He walked to the locker-room board and drew a heart on it. "Does anyone in here know what that is? Huh? I wouldn't think anyone in here would know what it is because it's a heart and no one in here has any. You just played twenty minutes of basketball that was totally devoid of any heart. No heart whatsoever. You've played like losers, you've acted like losers, you've wimped, you've whined, you've been sick, you cry, you're hurt. I hope you're proud of yourselves. I really wonder if you care about winning."

He left briefly, then returned.

"How many national championships do I have to win before you people will listen to me?" he said. "Four? Five? How many?

We told you and told you that you had to be ready to play tonight and look what happens. We told you nothing was automatic.

"I cannot coach you boys when you play like this. I can't take it anymore. I can't. I'm so discouraged and tired of you people not playing like you can that I don't know if I want to coach you anymore. I just can't take it anymore. But I'll do something about that after the game."

These last words genuinely scared the players. It was all timing. That afternoon, several of them had heard a report on television insisting that Knight was going to Ohio State. Now, he was standing in front of them telling them he didn't want to coach them anymore—that was hardly new—but adding, "*I'll do something about that after the game.*"

"Do you think he means it?" Kreigh Smith asked Joe Hillman as they left the locker room. Hillman just shrugged. Indiana's players may have moments when they can't stand Knight, when they think he is crazy, when they wonder why they ever came to Indiana. But most of the time, they want to play for Bob Knight. The thought of Knight's leaving scared them.

Knight had just been talking, of course. He had not talked to Ohio State, nor did he plan to. Ohio State knew this. In fact, Rick Bay would call Knight to ask him for a recommendation. But he would not call him to offer a job.

This was hardly the first time Knight had threatened to quit. In 1984, after a loss at home to Michigan State, Knight actually did quit. He walked in and told Ralph Floyd he didn't want to coach anymore. The team went on to Purdue for their next game without Knight. Floyd kept phoning asking him to come back. Knight kept saying no. Finally, he relented. Indiana won that game.

That had been a vintage year for mind games. Earlier in the season, after a loss at home to Purdue, Knight kicked the entire team out of the locker room. He ordered Garl to have all the carpeting taken up, the signs taken down and everything removed from the players' lockers because, "the SOBs don't deserve a locker room the way they're playing." He ordered the assistant coaches not to prepare for the next game against Michigan State, and he ordered Garl not to make any travel plans. He refused to take part in practice, sitting on a stationary bicycle while senior Cam Cameron and Dakich ran practice. At one point, he called Dakich over and told him, "If I were running this f—— practice I'd put Blab in the middle of a circle and have everyone throw the f—— ball at him until he learns to catch it!" While this was going on, assistant coaches Kohn Smith and Royce Waltman had locked themselves in the players' locker room so they could put together tapes because they knew that at the last minute Knight would want to prepare. When the team arrived in East Lansing, sure enough, Knight asked if the coaches happened to have any tapes with them. By golly, they just happened to have some. Indiana won that game, too. The players were restored to the locker room. Knight got off the bicycle and coached at practice again.

Tonight's ploy had the same end result. Indiana pulled together in the second half, but it wasn't easy. An Alford jump shot with 12:18 to go put them ahead 50–48. One minute later, Olson fouled out. Heineman, who had again played well against the team from his home state, went a couple of minutes later. Wisconsin ran out of players.

And Indiana got the boost it needed from Courtney Witte. This was the unlikeliest hero on the team. Once, during preseason, Knight had been so down on Witte that he deemed him not worthy of practicing with the team. Witte had been banished to the end basket to work on his own in scrimmage situations for several days.

But Witte had slowly worked his way back. He was never going to be a great player and had been recruited as something of a desperation measure. One year earlier, he had broken his foot twice and had to sit out the season. His weight ballooned and coming back had been difficult. But with Harris benched and Knight angry with Eyl for a poor first half, Witte got his chance.

He took advantage. Right away, he grabbed a rebound. Royce Waltman always maintained that Witte was one of those players who would always grab the first rebound anytime you put him in the game. That was what Witte did as a basketball player—he rebounded. Against Wisconsin, Indiana needed that. Before he was through, Witte had five rebounds and had converted them into six points. He even made a steal, and when he came out of the game the crowd became excited for the only time all night, giving him a standing ovation.

With Witte doing the job inside and Alford warming up outside for twenty-three points, Indiana finally pulled away—but not until the last three minutes. It was 66–63 when Alford hit a bomb with 4:12 left and Calloway hit a short bank thirty seconds later to make it 70–63. That was the biggest lead I.U. had enjoyed all night. Wisconsin crept to within five, but Witte rebounded a missed Daryl Thomas free throw and fed Alford for a jumper that made it 74–65 with 1:35 to go. Wisconsin was dead—finally.

There was little joy in the locker room. Witte was the one player everyone made a point of congratulating, but even that was bittersweet. Because as Witte accepted the pats and the handshakes, Joby Wright, standing nearby, cracked, "Hell, what's the big deal? Whopp's on scholarship. He's supposed to contribute, isn't he?"

The comment froze everyone. Wright had let his frustration with Harris show in front of the team. Wright had put heart and soul into making Harris a productive part of the program, and at that moment it looked like the whole project was going down the drain. Wright was at wit's end trying to figure out how to get to Harris. That feeling of hopelessness was never more evident than at that moment when he took his verbal swipe at poor Witte. Wright wasn't being mean—he is not a mean person. But the events of that week had drained him, and the words were out of his mouth before he knew how much they would sting.

For his part, Knight had little to say. "I just don't understand you people," he said. "I don't understand how you can continue to play this way. I think it's a damn shame to play this way against a team you know you can beat like this. You almost let them take this game away from you. I don't understand you boys, I'm sorry. I wish I did, but I don't. Tell you what, you come in tomorrow whenever the hell you want to."

He left. "Regular time," Robinson said, and everyone nodded. It was Alford who sounded the warning signal: "Let's make sure," he said, "that we don't let this turn into last year." Even at 15–5, the specter of last year just wouldn't go away. They had little to say to one another as they dressed. The victory hardly felt like a victory.

———

Nothing happened the next day to change that feeling. Garl had spoken to Dr. Bomba after the game, asking him to remind Knight that they had played sick against Wisconsin. Even the healthy players weren't really healthy. Remembering Japan, Garl didn't want to be the one to point this out, so he asked Bomba to do it.

Knight was not going to be waylaid in his anger by the old sick routine. He knew the players were not 100 percent, but he was still upset by their play. Once again, he began questioning the recruiting process. Mike Heineman, he decided, should have been recruited. "Not getting him was a disaster," Knight said. Dakich, Blab, Robinson, Morgan, and Alford should not have been recruited. "We'll never be any good until we've gotten rid of all of them. Alford will never, and I mean never, guard anybody. We've done a terrible job evaluating players."

Knight reacted to this victory almost as if it were a loss. He was looking ahead. After Northwestern on Saturday, five of the last seven games would be on the road. That scared him. His final words to the coaches on Thursday night were haunting: "Every time we play a f—— game I want to throw up at the way we've recruited for three years."

That was the mood Knight was in when they came in the next afternoon. There would be no practice. Instead, the players would have to watch the entire Wisconsin game on tape. "We don't need to practice," Knight said. "I know you can practice. What we've got to do is go through this tape so you people can see how bad you were in this game."

Actually, they would have been more than willing to take Knight's word on how bad they had been. But that wasn't about to happen. The tape session lasted two hours. Then they went to eat and came back for a walk-through on Northwestern. There was good news, though: Knight had left early to go to a high school game. That loosened things up considerably.

Knight had gone to see a game with Hammel and Bob Murray. Murray was a good friend and a business associate. He arranged most of Knight's coaching clinics during the off-season. Frequently, Murray made the four-hour drive from Chicago on Thursday and stayed through Saturday.

As they drove, Knight asked Murray how he would grade him on his bench behavior so far. "On a scale of one to ten," Murray answered, "I'll give you a six with the officials. I think most of the time you've controlled yourself. On dealing with the players, I give you a four."

"A four?" Knight said. "I think I've been a lot better than that."

"I don't," Murray said. "Last night sitting up in the stands I could hear you very clearly cursing when you got mad at the kids. There's no way I can give you more than a four."

Knight was surprised by his answer. Murray is an unusual friend in that he is willing to tell Knight what he thinks even if he knows Knight won't like the answer. It isn't easy to tell Knight the truth, especially where his temper is concerned, because he often doesn't understand the effect it has on the public's perception of him. Murray was one of the few people willing to tell Knight this. Hearing these things never improved Knight's mood. He wanted to be told he was terrific. Instead, Murray had told him he wasn't even close.

The next morning, the Wisconsin hangover was still evident. During the walk-through, Calloway, who had been three for ten against Wisconsin, missed a short shot. "Ricky, did you practice on your own at all yesterday?" Knight asked. Calloway shook his head. "This morning?" Same answer.

"Dakich, Bartow, why didn't you take some initiative and get Calloway out shooting last night? Why don't any of you people get on Calloway for not shooting or get on Harris for not going to class? Ricky, how can you shoot better tonight than you did on Thursday without practicing? Answer me, Ricky."

"I can't."

"That's right, you can't. So you won't play tonight. Get out of there. Stew, take his place."

Mind games. Calloway had been sick all week, probably sicker than anyone on the team. His poor game had been understandable. If Indiana had been playing someone tough instead of Northwestern, Knight never would have benched him for a crime so minor as not shooting on his own. But Knight wanted to jolt the team and this was one way to do it. He kept on them in the locker room before the walk-through that afternoon.

"You know, Randy Wittman is going to be here tonight, boys. When Wittman was here, he would haven't put up with Harris for five minutes. He would have told Harris to go to class or he couldn't play for his team. He would have been out there shooting last night with Calloway. I never once had to tell Randy Wittman anything, except to shoot the ball more. He was what Indiana basketball is about. None of you are."

Wittman would be amazed that night when he learned that he had been nominated for sainthood. This was the same Wittman who had been told not to come back for his fifth year by Knight, the same Wittman who had been banished from the locker room with his fellow seniors so as not to infect the others with their losing attitude, the same Wittman who had played on the four worst f—— teams in Indiana history. Now he was what Indiana basketball was all about.

There were guests at the walk-through that afternoon. Knight had invited the Loper family to the game that night. The Lopers were the people who had introduced themselves to Knight in the Bob Evans restaurant in Indianapolis with young Garland acting as spokesman for his deaf-mute father and brother. They had come to the game along with Garland's mother and sister.

After the walk-through, Knight took Garland and his father into the locker room. Through his son, Robert Loper told the players how proud he was of them and how much he was pulling for them. When Garland was through speaking, each player got up and shook hands with both Lopers. After they were gone, Knight looked at the players and said, softly, "And you guys think you have problems to overcome."

They overcame Northwestern with little trouble. Northwestern was beaten down by this point and could not have beaten Indiana if Knight had started himself at center. But the lead was only 38–26 at the half. Knight started Witte as a reward for his play against Wisconsin. Calloway was released from purgatory with seven minutes left in the half. He started the second half, and it was his breakaway dunk off a pretty Alford pass that got things rolling. Calloway made a steal and fed Steve Eyl for a dunk. Morgan hit from twenty feet. Alford hit. Then Morgan, then Calloway. They ran off fourteen straight points to build a 58–34 lead, and Knight finally relaxed. The final was 77–52.

Knight was so pleased he even talked in the press conference about how well he thought the team had done. "You know, in view of all the injuries and illnesses we've had, these kids have done a great job getting to where they are. They're 8–3 in the Big Ten and 16–5 overall, and that's more wins than we had all of last year. I'm not the greatest guy at passing out compliments, but these kids really deserve it."

Heck, someday some of them might be worthy of carrying Randy Wittman's jock.

Knight could go from sour to sanguine almost as quickly as he could go the other way. He was so delighted with the team's second-half performance that he took the coaches out for dinner and even had a little postgame sangria. They now had eight days off to get ready for the season's last big push. The rest would be needed. And what would they do about Harris?

As luck would have it, Harris's mother had come down for the weekend. When her son had told her why he was benched—he played ten minutes total in the two games—she had told him that she agreed with what Knight was doing. After the Northwestern game, she told Knight the same thing. "I think I've spoiled him," she said. "He's never had a strong male influence in his life. I think he needs it."

A few days later, Knight took Harris aside. "Andre," he said, "how about if you and I work together to get you going in the right direction? I like your mom too much to let you screw this all up. Okay?" Given a reprieve, Harris was eager to go along. That weekend would be the turning point of his season.

That night, though, Knight's mind was on what had been accomplished, not what was to come. "You know something," he said as he dug into a plate of chicken wings, "this season could turn out to be fun."

They were twenty-one and seven.

14.
Seven-Game Season

After the victory over Northwestern, Indiana was tied for first place in the Big Ten with Michigan. Both had 8–3 records, but Michigan would play five of its last seven games at home while Indiana played five of seven on the road. "We're not really in first place," Knight said. "That's just paper money. We can't beat Michigan."

Knight was more concerned with making certain of an NCAA tournament bid. He kept saying that nineteen victories would be good enough to get in. Actually, with Indiana's reputation and schedule, seventeen would almost certainly do it, but Knight didn't want to be borderline. His goal was nineteen wins; anything beyond that would be gravy.

With eight days to get ready for Ohio State (it was traveling-partner week again), Knight gave the players two days off while he went on another recruiting trip. Wright had convinced him to see Keith Smart again and to go to Chicago to meet with a high school coach named Landon Cox. Knight had been publicly critical of Cox in the past and hadn't recruited any of his players for several years. Wright had set up what amounted to a peace talk, and Knight was willing to go along.

Everyone needed the rest. The players were sore, sick, and, above all, tired. It had been four months since practice began, and there had been very few days off. With the toughest stretch of the season about to start, they needed a few days of not looking at or thinking about anything to do with basketball.

Knight came back from Chicago late Tuesday. His meeting with Cox had gone well. He had only one problem to deal with before he could turn his full attention to Ohio State. That was Ohio State.

The rumors about his taking the job there had persisted, and now a Cleveland TV station had reported that Knight would be the next coach. What flabbergasted Knight was that Rick Bay, when asked if that were true, had responded, "No comment." Knight knew the press would take a "no comment" to mean there might be truth to the story; it was time for him to get this over with. He put out a statement saying that not only was he not interested in going to Ohio State, but "I plan to finish my coaching career at Indiana."

End of speculation. Finally. The players—who had followed the rumors—were relieved.

The short practice had now become almost standard operating procedure. Even with the team rested, Knight knew that running them into the ground would be foolish. They practiced lightly getting ready for the Sunday game, and the tone of practice was calm.

It was so calm that as they ate breakfast on Sunday morning, Alford and Meier couldn't help but think back a year. Both felt their coach had turned around 180 degrees. Even with the occasional blowups, the mind games and all, this was a totally different Knight from the one they had seen in the past. He was patient. He reminded himself to teach and not to rail.

"It's like he knows he has to be more patient with this team," Alford said. "He seems to know when he can push and when he can't push."

The players didn't need much pushing for this game. The beginning of the nightmare had been here in Columbus last winter, when they lost to Ohio State by two. If Knight was ever given a truth drug and asked what one game he most wanted to win every year, he would answer either the game at Purdue or the game at Ohio State. He didn't like Purdue, and he seemed to still have something to prove to Ohio State. St. John Arena was the place where he had chafed on the bench, where he had just been another face in the crowd. Now, when he came home, he was a star, and, like any kid performing in front of people he had grown up with, he wanted to say, "Look what I've done." Winning was the best way to do this.

"There are some games," Alford told Calloway that morning, "that it is best not to lose." Calloway, an Ohio kid himself, knew what Alford meant.

They didn't lose. Finally rested, they played perhaps their best game, start to finish, since Notre Dame. They trailed early, once again having trouble with Sellers's size inside. But Harris was finally playing the way he had been coached to play since October.

He was staying near the basket, not wheeling and dealing with the basketball, and he was rebounding. Calloway had found his shooting touch. And Alford was, well, Alford.

He was the catalyst late in the first half when Indiana took control of the game. He made six straight free throws to give the Hoosiers a 27–23 lead. A moment later, he rebounded a Robinson miss for a basket. Harris came up with a pretty tip-in, and Thomas made two foul shots. Then Alford made a gorgeous backdoor cut, Harris found him, and it was a three-point play for a 38–28 lead. They got sloppy in the last two minutes, and the lead was just 38–34 at the half.

There were no explosions, though. Knight knew his team had played well. "Just stay patient and we're fine," he said. "As long as we're patient, we'll get good shots."

No problem. Ohio State got to within three early, but Alford and Calloway built the lead quickly back to nine. The game began to resemble the one in Bloomington: Ohio State would close the gap, Indiana would widen it. It got to 63–52 with 9:50 left after a Morgan steal. Ohio State sneaked back to 69–64 with 5:30 left. Knight called time. He wanted to spread the offense out and run some time off the forty-five-second clock on each possession. Shorten the game. He still had not raised his voice once in a huddle the entire game. Maybe he was remembering last year and controlling himself. Maybe *he* was rested.

There was one brief scare after the time-out. Thomas picked up his fourth foul, charging Sellers. The crowd was raising a ruckus. Ohio State could get to within three. But Hopson walked. A moment later, Calloway, using a brilliant first step, drove into the lane, and put up a soft seven-footer to make it 71–64. Sellers scored. Thomas answered. Alford missed, but Thomas rebounded. They ran some more clock before Morgan was fouled. He made both shots, and it was 75–66 with 2:24 to go. They just worked the clock from there, Alford making nine of ten free throws down the stretch to finish with (ho-hum) thirty-two points. Calloway had sixteen, Harris fourteen and seven rebounds. The final was 84–75.

"That," said Knight to the coaches, "was an awfully big win for the Hoosiers."

He was excited. He had watched his team play about as sound

a game as possible. "We told you all this week that it was a seven-game season now," he said. "Well, now it's a six-game season and we're 1–0. That's just where we want to be."

The most excited man in the room was Joby Wright. Again and again he patted Harris on the back. Finally, Harris had played. Finally, he had justified all the work and all the time and all the sweat Wright had put in. "What did I tell you about Andre Harris?" he said proudly to the other coaches. They were happy, too. Happy for Wright, happy for Harris. Most of all, happy to win.

The players were gurgling happily in the shower when the managers came in to get them. Woody Hayes was in the locker room, and Knight wanted the players back inside to meet him. "Is he going to hit us?" Alford asked laughing.

Hayes was in no shape to hit anyone. The old warrior was in a wheelchair. He was thin and his voice was a half-croak, though his words were as clear as ever. Knight had taken a class that Hayes taught when he was an Ohio State undergraduate, and he had remained loyal to Hayes even after Hayes had lost his job. In fact, Knight had been the one who talked Hayes into calling the player he had slugged to apologize, an act that had gone a long way toward exonerating Hayes in the eyes of many.

Knight wanted Hayes to talk to the team. Hayes told them that even though he had been pulling for Ohio State, he was proud of the way Indiana had played. "If you boys listen to what your coaches tell you, you'll do just fine," he said. "Always remember to listen. It's not as easy to do as it sounds."

One by one the players came by to shake his hand while Knight stood by the wheelchair with his arm around Hayes. "Bobby, this is so nice of you," he said.

"Nice of me?" Knight roared. "Are you kidding? This is as big a thrill as these kids will ever have, getting to meet you, coach. This is a really big thing for them. They all know who you are and what you accomplished."

If truth be told, the players would have preferred to have stayed in the showers. But Knight's words left Hayes aglow. He beckoned Knight toward him. Very softly he said, "They're good boys, you know, Bobby. You never really understand how much you love them until you aren't around them anymore. Remember that, Bobby. Enjoy them now."

Knight nodded. "I will, coach. I promise."

———

Ohio State had been conquered. The present looked bright on Sunday. But on Monday it was time to go glimpse the future. Knight had talked about Damon Bailey so much since he and Hammel had gone to see him play that it had become a running joke among the players and coaches. Whenever someone made an extraordinary play, the oft-made comment was, "That's good. Almost as good as Damon." Larry Bird was a great player. How great? "Almost as great as Damon."

The night before the Ohio State game, Knight had told Fred Taylor all about Damon Bailey. Taylor was skeptical. He began listing other phenoms that Knight had been head over heels in love with. No, Knight insisted, this was different.

It was time to see this paragon. Monday was the night. An expedition was arranged. Knight would play chauffeur for three of his professor friends. A second car would carry Felling and Waltman. Knight led the way, speeding down the back roads of southern Indiana towards Shawswicke. When a third car suddenly appeared, cutting between Knight and his followers, Waltman drew back in mock terror. "Oh my God," he cried. "It must be the Purdue staff. They're trying to beat us to Damon."

In the back seat, Felling was having a great time. "Yeah, I can see it now," he said. "Tomorrow's paper will have a headline: 'Bailey Signs With Indiana; Will Choose High School Later.' "

It was that way all the way to Shawswicke. When Knight started turning down tiny back roads, Felling began going on in lyrical tones: "This is what basketball is all about. A boy, a dream, a hoop. The back roads of southern Indiana on a cold winter's night. Coaches flocking from all over to see this young wonder. The gym appears in the gloaming. Hearts skip a beat. Could it be, yes it is. The Home of Damon."

The Home of Damon was a rickety, steamy old gym that was packed full with about 1,500 people. "Welcome to the home of the Farmers," said the sign. The Farmers had not lost in two years and were pounding their opponent, Oolitic, 16–0 after the first quarter. Bailey was about six inches taller (at 6-1) than anyone Oolitic had. He dominated. He made swooping moves to the basket. He went the length of the court. He put the ball behind his back. He also missed several jump shots and looked almost human at times. He was very, very good. A potential star. But still just a fourteen-year-old kid. The coaches and the professors sat high in the bleachers watching. Knight stood by the door. At halftime, he was like royalty at a party. Everyone lined up to shake his hand, say hello, and take his picture. They all knew why the legend was here. He was here to see Damon.

In the stands, Waltman turned to Felling. "What do you think?"

"I think," Felling answered, "that the mentor has slipped a cog."

Bailey was very mature. And a very nice kid. But there was no way he could even think of competing with any of Indiana's guards. No eighth grader could. Did he have great potential? Certainly. But to put any label on him at fourteen was premature at best, ludicrous at worst. Felling went so far as to say he had seen better eighth graders. "Maybe he'll be the greatest player ever," Felling said. "But who can tell now?"

They left before the game was over—Shawswicke was leading by forty and Damon had been taken out with thirty-four points—and headed for the cars. "What did you think?" Knight asked.

Waltman, ever the diplomat, shook his head and said, "He's pretty good. Very good."

"What about you, Felling?"

"Well, coach, he's good. But I thought Jay Shidler was better in eighth grade to tell you the truth and . . ."

Knight waved Felling off and got into his car. It took forty minutes to get back to Bloomington. As Knight got out of the car, he looked at Felling and said, "You know, Felling, I just knew, I *knew* you'd come up with an eighth grader who was better."

Felling was a brave man. "You know, Marty Simmons was pretty good in eighth grade too."

Knight was losing a fight with his mouth, which was curling into a grin. He had trouble staying angry with Felling. His mood was too good to be ruined anyway. Only four more seasons and then Damon could play for Indiana. And, in fact, the coaches were delighted to see Knight this eager and interested in the future.

*It is a crisp October day in 1990. Damon Bailey, Indiana fresh-
man, fails to help on defense. Knight stops practice. "You know,
Bailey, when we had Alford here he was so much tougher than
you it wasn't even funny. Why, I never had to talk to him about
playing defense even once in four years!"*

That was a ways off. For now, Damon Bailey's spot in the
Basketball Hall of Fame was secure.

———

Even if Indiana had had Damon Bailey in uniform, this would
have been the toughest week of the season. Playing at Illinois and
Purdue was never easy, and playing both three weeks after stealing
games from them in the final minutes in Bloomington would make
the task even more arduous.

But this was exactly the kind of week Knight cherished. His
team was already overachieving, with a 9–3 Big Ten record. It
had won the games it was supposed to win and a couple it probably
wasn't supposed to win. Now, facing games as an underdog, Knight
was right where he wanted to be. A victory in either game this
week would be cause for celebration. Even two losses, while disappointing, would not be devastating. Knight was in a kidding,
give-everyone-a-hard-time mood all week.

On Tuesday, when he walked into the locker room before practice, Felling was already there, clowning with some of the players.
"You got 'em ready for Illinois, Felling?" Knight asked.

"I thought I'd leave that to the main man," Felling answered.

"Yeah, well Garl [standing nearby] thinks you're chickenshit
for not doing it yourself."

"I'll deal with Garl later."

By now the players were making *ooh* sounds as if they expected
to see Felling and Garl rolling on the carpet at any second. It was
easily the loosest the locker room had been all season.

Harris, finally able to peek outside the doghouse after playing
well Sunday, was taking a beating because of his Grace Jones
haircut. Alford was getting it because he had been quoted in a
Columbus paper as saying he wanted someday to have a perfect
shooting game. The white kids were on the black kids for spending
so much time in the shower every day. The black kids were
questioning the bathing habits of the white kids.

Even mistakes in practice, while cause for concern, didn't bring about histrionics. When Kreigh Smith, who had only been back practicing briefly following his knee surgery, got two straight baskets, Knight asked, "Is Kreigh Smith paying you guys?" When Calloway missed an open man, instead of yelling, Knight asked him what he had done wrong. Calloway told him. "See, Ricky, in November you wouldn't have known what you did wrong. Now you do. That's progress."

Knight was also getting a good deal done off the court. With coaching vacancies opening around the country, he was into his annual game of musical coaches. Often, coaches call him asking for help in getting a job because they know that to many athletic directors Knight's word is golden. Sometimes, Knight makes recommendations without being asked.

Paul Giel, the athletic director at Minnesota, called that week to ask about Bob Donewald, the Illinois State coach. Donewald, a former Knight assistant, was happy at Illinois State, and Knight didn't think he would take the job. But, he told Giel, Tom Miller, the Cornell coach, would be interested and a good coach. Miller, another former Knight player and assistant coach, had been at Cornell five years. Knight thought it was time for him to move up the ladder. He likened Miller's situation to the one Mike Krzyzewski had been in when he went from Army to Duke.

"He's not that well known, Paul, but he's ready. He's a very smart young coach who will be everything you want on and off the floor." Invoking Krzyzewski's name was good strategy, since Duke was about to be ranked first in the country. Giel was intrigued and asked Knight if he would make a preliminary call to Miller. Knight was delighted.

Knight was extremely proud of his coaching protégés. He followed their fortunes closely and often called after big wins or big losses. Usually, after a big win, he would begin the conversation by saying something unpleasant. When Tennessee upset Illinois early in the season, Knight had called Don DeVoe, one of his early Army assistants, and demanded to know, "Why the hell did you shake hands with that sonofabitch Lou Henson?"

The Knight "family"—his former assistants and his coaching mentors like Newell, Taylor, and Iba—were renowned throughout the college basketball world. When SMU coach Dave Bliss was under NCAA investigation for alleged recruiting violations, someone asked Mike Krzyzewski if Bliss was still in the family. "He's living in the suburbs," Krzyzewski answered. Knight would never turn on a family member publicly, but he did get angry sometimes. When Donewald had interviewed for the Purdue job several years earlier and neglected to tell Knight about the interview, Knight had been upset, and hurt. To him, Donewald's not calling him was an act of disloyalty. That was the last thing you wanted to be considered as a member of the Knight family: disloyal.

The weather in Champaign when the team arrived on Wednesday was even worse than it had been in Bloomington. A dense blanket of fog hung over the town, so thick that the tops of buildings were invisible in a city where most buildings are only a couple of stories high.

Knight's theme for this game was simple: first ten minutes. "They'll come out all wound up and excited and the crowd will be into it, really fired up," he told the players. "We just need to get through those first ten minutes, get things settled down, and then go about winning the ballgame. We do that, we'll have a real chance. At Iowa, we let it get away the first five minutes. We can't do that here and win."

Knight repeated that speech on Thursday morning after they were through shooting in Illinois's Assembly Hall. Knight had two projects that morning: The first was to get Sam Carmichael, Knight's golf pro, to work with Steve Eyl on his shooting. Eyl was easily the poorest shooter on the team. He had been an outstanding option quarterback in high school and was an excellent natural athlete, a rare white player who could run and jump, but he had absolutely no confidence in his shot.

Carmichael had played on the pro golf tour for a while before buying the Martinsville Country Club, which was about twenty miles north of Bloomington. He and Knight played often during the summer, and Carmichael coached the Indiana women's golf team. Knight wanted him to talk to Eyl about the importance of swinging the same way every time in golf and liken it to shooting a basketball.

Almost every time Knight watched Eyl in shooting drills, he got upset. Eyl almost never shot the ball the same way twice. He jumped wrong or held the ball wrong. Knight would run over to work with Eyl, and Eyl would almost immediately tighten up. Shots that had been rolling off the rim began clanging off the front rim. Air balls began flying. Knight would get upset, and Eyl would shoot even worse. It was almost a ritual. Knight would walk away muttering that Eyl was the worst shooter he had ever seen, and Eyl would go back more confused and upset than he had been before.

"Steve Eyl," Kohn Smith said one day after one such session, "will be the death of us."

Smith wasn't down on Eyl. He understood the frustration of the player and the coach. Eyl worked as hard as anybody. When he came into games, he rebounded and played good defense. He was a good kid, a good student. But he was never going to be a good shooter.

Eyl was willing to try anything. He listened as Carmichael talked and demonstrated, swinging an imaginary golf club in the empty gym. When it was over, Eyl wasn't sure if he had learned anything. "I feel pretty good about my golf swing," he said, smiling. "But I'm not so sure about my shot."

While Carmichael and Eyl were talking, Knight was completing his second mission of the morning. The other guest on this trip was Steve Downing, who had been the starting center on Knight's first Final Four team in 1973. Downing was a huge, witty man who was an assistant athletic director at Indiana. He was one of those rare people who could get into a battle of wits with Knight and hold his own. Knight loved him.

Of course, Knight acted like he couldn't stand Downing most of the time. Downing received constant abuse and insults from Knight. When he and Hammel walked on the floor that morning to renew a long-simmering free-throw-shooting rivalry, Knight was watching. Downing made eight of ten. Hammel was not equal to that task.

"Give me the ball, Downing," Knight said, walking onto the floor. "I can whip you." Knight promptly made ten straight, much to the amazement of Downing, Hammel, and, most probably, Knight. "There's never been a day when I couldn't beat you, Downing," Knight said, reveling in his victory. "Hell, I remember when you made four in a row against Kansas in the last minute. It was one of the greatest f—— miracles of all time."

Downing was doubled over with laughter. He remembered, too.

Knight's looseness was never more apparent than at the team meeting that afternoon. When he asked Felling if everyone had arrived, Felling said that Witte was missing. Witte was sitting right there.

"Whopper," Knight said, "Felling was about to get you in trouble. What do you think about that?"

"Goddamn, Felling!" Witte answered, showing absolutely no respect for one of his supposedly respected coaches. The whole room broke up.

The laughter stopped quickly that night. Illinois, fired up just as Knight had predicted, broke to an 8–0 lead in the first three minutes. Alford finally broke the skein with a jumper four minutes into the game. One might have expected Knight to explode at the first TV time-out. He had emphasized the first ten minutes and they had come out and fallen behind immediately. Iowa all over again?

Knight didn't see it that way. "Boys, we're just fine," he said. "We're doing what we want to do, the shots just haven't dropped yet. We aren't a step behind like we were at Iowa. Just keep playing and we'll be right back in it."

Knight was right. From 8–0 down, the Hoosiers ran eleven straight points to lead 11–8. As it turned out, they never trailed in the game again. Alford was doing the work on offense and Harris was again excellent on the boards. But above all, Indiana was playing defense. Every possession was work for Illinois. There were no easy baskets to get the crowd going. Indiana, for the second game in a row, was playing textbook road basketball.

After ten minutes, it was 15–15. "Right where we want to be," Meier told Witte on the bench. Exactly. Indiana promptly scored the next seven points to lead 22–15. The only problem—again— was foul trouble. Daryl Thomas got his third with 7:33 left, and once again Todd Meier was thrown into the breach.

Illinois, with center Ken Norman almost unstoppable inside, closed the gap to 28–26, but Alford calmly knocked in three straight bombs, the last with one second left—a running, turn-around job—to make it 34–28 at the half.

The excitement in the locker room was palpable. Indiana had been blown out in this building two years in a row, but there would be no blowout this night. And there was a golden chance for a memorable upset.

The big question among the coaches was whether to start Thomas or Meier in the second half. Meier had played well and they had the lead. If they started Meier, they might be able to save Thomas and his three fouls for five minutes or so. But they could also get blitzed quickly and let Illinois back in the game. Felling and Walt-man wanted to start Meier. Knight finally agreed.

It was the right move. Meier hung in, and when Thomas came back the score was 43–36 with 14:51 left. But two minutes later, Thomas reached over Illinois forward Efrem Winters's back and picked up his fourth foul. Knight called time to settle everyone down. But things were getting tense. Harris threw an air ball. Dr. Rink was worried about Harris's stamina and thought he needed a rest. But with Thomas in foul trouble, Harris couldn't come out.

Right after Harris missed, Tony Wysinger hit for Illinois to close the margin to 45–44. More than eleven minutes were left. Indiana could unravel. But Alford wasn't going to let that happen. He promptly stuck a baseline jumper. Then Robinson, who had not played well since the last Illinois game, made another one, and it was 49–44.

Strangely, Henson was playing a zone. His team was bigger and quicker and playing at home. There was every reason to force the game's tempo, but Henson chose not to. Knight was off the bench after another Robinson jumper made it 51–44, sensing a chance to take control. "Defensive possession," he screamed. "Now, right now. Bear down."

They did just that. Harris, tired or not, deflected a Winters shot. Robinson grabbed the ball. Indiana set up. Harris drove and spotted Thomas open. He got him the ball. Layup. It was 53–44 with 8:56 to go. The crowd was silent. Henson called time.

"They're going to go inside on every possession now," Knight said. "Don't lunge inside! Just hold your position and we'll be fine."

A moment later, Harris lunged at a pass. Thomas, coming over to help, was a step late. It was his fifth foul. The lead was 53–48. Knight stared at the floor as Thomas went by him to the bench. The last seven minutes were like root canal. Every possession was critical. Alford hit to build the margin to seven. Harris, so pumped up he wasn't thinking, lunged again, and Norman made a three-point play. Alford hit another jumper. He never seemed to miss when Indiana had to score.

Norman missed at the other end. Harris scored. The lead was 59–51. Bruce Douglas missed outside and Harris rebounded. Less than six minutes, a chance to lead by ten. But Harris was called for an illegal screen. Another Illinois three-point play and it was 59–54. Knight decided to spread out and work the clock just as he had done at Ohio State.

Robinson hit, Wysinger answered. They traded turnovers and misses. Finally, Wysinger hit again with 1:50 left and it was 61–58. Knight called time ten seconds later. "We've got to suck it up for 100 seconds, boys, that's all. It's right there. Just play smart now. This is our ballgame."

They were hanging on now. Calloway walked with 1:13 left. The Indiana defense forced Illinois to take twenty-three seconds to get off a shot. Wysinger missed, but Glynn Blackwell rebounded and his shot made it 61–60. There were still fifty seconds to play.

Illinois was pressing. Robinson caught a quick pass from Alford right on the midcourt line. He had one foot in the frontcourt, the other in the backcourt. Referee Eric Harmon rushed in. Robinson, he said, had gone over-and-back, meaning he had gone into the backcourt after entering the frontcourt. Illinois ball.

But no. Referee Verl Sell raced over to Harmon. The rule on over-and-back had been changed one year earlier. It now said that until a player had both feet in the frontcourt, he could not be guilty of over-and-back. Robinson had never had both feet in the frontcourt. "Are you sure?" Harmon asked Sell. Sell was sure. Harmon changed his call. With forty-three seconds left, the ball went back to Indiana.

The Illinois crowd, not understanding the change, went berserk.

It was throwing things on the court. Henson was screaming. Knight called Sell over. "Verl, I promise I will never again give you a hard time in a game," he said. "That was one of the guttiest calls I've ever seen. It was the right call, but a gutty one."

The game was not over. Indiana would still have to shoot the ball if Illinois chose not to foul. The inbounds went to Calloway. He walked with the basketball. The crowd screamed. But the officials missed the call. They never saw it. The clock went down. Illinois didn't foul. Finally, with four seconds to go, Alford had to shoot. Douglas deflected the shot and Winters grabbed it and called time. Two seconds were left.

Illinois had to go ninety-four feet, from under its own basket to Indiana's, to win the game. Knight asked the coaches if they should put the 6-9 Jadlow in to distract the inbounds passer. They thought so. Knight wasn't sure. "Let's try it," he said finally.

Illinois wanted to pass the ball to midcourt, call time immediately, and then have another chance to inbound the ball from there. Douglas threw the ball to Norman, who was so intent on giving the time-out signal that he dropped the ball. Since he didn't have possession, he should not have been able to call time. But Tom Rucker, the third referee, Knight's old friend, awarded the time-out. What's more, somehow, the clock had never moved. There were still two seconds left.

Technically, this was possible. There could actually be 1.1 seconds left and the clock would show two. More likely, though, the Illinois clock operator had been conveniently slow. While the other coaches huddled—it was now Illinois's ball at midcourt—Waltman walked over to the timer.

"When did you start the clock?" he demanded to know.

"As soon as Norman touched the ball."

Waltman is, under most circumstances, the most low-key member of the coaching staff. "You lying sonofabitch," he said looking right at the timer. "You never even started the clock."

With that he stalked back to the huddle and spent most of the ensuing two time-outs—Indiana called one after Illinois had come out on the court—glaring at the timer.

With the ball at midcourt, Knight wanted to use Jadlow as an extra defender, leaving the inbounder unguarded. "No fouls," he said. "Get a hand up. Be smart. Boys, we've got to have two seconds of real smarts and real balls. Right now!"

Everyone in the arena was standing, including both benches. Douglas inbounded again. Illinois wanted to run a screen play near the top of the key, but Jadlow, the extra man, cut that angle off. Finally, Wysinger, who had been the hot shooter in the rally, came open on the baseline. Under the basket, Todd Meier saw the ball go to Wysinger.

Knowing there was no time for Wysinger to do anything but shoot, Meier left his man and ran at Wysinger, arms high in the air. From where he was standing, Knight thought Meier was going to collide with Wysinger. His heart stopped. Winston Morgan, standing near the top of the key, turned and saw Wysinger with the ball and turned his back: "I couldn't look." Alford, taken out of the game in favor of Jadlow, just held his breath.

Meier had made a brilliant play. He had run at Wysinger on an angle so that as he flew through the air, arms flailing, he was going past Wysinger, not into him. Wysinger, only 6–1, had to change his shot to get the ball over Meier. It came up way short. Flying past Wysinger, Meier never saw the shot. He just listened for the crowd. He heard no roar. He knew. The shot had missed. Time had finally expired. Indiana had won, 61–60.

This time they celebrated on the court. They hugged each other and grabbed and clutched and almost fell over from exhaustion. In a very real sense, this was the victory that brought Indiana all the way back from last year's depths of depression. The team that had dominated them twice in 1985 had now been beaten twice in 1986.

Knight had almost no voice left. But he was ecstatic. "I'm as proud of you right now as any team we've ever had," he told them. "Enjoy this one, boys. You earned it."

They enjoyed. Ricky Calloway was running around the locker room grabbing people and saying, "Do you know how long I've waited to play on a winner? A real winner?" And Stew Robinson spoke the words no one had spoken before: "Now we can win the Big Ten," he said. "We got to think about that now."

The long cold November nights seemed awfully far away now.

They flew home that night in sole possession of first place in the Big Ten. For the second time, Michigan State had upset Michigan. This time, they beat the Wolverines in Ann Arbor after Michigan guard Antoine Joubert had guaranteed a victory. Skiles responded with thirty-three points in leading the Spartans' victory and had sneered at Joubert during the game, yelling at him at one point, "Come on and shoot it, fat boy. Show me what you got."

That was the line of the year in the Big Ten, and Skiles was certainly the player of the year.

Thanks to Skiles, Indiana at 10–3 was alone in first place. Michigan was 9–4 and a host of teams were 8–5. The Hoosiers were also 18–5 overall, and Knight's nineteen-victory goal was starting to look conservative. When they arrived home that night—actually it was about 1 A.M.—Knight went to call Pete Newell. The coaches headed for the cave. "I have a feeling this is going to be a long night," Waltman said. "I suspect the mentor is thinking about more than an NCAA bid right now."

Waltman was partly right. Knight was starting to think big thoughts, but he was so giddy from the victory that they only looked at the tape once. This was a night to go home for at least a few hours and savor what they had accomplished.

The congratulatory calls came in throughout the next day. Jimmy Crews called early and turned the tables on his old coach. "I saw you shake hands with Henson," he said.

"I was just trying to confuse him," Knight answered, grinning. Others called. It was like the old days. Indiana was in first place in February and no one outside the team could believe it. If Knight had died that day he would have gone to heaven with a huge smile on his face.

There was, however, the rather large matter of playing Purdue in two days. Indiana traditionally had more trouble winning at Purdue than at any other arena in the Big Ten. Knight's record in Mackey Arena was 4–9; most of the losses had been in games where one play could have changed the outcome, and Knight could still recite most of them by rote. With Indiana in first place and Purdue attempting to nail down an NCAA bid, Gene Keady would make the game a crusade. Knight knew all this. He also thought that if his team could play the way it had at Illinois it would win.

Quinn Buckner was at practice Friday. He was now resigned to the fact that no NBA team was going to pick him up, and he and Knight were talking about what direction he should go in next. If Buckner had wanted a job in coaching, Knight would have almost undoubtedly found a way to give him a job at Indiana. But Buckner didn't want to coach. He wanted to try something else. In the meantime, though, Buckner would be at the rest of the team's games and sit on the bench next to Knight.

They bused to Purdue after a tight practice on Saturday. Knight knew this team had given him everything he could possibly ask for. He also knew that if they could find a way to win at Purdue, they would be in control of the Big Ten race. Knight has won seven Big Ten titles, but the last one was in 1983. He was dying to win this one in a year when no one—himself included—thought Indiana had a prayer at the start of the season.

The two-hour bus trip was a rare one for the Hoosiers. The team flies to every road game it plays, except Purdue. Louisville is just as close to Bloomington as West Lafayette, yet the team flies there. Busing to Purdue is as much tradition as anything else.

They went straight to Mackey Arena for a shoot-around; there would be no chance to shoot the next day since the game was in the afternoon. Walking onto the floor, Knight ran into Keady. Without so much as a hello, Keady told Knight to tell Alford and Robinson that he resented their coming up to shake hands with him after Indiana's overtime win in Bloomington the previous month. "They didn't shake hands with me last year when we kicked your ass," Keady said. "You can tell them I didn't appreciate that."

"Gene," Knight said softly, "they're just kids."

Keady stalked off. Knight had always had at least a civil relationship with Keady; the little episode was a clue as to how uptight Purdue was about this game.

Knight told the players what had happened. "Understand, they'll be looking at this as a season-maker. They'll play us harder than they play anybody. That's the way these people are. Now, you know I'm not very big on the people up here, including their coach, but you've never heard me say anything special about a Purdue game. But this game is a hell of an opportunity and it's one you people have created for yourselves."

Walking to the bus, Knight said softly, "I think it will be awfully hard for us to win this game."

That evening, Knight and the coaches walked down the road from their hotel to a Chinese restaurant. It was a bitterly cold night, but Knight seemed not to notice. Sam Carmichael was along again, having brought good luck with him to Illinois. "People like Sam are the reason I could never leave Indiana," Knight said as everyone struggled down the highway, cars roaring past. "I have friends I could never leave no matter what the job. Even if there was something I really wanted to do, I just couldn't leave people like Sam and Hammel and all the people around town who have been my friends over the years."

Knight and the coaches looked at tape until after 2 A.M. and then walked across the street to Bob Evans. Knight had apple pie à la mode and hot chocolate. He had not mentioned his weight for a month.

"I have to say that this team has really been fun to coach," Knight said, leaning back in his chair. "I can't remember when I've enjoyed watching a group of players get better any more than this one. And next year we should be even better. A lot better."

He smiled contentedly. It was 3 A.M. on February 23. Exactly one year had passed since he had thrown the chair.

———

Thirteen hours later, Purdue made its season. The Boilermakers were about as close to perfect as anyone can get. Early in the first half, they hit twelve straight shots. Long shots, short shots. Drives, jumpers, you name it. Indiana had no chance. A 10–7 Purdue lead after four minutes became a 41–19 lead after sixteen minutes. It was more devastating than Iowa. Basket after basket, with Keady up waving his arms to the crowd to keep it wild.

And it was wild. Mackey Arena is a strange place. It is not an old building, but it looks old. It is very dark, and all the seats are just benches. The crowd is easily the loudest in the Big Ten and just as certainly the most vulgar. It was on Knight from the moment he walked out from the tunnel and never stopped. The only way to stop a Purdue crowd is to win. That wasn't going to happen today.

Knight tried mightily to get his team into the game. He tried soothing. He tried screaming. He tried name-calling. Later, watching the tape, he would decide that the officials had set the tone early by not calling fouls that Purdue was committing inside. But the simple fact was that Purdue was having an extraordinary day. It shot 74 percent in the first half and led 46–29.

All of Knight's halftime pleadings were not going to save this one. They gave it a shot, whittling the gap to as little as 68–60 with seven minutes left. But Melvin McCants, Purdue's rapidly improving freshman center, powered over Thomas on the next possession to make it 70–60. Calloway missed a shot and Morgan went up and tangled with Todd Mitchell, Purdue's 6-8 moose of a forward, for the rebound. Morgan went down. The foul was on Morgan. Showing no class, Mitchell dropped the ball on Morgan's stomach. Morgan went after him. McCants stepped in. The proverbial cooler heads prevailed. Mitchell made the foul shots for a twelve-point lead. Indiana missed three layups on its next possession—Calloway, Alford, and Thomas—and Purdue scored again. It was 74–60. The brief run was over. The final was 85–68.

For the first time all season, Alford had been stopped. Purdue's guards had hounded and pounded him all day, and it had worked. Alford, shooting an extraordinary 56 percent coming into the game, was held to three for twelve shooting and a total of eight points. It was the only time all season he failed to score in double figures.

That it had taken twenty-three games for someone to shut Alford down was a tribute to Knight's offense and the way it freed Alford up for his shots, and to Alford, who often scored his points late because he wore defenders down with his relentless movement. Usually, if a good team decides it is going to stop a guard, it can do so. Most teams approached Indiana with the belief that if you stopped Alford you stopped Indiana. And yet, until Purdue, no one had been able to execute that strategy.

It usually took less to get Alford in the Knight doghouse than any other player. Knight had a knack for looking at a tape and not seeing any of Alford's shot making. In his third game at

Indiana, Alford scored twenty-seven points. Knight never said a word afterward. The next day in practice, Knight put his arm around Alford and said, "Don't think I didn't notice the points. But I don't talk about what's good—I talk about what's bad. I know you can shoot." Alford had improved considerably in all areas since then. But his strength as a basketball player lay in his shooting. He knew that and Knight knew that. Yet Knight constantly harped on Alford's weakness as a passer, his inability to find open men. Alford—never forgetting that first talk—was used to this. But he had been trained from high school forward to think shot first. Usually by the time he looked first for his shot and then to pass, the open man was no longer open.

Ideally, on a day like this one, Alford might have changed his game. Knight kept telling him throughout to look to be a feeder when the shot wasn't there. But Alford wasn't a feeder. He finished the game with one assist. Yet there was no explosion from Knight. After the other players had walked to the bus, Knight took Alford aside and walked him out of the building, his arm around his shoulder.

Quietly, he reminded Alford about how well he had played all year. "We wouldn't be where we are, Steve, without you. You've just done a great job. You had a bad day. Everyone does. Learn from it. Learn that there are some days you look to pass. You can be dangerous that way because of the way defenses gang up on you." He batted Alford on the back of the head as they walked out of the door. The only thing missing were the Lifesavers.

Knight's reaction to the defeat, given the margin and the opponent, was remarkable. He told the team it had played poorly and why. He told them he was disappointed in the way they had reacted to Purdue's aggressiveness. Little did he know that Purdue had finally discovered the Achilles heel that would ultimately do this team in. But that would be later. For now, as the bus lurched home in the middle of an ugly snowstorm, Knight told them to forget Purdue and remember where they had put themselves before Purdue.

"You still have a lot to be proud of, boys," he said. "You are still tied for first place and nobody but us thought we'd be where we are. Don't get deflated because of one game. This is the week we have to get ourselves into the NCAA. We have two home games [Minnesota and Iowa]. Let's win those two games, get ourselves into the NCAAs and the week after that we can worry about winning the Big Ten. That's our approach: the tournament this week, the league next week. Be thinking about that.

"Remember one other thing," Knight said before sitting down. "We're in first place in the Big Ten and there are eight sonsof-bitches including those assholes [Purdue] that aren't."

Knight sat down with the coaches. "There's just no point in beating on these kids. They've come such a long way. There's no sense getting all over them for one bad day."

The coaches were of the opinion, as they sat in silence for the rest of the trip, that their boss would have been incapable of such logic a year earlier. His players thought the same thing.

15.
Twenty Minutes to the Promised Land

There were now four games left in the season. Indiana and Michigan were again tied for first place in the Big Ten at 10–4. Michigan State, Purdue, and Illinois were all 9–5.

Minnesota would come to Assembly Hall on Thursday. The Gophers had come apart in the four weeks since Indiana had played there. They were not only losing, they were losing big. It would take an unreal collapse for Indiana to lose that game. Three days later would come Iowa, and Knight was worried about that game because his team had fared so poorly against the Iowa press in Iowa City.

That concern became apparent on Tuesday when a good deal of practice was devoted to working against the Iowa press. This was another first. Knight *never* worked on one opponent when another one was upcoming. But he felt that his team had not been ready for Iowa the first time and needed that extra work.

Naturally, having conceded to his team that he was concerned about Iowa, he had to prove that he was worried about Minnesota, too. So, on Wednesday, he put on a little display of "BK Theater." He screamed at Morgan and Robinson for poor passing. "Don't be throwing the ball like you're throwing it to an eighty-five-year-old woman," he yelled. He kicked the scorer's table when the defense broke down. "Shoot free throws," he said, throwing his arms up in disgust. "Maybe you can win tomorrow night shooting free throws. You sure as hell aren't going to win it with this defense."

They tried again. Calloway lost Kreigh Smith. "Ricky, you play that horseshit defense and I guarantee you that you won't play one goddamn minute next year."

Everyone knew what was coming next. Daryl Thomas bobbled a rebound. "That's it, I've seen enough of this shit. Take a goddamn shower. You don't want to win this f—— game, then neither do I."

Everyone understood. Knight had to be certain that the players thought he was worried about beating Minnesota. His only real worry was that they make sure to worry.

When the team came back later to walk through Minnesota, Knight sat on the sidelines acting as if he couldn't care less what was going on. When Felling asked him if he thought they had done enough, Knight shrugged. "Ask them," he said, gesturing towards the players. "They have all the answers."

Actually, Knight was right, they did have the answers. The best one came the next night when Minnesota was never in the game. It was 15–12 after seven minutes, but then the Hoosiers got on a roll. Alford was back to normal, bombing from outside. Morgan was dealing from the outside, and Harris was playing his best game of the season, controlling the inside. By halftime, the game was over, Indiana leading 49–25.

The only negative note was a Calloway dunk attempt that ended with Calloway landing hard on his butt. Calloway was very sore and Bomba recommended that he not play in the second half. That made sense. He was hardly needed. But Knight was nervous at halftime. He knew his team wasn't going to blow a twenty-four-point lead, but he worried that a flat second half would send them into their Iowa preparations on a flat note.

Iowa was very much on his mind when he called Alford and Robinson into the hallway. "I want you guys to make sure these other guys keep after it in the second half. I don't want any sleepwalking in the second half."

Ask and ye shall receive. Minnesota had no chance to play with Indiana. It was 72–38 when Knight began to clear the bench with eleven minutes still left. Even as he did, Knight summoned Murry Bartow, the designated message-writer. "Check with Hammel and find out the scores of our two losses to Iowa last year. Then go inside and write all three scores on the board."

Dutifully, Bartow walked up to Hammel's seat to find out the scores. Just as dutifully, Hammel looked them up. The three scores were there in bright red numbers waiting for the players when they walked through the door into the locker room.

There was one light moment before the 95–63 romp finally ended. With four minutes left and the lead at thirty-three, Knight called the wounded Calloway over. Calloway limped to his coach, wondering what words of wisdom he would receive. "Ricky," Knight said, "be sure to pick up all the warmup jackets for the *players.*"

The bench broke up. It was that easy an evening. They had now won nineteen games—Knight's goal. They were in the NCAA tournament for sure—even if Knight didn't want to admit it. How did they celebrate? By looking at tape of Iowa. The only break came when Knight went to his press conference. Phil Richards of *The Indianapolis Star*, a writer Knight liked, asked about the up-tempo that Indiana had played. How come?

"Well, Phil, that's an interesting question. Let me tell you what happened. This is an interesting story." Some poised their pens. Others leaned back, waiting for the put-on. "See, we were sitting in the locker room, and Todd Jadlow said, 'Hey coach, how about we play an up-tempo tonight so we can entertain Phil Richards?' And I thought that was really a hell of an idea."

With that Knight rejoined his players and his tape machine. After the players had been sent home, Knight went to tape his TV show, doing it on Thursday since there was no game until Sunday. That left the coaches to begin going through the tape.

There was also another tale in the continuing Damon Bailey

saga. Before the game, the principal of Shawswicke had given Kohn Smith a thick book of the Shawswicke season highlights. The front cover read, "Have Farmer Pride, Keep the Streak Alive." Included in the book were the team's complete statistics—Damon had averaged 31.1 points per game, shooting 64 percent from the field, and had gotten 14.7 rebounds and four assists a night—a history of the back-to-back 15–0 seasons, and details on the Farmers' summer workout plans. There were also pictures of Knight from the local newspapers: Knight watching Damon play, Knight holding court with the fans. And finally, there was a letter to Knight, thanking him for coming to two games and for his interest in Shawswicke basketball.

The coaches looked through the book wide-eyed. It was Felling who couldn't resist. "And just think," he said finally. "We've won nineteen games *without* Damon."

Indeed they had.

———

The roller coaster was working full-time the next two days. Knight was funny one minute, angry the next. Friday, when Calloway threw a pass while standing close to the basket, Knight stopped play. "Ricky, do you know the story of the Good Samaritan?" Calloway shook his head.

"The Good Samaritan is a biblical character, Ricky. Old Testament. He was a basketball player who kept throwing passes when he was only two feet from the goddamn basket. You know what God did? He cut him for overpassing."

A moment later, Calloway threw a pass three feet over Winston Morgan's head. Knight slammed a chair in disgust. "We cannot have this shit Sunday, boys. You throw passes like that, we're gonna get our ass beat."

Part of the problem in practice was that the white team was doing a good job imitating the Iowa press because they had spent the whole week doing it. Knight inserted himself in Robinson's spot and promptly threw a pass just as bad as the one Calloway had thrown. But he settled down and suddenly the press wasn't quite so ferocious. "Hamso," Knight said, coming out, "you think I have any eligibility left?"

This would be a hectic weekend. The game was on national TV, and several recruits had been invited to campus for the weekend. Saturday, two of them were there: Keith Smart, the junior college guard from Kansas, and Sean Kemp, the 6–10 sophomore from Elkhart. It was the first day of March, a cool but gorgeous day, and everyone was in an up mood—including Knight.

Before practice, he was trying to get Oliphant to dunk. At 6–6, it wasn't easy for Oliphant. He was a classic victim of "white-man's disease," and his feet never got very far off the ground. But he did dunk. In the locker room, Knight asked Pelkowski if he had seen Oliphant's dunk. Pelkowski nodded. "You ever see a slow white American dunk better than that?"

Pelkowski, still injured, laughed. "Magnus, are you going to practice today?" Knight knew the answer was no. "You know, Magnus, you have the best deal going. You have a better deal than the people getting U.S. aid in Colombia."

The comedy routine ended as soon as practice started. Joby Wright sat with Sean Kemp during much of the practice, selling. "Most places you go into, the only signs you see say, 'No smoking,' " Wright said, pointing to the championship banners at each end of the floor. "They're making a whole movie, *Hoosier*, about basketball in this state. That's a hell of a statement. You come here, it'll be hard, shit yeah, it'll be hard. But you'll be set for life when you finish at Indiana."

Kemp nodded. A few feet away sat Smart. A junior college sophomore and a high school sophomore—once, Knight wouldn't have wanted to mess with either. Now, he entertained both eagerly. "Keith," he said sitting down and putting an arm around Smart, "what do you think? Will we ever win another game?" Smart laughed.

Knight joined Kemp and his coaches. He was talking about how concerned he was with the Iowa press. "First time in fifteen years I ever prepared for one team before we had played another," he said. The coaches wanted to know if Knight holed the team up in a hotel the night before a game at home.

"No, never have," Knight said. He slapped Kemp on the knee. "I trust my players."

He sent those players home that night with a final word of warning: "Get a good night's sleep," he said. "You know there's no curfew, but if I were you guys, I'd be in at ten just in case I decided to phone you."

Robinson had a problem. As part of a class he was taking, he was supposed to go to a play that night. Knight grinned. "The old I-have-to-go-to-a-play routine, huh, Stew? Who are you going with?"

"Myself."

"You sure you aren't going with a girl?" Giggles.

"Sure."

"You better be sure, because if one of my friends who is going to that play tells me you're there with a girl, you'll be in big trouble." More giggles.

"What friends of yours are going?"

"None of your damn business." Nonstop guffaws.

———

Because of the CBS telecast, the tipoff was set for noon. That was very early, so early that Knight canceled the walk-through before the pregame meal.

Knight had more to say at the meal than he had said all season. There had been very little rhetoric in the past few days. There had been little talk about positioning or about tradition. Knight had focused squarely on basics, on handling the Iowa press. This was the last home game of the year, the last home game for Morgan, Robinson, and Witte. It was a chance for twenty victories, a chance to put themselves in excellent position in terms of seeding for the NCAA tournament, a chance to stay in a tie with Michigan for first place in the Big Ten.

Knight spoke first about what had to be done to win. "The first fifteen seconds of every possession their defense will attack you," he said. "But after that, we can attack them. You cannot be careless with the basketball and you cannot let up at any point in the game. They have the quickness to score a lot of points quickly if we let down."

Knight paused. Enough on how to win. It was time to tell them what winning meant and what they were playing for in this game. "Not a lot of teams get to this point," he said. "I want to give you an example of what playing here is all about. This weekend, you people are playing to get into the NCAA and to stay in first place in the Big Ten. All right, the whole program at Texas comes from here. [Bob] Weltlich coached here for five years and for two years with me at Army. At Texas today, they're playing for the Southwest Conference championship. If they win today, they win the championship.

"Last night, Cornell played at Princeton for the Ivy League championship. Tommy Miller played for us and coached for us here for five years and he had Cornell playing for the Ivy League championship last night. And today at Duke, Mike [Krzyzewski], who played for us and coached for us, is playing for the Atlantic Coast Conference championship and to be ranked number one in the country.

"That all came from here. That's all part of here. Those three teams in different parts of the country in different conferences, it's all part of this whole program. That's what you represent and that's what you're playing for and that's what you ought to be playing for.

"Because this is the best way to play basketball—*ever*. That's why so many people who play this way have a chance to do these things. That's why you've got a chance to do it. You've done a hell of a job getting yourselves into this position. Let's take advantage of it."

It was a striking speech, noteworthy not only because Knight wanted his team to know what it was part of, but because Knight seemed to be reminding himself that he had created something special. "The best way to play basketball—*ever*." That was Knight's assessment of what he had created as a coach.

The locker room was a zoo before the game. There was hardly room for the players, it was so crowded. Keith Smart was there and two juniors from Marion High School were there with their coaches. Morgan and Robinson's high school coach, Phil Buck, was there. Bill Shunkwiler, Knight's high school football coach, was there and so was Steve Bennett, one of Jim Crews's assistants, and Phil Eskew, an old Knight buddy who had run the Indiana High School Athletic Association for years. The regulars were there, too: Buckner, Abernethy, Steve Ahlfeld, Steve Green, Rink, and Bomba. If Knight had sold tickets he could have retired rich.

The game was worth the price of admission. George Raveling

got a technical before the game was a minute old. He stormed out of the coaching box in protest. Knight jumped up, screaming for another technical. When referee Darwin Brown, Knight's old friend from the first Ohio State game, came by, Knight demanded to know why Raveling hadn't gotten a second technical. "It's automatic, goddamn it," he yelled. As Brown went by, Knight brushed his arm—by accident. He drew a technical. This was all in the first ninety seconds.

The players seemed not to notice any of these histrionics. With Harris again playing like an All-American, Indiana jumped to a 14–6 lead. Harris had been averaging ten rebounds a game since his talk with his mother and Knight after his benching. In this game he would score fifteen points and get thirteen rebounds.

All the work against the press had been worth it. They were moving the ball quickly, before Iowa could trap, and Indiana was getting good shots on almost every possession. Knight continued his duel with the officials, but the players just kept playing. A Harris tip-in of a Thomas miss got the lead to 30–18. Alford produced a four-point play a minute later, swishing a long bomb falling down with Iowa's Gerry Wright on top of him. The foul on Wright came after the shot, so Alford shot one-and-one. He made both shots, and it was 40–22 with 3:24 left. The lead was still eighteen when Daryl Thomas went to the foul line with 1:17 left. But he missed and Iowa promptly got a three-point play from Andre Banks and a Roy Marble tip-in after a Robinson turnover. Those five points chipped the lead to 46–33 at the half. It could have been twenty. It was thirteen.

"Should have had them by twenty," Knight said, calmly, clinically. "You just can't let down, boys. Not now. Not when we're so close. Okay, spread yourselves out around the room and take deep breaths." The day had turned up unseasonably warm and the gym was hot. Playing against Iowa's incessant pressure, Knight was concerned about stamina.

The coaches huddled in the hall. Knight was pacing. Repeatedly, he asked how much time was left. "Longest goddamn halftime ever," he said finally. He went back inside.

"Boys, you've worked too hard not to give these twenty minutes everything you have left. When we come back in here we should all be ready to drop from exhaustion. That's how close we are. We've all worked since this summer, since October 15, to get to here. We're twenty minutes from the Promised Land now but it's got to be our best twenty minutes of the season."

It turned out to be the longest, toughest twenty minutes of the season. It began as an easy romp. Raveling picked up a second technical screaming about a Calloway basket after it looked like Calloway had been tied up. The bucket made the score 62–45. Alford's two free throws made it 64–45, and Indiana had the ball with a chance to push the margin over twenty. It was over.

Only someone forgot to tell Iowa. Harris turned the ball over and Bill Jones produced a three-point play. Daryl Thomas charged and Banks scored. Alford turned it over and Al Lorenzen scored. In two minutes the lead was down to eleven. Knight stood up, palms down. "Settle down," he said. They did for a moment, Alford hitting. But Iowa scored twice more to cut it to nine. The crowd rumbled nervously. A Harris tip-in built the margin back to 68–57 with 7:50 left. Comfortable. But the press was wearing Indiana down. Two quick turnovers led to two quick baskets and then Robinson missed a drive and Wright went all the way for a layup. It was 68–63.

Knight sat, arms folded, watching. Thomas was called for charging again. Jeff Moe, the Indiana kid who had buried the Hoosiers in Iowa City, hit two free throws to make it 68–65. Iowa was playing box-and-one on Alford now, denying him the ball when he had to have it most. Calloway came through with a soft bank shot to make it 70–65. Just when everyone was sighing with relief, Moe answered with a bomb. Alford tried to force his way to the basket and lost the ball. Ed Horton promptly posted inside, and his basket made it 70–69 with 3:10 left. In little more than ten minutes, Iowa had outscored the Hoosiers 24–6.

Alford had to have the ball now. He got it, made a move, and was fouled with 2:55 left. Just what Indiana wanted—Alford on the line for two automatic points. Somehow, Alford missed. The crowd groaned. Iowa could take the lead. Knight looked a little like Moses must have looked gazing on the Promised Land. Hammel was nearly hysterical. "It's just awful to ruin a great year like this. This is disastrous, just disastrous."

Iowa had time. It worked the ball around. Then, for some reason, 7-foot center Brad Lohaus tried a seventeen-footer. It had no chance, but Horton went over everybody for the rebound. He turned and had a wide open five-footer for the lead . . . it rolled off. Morgan rebounded. List Indiana's five biggest rebounds of the season and Morgan probably had four of them.

There was 2:30 left. Indiana had to score. Alford, never one to back off because of a mistake, wanted the ball. He flashed to the corner. Morgan whipped the ball to him and Alford never even paused. Twenty feet. Swish. It was 72–69. The building exploded. A moment later, Jones drove the baseline. Waiting, in perfect position as always, was Meier. The shot rolled off. Harris grabbed it. Indiana used the clock and ran the same play. This time Alford was in the other corner. Same result. Swish. It was 74–69 with 1:07 left. Ten seconds later, Horton walked. Finally—finally—it was over.

They were 20–6. Knight was ecstatic. One year earlier, a Knight-coached Indiana team had lost its final home game for the first time ever. Knight had been so distraught that he skipped the postgame ceremonies for Dakich and Blab. Now, he gleefully introduced Morgan, Robinson, and Witte. But first, a word from our sponsor.

"You know Indiana has the greatest basketball tradition in the world," Knight told the fans. "Last year, we were all kind of down because we didn't think we gave you the kind of basketball you people are used to seeing and enjoy seeing. I know I've enjoyed it greatly."

He left the floor to the seniors. It had been an almost perfect day. Duke had beaten North Carolina to win the ACC championship. True, Cornell had lost to Princeton and Texas had lost on a fluke shot by one point on the buzzer; Knight took that last one hard. But the Hoosiers had reached the Promised Land. And Moses had even entered it with them, at least for a few days.

16.
For the Championship . . . Thud

Knight might have been giddy after the Iowa victory, but the Michigan State game was on Wednesday and he did not want another loss to the Spartans. For one thing, Michigan State had beaten Indiana four straight. In the ten seasons that Jud Heathcote had been coach there, State had a 10–9 record against Knight; Heathcote was the only Big Ten coach with a winning record against Knight.

He also had a sharp enough wit to outdo Knight occasionally in one-liners. Once, when Knight had been feuding with other league coaches, he called Heathcote and said, "Jud, you're the only coach in this damn league that likes me."

"Bob," Heathcote answered, "Don't take anything for granted."

Knight certainly wasn't taking this game for granted. If he had believed in January that his team had lost at home to a mediocre team, the season had proved him wrong. Scott Skiles had been truly unreal, even with probable revocation of his probation hanging over him. He was averaging twenty-seven points a game, and Michigan State, picked seventh in the league preseason, was clipping at the heels of Indiana and Michigan with an 11–5 league record. The leaders were 12–4.

Knight hated the fact that Skiles was playing so well. As wonderful a season as Alford was having, Skiles was even better. Alford had no trouble admitting, "He's the best guard in America." But Knight would not so much as shake Skiles's hand as part of his last-game-against-a-senior ritual. Skiles's arrest record, in Knight's opinion, disqualified him from meriting such respect. In truth, if anyone merited a pat for being a competitor, it was Skiles.

If Knight's concern before the Iowa game had been the defense, his concern preparing for Michigan State was their offense. Led by Skiles, the Spartans had become a team that pushed the ball up the floor so quickly it was almost impossible for the defense to have time to set up. Skiles could not be allowed to score in conversion. Stopping him would not be easy.

But this was a team riding high. Since the opening two losses and the subsequent fishing trip, Indiana had won twelve of fourteen games. For the players, this meant relief. Last year's nightmare had not been repeated. The season had become fun. They were enjoying the winning, they were enjoying one another, and they were even enjoying their coach. The locker room was a loose, happy place. Alford would make several All-American teams that were being announced during this week—deservedly so. Calloway was the Big Ten rookie of the year. And Harris, owing to his play in the last five games, was tabbed by one magazine as a member of the "All-JUCO newcomer" team. In this era, there weren't many JUCO newcomers to choose from. But Wright grabbed the magazine and proudly showed it to anyone he could find—the coaches, the players, Harris, the secretaries, little old ladies on the street. He was entitled, though. No one had sweated longer or harder with a player than Wright had with Harris.

The team flew into East Lansing on a frigid, snowy night. When the coaches went to dinner, Knight sat down and found a woman standing over him with a menu, but not to take his order. "Coach, if you give me your autograph, I'll even bring you a chair."

She laughed hysterically at her cleverness. Fifteen weeks earlier, such hilarity had put Knight in a bad mood for an entire day. Today, he took the menu, signed, and said softly, "Ask the Spartans not to beat up on us too bad, okay?"

The angry young man of 1985 had become a very satisfied middle-aged coach in 1986.

———

Naturally, he wanted more. That was only human. The team had already met every preseason goal he had set, but now it had a chance to do more. A Big Ten championship with this team would rank very high on Knight's list of coaching accomplishments.

Skiles was going to be a problem. He was in a shooting groove not unlike the kind that baseball pitchers get into when they feel they can get every batter out. Skiles was so confident he thought he could make any shot he took. That kind of player is tough to stop.

East Lansing was hardly a cheery place. It was snowing when Indiana arrived and very cold even though it was March. On game day it started snowing at midday and snowed eight inches in a matter of hours. What's more, none of the hotel telephones were working. No calls could come in, none could go out—except from the lobby pay phones. The team felt as if it had been cut off from the outside world.

The morning practice on game day seemed destined to try Knight's patience. Jenison Field House is one of those old gyms that is an anachronism except on a game night, when it is packed and jammed and becomes alive and electric. There are no doors to shut in order to have a closed practice. Joggers abound, and on this morning, workmen were everywhere. The acoustics caused every sound in the building to echo all over.

Knight was uptight, but it wasn't the acoustics. It was poor Steve Eyl's shooting—again. "Steve, you're falling backward every time you shoot," Knight yelled, jumping from his seat as the players warmed up. He walked over to Eyl to demonstrate. He came back shaking his head. "I wish he had been a better football player," Knight said. "I'm not sure I can survive watching him shoot the ball for another two years."

Knight sat down and immediately noticed Eyl falling backward again. This time he called Alford over. "What's he doing every time he shoots?" he asked his best shooter.

"Falling backward," Alford said.

"Well, will you please go tell him that? Maybe he'll listen to you. You're a better shooter than I was."

Knight's frustration with Eyl's shooting had more to do with aesthetics than anything else. Eyl had done just about everything he had been asked to do coming off the bench. He had rebounded, played tough defense, and come up with a key follow shot here and there. But Knight was too much of a basketball purist to bear the sight of someone shooting a ball so incorrectly so often. He was like a conductor who kept hearing a note played wrong. Maybe no one else could hear it, but every time *he* heard it he winced. Watching Eyl shoot was painful for Knight.

Being watched was painful for Eyl, a quiet, easygoing sort who bore a remarkable resemblance to Ivan Drago, the Russian boxer in *Rocky IV*. Eyl was one of those players who had seen both ends of the Knight ladder up close. He had started for much of his freshman season and had been thought of in preseason as a starting candidate. He was one of the best athletes on the team, a player who could do everything on a basketball court except shoot.

But that malady hounded him, as did the misfortune of being named Steve on a team whose best player had that name. As a result, he was constantly referred to by everyone as SteveEyl as if it was one word. Even on the court, when other players wanted to get his attention, they would yell "SteveEyl" rather than just "Steve." This was not a problem for the team's two Todds—Jadlow and Meier—partly because their status was almost equal, but mostly because everyone called Todd Jadlow, "Jadlow." So there was Todd and there was Jadlow and there was Steve and SteveEyl.

SteveEyl was never going to be a shooter. He knew it and Knight knew it, yet the reality was often painful for both. With practice over, Knight went back to the hotel for some soup, trying all the while to push the mental picture of Eyl shooting out of his mind. The snow was so bad that he and Hammel skipped their walk.

It was still coming down hard when the team bused to the arena that evening, and the possibility of having to bus the 300 miles home was discussed. The very thought of a six-hour bus ride with Knight after a loss was enough to make everyone just a little tighter.

Jenison was jammed. Michigan State and Skiles had captured everyone's imagination because of their abandon and because of Skiles's charisma. Whatever one thought of his off-court behavior, it was impossible not to admire his guts and guile on the court. And the crowd was waiting for Knight. One sign hanging from the balcony identified one group as SACA—Students Against Chair Abuse.

To get to the floor from the locker rooms, the teams had to walk right between the bleachers. Even though a path was cleared, people pressed up against the ropes so that they were almost breathing in the faces of the coaches and the players. But this was not an ugly crowd like those at Kentucky or Purdue. They just wanted to be up close, to feel as if they were part of the game. Many even applauded Knight as he walked past them.

Also waiting for Knight when he walked onto the floor was Walter Adams. Walter Adams is a professor at Michigan State, a rabid fan of the basketball team who has sat for many years right behind the visitors' bench. He is a world-class heckler. One year, shortly after Knight's arrival at Indiana, Adams was all over Knight during a game. Knight turned around and pointed at Adams's wife. "If he's with you," Knight said, "I suggest you quiet him down so he can leave with you in one piece."

No one quite knew how to take that, but Adams quieted. The next year Knight showed up before the game looking for Adams. He had brought a gift, a peace offering. Give me peace, Knight was saying. Walter Adams did just that. The next year he showed up with a gift for Knight, and over the years their pregame exchange of gifts had become a tradition.

Knight, the history buff, had brought Adams a copy of the book *Grant and Lee*. Adams had brought Knight a green-and-white Michigan State seat cushion to sit on during the game, and a handsome framed plaque extolling the virtues of Knight. Adams was another Bob Knight convert; once he had gotten to know Knight, he not only liked him but would hear no words spoken against him. Knight took Adams's glasses from him to read the plaque. A crowd had gathered to watch the scene, as always, and both men enjoyed it immensely.

Finally, it was time to play. And Indiana was ready.

This night it all came together. Five months of work, all the yelling, all the hours, all the tape was worth it at least for these two hours. Everything clicked.

Skiles was still Skiles. He had twenty-one points by halftime and thirty-three for the game even though he played the second half with a hip-pointer suffered near the end of the first half. But Skiles could not beat Indiana alone and that was what he was left trying to do. His teammates were very mortal on this night. Larry Polec, the perennial Indiana-killer, had just four points. Carlton Valentine, who had come up with the twenty-one killing points in the first game, had just two.

In the meantime, Alford was matching Skiles shot for shot, scoring thirty-one points himself. Skiles and Alford put on a shooting duel for the national cable-TV audience the likes of which had not been seen for a long time. But Alford had more help. Calloway was superb with nineteen points. Daryl Thomas had fourteen. SteveEyl came off the bench to get two key baskets in the first half—from close in, of course—and Stew Robinson added nine. Harris had foul problems again and only played twenty-one minutes, but he managed ten points, six rebounds, and four steals while he was in the game.

Indiana, down 7–2 early, took the lead at 14–13 on a baseline jumper by Alford with 13:15 left and Michigan State never caught up. Alford and Calloway lit up creaky old Jenison and by halftime the lead was 48–35, Alford ending it with a spinning twelve-footer just before the buzzer.

Nothing changed after halftime. Knight made one small defensive adjustment to take the middle away from Skiles and that kept him off the foul line—he had been there eight times in the first half. The only suspense came when the Hoosiers went through a one for six free-throw shooting spell and let a sixteen-point lead melt to ten with 8:10 to play. But Skiles, doubled-teamed in the middle, missed an off-balance jumper, and SteveEyl rebounded. Alford fed Thomas for a pretty layup. The Spartans clawed back one last time, getting to within 81–73 with 3:13 left. Knight called time.

One adjustment: He wanted to go out of the regular offense and into a triangle—meaning that two players would go to one side of the lane and one to the other with two others outside. He wanted Alford inside, on the baseline, because he was convinced that if Alford drove baseline, Michigan State would be forced to foul.

It took Alford twelve seconds to draw a foul. He made both shots. One possession later, after an MSU miss, Alford drove baseline and fed Meier, who was fouled. The last three minutes were straight from a textbook. The Hoosiers outscored the Spartans 16–6 and the final was 97–79.

"They played just about a perfect game," Heathcote said. "It was a clinic."

Nothing makes Knight happier than watching his team put on a clinic. That they had done it on the road against a team that had given them fits for three years and had put themselves one game from a Big Ten championship made it that much sweeter. Knight enjoyed this one immensely. When a radio reporter trailed him out of the press conference to ask what changes Knight had made to bring about this team's turnaround, Knight said, straightfaced, "I think our zone defense has really been the difference. We've worked awfully hard on it."

The reporter, giving Knight just the response he wanted, nodded knowingly and said, "Interesting, since you never liked to play zone in the past."

Still straightfaced, Knight nodded just as eagerly. "That's right, but as you probably noticed tonight, we play a lot of different zones. Maybe someday we can sit down and talk about the concepts of our zone defense."

He walked away delighted with himself. Hammel, a step behind, groaned. Knight had scored yet another point in their running battle over the question, "Is the media really as stupid as Knight thinks it is?" On this night, the prosecution had some overwhelming evidence.

Inside the locker room, there were no qualifiers in Knight's praise of the team. Not a discouraging word was heard. "Look at what you've done now," he told the players. "You've got it down to one game for a conference championship. You can't ask for more than that, I can't ask for more than that. We're exactly where we wanted to be when we started on October 15. You should feel damn good about that. That's one hell of a turn-around."

They felt very damn good about it. As the players congratulated each other, Waltman put a tired arm around Felling. "Do you know what this means, Felling?" he said. "This means, we don't have to get into position to get into position anymore. We're *in* position."

Finally.

The bumpy flight home through the snow bothered no one—with the possible exception of Robinson, who was easily the team's most nervous flyer. Knight was already talking Michigan up front.

It was after two o'clock before they reached Assembly Hall. It was too late to look at tape, at least on a euphoric night like this. Knight was too wound up, too high to sleep, so he and Waltman went to the only open restaurant in town—Denny's—for something to eat.

An hour later, Knight pushed himself back from the milkshake he had treated himself to and looked at Waltman. "Remember how we felt a year ago tonight?" he said. "We had just lost to Michigan State at home and we knew we weren't going to the NCAAs. What a turnaround. I'm really proud of this group of kids. They deserve an awful lot of credit."

As he drove home that morning with his team 21–6, Knight had no way of knowing that Indiana had just won for the last time in this season. If he had known, he would have been shocked. Because at that moment, he had every reason to believe that the ending for this team would be a happy one.

———

Euphoria was still in the air the next afternoon. Knight almost sounded cocky talking to the players. "Hey, it doesn't matter that we're playing up there," he said. "We've proven all season it doesn't matter where we play. We can have a lot of fun with this game, boys. All the pressure is on them. The last place in the world they wanted to be Saturday was playing us for the Big Ten championship."

That was certainly the way the game shaped up. Both teams were 13–4 in the league. Everyone else had at least six losses. It was a two-team race, one game for first place outright. A bad Indiana team had won in Crisler Arena in 1985, and there was no reason to believe a good one couldn't repeat in 1986. The pressure was on Michigan because it had been the preseason Big Ten favorite. Frieder even admitted the pressure was on his team.

"It may not be fair, but I told our seniors that in spite of everything they've done here, their whole careers may very well be judged on this game," he said. "When you've won as much as they have, that isn't right. But it's true."

True or not, Frieder had apparently decided to take the tack of telling them that was the way it was. He apparently wanted pressure on his team in this game. On the surface, that didn't seem like a brilliant strategy.

For Indiana, this was a chance to make a very good season a magic one. There was no reason to think the game wasn't winnable. They had handled playing on the road most of the season without any trouble. Knight was brimming with confidence. "Michigan has played like dogs a lot this year," he told the players. "But I guarantee you they'll play very hard on Saturday. That's okay, though, because it will just open up some things for us on the inside."

They were so high the plane hardly seemed necessary to get to Ann Arbor. On the flight, Knight had an assignment for Hammel. "In fifteen years, nine Big Ten teams each year have had a chance to finish ahead of us in the league," he said. "How many have done it?" Hammel spent most of the trip burrowing through his record books. Just before landing he had the answer: Out of the 135 teams that could have finished ahead of Indiana, Michigan, by winning on Saturday, could be the twentieth team to do so. Six of those twenty had come in one year—1985.

"That just might be the most impressive thing we've done here," Knight said, settling back with a satisfied smile.

They went straight to the arena after arriving, since the game the next day was in the afternoon. Knight was greeted by an assistant football coach who told him that Michigan football coach Bo Schembechler was away but wanted to be sure Knight got a gift that he had left for him. It was a Michigan football Fiesta Bowl sweater. That sweater was a reminder of the comeback season Michigan had had in football. It also reminded Knight of a speech he had given his team in November, comparing Indiana basketball to Michigan football. His players had lived up to his plea that they make this a comeback season like the one Schembechler's team had.

Crisler Arena was hot that evening because the CBS technicians had turned on the TV lights so Indiana would have some notion of how the lighting would feel during the game. Knight was loose; Steve Eyl actually made it through the session without having his shooting disparaged. When it was over, Knight called them into a circle at center court. His voice wasn't very loud, but in the empty arena his words seemed to echo off the seats.

"You do not have to do anything in here tomorrow except play as well as you can play," he said. "You do not have to play the greatest game ever played. It really doesn't matter what you're playing for tomorrow in terms of how you play because you should play as well and as hard as you can every time you play. That's what you've done this season. The teams that do that are the teams and the players that end up playing for championships."

Michigan was an exception to this rule, however. Indiana had come very close to playing hard and well in every game it had played all season. Michigan had been superb in one game, awful in the next. It had been the kind of inconsistent team that would drive Knight crazy. Indiana, even knowing the special nature of this game, probably could not take its level of play much higher than where it had been for the past several weeks. Michigan, if ready, could play several notches higher. From an Indiana viewpoint, that was the scary part.

But on that frigid evening, that hardly seemed possible. Indiana had just played its best game of the season. It was peaking. And if anyone had a reputation as a big-game coach, it was Bob Knight. It was Tim Garl who said it best that evening: "We've caught all the fish. Now, we're going for Moby-Dick."

If Garl had remembered the ending of *Moby-Dick*, he might not have spoken so quickly.

Saturday dawned ugly: overcast and windy, a gusty wind that practically knocked you over when you walked outside. With the moment at hand, Knight wanted nothing left undone. The post-breakfast walk-through was the longest of the season. When it was over, everyone went back up to Knight's suite for one more look at the tape.

"We can have a lot of fun against this team," Knight said, repeating the theme he had been harping on since Thursday. "They're out of shape and they wish they weren't playing you people today."

On the bus, he said it all again: "There aren't a half dozen teams in the country in the position you're in. You put yourselves here by doing what you're capable of. All of the pressure is on them."

Perhaps. But Michigan was going to be ready for that pressure. Crisler Arena was alive long before tipoff. This was the last home game for a distinguished senior class: Roy Tarpley, Butch Wade,

Richard Rellford, and Robert Henderson. It was a game for a second straight league title against a vaunted and hated opponent. A huge banner hung from one balcony. It read: "Who Says We're a Football School?"

The Indiana locker room was tense. Knight was fine, calmly going through mail in the anteroom while conversing with Buckner and Kent Benson, who had driven over from Detroit for the game since the Pistons weren't playing. But everyone else was wound a little bit tight. Even Dakich, who had predicted victory before every game all season, admitted, "I'm nervous. I don't why. It's the first time all season."

Maybe he knew something. The arena was so loud after the player introductions that Knight could barely be heard, even in Indiana's tight huddle. "Forget what is going on around us," he said. "This game is going to be decided out there, inside the lines. Nothing happening off the court is going to have anything to do with who wins this game. The buckets are still ten feet. We've been through it all before. You people would not be here if you weren't good enough to win this game.

"Just like Illinois now, get it settled down the first ten minutes and then let's win the basketball game."

If a home crowd doesn't necessarily intimidate a visiting team it can certainly charge up a home team. Michigan was charged up. The bored looks that the Wolverines had worn for so much of the season were nowhere in sight. Their eyes shone with intensity as they walked out amidst the din.

Rellford began the game with a thunderous dunk. The noise was earsplitting. Indiana hardly seemed rattled. Thomas hit a short jumper to tie it and Morgan followed an Alford miss for a 4–2 lead.

And then the roof fell in. Indiana couldn't get a rebound. Tarpley, Wade, Rellford, and Joubert looked like they were running a tip drill among themselves. It was 8–4 at the first TV time-out and Knight's voice was tense. He seemed to sense trouble. "I told you boys patience would win this game. Where is it? Move the ball, look for shots, and be patient."

They tried. Michigan wouldn't let them. Thomas picked up a second foul five minutes into the game reaching in on Tarpley.

Normally mild-mannered, Tarpley whirled and started talking trash to Thomas. Michigan was that intense. Thomas looked surprised at Tarpley, then laughed. It wasn't funny.

With Michigan leading 10–8, Joubert scored eight straight points. Chunky, cocky, often lazy, Joubert would not have lasted five minutes at Indiana. But he knew how to beat Indiana. Beginning with Joubert's spree, it was Purdue all over again. Tarpley went over Thomas for a dunk. Tarpley swished a hook. Thomas turned the ball over, lunged, and committed his third foul. He came out and was greeted by a blast from Knight. Harris shot an air ball, Michigan rebounded and raced downcourt, and Tarpley hit again. It was 24–12.

The next time-out was the Daryl Thomas show. "Why even bother showing up, Daryl? Back to the same old shit, Daryl. Back to where you were. Are you scared? What the hell are you scared of?"

Todd Meier, in for Thomas, threw the ball away and Glen Rice dunked. Gary Grant hit from outside, then stole another bad Meier pass for a dunk. It was 32–16. Even Alford was shaken. He tossed a brick and Joubert hit again. Rellford, a nonshooter, hit a fifteen-footer. The half ended with Alford holding for the last shot as he had done with so much success all season. This time, Grant blocked the shot. It was 44–25 at intermission.

There were no halftime hysterics. No speeches. No declarations. Just disappointment. "I've never had a team play scared in a big game before," Knight said. "I don't know why you're scared. You got right out of what we wanted to do and never got back into it. You guys are out there playing your own game out there. Playing my game is what got you here, boys, not playing your game.

"Steve, if you see them not moving, put the ball on your hip and direct them. You haven't done that once. Well, let's see if we can play a half of basketball. Let's see if we can salvage something here. But you better think about how tight you've played. They came at you and you were totally intimidated. Why can we play at Illinois, at Michigan State, at Ohio State, and come out here and be scared to play? Boys, I just don't understand it."

The coaches didn't understand it either. In the hallway, they had no answers. In truth, there were none. Wright made a comment about the Michigan people lacking class. "Forget that bullshit," said Knight, who often got completely tangled up in it. "Let's worry about ourselves. We're getting our ass kicked out there."

He didn't even talk to the players about coming back to win the game. Instead, he talked about why they had to play better in the second half. "What surprises me is that you've shown you can play with good teams," he said. "If you have any thought about competing nationally, this is what you've got to beat. If you want to play with North Carolina, Duke, Kansas, Georgetown, Georgia Tech, this is what you've got to beat. The country is full of teams like this. This is not an isolated case.

"I almost feel like you are right back where you were at the start of last season. I wonder if any of you thought about this: 'Hey, we got here by doing exactly what we were told to do. The minute we deviate from that, we're going to get our ass beat.' You are not good enough to not listen to us and be any good. Let's see if we can get back to doing what we can for a half."

They couldn't. It took Thomas exactly twenty-three seconds to pick up his fourth foul—an offensive foul. It was almost as if he subconsciously wanted to come out of the game. Knight put Jadlow in for Thomas. That turned out to be the one bright spot of the day. Jadlow played with abandon. He scored eleven points, he mixed it up inside, he went after people. When Rellford threw an elbow in his direction Knight jumped off the bench and yelled, "If he throws an elbow hit the sonofabitch in the mouth, Todd!"

It was all a long roar into the wind. Indiana never cut into the halftime margin. It just built and built. It was twenty minutes of humiliation. With the score 53–29, fourteen thousand voices began chanting, "Throw a chair, Bobby, throw a chair." A banner was unfurled, reminding Knight of his fishing speech after the Purdue game: "Bobby, wouldn't you rather be fishing?" Knight would rather have been anywhere else in the world.

Michigan kept running and dunking until the final minutes when Frieder took the seniors out one by one. Indiana had to endure each ovation, each set of hugs and high fives. It stretched on and on. In the final minute, Knight was reduced to telling Thomas that Jadlow had played harder than he had and that was a disgrace. Finally, it ended at 80–52. The walk off the floor and up the ramp was painful. The catcalls echoed in their ears, the laughs. They had worked so hard for so long to get to play this game, and it had been a complete, unmitigated disaster.

Knight knew how hard they had worked, and he knew how awful they felt. He reminded himself of that as he looked around the room at his stunned team. It was back to his old mental tug-of-war. "Jadlow did a hell of a job, he competed, he fought, and he played hard. The rest of you, nothing. You were totally intimidated and they just beat the shit out of you from the start."

Pause. "Hey, don't get your heads down. I'm really proud of you. You did a hell of a job with this season. We had a tremendous turnaround from last year's team, a great turnaround, and I know that you worked awfully hard to do it."

Pause. "But you played against the kind of people today that you've got to beat to be any good nationally. Ricky, you didn't do shit out there all day. You played like a damn scared high school kid all day. We've told you about building your body and your hands. If you don't get stronger, you won't play next year. Daryl, same thing. We got the shit beat out of us on the boards. You want to play, you got to compete. Harris, you paid no attention to what we wanted. You won't play either. We have too many players next year. You won't play. There's no way. Four of our best players are being redshirted right now and we got two more coming in who will be right with those four. You people want to play, you better take stock or your ass will be on the bench next year. I guarantee you that.

"Steve, not once did you go up and grab Daryl by the jersey and say, 'Get in the f—— game, Daryl, goddamn it. Quit playing like a pussy!' You know how many times Buckner did that to Benson? Do you know? You want to be a leader, Steve, you got to do that. We got nothing from you, nothing from anyone except Jadlow. And Winston, I thought Winston gave us everything he had. The rest of you didn't scratch or scrape at all. Not at all."

Pause. "Okay. The hell with this game. Don't even think about it. It's over. You've had a hell of a regular season, one you should be proud of. Now we've got a tournament to play. We can still get the job done there. All of you know we're capable of it. It's one bad day, boys, it doesn't have to ruin everything that we've done. Let's get the hell out of here."

And so it went all the way home. One minute Knight was telling Hammel and Felling how bad the team had been, the next he just shook his head and said, "Ah, what the hell. Michigan's got as much talent as anyone in the country. We're still right where we want to be."

17.

Back to the Brink

Knight spent the next two days reminding himself that Michigan had been an aberration, not part of a pattern. Still, he was torn. He could not just let go of a twenty-eight-point loss on national television for a Big Ten championship without at least one tantrum.

It didn't come right away, though. Sunday, Knight's mood was good, especially when the pairings for the NCAA tournament were announced. Indiana had been placed in the Eastern Regional as the number three seed. That meant that the NCAA Tournament Committee, looking at Indiana's season, had rated Indiana somewhere between ninth and twelfth in the country. The way the tournament is set up, the top four teams are seeded number one in the four regions; the next four are seeded number two, and so on right through the last four teams, who are the four sixteenth seeds.

As a number three seed, Indiana drew the fourteenth seed in the East as its first-round opponent. That was Cleveland State, a little-known team that had only become a factor in basketball in the last three years. This would be Cleveland State's first appearance ever in the NCAA tournament. The Vikings were 27–3 for the season. Their most impressive victory had been a rout of a struggling DePaul team in Chicago. They had played two Big Ten teams—Ohio State and Michigan. At Ohio State, they had lost 99–95. At Michigan, after trailing just 47–45 at halftime, they had lost 105–85. Of course Indiana knew about getting blown out at Michigan.

Looking at the tapes of those two games, Knight concluded that this would not be an easy game: Cleveland State was quick, deep, and it pressed all over the floor. The press had given Indiana trouble during the season. But with a week to prepare before playing the game on Friday in Syracuse, Knight certainly saw it as winnable.

In fact, Knight was excited by Indiana's draw. The first seed in the East was Duke, Mike Krzyzewski's team. The second seed was Syracuse. If Indiana won its first-round game, it would face either St. Joseph's or Richmond. That game would be eminently winnable. Then, in the round of sixteen, the likely opponent was Syracuse, a talented but undisciplined team. Again, a winnable game. And, if Duke were the opponent in the regional final, well, Knight had felt all year that Duke was a vulnerable team that had gone 32–2 largely because of Krzyzewski's coaching.

"And if we did lose to Duke, I wouldn't feel very bad about it," Knight said. "Because at least that way one of the good guys would be in the Final Four."

In short, Knight believed they could win the regional. There was no team he felt would overwhelm his team. And that is just what he told his players. "You will have to play like hell in every game in this tournament," he said. "Cleveland State is a very good team, a quick team, a tough team. But if you play from buzzer to buzzer you can beat any team in this regional. Any one of them. It's all right there for you."

This was Monday. On Sunday, they had waded through the Michigan tape for ninety minutes and then met briefly that evening after they had learned who they would be playing. Now, he wanted them to begin looking at some Cleveland State tape while he went through the Michigan tape one more time. Before he left, he had to remind them that he had not forgotten Michigan yet.

"Daryl, if we're going to win in this tournament, you have to play," he said. "You can't hide like you did Saturday. Now, I want to know right now, are you going to play or are you going to hide?"

"I'm going to play."

"Okay, you better. Because if you go out there and hide again I have absolutely no interest in having you play next year. You've made some great strides this year, Daryl, but you haven't played a really outstanding game since Illinois. You've gotten in foul trouble almost like you don't want to play. I won't tolerate it."

He left to review the Michigan tape. Waltman and Felling began to talk about Cleveland State. Ten minutes later Knight was back. He was angry. "I just started looking at this tape for the fourth time and I'm getting angrier each time I look at it. I want to show you the first two plays of this game because that's all I needed to see to analyze how much you people wanted to win this game."

He set the tape up. The first play showed Calloway going for a head fake and leaving his feet on defense. "How long has this gone on, Ricky? I'm getting tired of seeing the same mistakes." The shot was missed, but Harris had missed the box-out. "Tough to box out, isn't it, Andre?"

Play two: Harris missed a shot. "You drifted, Andre. The shot had no chance." Thomas almost tipped it in, a play that at first glance looked like a good effort that didn't go down. Not according to the tape. "Look at this, Daryl. You did not run down the court hard. In the first minute of the game, you aren't running hard. If you had been, you would have tipped it in easily. Instead, you had to half-lunge at the ball."

He snapped the tape off. The lights stayed out. "Boys, I am not used to having teams come in and lay an egg in a game this important. That is *not* the way you go after a championship. I just can't believe how bad you were. This tape is making me sick. Daryl, you sucked. You chickened out. You all better think about what I expect in this tournament."

There was some BK Theater involved in this outburst. Knight had treated the team with kid gloves with few exceptions since the painful aftermath of the first Michigan game. Now, with the tournament upon them, it was time to turn up the fear level at least a little bit. He wanted them reminded that the last five months had been to prepare for this month, these games, and that he would judge their season on what they did in March. He wanted no letdowns.

Knight went back to the cave with Kohn Smith. A few minutes

later, Smith was back. Time for some more BK Theater: guest star, Kohn Smith. "Hey, I just walked out of there, he's so mad," Smith told them. "It's like being in a cage with him in there. He's stayed off you all season long and then you go into that game with everything at stake and you play with your heads up your ass. You can't let that happen again. Coach shouldn't have to rant and rave and throw guys out of practice to get you ready to play in big games.

"You guys have to have some pride. Daryl, aren't you sick of being called a pussy? Andre, aren't you tired of being told you play dumb? Hey, we don't like it when he goes nuts and starts throwing things and cursing and ripping up carpets. We work our ass off to keep that from happening. We'll all look back at Michigan and say, 'It could have been.' But that opportunity is gone—forever. Now we've got a chance in the NCAAs. Let's not blow it."

Smith told the players that Knight had not sent him to talk to them. They knew he was lying and he knew they knew he was lying. It was back to the old Knight mind games. Rather than come back and scream again, Knight sent Smith to tell the players he was on the *verge* of screaming again. Smith was not the tough talker on the staff. It was not his role and not his forte. He knew it. Walking out of the locker room, he shook his head. "That was terrible," he said. "They didn't buy a word of it."

How could they? They knew that one of the coaches would never walk out of the cave on Knight to deliver a speech to the players. Especially not Smith. If he was giving a tough talk it was because he had been told to give a tough talk.

It was that way all evening. Mind games. They went on the floor to begin walking through Cleveland State, and Knight, sitting with Ed Williams, called them over to say he had just told Williams he thought they would win the regional. Then, back inside the locker room, the managers handed out Xerox copies of a newspaper story quoting Cleveland State coach Kevin Mackey as saying he was excited to play Indiana.

Again, he told them they could beat anybody. Then, one more time, he told them they had been awful on Saturday. Back and forth. "Cleveland State will look at this like an unknown heavyweight getting a shot at the champ." "Syracuse, boys, we can handle Syracuse. I guarantee it." "Ricky, why were you so bad Saturday? Have you even thought about it?"

And on and on and on. It hadn't been this way for a long time. It was last year's daily routine.

When Knight finally sent the players home, his message for the week was clear: Play well and Michigan will be forgotten; play poorly and it could be a long off-season. In spite of the mind games, everyone's mood was generally good. The players were making their usual bets—the average bet ranges from a soda to a dollar—on various first-round matchups and on the other regionals. The coaches were giggling about Purdue's draw, a first-round game against Louisiana State at Louisiana State. Keady had whined to Knight just two weeks earlier about "always getting screwed by the NCAA Tournament Committee." Now, he had truly been screwed and everyone at Indiana was amused.

The other thing that made Knight's postpractice mood bright was the news that Keith Smart, the junior college guard from Kansas, wanted to come to Indiana. Knight had given Hammel the story for the next day's newspaper and was almost giddy. The junior college experiment, judged a failure in January, was now judged an unqualified success. Harris had played well down the stretch and Jadlow had been the team's best player at Michigan. Knight was so excited about Jadlow that he was comparing him to Mark Alarie, Duke's silky-smooth All-American forward. With Smart committed and 6-11 junior college sophomore Dean Garrett already signed, Indiana would have four JUCOs on its roster in 1986-87. "We'll redshirt Jadlow," Knight said. "The other three will probably start."

Indiana—JUCO heaven.

Spring arrived in Bloomington the following day. The sun was out and the temperature climbed into the seventies. That alone was enough to brighten moods and energize everyone. Everyone was in early. The graduate assistants had by far the most arduous task of the week. They had to call around the country to track down tapes of possible opponents. More Cleveland State, lots of St. Joseph's and Richmond, and be thinking about the following week, too.

This was not an easy job. College basketball teams routinely trade tapes with one another, but some schools and conferences have rules against tape trading, and some coaches won't give a stranger tape on a friend's team. Dakich and Bartow sat in their little office with lists of phone numbers and made arrangements to acquire as many tapes as possible. How many would be enough? There was no such number.

The coaches spent the morning going over Cleveland State tapes again before retiring to Smitty's for lunch. Knight was in an expansive mood, remembering his days at West Point when the team would get ready to play the NIT each March while talking yet again about how much the JUCOs had helped the program.

Practice began that afternoon as strictly business—no games—but went straight downhill. The red team was having trouble with the press. Knight had seen this show before and it didn't please him. The only time all season that Indiana had faced a really good press and handled it had been the second Iowa game. In that game the players had been keen and honed in because they had been embarrassed at Iowa. Cleveland State's press had at least as much potential to create trouble as Iowa's. But the players were not apt to take Cleveland State as seriously as Iowa.

"The problem you had against Michigan, boys, was that you developed an inflated opinion of yourselves after Michigan State. You did not have a tough mentality for that game. Cleveland State will have a tough mentality, I promise you that. You are going to have to play an entire game Friday and an entire game Sunday or you have to wait until October 15 to play again. There's no second chance. If you aren't ready, it's over. The first guy I see trotting out there on Friday is coming out. If you want to play in this game you are going to have to bust your ass from start to finish."

Knight thought that Cleveland State could hurt Indiana with its press. He also thought that Cleveland State was too quick for Indiana to go out and pressure on defense. He wanted his team to play in a defensive shell. It would look like a man-to-man but it would do what a good zone does: force a lot of jump shots. "From twenty feet in we have to be red-tail bitches," Knight said. "Make them shoot outside. Inside twenty feet we can't give up anything."

This was a day for spectators. Most of Knight's friends knew it was a good idea to stay away on the Monday after a loss—especially one like Saturday's—so they were out in force on Tuesday. In spite of the intensity he directed at the players, Knight was much looser than he had been the day before. At one point he sat with his crew of professors discussing the significance of degrees: "Here's the way I look at it," he said, 'A BS is just what it stands for, an MS is More of the Same, and a PhD is Piled Higher and Deeper.''

Knight was just finishing his speech when he looked up and saw Thomas fail to get open. "Goddamn it, Daryl, you got to be hard to guard!" he screamed.

From there, the tension built. A Calloway turnover precipitated a ball's being kicked fifteen rows into the stands. Morgan went from red to white, then the Todds began switching back and forth. The turnovers continued. "There isn't a white shirt in here as quick as anyone on Cleveland State," Knight roared, kicking the chair he had been sitting on. "This crap is no better than the crap I watched on Saturday. Get out of here. Go home. If you don't want to play any more than this then f— it.''

They went into the locker room. The screaming continued for several more minutes. What had started as BK Theater had escalated into real anger. Knight walked out of the locker room and punched one of the mats underneath a basket on his way back to the cave. He calmed down quickly, though.

"Boys," he said to the coaches, "let's go eat a steak tonight.''

Whether it was the steak or the return to normal weather the next day—rain—Knight's mood was considerably brighter. This would be the team's last practice at home before leaving for Syracuse on Thursday morning. Under NCAA rules, each school has to be at the game site the day before it plays and is assigned one hour of practice time on the floor that day. Since the practice is required to be open, a lot of teams practice a second time somewhere private.

Because of the travel schedule, Knight didn't want to schedule a second Thursday practice unless he had to. It was important, then, to get a lot done on Wednesday.

But this was one of those practices that was cursed from the start. It was almost reminiscent of the day when Daryl Thomas got hurt and Calloway and Pelkowski both sprained ankles before Thomas went down. It started early, when Alford, reaching for a pass, jammed the thumb on his shooting hand. Bartow, standing nearby, bolted for the training room in search of Garl.

Alford tried to come right back, but couldn't hold the ball. Knight ordered him out. Alford stood on the sideline icing the thumb while everyone else kept casting nervous glances in his direction. Knight could make a million speeches about how to play the game and they wouldn't do any good without Alford.

Even with Alford out, the team was sharp. So was Knight. When Thomas made a mistake and began to explain what he had done wrong, Knight interrupted. "Daryl," he said, "remember this old saying: Never complain or explain."

A moment later, when Thomas set a good screen, Knight stopped play again. "Daryl, was that an accident or did you actually figure out what to do?"

Buckner, who would be making the trip to Syracuse, was at practice, and he spent a good deal of time working with Robinson, Morgan, and Calloway. Buckner was a natural floor leader as a player, just the kind of general that Knight thought this team lacked. His presence always seemed to comfort Knight.

Disaster two came shortly after Alford, thumb taped, had come back in. Calloway, picking his way through the lane, ran smack into a Courtney Witte elbow. Witte didn't throw the elbow, Calloway just ran into it. He reeled and keeled over like a bowling pin. He was out cold. Garl, who was having a very hard time getting a free minute to finalize travel plans, was sent for again. Everyone was shooting free throws. The nervous glances were now directed at Calloway.

It took Garl a couple of minutes to get Calloway up. He struggled up like a boxer looking for his corner. "Ricky," Knight asked from ten feet away, "how many fingers am I holding?" Calloway correctly answered one. "Now, how many?" Knight asked, still holding up one finger. Calloway stuck with one. "Ricky, you're going to be all right."

Two plays later, Robinson got nailed in the groin. He went down in considerable pain, the kind that everyone grins at because they know how much it hurts but also that it will pass quickly.

"Stew," Knight asked, "you weren't planning on using them tonight were you?" Robinson shook his head. "Then let's go."

Calloway was okay, so was Robinson. Alford said he was okay. Knight cut practice off soon after Robinson's mishap as if remembering not to push his luck on a day like this one. As he and Buckner walked to the locker room before the evening walkthrough, Knight nodded his head as if he had just reached a decision.

"Quinn, if we can beat Cleveland State, I really think we can win this whole regional."

His eyes were lit up like a little boy who thinks he's getting that red fire engine on Christmas. But there would be no fire engine this year; Indiana had just held its last practice of the season in Assembly Hall.

———

The trip started poorly and went downhill from there. The trouble began when Hammel of all people was late for the bus. This was very unlike Hammel. He was always careful to arrive in plenty of time because he always believed that Knight would leave him behind without batting an eye.

Knight waited. He waited fifteen minutes before Hammel chugged up. He and Garl had gotten their signals crossed; Garl had said the team would leave at 9:30, meaning from the airport, but Hammel thought he meant from Assembly Hall. It was a measure of the depth of the Knight-Hammel friendship that on the day before an NCAA tournament game, Knight waited for him. If a player—any player—had been that late, Knight probably would have left without him.

Of course, Knight was not going to let such an act pass without mention. "Hamso," he said, "any chits that were out are even now." Hammel nodded. No one knew this better than he.

They arrived in Syracuse on a gray, ugly day, even grayer and uglier than most days in Bloomington. If there is a gloomier town anywhere in America than Syracuse, it has not yet been discovered. The sun in Syracuse is considered a myth along the lines of the Greek gods.

The bus went directly from the airport to the cavernous Carrier Dome, one of those awful indoor football-basketball arenas that have sprung up in the 1980s. Domes are a terrible place to watch basketball, but the NCAA loves them because they seat lots and lots of people who pay lots and lots of money for tickets. As domes go, the Carrier Dome is not as bad as some others because a giant curtain is drawn right through the middle of the building. It certainly isn't intimate, but with thirty thousand people in for a Syracuse game the place does shake.

It was cold and almost empty Thursday. Reporters milled around, most wondering exactly what to write. The NCAA tournament is tough on writers because by the time you reach the game site, there are so many reporters around that all interviews are like gang bangs. If one shows up at these practices looking for a story, one is generally in big trouble.

Still, a lot of writers were hoping to write something about Knight off of the mandatory postpractice interview session. If anyone in America would eschew the usual pregame clichés and say something interesting it was Robert M. Knight.

But Knight had no interest in entertaining the press on this day. He was honed in now, his mind focusing only on Cleveland State. After the practice session, before he went to the interview room, he asked the coaches what they thought about practicing again in the evening. He left them to mull that one over as he went to see his friends with the notebooks and microphones.

The session was calm, except for the presence of an idiot TV reporter from Cleveland who wanted somehow to create news where there was none to create. "Coach," he began, "most people in Cleveland think that Cleveland State has two chances in this game, slim and none. What do you think?"

Knight, who was very nervous about this game, answered honestly. "If that's true," he said, "then the people in Cleveland don't know very much about basketball." Note that Knight said, "If that's true."

Kevin Mackey had not followed Knight into the room by more than two minutes when the same guy said to him, "Coach, Bob Knight was just in here and he said the people in Cleveland don't know much about basketball."

There are days when Knight's complaints about the media ring disgustingly true.

The coaches were against another practice. The players had been up since 7:30; they had traveled and practiced and not had any rest. Better to let them rest, eat, and do a walk-through at the hotel than get on another bus and get dressed to practice again. Knight agreed. The kids got their rest and the coaches ate a wonderful Italian dinner. Yes, there was a reason for Syracuse to exist: a restaurant called Grimaldi's.

They went to bed early, hoping for sunshine and a victory.

It rained all day. The temperature never climbed out of the thirties. Knight, who would normally eat breakfast with Hammel while the team was at pregame meal, skipped breakfast. He was tight, noticeably tight. In a way, that was a good sign. The loosest he had been all year had been the three days leading up to the Michigan game.

Everyone was ready to play. Alford had quieted any doubts about his thumb by making fifteen straight shots during Thursday's shooting drills. The assistants left early to scout the noon game between Richmond and St. Joseph's. Indiana would meet the winner Sunday. Coaches from both schools had already been talked to about borrowing tapes from the loser of that game.

Everyone and everything was prepared. Most of the Indiana family was there: the redshirts, who normally didn't travel, had traveled. So had Ralph Floyd, Ed Williams, and Quinn Buckner. The weekend looked a lot brighter than the weather. Knight, though, fretted. As the team warmed up he walked around the huge locker room, unable to sit still—unusual for him. "Are we all right?" he asked repeatedly.

They came back in for a final word. "Boys, we've told you and told you that every minute you play in this tournament has to be all-out," Knight said. "But I want to tell you something. No one in this tournament has worked harder to get here than you have. It's five months exactly today. You know what you've been through and it was pointing towards this. We are right where we want to be right now. So let's go out and make sure we didn't do all this work for nothing."

Knight wanted a good start. He believed, with good reason, that in spite of all the brave talk, a quick Indiana start might make Cleveland State think it was in over its head. Get their confidence down early and the game might not be as tough as he had thought it would be.

Naturally, the start could not have been much worse. Morgan took the first shot and nailed it for a 2–0 lead. It was to be the only shot he took all day. Clinton Ransey, who would prove unstoppable on this day, promptly answered to make it 2–2.

Cleveland State set up its press. All week long, Indiana had worked with Morgan taking the ball out of bounds to get the offense started. The first three times he touched the ball, Morgan could not get the ball inbounds. By the time the sequence was over, Ransey had four more points, the score was 6–2 Cleveland State, Knight had yanked Morgan in favor of Robinson, and any hope for a quick start was long gone.

It would be a struggle, just as Knight had feared.

Indiana got its bearings after the shaky beginning and the two teams seesawed for ten minutes. A Daryl Thomas layin made it 26–25, Indiana. But then the press offense turned shaky again and Cleveland State ripped off six straight points, just as it had done at the start. Punching the ball inside—Indiana's defensive shell was showing cracks all over—the Vikings built the lead to 37–28 with 6:30 left.

But Alford revved up and brought the Hoosiers back. They got to within 43–41 before a follow shot by Clinton Smith, on a play where he went around Todd Meier, made it 45–41 at the half.

Still, there was no need to panic. They had survived the bad start and come back from a nine-point deficit. Nothing had really changed. If they handled the press, they would win the game. Knight was clinical with the players as he went through their mistakes. Only when he and the coaches retreated to the bathroom to talk did he get angry.

"I ought to fire all of us for setting up that way against the goddamn press," he said angrily, kicking a nearby stall in frustration. "All we have to do is get it in before they set up and we're alright. Morgan is just so slow. We have to go with Robinson in the second half, we have no choice. Jesus, I didn't want to be behind in this game."

The only change they made was on the inbounds pass. In order to keep the press from setting up, Knight wanted the person nearest the ball to grab it right away and throw it in. "We're all right, boys," he told them. "We told you this was going to be a tough game so this is no surprise. They are going to come out and go right at us in this second half and that's just fine.

"Be patient, look for openings. Let's get started right this time and play like hell the first five minutes. It's just like the score is 4–0 and we've still got twenty minutes to play. Plenty of time. Let's go."

They did play like hell the first five minutes. Hell as in bad. Daryl Thomas picked up his third foul right away—on an offensive foul—and Cleveland State scored the first six points. Knight had to call time. Now it was 10–0 and there was less than eighteen minutes to play. Morgan was given a brief reprieve, going in for Calloway, who had just committed another turnover.

Knight tried to repeat Minnesota. There, he had talked them back into the game after a horrendous second-half start. He screamed at Thomas, he told them they were backing down. They listened. They went back and began playing even as Knight continued to rail at Thomas on the bench. Robinson broke the Cleveland State spell with a jumper to make it 51–43.

But Cleveland State was firmly convinced that it was going to win. Each time Indiana crept closer, someone, usually Ransey, would get a bucket. The Hoosiers got to within striking range once. An Alford drive cut the lead to 66–61 with 8:55 left. Ransey then made one of two foul shots to make it 67–61. Alford drove baseline again, was fouled and made both shots. It was 67–63. Back to 4–0 and still more than eight minutes left.

But after Eric Mudd, CSU's center, got inside (again the shell cracked) to make it 69–63, Robinson missed the front end of a one-and-one that could have cut the margin back to four. Time was now slipping away. The lead seesawed between six and eight. Harris cut it to six, but Ransey answered with six minutes left. Harris missed and Smith rebounded. Cleveland State called time. Mackey wanted to spread out and kill some time. Knight glanced at the clock. Five minutes. And it was 8–0.

A moment later it was 10–0. Ransey again. He would score twenty-seven points before it was over, three more than Alford. With CSU spread out, Indiana was in desperate trouble. The last thing it wanted against a quicker team was to have to chase. Now, it had to chase.

This was not Indiana basketball. The Vikings were killing time and holding the lead. It was still 81–73 when Harris followed a Calloway miss with sixty-seven seconds left. Ransey, to prove he was human, threw the ball away, and Eyl, not worrying about missing at this stage, drove for a layup to make it 81–75 with forty-three seconds left. They fouled Mudd on the inbounds. He missed and Alford hit a drive with thirty seconds to go.

It was back to 4–0. But now almost all of that twenty minutes was gone. They had to steal the inbounds pass. There were no time-outs left. Cleveland State threw a long inbounds pass. Smith caught it and went right to the basket. Eyl went right up with him. He blocked the shot. The whistle blew. The block looked clean. Would it be a jump ball? No. Referee Tom Fraim said Eyl had fouled Smith with his body going up. If the call had gone the other way, Indiana might have had a chance for a miracle. But it would have taken that. There were only twenty-one seconds and no time-outs left.

But there would have been hope. Now, there was none. Smith made both foul shots to make it 83–77. Alford made the last basket of the season. The clock ran to zero. It was 83–79. Still 4–0. But now time had run out.

There were no tears in the Indiana locker room. People don't cry when they are in shock. Knight didn't rant. It would take a while for his anger to escalate, although it surely would. He told them he was disappointed, that they had backed down—again. No screams. But it would get worse.

Knight's only outburst was brief. It came when he turned and saw Dakich, who was trying very hard—like everyone else—to be invisible. "Jesus," Knight said angrily, "I have to watch this f—— team play like it did last year and then I turn around and the first person I see is goddamn Dakich."

There was not much to say. The press had killed them. They had needed to be tough inside and they had been hammered inside. Thomas, who finished with eleven points, had scored nine of them in the first half. Three of his four rebounds had come in the first half. Harris had played well with sixteen points and ten rebounds.

Alford had been Alford. Calloway had been respectable with ten points, seven rebounds, and just two turnovers.

But it had not been enough. They had needed something extra and no one had found it. For Morgan and Robinson, it was a bitter end after all the ups-and-downs. Robinson had shot just three of nine from the field and had missed a crucial free throw when the deficit had only been six; Morgan had turned the ball over five times. Even more important, his first two turnovers had come in those nightmarish early minutes, helping Cleveland State establish confidence at a time when a quick Indiana start might have rattled a team playing in postseason for the first time. As always, they had given everything they had. Sadly, as had often been the case in the eyes of their coach, that had not been enough.

In truth, pointing fingers at individuals was foolish. Cleveland State had played well, Indiana had not. In his postgame press conference, that is exactly what Knight said. He was calm, collected, and gracious. The ifs and buts and the self-questioning would come later.

The players dressed in record time. Thirty minutes after their season had ended, they were on a bus heading for the airport. The media never got a chance to ask them what had gone wrong. It was just as well. None of them had any answers.

The flight home could have been worse. Knight slept for a while, told Hammel he didn't know if he could take this any more, and then got up to tell the players how disappointed he was. They should have been tougher, smarter. They should have handled the press better.

The campus was empty when the bus pulled up to Assembly Hall. Friday had been the last day of class before spring break, and almost everyone had taken off for Florida or home. Once again, the players found themselves on a deserted campus under the most depressing of circumstances. This time, though, they would escape—eventually.

The rituals had to be finished first. They met for the last time as a group in their regular meeting room. One year ago, Knight had dismissed his most disappointing team ever from this room. This team had given him many happy moments. But all that was forgotten now. First, the three seniors had to be excused. "Stew,

Winston, you can go," Knight said, forgetting Courtney Witte. Witte paused a moment, unsure what to do, then got up and followed Robinson and Morgan to the door. Knight asked Morgan to wait outside for him for a moment.

Then he turned to the twelve players who would return. The redshirts, who had made the trip, were in the room, too. Knight had talked earlier in the week to the coaches about the possibility of practicing after the final game, assuming the team did not reach the Final Four. NCAA rules stipulate that a team may practice until the day of the national championship game.

When Knight first brought up the idea, he was thinking about getting some extra work for the redshirts and of getting some practice work on tape. Now, as he stood in front of his remaining players, those rational thoughts were far from his mind.

"You people have a lot of work to do if you want to be any good next year," he said. "A lot of work. The way you played these last two games won't beat anyone. Not anyone. We'll see you here a week from Sunday at four o'clock."

That was it. The season was over, but the suffering was not. The good times had ceased to exist. Notre Dame, Illinois, Purdue, Michigan State, Iowa—all forgotten. All Knight could see in his mind's eye at that moment was Michigan and Cleveland State. Humiliation. Defeat. All the questions and self-doubts came racing back to him.

But the year had not been a lost cause. As the others left, Knight called the waiting Morgan back into the room. On this same spot, Knight had told Morgan he didn't want him back for his last year, that he was finished playing basketball at Indiana. Now, Morgan was finished after five long years.

"Winston," Knight said softly, "I just want you to know that I know you gave us everything you had this season and I appreciate it."

Ten years ago, five years ago, one year ago, Knight would probably have been unable to reach out to one of his players this way after such a crushing loss. It was a final first in a season of firsts. Morgan looked at his former coach. Five springs earlier, Knight had given him a dollar and told him he would never give him anything else for free. Knight had been telling the truth. Because Morgan had truly earned these last words.

As the others left, they knew what awaited them the following Sunday: an angry coach. The tape would have been looked at and looked at, the mistakes dissected. Every one of them would be found at fault at some point in some way. It would be a long day and a longer week. They would once again have an angry, frustrated coach, one trying to deal with a defeat he was incapable of dealing with.

They would be in jeopardy once again. They had achieved and achieved for five months but all that had been virtually wiped out in a week. They were back in trouble again.

They were back to the brink.

Epilogue

In the days following the end of the season, Knight was haunted by the way it had ended. Again and again he replayed the last two games in his mind. He questioned himself, his coaches, his players. He was angry, not at anyone specifically—with the possible exception of Daryl Thomas, whose manhood was once again in constant question—but with the world.

Indiana had been upset in a year of upsets in NCAA play. On the same day that Cleveland State beat Indiana, Notre Dame was stunned by the University of Arkansas at Little Rock, another team that was making its NCAA tournament debut. Two days later, Syracuse, playing on its home floor, lost to Navy by twenty points, an embarrassment well beyond what had happened to Indiana. Michigan, which had beaten Indiana by twenty-eight points eight days earlier, lost to Iowa State—the same Iowa State Indiana had beaten by twenty-one points in December.

But Knight saw none of this. All he could see was *his* loss and *his* humiliation. Once again, Knight somehow saw himself diminished by defeat. Knight had never before lost a first-round NCAA tournament game. It tore him up.

Which was a shame. Because overall, 1985–86 was a season Knight should be able to smile about. He and his team achieved or surpassed every preseason goal he set. He had hoped for nineteen victories; he got twenty-one. He had hoped for twelve Big Ten victories; he got thirteen. He wanted to get back into the NCAA tournament; he did. He wanted people to respect Indiana again; they did. The fact that the NCAA Tournament Committee, with all its computer printouts and scouting reports, rated Indiana among the top twelve teams in the country was proof of that.

Individually, Knight wanted Steve Alford to play up to the potential he had flashed as a freshman. Alford did just that. He was consistent, he was tough, and he improved the nonshooting aspects of his game. He was an All-American, so much so that when someone criticized Alford's selection as an All-American one night at dinner, Knight said, "How could you not vote for Steve?" Alford would have enjoyed hearing those words.

Daryl Thomas, asked to play center at 6–7, averaged 14.5 points a game and was brilliant at times. He did not have a good finish and was not the same player he had been in the last twelve games of the season, but the potential he showed was encouraging.

Andre Harris, after going through a preseason in which he could do no wrong and an early season in which he could do no right, justified Joby Wright's faith in him during the season's last eight games. Ironically, he almost reversed roles with Thomas. Harris emerged as the team's best rebounder (he finished with a 5.6 average, high on the team) and began to take better shots and make smarter passes.

Rick Calloway had about as good a freshman season as anyone could possibly have hoped for. He averaged 13.9 points and 4.9 rebounds and finished the season as a player with a limitless future.

Right there was a solid four-man nucleus—if Harris overcame his academic problems to stay eligible. Todd Meier and Steve Eyl would also be back to supply depth, and the five redshirts—Kreigh Smith, Magnus Pelkowski, Joe Hillman, Brian Sloan, and Jeff Oliphant—all showed potential. Sloan in particular showed remarkable improvement.

The three recruited players all had to be considered question marks until they proved themselves. But at 6–11 and 230 pounds,

Dean Garrett would at the very least give Indiana someone big and strong in the middle. Keith Smart was an excellent athlete, the kind of player whose quickness would be valuable against a press like Cleveland State's. And David Minor, the only high school recruit, was reportedly a lot like Calloway but a better shooter. If he turned out anything at all like Calloway, Indiana would have a terrific player.

In short, all the elements were in place for Indiana once again. There was experience, players who had proven themselves capable of competing with almost anyone in the country. With the advent of a three-point shot from the ridiculous range of 19 feet, 9 inches, Alford would be easily capable of averaging thirty points a game—if necessary.

There was also the semiexperience of the redshirts, players who understood the program and now had to put that knowledge to use. And there was the raw potential of the recruits. Indiana would begin 1986–87 ranked at least in the top ten, perhaps in the top five.

And then there was the coach. If 1985–86 proved anything it proved beyond a shadow of a doubt that Bob Knight remains as good a coach as there is, perhaps the best. For twenty-seven games he got as much from his basketball team as any coach in the country, maybe more. That the last two games were a disaster does not diminish that fact.

Knight seemed to have learned from the debacle of 1985. He was more patient than he had ever been, more understanding, more restrained. All of these are relative terms. There were still moments when he went out of control and days when he played silly mind games with everyone. But more than anything, Knight taught, coached, and pushed his team, and made it about as good as it could possibly be.

The question then is this: Can he do it again? Knight began this past season uncertain about his team. He wondered whether a team with a 6–7 center that depended on a 6–1 guard to do most of its scoring could beat anybody. The answer was yes. Now he will begin the season with a team picked to do great things again. Knight will expect great things, too. He will expect Garrett, Smart, and Minor to be better than Witte, Morgan, and Robinson. He will expect the redshirts to play a lot and play well. He will expect more than twenty-one victories, more than thirteen Big Ten victories, and much more than the first round of the NCAA tournament.

With those expectations will come potential pitfalls. What will happen after the first loss? A loss at home in the Big Ten? Will Knight once again be patient? Will he go fishing or will he go head-hunting? As bright as Knight is, as brilliant a coach as he is, the answers to these questions should be simple, but nothing about Bob Knight is simple and few things in his life are easy. He couldn't stand the comfort.

Two weeks after the Cleveland State loss, Knight has not stopped brooding. He had made life miserable for the players during the first two days of their postseason practices, sitting in the stands while they scrimmaged. He even yelled at Bartow and Dakich for doing a poor job of refereeing on that first Sunday. When he left for Dallas on Thursday to go to the Final Four, everyone breathed a sigh of relief. The assistants ran scrimmages until the following Monday—the last day allowable under NCAA rules.

In Dallas, Knight was reunited with his coaching family. This is an annual affair, because the Final Four is also the site of the National Association of Basketball Coaches convention. Knight rooms each year with Pete Newell, and he spent the weekend with people like Fred Taylor, Henry Iba, Bob Murray, and all his former assistants. On Friday night, the annual family dinner was held at a local Italian restaurant.

Knight spent a good deal of time during that weekend with Mike Krzyzewski, whose Duke team reached the championship game before losing to Louisville, 72–69. Knight wore a Duke button everywhere he went, spoke to Krzyzewski's team about playing in the Final Four, and went to Krzyzewski's room after the final to console him. There was irony here: Knight would have been inconsolable after such a loss, yet he insisted on trying to help console Krzyzewski.

In the days following the final, Knight called Krzyzewski several times to make sure he was okay. Krzyzewski was fine. He was far better equipped to deal with a crushing loss than his mentor was.

In fact, Knight was still brooding about the Cleveland State loss in Dallas. When a friend asked him why he wasn't going to the NABC banquet, Knight answered, "I'm laying low. I'm kind of struggling right now."

Why?

"Our team just isn't very good."

But, it was pointed out, he had done all that could be done, squeezed all there was to squeeze for twenty-seven games.

"But we played twenty-nine."

Knight paused. Then he added, "And Daryl Thomas is still a pussy. I don't know what to do about him."

So there it was. To Knight, the epitaph for 1985–86 was that Daryl Thomas was still a pussy and Indiana had lost two games in embarrassing fashion. Undoubtedly, that would pop into his mind again and again during fall practice, after the first bad half, after the first loss. . . .

The key for Bob Knight remains the same: He is as brilliant a coach as there is. He is an extraordinarily compassionate, caring, sensitive person. No one has ever had a better or more loyal friend. And yet everyone who cares about him remains concerned about his ability to hurt and to cause pain. And the person he hurts most often is Bob Knight.

People around him—friends, coaches, players—want, like Isiah Thomas, to hug him and tell him that they love him. Yet he shies away from that, often acting as if he doesn't think himself worthy of that kind of feeling and then going out and doing something to prove it.

He has won 438 games as a coach, and if he were to coach another twenty years, he could well break Adolph Rupp's all-time record of 880 victories. There is no reason for him not to coach another twenty years. He loves the game, the challenges, and the players. And yet, he still remains unhappy so much of the time. Losses destroy him, and when they do he seems to feel obligated to make everyone and everything around him as miserable as he is. Often, he succeeds.

If only he could let go of things: losses, grudges, tantrums. He is rich and he is famous. In a good mood, there is no one in the world more delightful to be around because he is so bright, so well-read. In a bad mood, there is no one worse. Just as he sees everything in black-and-white terms, he, too, is black and white. Bob Knight never has an average day.

In 1985–86, he saw firsthand what patience could do for a basketball team. He found that he did not have to make a major issue of each defeat in order to get his team to bounce back. He found that if he made the effort, he could control his temper. One can only hope that he will remember these lessons and use them.

He has so much to give—and has given so much. And when he begins his twenty-second season as a college basketball coach this fall, he will only be forty-six years old. A young man with a bright future. If he doesn't destroy it.

Moby Dick

The 1986 season did not end at Indiana until seventeen days after the stunning loss to Cleveland State. True to his word, Knight had the players back scrimmaging during the final week of NCAA tournament play. It was, to say the least, less than fun for the players.

Knight's mood was so dark that he even barked at Dakich and Bartow for refereeing poorly. On one particularly unpleasant afternoon Uwe Blab, the leading scorer from the still-remembered 1985 disaster, came to practice. Blab, who was playing in the NBA for the Dallas Mavericks, had let his hair grow and was wearing a ponytail and an earring. Knight ignored him. When the practice was over he told the players in the locker room, "I better not ever catch any one of you coming back here looking like that."

Fortunately for everyone—including Knight—Knight went to Dallas for the Final Four, leaving the assistant coaches in charge of the last few days of scrimmages. The Final Day finally came on March 31. While Knight was parading around Dallas wearing a Duke button on his sweater (a show of support for Mike Krzyzewski) his team scrimmaged for the last time.

The atmosphere that last day was loose. There was a sense of relief because the angry coach wasn't there, and because the players knew they would not have to see another formal practice until October 15. But there were also questions, the unpleasant residue of the Michigan and Cleveland State debacles.

As the players dressed after the final practice, many of them were as bewildered as they had been the year before after the loss in the NIT final. They had little idea as they left Assembly Hall that evening that exactly one year later they would be rolling on top of one another in the Superdome, celebrating a national championship that even Knight had to concede was a remarkable feat.

There were changes during the off-season. Andre Harris, without basketball as a motivator, had slipped back into bad habits academically. He flunked out at the end of the semester and, as promised, Knight did not offer to help him gain readmission. Harris transferred to Austin Peay.

That certainly did not leave the junior college experiment on solid ground. Harris, with all his ability, had been a headache from the beginning. Jadlow had shown potential in flashes, but would be redshirted in '86–'87. He needed time to mature.

The new JUCO arrivals were Dean Garrett and Keith Smart. Garrett, 6-10 and raw, had been signed early when Knight still had stars in his eyes from watching Harris run and jump during the early workouts. Smart's signing, however, was testimony to Joby Wright's persuasiveness. Knight's initial reaction to Smart— "He wears gold chains"—had come at a time when Harris and Jadlow had already spent considerable time in the doghouse.

And yet, Wright had kept after Knight, convinced him to invite Smart in for a visit and to go back and see him play. Smart had been so impressive, both on and off the floor, that Knight decided to give the JUCO project one more all-out shot. It turned out to be one of the crucial decisions of his coaching career.

There were other decisions to be made during the off-season. In June, Knight filed for divorce after twenty-two years of marriage to Nancy Knight. He knew that this decision, though not surprising, would be traumatic for both his sons, especially Patrick, who would turn sixteen in September. But he honestly believed it was the best thing for everyone—including Nancy.

The decision came as a surprise to no one inside the basketball program. Everyone knew that Knight had purchased a house in

Ellettville the previous summer to prepare for just such an eventuality, and the general sentiment was relief that the issue was finally going to be resolved.

There was one hitch, though. As soon as the divorce papers were filed and became a matter of public record, the *Bloomington Herald-Telephone* reported it. Somehow, Knight had thought he could keep the move a secret. When the story hit the paper, he was furious. Naturally, Hammel was caught in the middle of the whole debacle.

Later in the summer Hammel was talking about what had happened and Knight's anger with the newspaper. "But doesn't he understand that filing for divorce is public record?" Hammel was asked.

"Wait a minute," Hammel answered, half joking. "Are you using understand and Bob Knight in the same sentence when it comes to the media?"

The summer was not without its funny moments. Knight went off to Spain for the world championships to be a TV analyst and to conduct several clinics for Adidas. One night, driving on a country road, Knight's car broke down. He began walking, looking for help. Finally he spotted a house with lights ablaze. He knocked and asked if the people there would help him. Could they help? They could help him with just about anything he wanted.

He had stumbled into a brothel.

Remembering the wild rumors that had circulated the year before when word had leaked out about his purchase of the Ellettville house, Knight couldn't help but laugh when he returned home and told friends the story.

Knight also spent a couple of days in the early fall visiting his old friend Bill Parcells, the New York Giants' coach. The two had been buddies when they had coached at West Point, and they remained close. When Parcells took Knight into his locker room shortly before kickoff one Sunday, Lawrence Taylor, the Giants' All-Pro linebacker, spotted him immediately.

"Hey," Taylor said. "Look, everybody, it's the chairthrower."

Maybe Knight was in a good mood or maybe he looked at Taylor's chiseled, 6-foot-3-inch, 245-pound body closely. Either way, he didn't snap. There were no cracks, as one might have expected, about Taylor's off-season drug treatment.

"You just worry," Knight told Taylor, "about getting out there and tackling somebody." Taylor tackled, the Giants won easily and Knight returned home full of stories about his buddy Parcells. The Giants would go on to win the Super Bowl, a victory that gave Knight almost as much pleasure as what would take place in March.

The team that gathered to begin practice on October 15 had almost as many question marks as the one that had started practice twelve months earlier. Gone, in addition to Harris, were '86 seniors Winston Morgan, Stew Robinson and Courtney Witte. Knight was less than pleased with Robinson, who had failed to graduate.

Morgan and Robinson had, in essence, shared one starting spot the previous season, and Harris had been the power forward and the leading rebounder. Ideally, those two spots would be filled by Garrett and Smart. Both had a lot to prove, however.

There were some givens. Alford, who had played superbly as a junior, was locked in, not just as a starter but as the captain and leader Knight had spent most of the previous season convincing him he had to become. Alford was now just that. This would be his team, just as the '76 team had been Quinn Buckner's team, just as the '81 team had been Isiah Thomas's team.

Daryl Thomas would start at Harris's forward spot—*if* Garrett could produce at center. He had done a good job playing center at 6-7 in '86, had handled more abuse from Knight than anyone not named Alford and would be more comfortable playing forward as a senior. The other forward spot belonged to Rick Calloway. He was a sophomore now, established as a rising star.

The other two spots would be competitive, though, and that was healthy. The five redshirts from a year ago—Joe Hillman, Kreigh Smith, Brian Sloan, Magnus Pelkowski and Jeff Oliphant —would get a chance too. So would Todd Meier, the third senior who had played so well in spots the year before in spite of his aching knees.

And then there was Steve Eyl, or, as the players called him, SteveEyl. As good an athlete as Eyl was, basketball did not come easy to him, especially shooting a basketball. Knight had tried everything to make Eyl a better shooter, but had succeeded mostly in making Eyl tight as a drum every time he felt his coach's watchful eye upon him.

But during the offseason pickup games, there was little doubt among the players about who the most improved player around was: SteveEyl. He was shooting better, more consistently. Feeling more confident as a shooter made him more confident as a player. By the time practice started Eyl had come a long way from the day in Wisconsin when Knight had told Eyl if one of his assistants ever recruited another player like him he would be fired.

As always, the preseason had its share of rotten evenings. That was no surprise. It was part of the routine. But three weeks into practice, the players were hit by a lightning-bolt that shook them and put the whole season in jeopardy.

They were sitting in the locker room waiting for Knight to come in and give his pre-practice talk. The next night, they were scheduled to go to Fort Wayne for the annual red-white scrimmage. Knight walked in, the assistants following, looking somber. Knight had a piece of paper in his hand. He began reading from it.

It was a letter from the academic staff. One of the players—Knight didn't use his name while reading the letter—had been cutting class. He was in danger of failing a course. This had been going on for several weeks. When Knight finished reading, he turned to Alford.

"Steve," he asked, "what do we usually do in situations like this?"

Almost in a whisper, Alford answered, "Well, usually the guy would be gone."

"That's right," Knight said. He looked across the room at Thomas. "Daryl, you're gone."

It looked like Mike Giomi revisited. Thomas, a good student, was not failing by NCAA or Indiana standards. But he was cutting class, and that was below Knight's standards. He knew the rules and he had broken them. The team made the trip to Fort Wayne without Thomas. A brief Indiana press release said Thomas had been thrown off the team for cutting class.

These were nervous days for the players. Most preseason publications were picking Indiana in the top five and, after watching Smart and Garrett practice, the players and coaches really believed this team could be very good. But not without Thomas. He was, by consensus, the second best player on the team. He was a senior, he was smart, he was experienced and he had been toughened by three years under Knight. For the Hoosiers to excel, Thomas *had* to play.

Knight knew all this. But he certainly was not about to compromise his academic standards. And yet, Knight is not inflexible. Recidivism in his program is inexcusable, but first offenders, especially if they have been solid citizens in the past, get a second chance.

"Only two things I will never ever excuse," Knight had once said. "One is lying, the other is using drugs."

On the second issue, Knight had once given a player who had been a solid person a second chance when he had tested positive for marijuana. And so, Daryl Thomas, good kid, good student, would get a second chance. Make up the missed class time and the missed work and you can come back, Thomas was told. He did just that. One week after the incident in the locker room, Thomas was returned to the team. Three nights later, he scored twenty-two points in an exhibition victory over the Russians.

The season's first crisis had been survived.

If there was another significant event during preseason, it was the gradual change in the Knight-Alford relationship. Even as he drove him and haunted him and attacked him during the winter of '86, Knight had been mellowing on Alford. He had started that season threatening not to start him, throwing him out of practice, questioning whether he could ever be the leader he had to be for the team to succeed.

At times, he had been brutal after Alford had not played well. More than once, he had told the coaches, "We'll never be any good until we get rid of Alford."

But deep down, Knight knew that wasn't true. He knew how hard Alford had worked to please him, and how much he had improved. That didn't mean there weren't going to be moments during this final season when Alford got ripped. There were. But with Alford's last days in an Indiana uniform approaching, Knight knew it was time to use the boxing gloves less and the kid gloves more. Alford had earned at least that.

And so, on the day after Thanksgiving, twenty-four hours before the season would begin with a game against Montana State,

Knight called Alford into the cave. Alford had been there before but usually because he—or the team—was in some kind of trouble. Now though, Knight didn't scream or yell. As Alford told friends later, his voice and his words were soft.

"I just wanted you to know," Knight said, "how much I appreciate you. You stand for everything this program is about...I don't think I could care about you more than I do if you were my own son."

Alford was both stunned and touched by this gesture. He knew this side of his coach existed; he had seen it in things he had done for others over the years. But this was the first time Knight had ever really reached out to him this way.

"Coach," Alford said at the door, "I can't tell you how much I appreciate what you just said."

"Steve," Knight answered, "I hope you know how much I appreciate you."

Finally, Alford knew. When he told friends about the incident, none of them was amazed as he was. They had always known how Knight felt about Alford. Only Alford hadn't known. Perhaps Knight had sensed that.

The season began with a walkover victory over Montana State. Hillman, at least for the moment, had beaten Smart out for the second starting spot at guard. Garrett, despite a shaky preseason, was the starting center.

The win was a costly one. With 17:28 left in the game and the Hoosiers leading comfortably 48-35, Calloway went down with a knee injury. Initially, it looked very serious, perhaps season-ending. He would be gone, it was thought, at least a month.

This was a potential disaster. Calloway would miss several tough December games. More importantly, he would miss time developing, getting used to the new players, improving his own game. Even after the 90-55 victory, the season had not gotten off to a good start.

Notre Dame was next. Smart started in Calloway's place. As it turned out, this was to be a historic night. Indiana's 67–62 victory was expected. That was no surprise. What was a surprise, even a shock, was the zone defense in which the Hoosiers opened the game.

Knight had talked about playing zone as far back as the end of the '85 season. He had even practiced it a little that summer on tour. He had practiced it even more during this preseason. A year earlier, prior to playing Notre Dame, he had thought that a zone would be the best defense against David Rivers, Notre Dame's penetrating guard. He had even thought about playing it for one possession at the start of the game, just to throw the Irish off.

But he had not done it that night or any night in '86. But now, having practiced it, Indiana was ready to play it. Ironically, when Digger Phelps had read that Knight considered playing zone against his team, he had considered it a slap in the face. When Indiana arrived at Notre Dame on the morning of the game an angry Phelps was waiting for Knight. The two good friends retreated to Phelps's office, where Knight spent close to an hour explaining to Phelps that playing zone was not a slight to Notre Dame but testimony to Rivers's ability as a penetrator.

Phelps was mollified. Indiana played zone most of the game. It was Hammel who asked the question in the postgame press conference: "What about the zone?"

"What zone?" Knight answered with a straight face. "Did you see a zone out there?"

If the Notre Dame game did nothing else, it showed how far Knight had come in terms of flexibility. The once man-to-man, walk-it-up, don't-recruit-outside-the-Midwest, don't-touch-JUCOs and don't-redshirt-players coach had in one night played zone, pushed the ball up the floor, started two Californians (Hillman and Garrett), two JUCOs (Garrett and Smart) and played three redshirts of a year before (Hillman, Smith and Pelkowski).

Living proof that you *can* teach an old coach new tricks.

Kentucky was next at home, and the 71–66 victory was a sweet one even though the Wildcats weren't nearly the team they had been the previous season. This was revenge for the bitter loss in Lexington on the night that Alford had been suspended by the NCAA because of his posing for the sorority charity calendar.

Knight had talked the previous year about announcing that he was canceling the Kentucky series after beating them—he would never make such an announcement after a loss—but he had changed his mind by the time the two teams played this game.

"I think [Eddie] Sutton will run the program a hell of a lot differently than [Joe B.] Hall did," Knight said after the game, a reference to published reports of payoffs to players during Hall's tenure. "If he does, then this will continue to be a hell of a rivalry."

It was a not-so-subtle message. Knight was willing to take Sutton's word that he was going to clean the program up—for now —after a victory. Time would tell.

The Hoosiers were now 3–0. As always, the Notre Dame and Kentucky games had been draining.

Knight always worried about the game that followed Notre Dame and Kentucky, regardless of the opponent. One year earlier, the Hoosiers had come up flat at home against Kansas State and had almost lost to a team that would finish that season at the bottom of the Big Eight. Now, they had to go on the road to Vanderbilt.

The opponent itself made the game unusual. Knight does not normally like to play against friends, and C.M. Newton was a friend. He had been one of Knight's assistant coaches with the Olympic team. But playing Indiana at home was a coup for Newton as he tried to rebuild the Vanderbilt program. Beating the Hoosiers would be a breakthrough.

For Vanderbilt, the game was a breakthrough; for Indiana, a nightmare. The Hoosiers led by nine early in the second half but couldn't hold on. With Vandy guard Barry Goheen running wild for twenty-six points and the crowd roaring, Vandy pulled the upset, 79–75. Knight was gracious afterwards, crediting Newton and his players. "I know they've built toward something like this," he said. "I hate to see it be us, but I'm happy for them. We just didn't deserve to win the basketball game."

That was the message Knight took back to his players: they had not deserved to win the basketball game. The next two days were a return to the bad old days. There was BK Theater, lots of screaming and yelling, and a mass kickout/harangue on Thursday. Part of this was a result of the Vanderbilt loss. Part of it was the upcoming weekend. It was Indiana Classic time again, the thirteenth annual tournament in which Indiana invites three teams to come play patsy for it.

The opening-night opponent for Indiana was North Carolina-Wilmington, not exactly a name that would get the same reaction from the players as Notre Dame or Kentucky. Knight juggled his lineup, starting Sloan, Pelkowski and freshman David Minor. Smart and Garrett were on the bench.

As always, playing a no-name team made Knight nervous. He had good reason. After playing a good first half and leading 43–29, the Hoosiers collapsed in the second half.

With center Brian Rowsom running another 35 points, 18 rebounds—UNC-W came back. And came back. It got to within 73–72 with thirty-eight seconds left, and UNC-W even had the last shot, a squared seventeen-footer by Rowsom. But the ball spun out, and one of the most embarrassing upsets in Indiana history had been averted.

Knight didn't even stick around for the press conference. He sent Wright, who explained Knight had left to go watch Patrick play.

If there was going to be a major explosion it was likely to come after a victory like this one. A lead had been blown against a team that should have been blown out. This, three nights after a loss. But Knight didn't go wild, didn't rant or rave. The walk-through on Saturday morning was firm but calm. The Hoosiers—with Garrett and Smart restored to the starting lineup—came out flying against East Carolina in the final. It was 49–22 at halftime, and the final was 96–68.

What was most remarkable was what Knight said after the game. "We didn't come back well after Vanderbilt, and that was my fault. We were too hard on them and went after it too hard."

My fault? Went after them too hard? Was this really Bob Knight talking?

It was. This was a Knight who had started the process of trying to be more patient almost from the moment he hurled the chair. He had made some progress in '86. Now, with a good team that he knew was playing hard even when it didn't play well, Knight was as calm (for him) as he had ever been in his coaching career.

The rest of December went smoothly. Cailoway, whose injury had not proved as serious as first feared, returned for the Morehead State game, an easy 84–62 victory. Louisville was next, another revenge game. Like Kentucky, the Cardinals, defending national champions, were not nearly the same team that had beaten Indiana a year earlier.

Even so, the game wasn't easy. Alford was 4-for-17, and Louisville led 49–42 with 9:07 to play. But Indiana strung eleven straight points together, capping the rally on a leap-and-lean three-point play by Calloway with 6:36 left. The lead was 53–49, and IU coasted from there to win, 67–58. After that came two easy victories in the Hoosier Classic. The record going into Big Ten play was 9–1.

———

It had been four years since Indiana had won a Big Ten title. The 1983 team, led by Ted Kitchel and Randy Wittman, had won the league the season before Alford, Thomas and Meier had arrived as freshmen. No group of Knight-coached seniors had ever left Indiana without a Big Ten championship. Knight reminded them of this fact. That would be one of his themes throughout the next eighteen games, getting a Big Ten championship for the three seniors.

The start was shaky. Playing at Ohio State should not have been that tough a task. Indiana had beaten a more talented Buckeye team twice in 1986. This team had a new coach, though, the very aggressive Gary Williams. But with Dennis Hopson, who would go on to beat Alford out for Big Ten Player of the Year honors, struggling with the flu (four points in ten minutes), it should have been easy.

It wasn't. Indiana blew a seventeen-point lead and actually trailed 75–74 with 4:26 left. But, as would become part of their pattern, the Hoosiers righted themselves just in time and blew to an easy 92–80 victory down the stretch. It was a road win and, struggle or no struggle, a better start than last year's 0–2 that had led to Knight's fishing trip in Assembly Hall.

They won easily at Michigan State and then went to Michigan for a Monday night TV game. This had been the scene of the most embarrassing loss of the year before, the 80–52 debacle in the regular-season Big Ten showdown finale.

Knight does not easily forget such a loss. His memories of that afternoon and of the taunting Michigan fans were vivid. He reminded the players about the embarrassment several times prior to the rematch.

Once again, it looked simple. With Alford hot, the Hoosiers ran off a 12–2 string at the end of the first half and led 51–34. The Michigan fans, who had been all over Knight at the start of the game, were quiet. But the lead didn't hold. Garrett was being outplayed inside by the lumbering Mark Hughes, and Michigan's three guards kept knocking in jump shots. The lead dwindled quickly. The crowd was berserk.

It was still 80–71 with 3:50 left. But the Wolverines were on a 12–1 skein, and when Gary Grant nailed a jumper with 1:07 left, Michigan led 83–81. A fourth straight loss to Michigan? Unthinkable. And yet, as the players leaned into the huddle to hear Knight yelling to be heard over the crowd, the possibility was quite real.

With forty-five seconds left Eyl was fouled. Eyl, the nonfree throw shooter of a year ago, would have had no chance in such a situation. Now, he calmly made both shots to tie the game at 83 apiece.

But with eight seconds left, Eyl drew his fifth foul, on Grant. The first free throw was good for 84–83. The second missed. Knight called time. His message in the huddle was simple and direct. "Steve," he said to Alford, "I want you to take the ball and score. Not shoot, score. Understand?"

Alford understood. He went the length of the floor, spun at the side of the lane and put up a twelve-footer. It rolled around the rim, hesitated and dropped in with one second left. It was 85–84. Michigan couldn't get a shot.

It should be remembered that Knight has walked off the floor after winning national championships without so much as cracking a smile. Now, he turned to the crowd behind him, thrust his arms high and leaped into the air, shaking a fist. He was overjoyed. He ran—yes, ran—from the floor, still celebrating.

Someone asked Alford later if he had ever seen his coach that happy. "Not even close," Alford answered.

They bombed Wisconsin and Northwestern at home. Their Big Ten record was 5–0. Iowa, at Iowa, was next. Indiana had already avenged three of the previous year's losses—Kentucky, Louisville, Michigan. This was another chance. Iowa had bombed IU in Iowa City two years in a row. Now, under rookie coach Tom Davis, the Hawkeyes were unbeaten and ranked No. 1 in the nation. Indiana was No. 3.

Iowa was ready for Indiana. The Hawkeyes led 34–22, before the Hoosiers closed to 46–44 at halftime. Indiana led briefly in the second half, but Iowa turned the jets up again, destroying IU inside. The final rebounding margin was an extraordinary 46–19. The final score was an equally amazing 101-88. It was amazing because it marked the first time in Knight's twenty-two years as a coach that an opponent had scored 100 points on one of his teams. Even though the screwy three-point rule skewed matters, Iowa would have scored ninety-seven without the rule. That was lots of points.

A year earlier, after the loss at Iowa, Knight had raged through the trip to Minnesota, and the Hoosiers had almost lost to a crippled Minnesota team. There was no rage now, just a message: "We have to keep winning until we get to play Iowa at home." They began with a romp, 77–53, at Minnesota.

They kept going the following week with tough but solid victories at home over Illinois and Purdue. The Purdue victory was particularly impressive because the Boilermakers had won three of four from Indiana coming in, and the only IU victory had been the Miracle at Coogan's Bluff game the year before, when Purdue had scored only one point in the last nine minutes and IU, with the whole front line out of the game, scraped to a 71–70 overtime victory.

This time, it was easy. Indiana took the lead for good on two Alford free throws with 16:17 left and led by as many as seventeen before easing to an 88–77 win. The record was now 17–2.

The Michigans came to town the following week. Naturally, the players were reminded time and again about the fact that they had lost to both these teams at home two years in a row. But this was a very different team than the ones that had lost those four games. What's more, the Michigans had lost players like Sam Vincent and Scott Skiles (State) and Roy Tarpley and Butch Wade and Richard Rellford (Michigan).

Michigan State hung tough most of the night, cutting a fifteen-point lead to five with 3:44 left. But Alford just kept hitting shot after shot. When it was over, Indiana had an 84–80 win, and Alford had a career-high forty-two points. After the game Knight sounded as if he was talking about Buckner when Alford's name came up.

"We won it because Steve Alford plays for us," he said. "He's an all-American and he played like an All-American. . . . Without Alford, Michigan State wins the ball game going away. Steve's played that way since he was a freshman *[What!?]* He's remarkable for the kind of athlete he is to be able to produce what he does."

Reading these comments in the paper the next morning, Alford undoubtedly thought that perhaps it would be reasonable to suggest that the next time the team was drug-tested, the head coach join the line.

"I'm almost as good right now," he joked, "as Damon."

Damon as in Damon Bailey, the boy-wonder eighth-grader Knight had fallen in love with the previous season. Damon was now a freshman at Bedford High School, and would lead that team to the state Final Four in March. He was playing superbly, averaging twenty-three points a game. Knight had gone back to see him play, and was already setting Alford up as Bailey's role model. Damon and his family were frequently at home games, and in the locker room afterwards. Knight even had Alford take Damon and his family to dinner one night.

Three days after Michigan State, Alford was "held" to thirty points by Michigan. This game was an old-fashioned blowout, the Hoosiers for once building a big halftime lead and then pulling away, leading by as many as twenty-four points before winning 83–67.

After the game, Knight was asked on CBS-TV if he thought this team was good enough to win the national championship. "I've coached teams that good," he said. "I don't think this one is."

Maybe not, but the Hoosiers were doing a decent imitation. They were 19–2 heading into what should be an easy stretch: games at Northwestern and Wisconsin and a home game with Minnesota before the rematch with Iowa. The three weakest teams in the league. No problem. As it turned out, the next ten days would be the most difficult and traumatic of the season.

———

To think that Northwestern might be the site for an Indiana debacle was a joke. The Wildcats were starting from scratch under rookie coach Bill Foster, and were destined to finish the season

7–21. The score in Bloomington had been an embarrassing 95–43, and it could have been worse.

But from the beginning everything went wrong. The Hoosiers led the entire first half, but could never gain control. Alford was one-for-five. Jeff Grose, the 1985 Mr. Indiana who seemed to struggle against everyone but Indiana, came off the bench to score eight points. The half ended with a dunk by the Northwestern center that cut the margin to 34–32.

That was bad enough. What was worse was the Northwestern band. At Northwestern, the band sits adjacent to the visiting team's bench. It likes to chant things at the opponents, get things riled up a little. Naturally, the band had plenty to say to Knight throughout the half. As he walked past the bleachers where the band was seated at halftime, one band member kept yelling over and over, "Knight, you suck."

Most of the time Knight just keeps his head down and ignores such clever repartee. But with the team playing poorly, his rabbit ears were on. Suddenly, he stopped a few feet from the youngster, reached over the railing, grabbed him and tried to yank him out of the bleachers.

Dakich, trailing Knight by a couple of feet, immediately grabbed his coach and tried to pull him away. Knight, angry, is a handful. Dakich was able to keep Knight from doing any damage, but he couldn't pull him loose. Finally, Wright, who had turned around in the hallway and found that he had lost Knight, raced back and used his 6–8 bulk to pry both Knight and Dakich loose. He pulled them into the hallway.

"Let go of me, Goddammit," Knight screamed. "Let go!" Wright and Dakich let go. But the incident wasn't over. Knight sought out a campus policeman. Pointing to the youngster, Knight said, "If he's still here when we come back for the second half, there won't be a second half."

Then he left for the locker room. The police removed the offender. The Hoosiers played the second half—barely. They hung on to win 77–75, only because Thomas scored thirty-two points on a night when Alford was four-for-thirteen and Dean Garrett produced three points and three rebounds.

Knight was wild in the locker room afterwards. At one point, he grabbed a stat sheet and pushed it up against Garrett's chest. "Three rebounds," he roared. "Three!" Then, turning to Wright, he said, "You ever recruit another junior college pussy like this one and I'll fire you!"

Knight also berated the media for doubting him when he said the team wasn't that good. He ripped Garrett and Alford. ("We got absolutely nothing out of Alford tonight.") It was unfortunately like old times, including the old question about Knight's self-control.

What if Dakich, who was on the trip (graduate assistants rarely travel) only because Chicago is near his home, hadn't been right behind Knight when he went after the band member? What if Knight had succeeded in yanking him from the bleachers? What then? Woody Hayes II? After working for two years to get away from such outbursts, Knight had almost wiped himself out in one frustrating swoop.

It didn't get much better at Wisconsin. Alford's first basket of the game made him the school's all-time leading scorer, but he would finish the night four-for-nineteen. Suddenly, after being unable to miss against the Michigans, he couldn't buy a shot. In practice, the shots were dropping as they always did. But in games, he was missing and missing badly. Usually when Alford misses, the ball rims out. Now, he was chipping paint off the rims.

Indiana should have lost to Wisconsin. The Hoosiers trailed by six with four minutes left in regulation and through much of the three overtimes. But Garrett saved the game by grabbing a Hillman air ball from the corner and banking it in with four seconds to go for an 86–85 miracle. The imprint of the stat sheet undoubtedly still on his chest, Garrett had produced twenty-one points and eleven rebounds.

Playing Minnesota at home was no easier. There were fourteen lead changes and twenty ties before Garrett played hero again, making two free throws with three seconds to go for a 72–70 victory. Alford's slump continued. He was seven-for-twenty. That made fifteen-for-fifty-two in three games. He had not shot that poorly since about fourth grade.

Knight didn't panic, though. Nothing was wrong with Alford mechanically. There was no sense beating him up emotionally because everyone knew Alford was doing everything he could to break the spell. The rematch with Iowa was next. The Hoosiers, in spite of their struggles, had done what Knight had asked: They had won all their games after the Iowa loss to set up the rematch. After three straight poor performances, though, the question was, Would they break loose or break down?

They broke loose. Alford's touch returned. He was five-of-seven in the first half. Everyone sizzled. Leading 27–21 with 10:30 left, Indiana went on a rampage, outscoring Iowa 19–6 the rest of the half. Assembly Hall was rocking as it almost never rocked. Iowa made it closer during garbage time, but the final was 84–75.

Knight walked off the floor twirling Al McGuire's red handkerchief—having stolen it from him during the postgame TV interview. He was giddy. He knew his team, faced with a big game, had responded in a big way. What's more, the Hoosiers were in first place in the Big Ten with a 14–1 record. If they could win at Purdue, they would clinch at least a tie for the title.

But they didn't win at Purdue. In foul trouble right from the start, they fell behind by nine at halftime and never caught up. They got to within one, but could never get even. Garrett fouled out with just two points. Thomas and Smart also fouled out.

It was an aggravating loss, because unlike the game the year before at Purdue, this one had been winnable. Still, if they won their last two league games—at Illinois, and against Ohio State at home—they would do no worse than tie for the Big Ten championship.

But Illinois produced another loss. The Illini had lost three straight close games to the Hoosiers, and the law of averages, if nothing else, was on their side. Alford had another poor shooting day (six-of-sixteen), and Illinois led almost the entire second half. The game ended with Alford's desperation halfcourt heave being blocked at the buzzer with Illinois leading 69–67.

Now they had lost two straight. Worse, they were one game behind Purdue. If Purdue won at Michigan State and Michigan, it would win the league title, regardless of what Indiana did against Ohio State. This did not please Knight. The week following the Illinois loss was a long one, the practices tough. Knight hated having to depend on someone else—especially someone like Michigan coach Bill Frieder.

But that's the way it turned out. Frieder's team did to Purdue exactly what it had done to Indiana on the last day of the season in '86. The Wolverines humiliated the Boilermakers, 104–68. When Indiana, trailing by eight midway in the second half, came back to beat Ohio State 90–81 in the home finale for Alford, Thomas and Meier, the two teams had tied for the Big Ten title with 15–3 records. It was Knight's eighth Big Ten championship as a coach, breaking the record of seven held by Fred Taylor. Knight had played on three of those seven Taylor-coached teams at Ohio State, meaning that in nineteen Big Ten seasons as a coach and player he had been part of eleven championships.

At least as important as the title, Purdue's loss changed the seedings for the NCAA tournament. If Purdue had beaten Michigan, it would have been the No. 1 seed in the Midwest Regional. Indiana would have gone back to the Eastern Regional—and back to Syracuse, site of the Cleveland State nightmare—as a No. 2 seed. But when Purdue got hammered, it dropped from a top seed to a No. 3 seed, and the Hoosiers slid right into their No. 1 spot in the Midwest.

That meant that to reach the Final Four, Indiana would only have to travel forty-five miles north to Indianapolis, and then a hundred miles east to Cincinnati. Home cooking, but more important, lots of home fans.

They proved important that first weekend. The opening game was a 92–58 breeze past Fairfield, hardly surprising since Indiana was the No. 2 seed in the sixty-four-team field, and Fairfield was No. 63. But the second-round game was against Auburn, one of those talented but inconsistent Southeast Conference teams.

The Tigers came out blazing. Within six minutes they led 24–10, and the 34,576 in the Hoosier Dome were in shock. But Thomas and Alford got hot, the officials—apparently intimidated by Knight—made some strange calls against Auburn, and the game swung completely around very quickly. IU got even at 40–40 with 5:38 left, led 53–48 at the half and blew to a 107–90 victory. That they were able to play at that quick a pace that effectively against athletes like Auburn had was very encouraging to Knight. He would admit later that after the Auburn game he began thinking his team just might be good enough to win the whole thing.

The Auburn victory set up one of those matchups Knight would just as soon never deal with. The round-of-sixteen opponent would be Duke, and that meant coaching against Krzyzewski. Of all his proteges who have gone on to become head coaches, Krzyzewski is not only the most successful, but the one closest to Knight. He had done a brilliant job getting this Duke team to the round-of-sixteen one year after it lost four starters off the team that reached the NCAA championship game.

It was an awkward week for both men. Indiana was clearly the better team, but Krzyzewski harbored the belief—quietly—that if he could get a good performance from his best shooter, guard Kevin Strickland, an upset was possible. The two coaches talked early in the week. Knight even offered to talk to any members of the North Carolina media Krzyzewski asked him to talk to. Krzyzewski was asked about the relationship so many times that he finally said one day, "You know, this game is turning into forty ways to say I love you."

There was no sign of love once the game started. Duke was ready to play, and led 29–21 early. But, just as it had done against Auburn, Indiana got on a roll. A couple of stupid plays by Duke, some hot shooting by Smart and Calloway, and it was 49–39 at halftime. Duke hung in, though, and when Tommy Amaker buried a three-pointer with three minutes left, the lead was 78–76.

Suddenly, the Hoosiers faced a crucial possession. They had not expected this kind of comeback. Duke had confidence on offense, and the way it played defense, if it ever got a lead . . .

It never did. Alford shot-faked, drove the lane—a surprise to the Duke players—and coolly hit a reverse layup. It was 80–76. Strickland missed a jumper and Smart hit a drive of his own. That was it. Ballgame. Strickland had shot five-of-fifteen. Krzyzewski had been right. If he had played well, Duke might have pulled the upset.

But it didn't, and the Hoosiers were in the final eight. Knight was subdued after the game. There was no real joy in beating Krzyzewski. He and the coaches went to work preparing for LSU as soon as they returned to the hotel that night.

LSU. That meant Dale Brown, one of Knight's least favorite coaches, and Knight's least favorite group of fans, dating back to the Tiger-bait incident in Philadelphia in 1981. What's more, although LSU was only 24–14, it had the kind of athletes that could give Indiana trouble. Looking at the tape Saturday night, Knight commented, "How in the world did that son-of-a-bitch [Brown] ever lose fourteen games with this team?"

That seemed like a reasonable question the next day. From the start, Garrett could not handle 6–8 Nikita Wilson inside. LSU's guards were quick and slick. Indiana was leading 18–17 with 11:39 left in the first half when Thomas was called for three seconds. Knight did not see and could not hear the call. He asked for an explanation. He got none. Angry, he walked out of the coaches' box to find out what the call was.

As soon as he left the box, referee Tom Fraim had no choice. He nailed Knight with a technical foul. Knight went slightly crazy. He screamed. He yelled. He stormed to the scorer's table, where Gene Corrigan, representing the NCAA Tournament Committee, was sitting. He told Corrigan just what he thought of the situation, banging his hand on the table and on the phone next to Corrigan. Amazingly, Knight was not hit with another technical. Almost as amazingly, the technical was only Knight's second of the season, proof of his newfound self-control on the bench. Now, though, facing Dale Brown with a Final Four trip on the line, he was not so controlled.

This was also a classic case of an official being intimidated by Knight. Fraim, one of the best officials in the country, would admit later that he probably should have given Knight a second technical. Furthermore, he conceded that he had hesitated because he believed if he gave Knight another tech, Knight would get even angrier and probably earn a third technical—and ejection from the game. Not wanting to deal with that, Fraim let Knight run amok.

Interestingly, none of the three officials working the game advanced to the Final Four. The main reason, as it turned out, was their failure to deal more firmly with Knight.

The technical cost the Hoosiers only one point, and they led at halftime, 47–46. But LSU took command early in the second half, leading 63–51 after a ferocious Wilson dunk with 12:24 left. It didn't look good for the Hoosiers. It looked worse several minutes later when Calloway went down, his knee hurt again. He limped off with Garl, his season—and his team's—seemingly over. By the time the two of them came back to the bench, it was 75–66 LSU, and the clock was down to 4:38.

Under the stands, Calloway had told Garl he felt okay, that he could play. Garl had no choice but to take his word. He told the coaches Calloway could play.

Slowly, Indiana rallied. Hillman came off the bench to produce a vital three-point play. Brown helped by going to a spread offense. That kept the ball away from Wilson. The Hoosiers kept creeping back. Smart made it 76–75 with forty seconds left. Indiana would have to foul. It did, going after freshman point guard Fess Irvin with twenty-six seconds to go. Irvin had played superbly, with fourteen points and three assists. But the pressure got to him. His free throw was a brick.

Down came Indiana with a chance to win. Knight would never call time in this situation. He always felt his players had a better handle on what to do than the opponents. The clock ran down. The ball went inside to Thomas. He shot-faked and went up, thinking he was going to get hammered. He was off-balance when he shot from ten feet out in the lane, and the shot was woeful— short and to the right. An airball.

But there was Calloway, swooping in as if he had never had a knee injury. He grabbed the ball in the air, and in one motion banked it in. It was 77–76, Indiana. Basket by Calloway. Calloway, from Cincinnati, in Cincinnati. Calloway, who had been reminded time and again in practice that he had played for a loser in high school and would have to prove to his college coach that he was a winner. "Talent will only take you so far, Ricky. . . ."

It wasn't talent that had put Calloway in that spot. It was grit and smarts and, above all, being a winner. In the stands, Calloway's divorced parents each leaped straight into the air as their son's shot fell through.

LSU still had six seconds to get off a shot. It got a good one, a turnaround jumper in the lane by Wilson. But it hit the front rim. Time ran out. Indiana was going to New Orleans. Knight couldn't resist one final swipe at Dal Brown. Describing the last play on national TV, he made direct reference to Brown's changing defense, the "freak defense," as Brown called it. "On the last play," Knight said, "we used our freak offense."

The Final Week would be hectic. This would be an entourage week for Knight. Friends would fly into New Orleans from all over the country to hang out with Knight. Johnny Bench, the former Cincinnati Reds catcher, was there. John Havlicek, Knight's old teammate. David Israel, the former *Chicago Tribune* columnist, now working in television in Los Angeles. And others. And the usual members of the entourage. The Indiana plane had to make three separate trips to New Orleans *before* the team left on Friday.

They arrived Friday afternoon, almost forty-eight hours after Syracuse, Providence and Nevada–Las Vegas, and late for their scheduled practice because of hundred-mile-per-hour headwinds. Knight was in a good mood, happy to be in the spotlight and in his fourth Final Four.

The semifinal opponent was Nevada-Las Vegas. The Rebels were 37–1, ranked No. 1, and the favorites to win the tournament—except among basketball people, most of whom picked Indiana. Knight was worried about Armon Gilliam, UNLV's 6-9 All-America, a superb player. He was afraid he might dominate the game.

He wasn't far wrong. Gilliam, despite double- and triple-teaming, scored thirty-two points. What's more, Freddie Banks, UNLV's mad bomber, banged in thirty-eight points, making ten three-point shots from every conceivable spot on the floor. But Gilliam and Banks didn't get enough help. Knight had decided not to guard point Mark Wade, a great passer but a poor shooter. Wade didn't hit a shot until the last five seconds of the game.

In the meantime, Alford was superb, hitting ten-of-nineteen from the floor and eleven-of-thirteen from the foul line. Both misses came on a two-shot foul in the second half, the first time in his college career Alford had missed twice in one sequence. He never missed again, though.

The game was Indiana's almost throughout. Vegas made a last desperate run, cutting a 90–80 lead to 92–88 with 1:11 left. But Banks ran out of ammunition in the final minute, missing two shots from the field, and a free throw when the lead could have been cut to two. The final was 97–93. Indiana would play Syracuse for the national championship.

By now, Knight was as thrilled with this team as with any he had ever coached. This was not a dominating team like the two that had won national championships for him in the past. Those teams had run over the NCAA tournament like an eighteen-wheel truck. This team had been behind in every game it played in the tournament—except against Fairfield—and kept finding ways to win.

And then there was Alford. With the end of the Little Kid's career now plainly in view, Knight was already becoming nostalgic. He talked about how Alford got so much out of his talent, how much he admired his toughness, how much he would be missed.

Alford was already taking his place in that great tradition of Indiana basketball under Knight. The way the inner circle told it now when the Mentor wasn't around, Quinn Buckner was the man who invented basketball, Randy Wittman was the man who perfected basketball, Alford was the man who played basketball the way it should be played and Damon Bailey would be the man who took basketball to a new dimension.

Alford laughed at all this, remembering the many evenings when he had been the world's worst player. At the Sunday press conference before the title game someone asked Alford to talk about his four years under Knight. With a glance at his coach, Alford said, "I've survived four years and I've only got one game left. I'm not going to blow it now."

He didn't say another word. The Little Kid had always been smart.

They went through all the rituals in those last twenty-four hours. There was a small glitch when they arrived at the Superdome to practice Sunday. Syracuse's practice uniforms had been stolen and their practice had started forty-five minutes late. They were still on the floor. Knight was angry until what had happened was explained to him. "Tell them to take all the time they need," he said.

They looked at tape in the locker room until Syracuse left. Later, Knight would tell people that practicing that day had probably been a mistake. The team was drained from the up-and-down game against Vegas. Just shooting and walking through would have been a better idea, Knight thought.

On game day, they walked through at the hotel and listened to Havlicek and Buckner, just as the '81 team had done before playing North Carolina. Before they left the hotel, Garl made arrangements for a postgame feast. "If we lose," he told the banquet manager, "we'll still pay, but we won't be here to eat."

The game was everything a national championship game should be. It was 34–33 Indiana at halftime when Alford tossed in a three-pointer at the buzzer. Remembering that Wittman had made a jumper to put IU ahead of North Carolina 27–26 in 1981 never to trail again, Hammel saw the shot as a potential harbinger.

"Randy Wittman," he said softly as the teams left the floor.

Not this time. Syracuse took the lead on two free throws by Seikaly fifty-two seconds into the half. Seikaly had collided in the lane with Calloway on the play. Calloway went down, a bone in his wrist broken. But he said nothing at the time and kept playing. Only after the game did he tell Garl, "I think I broke my wrist."

Syracuse, playing in its first national championship game, was not going to go away. The Orangemen led 52–44 with 13:09 left. Indiana somehow came up with a 10–0 surge. Hillman was playing now for Calloway, who would not score in the game.

Hillman had initially come in for Smart, who had been yanked with 16:41 left because of a bad pass. But Knight wasn't angry; he just wanted to settle him down. As Smart came out, Knight tapped him on the rear end and said, "Be ready to go right back in." Kohn Smith grabbed Smart and reminded him that there was plenty of time left and no need to rush anything.

Smart came back for Hillman with 12:12 left. Eight seconds later, Hillman replaced Calloway for the rest of the night.

The last ten minutes of the game belong in a time capsule. Every possession was tight-throat time, a little bit tighter each time. The lead and the momentum seesawed until Syracuse's Howard Triche hit a jumper from the lane to make it 72–70 Syracuse with fifty-seven seconds left. This was ironic. Knight had ordered his players to let Triche shoot most of the night, and the strategy had paid off. He was two-for-eight until that shot. But it dropped.

Then Smart, who had been spectacular down the stretch, missed a baby-jumper on the baseline. Triche grabbed the weak-side rebound with thirty-eight seconds left, and Alford fouled him immediately.

The game was in Syracuse's hands now. Triche made the first free throw, but missed the second. Smart grabbed the rebound, raced through the defense and hit from the lane to make it 73–72 with thirty seconds to go. Indiana called time.

If Jim Boeheim, who had coached a wonderful game all night, made a mistake, it was here. Instead of running an inbounds play to get the ball to one of his guards, Sherman Douglas or Greg Monroe, both good foul shooters, he inbounded to Seikaly, who passed to freshman Derrick Coleman. He was fouled with twenty-eight seconds to go. Knight called time again to let Coleman think.

Coleman had been remarkable all evening, with nineteen rebounds. But here, he turned freshman, missing the free throw badly. Thomas rebounded—Syracuse kept all its players back to avoid fouling—and Indiana came down with the national championship hanging in the balance.

Once again, Knight didn't call time. Whether it was Assembly Hall in October or the Superdome in March, it was just a matter of running the offense. Alford, who had twenty-three points, was the first choice to shoot. But Syracuse was in a box-and-one defense, with the very quick Douglas dogging Alford's every step.

Thomas, looking to screen for Alford, finally stepped into the low post. Ten seconds were left when he took the ball and turned to find Coleman in his face. Instinct took over here—four years of developed instinct. It was almost as if Thomas could hear Knight's voice inside his head: *"Shot-fake Daryl, shot-fake!"* He shot-faked. Coleman didn't budge.

Almost any player in that situation, time running out, national title at stake, would have panicked. But all those dreary nights in Assembly Hall were at work now. The voice was inside Thomas's head: "Don't force a bad shot. *Never* force a bad shot."

Thomas looked and spotted Smart cutting from the top of the key towards the baseline. Calmly, as if it were just another Sunday scrimmage, he flipped the ball back to him. Smart took one dribble to his left, flew into the air and shot. Triche, who had seen Smart come open, flew at him, arms waving. Smart was slightly off balance as he went up from sixteen feet, but the shot was true all the way. It hit the bottom of the net as the clock rolled from five seconds to four.

The Syracuse players were stunned. For almost three seconds, no one moved to call time out. By the time they did, only one second was left. It was not enough time. Smart stole the last desperate in-bound pass and hurled the ball to the heavens.

They jumped on each other, pummeled each other and cried. Alford kept screeching *"Yes, yes"* to anyone who would listen. Kohn Smith, who had soothed so many tears, shed his own unabashedly. Knight just watched it all, accepting congratulations all around, knowing he had become only the third coach in history to win at least three national titles. (John Wooden had ten; Adolph Rupp, four.)

When they gave him his championship watch on the victory podium he looked up at the thousands of red-and-white-clad fans and waved, a huge grin on his face. Truly, he was overjoyed by this championship.

Finally, they went back to the locker room. When there was quiet, Knight spoke briefly. "What you did," he told them, "was refuse to lose. You've been that kind of team all year. I want you to know I would have been just as proud of you if you had lost."

Then he left them to the celebration they had worked so hard to earn. The victory meal cost $3,500. No one at Indiana would mind a bit. It had been 765 days since Knight had thrown the chair. He had come a very long way from that moment to this one.

———

In the aftermath of victory, there was still the future. Alford, who finished his career with 2,415 points, would move on to the NBA and huge endorsement dollars. They were banging on his door from the morning he got home from New Orleans.

Indiana, even without Alford, Thomas and Meier, would be very good again in 1988. Two freshman guards, one a shooter, one a pure point guard (something the team has not had since 1981), had been signed from Marion High School, the three-time state champion. One of Garrett's teammates from San Francisco City would also become a Hoosier. The JUCO experiment was now a part of life at Indiana. Already a JUCO from Kansas had committed to attend in the fall of 1988.

Knight had signed a contract extension at midseason that would keep him at Indiana until 1997—at least. If he averaged twenty-seven victories a year in those ten seasons he would have (a reasonable figure to hope for) 738 career victories at age fifty-six, and would only be 137 shy of Adolph Rupp's all-time record.

There was one final irony at the end of the two-year road that had led from the chair-throw to Smart's jump shot. Three days after winning the championship, Indiana was honored by President Ronald Reagan at the White House. This was standard fare for championship teams, but a thrill for Knight, a staunch Republican who twice voted for Reagan.

But a few days later, Knight received a letter from another Republican president: Richard M. Nixon. The former president congratulated Knight on his team's victory and praised him highly. Finally, Nixon wrote, "This has been a great year for you. Not only did your team win the national championship, but your autobiography is No. 1 on the national bestseller list."

The autobiography has yet to be written. But the story that Knight, his coaches and his basketball players wrote in the last two years is truly an extraordinary one.

Acknowledgments

When reading the acknowledgments at the start of a book I have often thought that it is absolutely impossible for all those people to have played a significant role in the creation of one book. Now, having gone through the experience, I think I understand. For me, there are a lot of people to thank.

First, my employers at *The Washington Post*, who graciously allowed me the leave time I needed to spend the season at Indiana. Specifically, I would like to thank executive editor Ben Bradlee and managing editor Leonard Downie, and give special thanks to my boss, George Solomon, who not only encouraged Bradlee and Downie to grant the leave but kept telling me throughout to be patient and to learn from the experience. I would also like to thank all the people at the paper who helped me while I was away: Barbara Lupica, Debbie Schwartz, David Levine, and Bob Lohrer were remarkably patient week in and week out and kept me in touch with the real world, while Deputy Sports Editor Leonard Shapiro and assistant sports editors Sandy Bailey and O. D. Wilson were generous with advice and encouragement.

The people I came in contact with during my five months in Bloomington could not have been nicer to me. Bob Knight's four full-time assistant coaches—Ron Felling, Kohn Smith, Royce Waltman, and Joby Wright—were terrific to be around from start to finish. My memories of the time I spent with them will always be warm. The same is true of the three graduate assistants—Dan Dakich, Murry Bartow, and Julio Salazar—who all made the time I spent in Indiana much more pleasant than it would have been had they not become my friends. The same is true of trainer Tim Garl and his assistant, Steve Dayton. Tim cannot be given enough credit for the work he does at Indiana. He supplied me with aspirin, orange juice, bad stock tips, and endless patience. The four senior managers—Bill (Jim) Himebrook, Jim (Jim) Kelly, Mark (Jim) Sims, and Jeff (Jim) Stuckey—never lost their sense of humor. That in itself is an achievement. I can't thank them enough for their help. The same is true of SID Kit Klingelhoffer, promotion director Chuck Crabb and the staff: assistant John Johnson, student assistants Eric Ruden, Mike Sobb, and Jan Brown, who is the office saint. I would also be remiss if I didn't thank athletic director Ralph Floyd, whose loyalty to Bob Knight and Indiana goes beyond anything I can put into words here.

As for Bob Hammel, let me put it this way: without him I would not have survived the season. He was not just a friend, but a mediator when the mentor and I needed one. I can't thank him enough.

Last, but certainly not least at IU, the players. If a man is a measure of the people he surrounds himself with, then Bob Knight must be all right, because the sixteen players who were on the 1985–86 team were as good a group of people as one could hope to find. That sounds corny. It's also true. They could not have been nicer to me. Not once did I have the sense that having an outsider lurking around the locker room with an ever-present tape recorder bothered them. If they were 21–8 as basketball players, they were unbeatable as people, at least in this book.

Of course I never would have made it to Indiana if not for my agent, Esther Newberg, and my editor at Macmillan, Jeff Neuman. They both had faith in the project from the start and if not for them, there would have been no project. They also provided encouragement throughout, especially during the writing process when it was needed most.

Then there are the people who know best what was involved in putting this book together because they were virtually forced to live through it with me: Keith and Barby Drum, Ray Ratto, Tony Kornheiser, David Maraniss, Lesley Visser, John Hewig, Michael Wilbon, Ken Denlinger, Dick (Hoops) Weiss, Sally Jenkins, Loretta Tofani, Lexie Verdon, Linda Reynolds, Dave Kindred, Bob DeStefano, John Caccese, Jackson Diehl, Fred Hiatt, Margaret Shapiro, Martin Weil, Tom Mickle, Mike Krzyzewski, Bud Collins, Juan Williams, and of course, my family. Special thanks to Keith Drum, Kornheiser, Maraniss, and Visser, who urged me to go ahead with the idea when it was just that: an idea.

Finally, a few words on Robert M. Knight. It will be readily apparent while reading this book that the access he granted me was extraordinary. The last thing in the world any basketball coach needs is someone trailing after him recording his every word and act. Yet that is exactly what he let me do. Without this access, this book would not have been possible. The book was not Bob's idea, it was mine. He had little to gain by my constant presence and much to lose, and yet he never once backed away from the project even at times when he was undoubtedly sick and tired of turning around and seeing my face and my tape recorder.

That is why, as I finish this, I am reminded of an incident that took place in January. After the Indiana-Illinois game during which Bob kicked and slammed a chair, and kicked a cheerleader's megaphone, Dave Kindred, the superb columnist for *The Atlanta Constitution,* wrote that he was disappointed to see Knight acting this way again. Kindred, a longtime friend of Knight's, ended the column by writing, "Once again I find myself wondering when it comes to Bob Knight if the end justifies the means."

A few days later, Knight called Kindred. "You needed one more line for that damn column," Knight said. "You should have finished by saying, 'And one more time, I realize that it does.'"

Kindred thought for a moment and then said, "Bob, you're right."

I agree.

———

One year ago I wrote that this book would not have been possible without the extraordinary access that he gave me. It should now be said that the success of this book was almost entirely the result of that access.

Shortly after the book came out, when Bob had made his disdain for it—and for me—clear, I wrote to him. In the letter I said that while I was disappointed that he didn't like the book, I wouldn't change a word of it because I believed it had done exactly what he and I set out to do: give people an idea of what living through a season with him is like.

I still feel that way. Throughout this past season I was asked repeatedly why I thought Knight had given me such remarkable access when he had nothing to gain, financially or otherwise. The reason, I think, is this: Knight honestly believed that a close-up coach who cared about his players and about education, a coach who played by the rules and who recruited players who not only graduated but were a credit to their school.

I think Knight's assessment was correct because that is exactly what I discovered. I did not discover or write about a saint, but about a driven and brilliant coach: a flawed man, but a good man.

I felt that way about him when I started the project. I felt that way about him when I finished it. And, after all the name-calling, I feel that way about him now. A few profanities didn't change the way most people felt about Bob Knight. Even when directed at me, they won't change the way I feel about him either.

—John Feinstein, Shelter Island, N.Y.
May 1987

About the Author

JOHN FEINSTEIN is the author of many bestselling books, including *A Good Walk Spoiled* and *One on One*. He writes for the *Washington Post, Golf Digest,* and is a regular contributor to the Golf Channel.